The Book of
British Birds

The Book of British Birds

Published by The Reader's Digest Association Limited
LONDON • NEW YORK • SYDNEY • MONTREAL

Contents

How to use this book

This comprehensive guide covers all the regular British species, including residents, those that come to breed in summer, winter visitors and passage migrants – birds that pass through each spring and autumn.

Identifying birds depends on several factors and knowing what to look for is half the battle. Guidelines on this are followed by pages of illustrations grouping birds by colour and shape in flight. Equally important is where they live, so species are arranged by habitat, although since birds are no observers of boundaries, they often move from one area to another, rarely fitting neatly into just one category. Each species is illustrated and, unless a note indicates the sex, age or season depicted, the bird is an adult, male and female are alike and the bird's plumage does not change appreciably from one season to the next.

Scientific names, based on Latin or Greek, show how each bird is related to other species. A species comprises individuals capable of breeding to produce fertile young. Those showing similarities through common evolution are grouped into a genus. The first word of the scientific name shows the genus; the second makes each species unique. A blackbird, for example, is in the genus *Turdus* and its species is *Turdus merula*. The genera are grouped into families, families into orders and the orders make up the class Aves – birds.

Some birds are seen in Britain very occasionally and these have a section to themselves. They may be vagrants driven by storms or simply lost on their long-distance migrations, or they may be newcomers, attracted by the changing climate to extend their breeding ranges. While climate change may bring new species, others, such as wood warblers and spotted flycatchers, are declining. Anything that influences food supply (including the timing of peak availability), length of breeding season and winter mortality is bound to affect numbers. The drastic reduction in sand eels in the North Sea, for instance, thought to be a consequence of climate change as the seas warm up, has meant a succession of catastrophically poor breeding seasons for seabirds such as kittiwakes. Also many summer migrants are arriving too late to take advantage of the spring caterpillar crop.

In recent years the rate of climate change has grown alarmingly, and indications are that it will speed up. The section on bird society emphasises how birds' behaviour is dictated by the need to feed, to establish and defend a territory, to reproduce and to nurture their young. One effect of a faster rate of change is that birds will not have as much time to adapt as they had in the past. Specialised species in particular, such as the ptarmigan and redshank, are likely to suffer.

On the positive side, milder conditions suit some birds, so while numbers of dunlins and ringed plovers wintering in Britain are declining, little egrets are increasing, and blackcaps from central Europe are coming here rather than flying south.

How to read the maps

The distribution maps show when and where each species is most likely to be seen, which can be useful clues to a bird's identity. Check timing and location carefully, and make a note, especially if you think you have seen an unusual species.

- RED DOTS show the sites of breeding colonies
- PURPLE shows the usual breeding range of summer visitors
- GREEN shows the areas where a resident species breeds and remains all year round
- BLUE shows the areas where a species is found in winter
- GREY indicates where passage migrants occur
- DIAGONAL STRIPES indicate where rare passage migrants, vagrants or newcomers have been seen.

The winter range of birds and the range of passage migrants are less precise than the breeding range of resident birds or summer visitors because they depend on factors such as the severity of the weather. Some birds, particularly passage migrants, may sometimes be seen outside their usual range, while others such as the red grouse, are highly unlikely to be found away from their regular range and habitat.

Identifying Birds

For most people, an interest in birds begins with identification – with the pleasure to be had from being able to put the right name to a bird, whether studied at leisure in a town park or glimpsed fleetingly on a drive through the country. The following pages are a comprehensive guide to the species regularly seen in Britain. Familiarity with them will make recognition quick and easy.

The points to look for when identifying birds

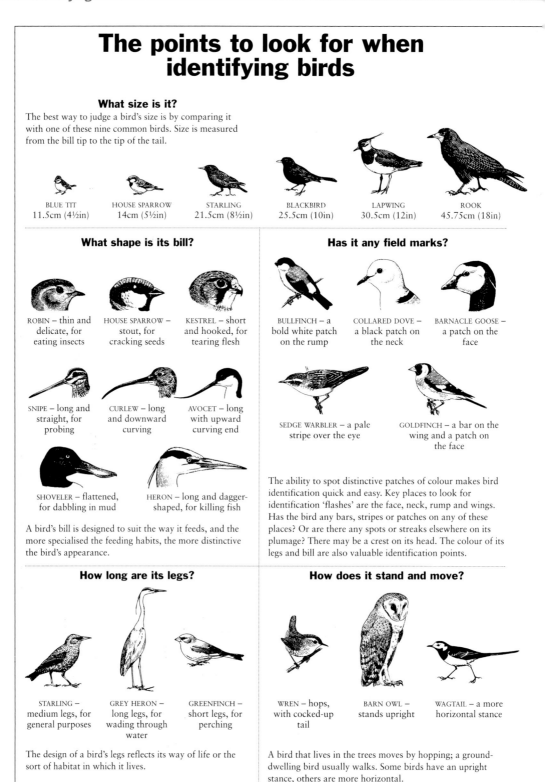

What size is it?

The best way to judge a bird's size is by comparing it with one of these nine common birds. Size is measured from the bill tip to the tip of the tail.

BLUE TIT
11.5cm (4½in)

HOUSE SPARROW
14cm (5½in)

STARLING
21.5cm (8½in)

BLACKBIRD
25.5cm (10in)

LAPWING
30.5cm (12in)

ROOK
45.75cm (18in)

What shape is its bill?

ROBIN – thin and delicate, for eating insects

HOUSE SPARROW – stout, for cracking seeds

KESTREL – short and hooked, for tearing flesh

SNIPE – long and straight, for probing

CURLEW – long and downward curving

AVOCET – long with upward curving end

SHOVELER – flattened, for dabbling in mud

HERON – long and dagger-shaped, for killing fish

A bird's bill is designed to suit the way it feeds, and the more specialised the feeding habits, the more distinctive the bird's appearance.

Has it any field marks?

BULLFINCH – a bold white patch on the rump

COLLARED DOVE – a black patch on the neck

BARNACLE GOOSE – a patch on the face

SEDGE WARBLER – a pale stripe over the eye

GOLDFINCH – a bar on the wing and a patch on the face

The ability to spot distinctive patches of colour makes bird identification quick and easy. Key places to look for identification 'flashes' are the face, neck, rump and wings. Has the bird any bars, stripes or patches on any of these places? Or are there any spots or streaks elsewhere on its plumage? There may be a crest on its head. The colour of its legs and bill are also valuable identification points.

How long are its legs?

STARLING – medium legs, for general purposes

GREY HERON – long legs, for wading through water

GREENFINCH – short legs, for perching

The design of a bird's legs reflects its way of life or the sort of habitat in which it lives.

How does it stand and move?

WREN – hops, with cocked-up tail

BARN OWL – stands upright

WAGTAIL – a more horizontal stance

A bird that lives in the trees moves by hopping; a ground-dwelling bird usually walks. Some birds have an upright stance, others are more horizontal.

Success in identifying birds depends largely on knowing how to look at them. This is not simply a matter of being alert, but is a technique that can easily be learnt. The most important clues to a bird's identity are: size; shape, including the shape and length of the bill and the length of the legs; general colouring of the plumage; any particular field marks; behaviour; song and calls; when and where the bird was seen.

Many birds are programmed to fit into a particular habitat, making the task of identification much easier – birds that are similar in appearance may occupy very different habitats. What looks like a partridge beating low over the moors is much more likely to be a red grouse. A pipit on a rocky shore is far more likely to be a rock pipit than a tree pipit or a meadow pipit, although birds can and do move from habitat to habitat.

MALLARD 58.5cm (23in)

PHEASANT 83.75cm (33in), including 45.75cm (18in) tail

MUTE SWAN 153cm (60in)

What shape are its wings?

BARN OWL – round-winged

ROOK – deeply slotted wing-tips

KESTREL – long and pointed

SWIFT – long and swept back

Even when a bird is flying too high for any features to be picked out, its silhouette is often enough to place it in a broad group.

What shape is its tail?

PHEASANT – long

SWALLOW – forked

LINNET – cleft

BLACK-BACKED GULL – square

BUZZARD – blunt and rounded

The shape of a bird's tail, like the shape of its wings, can be sufficiently distinctive to be a useful recognition feature, even when it is flying high.

How does it fly?

The starling flies in a direct line. The woodpecker has an undulating flight

Birds glide, soar, flap, hover and perform a multitude of aerobatic tricks, and the way in which they fly can be very distinctive. A kestrel is unmistakable when hovering. So is a spotted flycatcher when it darts from its perch to catch an insect. Some birds rise and fall as they fly, first beating their wings rapidly, then holding them closed.

What features show in flight?

WOODPIGEON – bar on the wings

WATER RAIL – legs are trailed

Wing-bars and 'flashes' on the tail often show up in flight. Other points to note are how a bird holds its legs and neck, whether it flies in loose flocks or in formation and whether it sings in flight.

The 216 birds in the section beginning on page 30 are grouped by the habitats in which they are most likely to be seen.

Since some birds visit Britain only in the summer, others only in the winter and yet others mainly in the spring and autumn, the time of year when a bird is seen may be a valuable clue to its identity. It may help, for instance, to distinguish a hen harrier, a winter visitor in the south, from a Montagu's harrier, which is unknown in these islands in winter. The calendars under the maps that accompany each entry show at a glance when that particular bird is most likely to be seen.

Armed with this information it should be possible, by using the identification keys in the following pages, to recognise any of the birds commonly seen in Britain.

Identifying birds by colour

Colour is the first feature to strike most people about a strange bird, but in the British Isles there are too many small brown birds to make instant identification easy. For this reason, the birds in this colour key are separated into manageable groups, with similar-looking birds placed close together so that minor differences show up immediately.

As a first step, the birds are grouped according to where they are most likely to be seen. Land birds are those seen mainly on or over land. Waterside birds are those normally found close to water – either inland or on the coast – but not normally seen swimming. Waterbirds are those usually seen on water or flying over it.

Birds do not keep rigidly to these categories, but the broad groupings are a good general guide and can save time in identifying an individual bird. Within the three categories, birds are grouped according to colour. Here, it is the general effect that counts. A starling, for instance, turns out on close scrutiny to have a spangled plumage, shot with iridescent purples, blues and greens, but from a distance it looks black, so it has been classed as black in this colour key.

When both male and female are illustrated, they are grouped according to the colour of the male's plumage. Hen-harriers and Montagu's harriers, for example, are both given as grey birds because this is the colour of the male, although in both cases the female is brown.

The sizes given are for the length of a bird from the tip of its bill to the end of its tail. A guide to judging sizes is given on pages 8 and 9. For more information about each bird shown in the identification keys – and to distinguish between two similar birds covered here by a single illustration – refer to the main entry on the page indicated.

Land birds: black

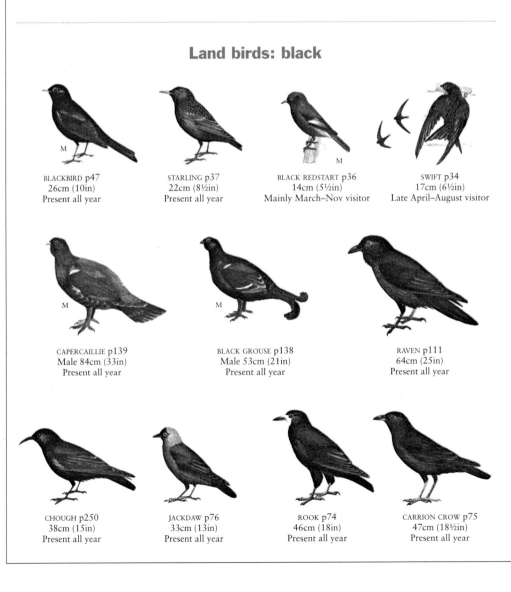

BLACKBIRD p47
26cm (10in)
Present all year

STARLING p37
22cm (8½in)
Present all year

BLACK REDSTART p36
14cm (5½in)
Mainly March–Nov visitor

SWIFT p34
17cm (6½in)
Late April–August visitor

CAPERCAILLIE p139
Male 84cm (33in)
Present all year

BLACK GROUSE p138
Male 53cm (21in)
Present all year

RAVEN p111
64cm (25in)
Present all year

CHOUGH p250
38cm (15in)
Present all year

JACKDAW p76
33cm (13in)
Present all year

ROOK p74
46cm (18in)
Present all year

CARRION CROW p75
47cm (18½in)
Present all year

Land birds: black and white/grey

LAPWING p68
30.5cm (12in)
Present all year

MAGPIE p73
46cm (18in) including
20–26cm (8–10in) tail
Present all year

HOODED CROW p110
47cm (18½in)
Present all year

LONG-TAILED TIT p130
14cm (5½in) including
8cm (3in) tail
Present all year

PIED WAGTAIL p165
18cm (7in)
Present all year
M

HOUSE MARTIN p35
13cm (5in)
April–Oct visitor
M summer

PIED FLYCATCHER p129
13cm (5in)
April–Oct visitor
M in winter; or F

RING OUZEL p109
24cm (9½in)
March–Oct visitor
M

WHEATEAR p89
14.5cm (5¾in)
March–Oct visitor
F   M

LESSER SPOTTED WOODPECKER
p121
14.5cm (5¾in)
Present all year
F   M

GREAT SPOTTED WOODPECKER
p120
23cm (9in)
Present all year
F   M

Land birds: brown

RED KITE p114
Male 56cm (22in)
Female 61cm (24in)
Present all year

GOLDEN EAGLE p101
Male 76cm (30in)
Female 89cm (35in)
Present all year

BUZZARD p116
Male 51cm (20in)
Female 58cm (23in)
Present all year
F

KESTREL p62
34cm (13½in)
Present all year
M

PHEASANT p61
Male 84cm (33in) including 46cm
(18in) tail; female 59cm (23in) includ-
ing 23cm (9in) tail
Present all year
M   F

RED GROUSE p99
Male 38cm (15in)
Female 34cm (13½in)
Present all year
M

QUAIL p60
18cm (7in)
May–Oct visitor
M

GOLDEN PLOVER p104
28cm (11in)
Present all year
Summer   Winter

STONE CURLEW p84
41cm (16in)
March–Oct visitor

WOODCOCK p117
34cm (13½in)
Present all year

CORNCRAKE p63
27cm (10½in)
April–Sept visitor

Land birds: brown

TAWNY OWL **p41**
38cm (15in)
Present all year

SHORT-EARED OWL **p107**
Male 36cm (14in)
Female 42cm (16½in)
Present all year

LONG-EARED OWL **p140**
36cm (14in)
Present all year

JAY **p134**
34cm (13½in)
Present all year

NIGHTJAR **p86**
27cm (10½in)
May–Oct visitor

WRYNECK
p119
22cm (8½in)
Late March–Oct visitor

WOODLARK **p87**
15cm (6in)
Present all year

SKYLARK **p69**
18cm (7in)
Present all year

MEADOW PIPIT **p108**
15cm (5¾in)
Present all year

TREE PIPIT **p88**
15cm (6in)
April–Oct visitor

SONG THRUSH **p49**
23cm (9in)
Present all year

REDWING **p71**
21cm (8¼in)
Present all year

WAXWING **p43**
19cm (7½in)
Oct–April visitor

HAWFINCH **p136**
18cm (7in)
Present all year

GRASSHOPPER WARBLER **p94**
13cm (5in)
April–Sept visitor

GARDEN WARBLER **p125**
14cm (5½in)
April–Oct visitor

WREN **p44**
10cm (3¾in)
Present all year

NIGHTINGALE **p123**
17cm (6½in)
April–Sept visitor

CRESTED TIT **p142**
12cm (4½in)
Present all year

CIRL BUNTING **p79**
16cm (6¼in)
Present all year

CORN BUNTING **p80**
18cm (7in)
Present all year

TWITE **p112**
13cm (5¼in)
Present all year

Land birds: grey-brown or brown and white

RED-LEGGED PARTRIDGE p58
34cm (13½in)
Present all year

PARTRIDGE p59
31cm (12in)
Present all year

DOTTEREL p103
22cm (8½in)
April–Oct visitor

BARN OWL p66
34cm (13½in)
Present all year

Winter Summer

PTARMIGAN p98
36cm (14in)
Present all year

HOOPOE p42
29cm (11½in)
April–Sept visitor

TURTLE DOVE p118
28cm (11in)
April–Sept visitor

COLLARED DOVE p40
32cm (12½in)
Present all year

MISTLE THRUSH p48
27cm (10½in)
Present all year

FIELDFARE p70
26cm (10in)
Present all year

LITTLE OWL p67
22cm (8½in)
Present all year

SPOTTED FLYCATCHER p52
14cm (5½in)
May–Sept visitor

TREECREEPER p133
13cm (5in)
Present all year

DUNNOCK p45
15cm (5¾in)
Present all year

WHITETHROAT p92
14cm (5½in)
April–Sept visitor

LESSER WHITETHROAT p93
13cm (5¼in)
April–Sept visitor

BLACKCAP p126
14cm (5½in)
March–Oct visitor

MARSH TIT p131
(willow tit similar) 12cm (4½in)
Present all year

TREE SPARROW p77
14cm (5½in)
Present all year

HOUSE SPARROW p38
15cm (5¾in)
Present all year

Land birds: grey

PEREGRINE p238
Male 38cm (15in)
Female 48.25cm (19in)
Present all year

HOBBY p83
33cm (13in)
Late April–Sept visitor

SPARROWHAWK p115
Male 28cm (11in)
Female 38cm (15in)
Present all year

MERLIN p102
Male 27cm (10½in)
Female 33cm (13in)
Present all year

MONTAGU'S HARRIER p82
43cm (17in)
Late April–Sept visitor

HEN HARRIER p100
Male 43cm (17in); female 51cm (20in)
Present all year

CUCKOO p85
33cm (13in)
April–Sept visitor

WOODPIGEON p65
41cm (16in)
Present all year

FERAL PIGEON p33
33cm (13in)
Present all year

STOCK DOVE p64
33cm (13in)
Present all year

COAL TIT p143
11cm (4¼in)
Present all year

Land birds: green, yellow or red

CHIFFCHAFF p127
(willow warbler similar)
11cm (4¼in)
March–Dec visitor

GREEN WOODPECKER p122
32cm (12½in)
Present all year

GOLDCREST p141
9cm (3½in)
Present all year

WOOD WARBLER p128
13cm (5in)
April–August visitor

SISKIN p144
12cm (4¾in)
Present all year

GREENFINCH p55
15cm (5¾in)
Present all year

CROSSBILL p146
17cm (6½in)
Present all year

YELLOWHAMMER p78
17cm (6½in)
Present all year

GREAT TIT p51
14cm (5½in)
Present all year

BLUE TIT p50
12cm (4½in)
Present all year

Land birds: red or orange on head or breast

GOLDFINCH p53
12cm (4¾in)
Present all year

CHAFFINCH p54
15cm (6in)
Present all year

M

REDPOLL p145
13cm (5in)
Present all year

Another form
of the same
species

LINNET p96
13cm (5¼in)
Present all year

F

M

F

Summer

Winter

BRAMBLING p135
15cm (5¾in)
Late Sept–April visitor

M

F

WHINCHAT p91
13cm (5in)
April–Sept visitor

M

F

STONECHAT p90
13cm (5in)
Present all year

F

M

BULLFINCH p56
15cm (5¾in)
Present all year

M

DARTFORD WARBLER p95
13cm (5in)
Present all year

ROBIN p46
14cm (5½in)
Present all year

SWALLOW p72
19cm (7½in)
March–Oct visitor

NUTHATCH p132
14cm (5½in)
Present all year

F

M

REDSTART p124
14cm (5½in)
April–Sept visitor

Waterside birds: brown

M

F

MARSH HARRIER p151
53cm (21in)
Present all year

BITTERN p148
76cm (30in)
Present all year

M

F

Males in
summer

RUFF p155
Male 28cm (11in); female 23cm (9in)
Present all year

CURLEW p105
56cm (22in)
Present all year

WHIMBREL p212
41cm (16in)
March–Oct

JACK SNIPE p157
19cm (7½in)
Oct–April visitor

SNIPE p156
27cm (10½in)
Present all year

REED WARBLER p169
(marsh warbler similar)
13cm (5in)
April–Oct visitor

SEDGE WARBLER p168
13cm (5in)
April–Sept visitor

ROCK PIPIT p249
17cm (6¼in)
Present all year

M

F

BEARDED TIT p171
17cm (6½in) including
8cm (3in) tail
Present all year

Waterside birds: white and black/brown

OSPREY p150
56cm (22in); April–Oct visitor

AVOCET p206
43cm (17in); present all year

BARNACLE GOOSE p203
59–69cm (23–27in); Oct–April visitor

GREEN SANDPIPER p161
23cm (9in); present all year

COMMON SANDPIPER p160
18cm (7¾in); April–Oct visitor

Winter

Summer

TURNSTONE p223
23cm (9in); present all year

LITTLE RINGED PLOVER p154
15cm (6in); March–Oct visitor

RINGED PLOVER p221
19cm (7½in); present all year

OYSTERCATCHER p220
43cm (17in); present all year

DIPPER p170
18cm (7in)
Present all year

M Winter

M Summer

SNOW BUNTING p230
17cm (6½in)
Present all year

M

F

REED BUNTING p172
15cm (6in)
Present all year

SAND MARTIN p164
12cm (4¾in)
March–Sept visitor

Waterside birds: grey-brown

GREENSHANK p106
31cm (12in); present all year

WATER RAIL p152
28cm (11in); present all year

SPOTTED CRAKE p153
23cm (9in); March–Oct visitor

Winter

BAR-TAILED GODWIT p211
38cm (15in)
August–May visitor

BLACK-TAILED GODWIT p158
41cm (16in)
Present all year

REDSHANK p159
28cm (11in)
Present all year

Bean goose

WHITE-FRONTED GOOSE p201
66–76cm (26–30in);
Lesser 53.25–63.5cm (21–25in)
Oct–April visitor (Lesser Dec–March)

PINK-FOOTED GOOSE p200
61–76cm (24–30in);
bean 71–89cm (28–35in);
both Oct–April visitors

GREYLAG GOOSE p202
76–89cm (30–35in)
Present all year

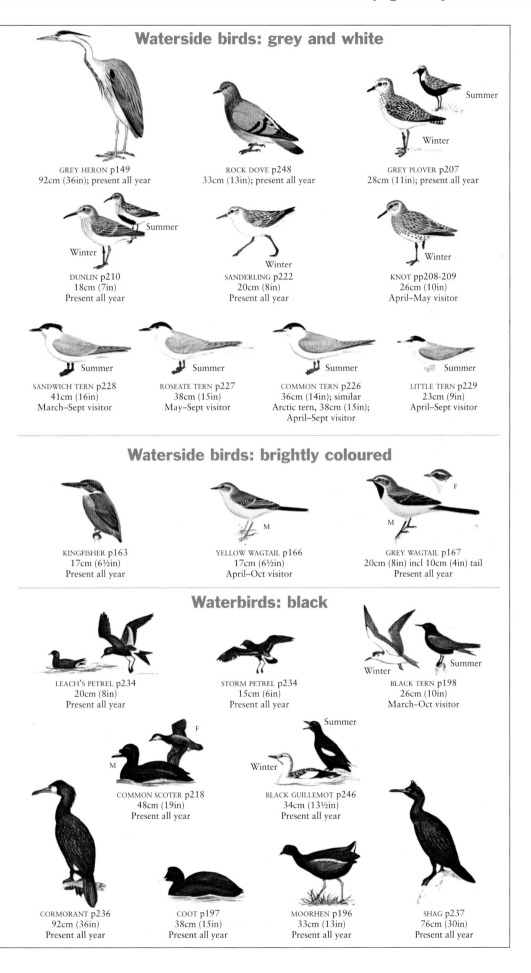

Waterside birds: grey and white

GREY HERON p149
92cm (36in); present all year

ROCK DOVE p248
33cm (13in); present all year

Summer

Winter

GREY PLOVER p207
28cm (11in); present all year

Summer

Winter

DUNLIN p210
18cm (7in)
Present all year

Winter

SANDERLING p222
20cm (8in)
Present all year

Winter

KNOT pp208-209
26cm (10in)
April–May visitor

Summer

SANDWICH TERN p228
41cm (16in)
March–Sept visitor

Summer

ROSEATE TERN p227
38cm (15in)
May–Sept visitor

Summer

COMMON TERN p226
36cm (14in); similar
Arctic tern, 38cm (15in);
April–Sept visitor

Summer

LITTLE TERN p229
23cm (9in)
April–Sept visitor

Waterside birds: brightly coloured

KINGFISHER p163
17cm (6½in)
Present all year

M

YELLOW WAGTAIL p166
17cm (6½in)
April–Oct visitor

F

M

GREY WAGTAIL p167
20cm (8in) incl 10cm (4in) tail
Present all year

Waterbirds: black

LEACH'S PETREL p234
20cm (8in)
Present all year

STORM PETREL p234
15cm (6in)
Present all year

Winter

Summer

BLACK TERN p198
26cm (10in)
March–Oct visitor

F

M

COMMON SCOTER p218
48cm (19in)
Present all year

Summer

Winter

BLACK GUILLEMOT p246
34cm (13½in)
Present all year

CORMORANT p236
92cm (36in)
Present all year

COOT p197
38cm (15in)
Present all year

MOORHEN p196
33cm (13in)
Present all year

SHAG p237
76cm (30in)
Present all year

Waterbirds: black and white

Winter

Summer
GREAT NORTHERN DIVER
p219
Male 84cm (33in)
Female 76cm (30in)
Oct–May visitor

Winter

Summer
BLACK-THROATED DIVER
p191
69cm (27in)
Present all year

BRENT GOOSE p204
57cm (22–24in)
Sept–April visitor

M
SHELDUCK p214
66cm (26in)
Present all year

F
M
EIDER p216
61cm (24in)
Present all year

F
M
SCAUP p215
48cm (19in)
Sept–April visitor

F
M
TUFTED DUCK p185
43cm (17in)
Present all year

F
M
GOLDENEYE p186
46cm (18in)
Present all year

M Summer
F
M Winter
LONG-TAILED DUCK p217
59cm (23in)
Sept–April visitor

F
M
SMEW p187
43cm (17in)
Nov–March visitor

Lesser black-
backed gull
LESSER BLACK-BACKED GULL
p241
53cm (21in)
Present all year

Great black-backed gull
GREAT BLACK-BACKED GULL
p242
69cm (27in)
Present all year

Summer

Winter
GUILLEMOT p244
42cm (16½in)
Present all year

Summer

Winter
RAZORBILL p245
41cm (16in)
Present all year

Summer
PUFFIN p247
31cm (12in)
Present all year

MANX SHEARWATER p233
36cm (14in)
Feb–Oct visitor

Waterbirds: brightly coloured

F
M
SHOVELER p183
51cm (20in)
Present all year

F
M
GOOSANDER p189
66cm (26in)
Present all year

F
M
RED-BREASTED MERGANSER
p188
59cm (23in)
Present all year

F
M
MALLARD p179
59cm (23in)
Present all year

F
M
TEAL p181
36cm (14in)
Present all year

Winter

Summer
BLACK-NECKED GREBE p194
31cm (12in)
Present all year

Winter

Summer
SLAVONIAN GREBE p195
33cm (13in)
Present all year

Waterbirds: grey/brown

GREAT SKUA p239
59cm (23in)
March–Nov visitor

Dark phase   Light phase
ARCTIC SKUA p240
46cm (18in)
April–Oct visitor

Winter   Summer
LITTLE GREBE p192
23cm (9in)
Present all year

WIGEON p177
46cm (18in)
Present all year

POCHARD p184
46cm (18in)
Present all year

GARGANEY p180
38cm (15in)
March–Oct visitor

GADWALL p178
51cm (20in)
Present all year

CANADA GOOSE p176
97cm (38in)
Present all year

Summer
GREAT CRESTED GREBE p193
48cm (19in)
Present all year

Summer   Winter
RED-THROATED DIVER p190
61cm (24in)
Present all year

Waterbirds: white or grey and white

PINTAIL p182
56cm (22in)
Present all year

FULMAR p232
47cm (18½in)
Present all year

F Summer   Winter
RED-NECKED PHALAROPE p162
18cm (7in)
April–Oct visitor

HERRING GULL p224
59cm (23in)
Present all year

COMMON GULL p225
43cm (17in)
Present all year

KITTIWAKE p243
41cm (16in)
Present all year

Summer   Winter
BLACK-HEADED GULL p32
38cm (15in)
Present all year

Juvenile
Adult
GANNET p235
92cm (36in)
Present all year

Summer
SPOONBILL p205
86cm (34in)
Present all year

MUTE SWAN p175
153cm (60in)
Present all year

Whooper   Bewick's
WHOOPER/BEWICK'S SWAN
p174
Whooper 153cm (60in)
Bewick's 122cm (48in)
Oct–March visitors

Identifying birds in flight

A bird in the air gives many clues to its identity. The first is pattern of flight. Is this direct, or meandering? Powerful or fluttering? Does the bird fly in rapid bursts, or is its flight sustained? Then there is the method of flight. A bird may use its wings almost all the time in flapping flight, or it may glide, coasting along with wings outstretched. It may hover in one place or it may soar, using up-currents of air to gain height. Flight that consists of flapping and gliding in a fairly regular pattern is called undulating. Knowing which bird uses which method often aids identification.

Further points to watch for are the size and shape of the wings, the speed at which the wings move, the depth of the wing-beats and the general appearance of the plumage.

Divers and grebes

On land they are clumsy, but in the air they come into their own. They fly swiftly on short, pointed wings, with necks stretched out

Summer

RED-THROATED DIVER p190
Large, with heavy body and small wings; takes off easily from water and flies fast and direct

Summer

LITTLE GREBE p192
Small with predominantly brown plumage and small wings; weak, whirring flight

Summer

GREAT CRESTED GREBE p193
Heavy-bodied with long neck; wings small and pointed with prominent white patch

Petrels and storm petrels

With their narrow, pointed wings these birds fly far out to sea, skimming over the waves to pick small creatures from the surface

STORM AND LEACH'S PETRELS p234
Storm petrel (left) black with white rump; Leach's larger with forked tail; both have fluttering flight

MANX SHEARWATER p233
Small body; long, pointed wings; black above, white beneath; glides and banks in flight

FULMAR p232
Heavy body and 'bull-necked' appearance; grey above, white beneath; gliding, banking flight

Gannets and cormorants

These large birds live on or near the sea and dive for their fish, either from the surface or from the air. They fly with slow, powerful wing-beats, and carry their long necks well forward

Juvenile

Adult

Juvenile

Summer

GANNET p235
Adult white with long, black-tipped wings; young dark, later brown and white

SHAG p237
Large with long neck; crest in spring and summer; flight slow and flapping

CORMORANT p236
Larger than shag, with slower wing-beats and flapping flight; white thigh-patches in summer

BITTERN p148
Broad wings, plumage buff streaked with brown; long, green legs trail in flight

GREY HERON p149
Long wings, grey and black; heavy flapping flight, legs trailing, head drawn back

Herons

Despite being adapted for stalking in deep water, herons are powerful flyers. Once in the air, they trail their legs behind them

Ducks

Superb performers on water, ducks are equally at home in the air. They have stout bodies, long, pointed wings and powerful breast muscles. They fly fast and direct, with long necks stretched out and rapid flapping of the wings, gliding only as they land. They often fly in flocks

GOOSANDER p189
Long neck and straight, slender bill; male has grey rump and white wing-patches

RED-BREASTED MERGANSER p188
Neck and bill long; breast chestnut; white wing-patch

SHELDUCK p214
Wings have black tips, white foreparts and lustrous green patch; slow wing-beat

EIDER p216
Biggest British sea duck; flies powerfully in long lines close to water

LONG-TAILED DUCK p217
Small; dark wings, dark brown and white body; wings beat mainly below body

SHOVELER p183
Heavy bill broadened at tip; pale blue leading edges to wings in both sexes

WIGEON p177
Drake has chestnut head, large white patches on wings and grey back; duck mainly brown

PINTAIL p182
Drake mainly grey, with brown head and neck; light trailing edges on wings

MALLARD p179
Both sexes have blue patch on rear of wing; drake has green head and white collar

COMMON SCOTER p218
Heavily built; drake black with yellow patch on black bill; duck brown with pale buff cheeks

POCHARD p184
Wings grey with indistinct pale stripe; drake has chestnut-red head and black neck

TEAL p181
Small and fast-flying; both sexes have green patch bordered with black and white on rear of wings

GOLDENEYE p186
Squat shape; large white wing-patches; drake has black head with white patch near eye

TUFTED DUCK p185
Black wings with white stripe; drake has black head and neck, with white breast; duck brown

SCAUP p215
Dark wings with white stripe; drake has dark green head and black breast; duck brown

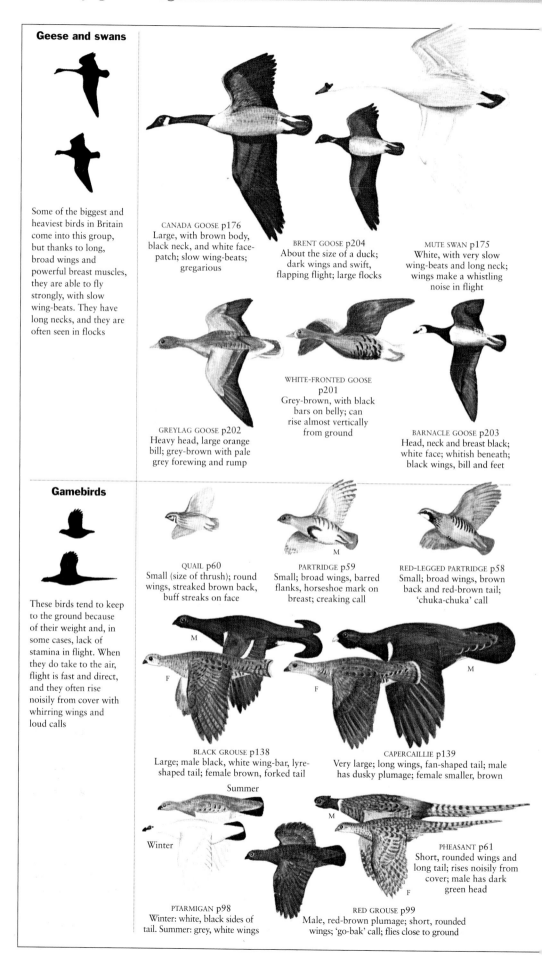

Geese and swans

Some of the biggest and heaviest birds in Britain come into this group, but thanks to long, broad wings and powerful breast muscles, they are able to fly strongly, with slow wing-beats. They have long necks, and they are often seen in flocks

CANADA GOOSE p176
Large, with brown body, black neck, and white face-patch; slow wing-beats; gregarious

BRENT GOOSE p204
About the size of a duck; dark wings and swift, flapping flight; large flocks

MUTE SWAN p175
White, with very slow wing-beats and long neck; wings make a whistling noise in flight

WHITE-FRONTED GOOSE p201
Grey-brown, with black bars on belly; can rise almost vertically from ground

GREYLAG GOOSE p202
Heavy head, large orange bill; grey-brown with pale grey forewing and rump

BARNACLE GOOSE p203
Head, neck and breast black; white face; whitish beneath; black wings, bill and feet

Gamebirds

These birds tend to keep to the ground because of their weight and, in some cases, lack of stamina in flight. When they do take to the air, flight is fast and direct, and they often rise noisily from cover with whirring wings and loud calls

QUAIL p60
Small (size of thrush); round wings, streaked brown back, buff streaks on face

PARTRIDGE p59
Small; broad wings, barred flanks, horseshoe mark on breast; creaking call

M

RED-LEGGED PARTRIDGE p58
Small; broad wings, brown back and red-brown tail; 'chuka-chuka' call

M

F

M

F

BLACK GROUSE p138
Large; male black, white wing-bar, lyre-shaped tail; female brown, forked tail

CAPERCAILLIE p139
Very large; long wings, fan-shaped tail; male has dusky plumage; female smaller, brown

Summer

Winter

M

F

PHEASANT p61
Short, rounded wings and long tail; rises noisily from cover; male has dark green head

PTARMIGAN p98
Winter: white, black sides of tail. Summer: grey, white wings

RED GROUSE p99
Male, red-brown plumage; short, rounded wings; 'go-bak' call; flies close to ground

Birds of prey and cuckoo

GOLDEN EAGLE p101
Very large; long, broad wings and dark plumage; often soars for long periods

BUZZARD p116
Broad wings; wide, rounded tail; soars, hovers, and flaps wings slowly

RED KITE p114
Long wings; long, forked tail; often soars for long periods

Birds of prey and cuckoo

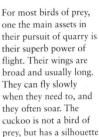

For most birds of prey, one the main assets in their pursuit of quarry is their superb power of flight. Their wings are broad and usually long. They can fly slowly when they need to, and they often soar. The cuckoo is not a bird of prey, but has a silhouette similar to that of some birds in this group

HEN HARRIER p100
Long wings and tail; flight slow and flapping; male has white rump

MONTAGU'S HARRIER p82
Long wings and tail; flight slow and flapping; male has black wing-bars

SPARROWHAWK p115
Short, rounded wings, long tail; fast, direct flight; sometimes soars

CUCKOO p85
Pointed wings, long tail; direct flight, shallow wing-beats

MARSH HARRIER p151
Large; long wings and long tail; male buff below with grey band and black wing-tips; female rusty brown

OSPREY p150
Very large; dark above, speckled white below; dark mark under 'elbow' of wing

Falcons

Peregrines dive almost vertically to catch prey, and all falcons are able to manoeuvre superbly in chases after small birds, flying fast and using rapid, shallow beats of their long wings

PEREGRINE p238
Long tail, slate-grey back; fast, direct flight; soars and glides at times

HOBBY p83
Long, scythe-like wings, slate-grey back, red thigh-patches

KESTREL p62
Small and slim; pointed wings and long tail; distinctive hovering flight

MERLIN p102
Small; streaked underparts; fast, direct flight, rapid wing-beats

Rails

Heavy bodies and small, rounded wings limit the rails' airborne activity. Their flight tends to be weak and whirring, often with legs trailing

COOT p197
Black; white wing-bar, white shield-patch on head

MOORHEN p196
Small; black; white at sides of tail; flight weak, legs trailing

CORNCRAKE p63
Short, rounded wings; flight weak, pink legs trailing

WATER RAIL p152
Small; rounded wings; flight weak, legs trailing

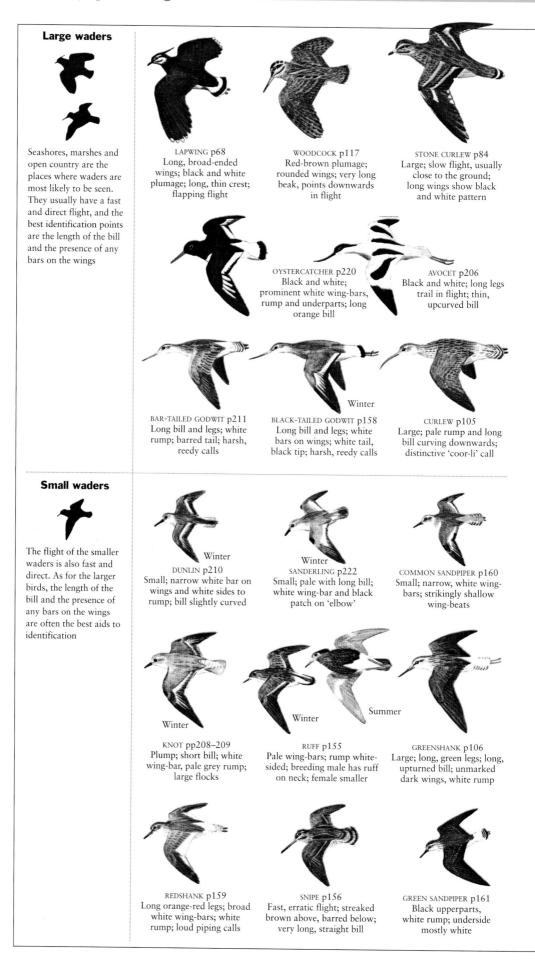

Large waders

Seashores, marshes and open country are the places where waders are most likely to be seen. They usually have a fast and direct flight, and the best identification points are the length of the bill and the presence of any bars on the wings

LAPWING p68
Long, broad-ended wings; black and white plumage; long, thin crest; flapping flight

WOODCOCK p117
Red-brown plumage; rounded wings; very long beak, points downwards in flight

STONE CURLEW p84
Large; slow flight, usually close to the ground; long wings show black and white pattern

OYSTERCATCHER p220
Black and white; prominent white wing-bars, rump and underparts; long orange bill

AVOCET p206
Black and white; long legs trail in flight; thin, upcurved bill

BAR-TAILED GODWIT p211
Long bill and legs; white rump; barred tail; harsh, reedy calls

BLACK-TAILED GODWIT p158
Winter
Long bill and legs; white bars on wings; white tail, black tip; harsh, reedy calls

CURLEW p105
Large; pale rump and long bill curving downwards; distinctive 'coor-li' call

Small waders

The flight of the smaller waders is also fast and direct. As for the larger birds, the length of the bill and the presence of any bars on the wings are often the best aids to identification

DUNLIN p210
Winter
Small; narrow white bar on wings and white sides to rump; bill slightly curved

SANDERLING p222
Winter
Small; pale with long bill; white wing-bar and black patch on 'elbow'

COMMON SANDPIPER p160
Small; narrow, white wing-bars; strikingly shallow wing-beats

KNOT pp208–209
Winter
Plump; short bill; white wing-bar, pale grey rump; large flocks

RUFF p155
Winter Summer
Pale wing-bars; rump white-sided; breeding male has ruff on neck; female smaller

GREENSHANK p106
Large; long, green legs; long, upturned bill; unmarked dark wings, white rump

REDSHANK p159
Long orange-red legs; broad white wing-bars; white rump; loud piping calls

SNIPE p156
Fast, erratic flight; streaked brown above, barred below; very long, straight bill

GREEN SANDPIPER p161
Black upperparts, white rump; underside mostly white

Small and medium-sized plovers

These short-billed wading birds fly fast and direct on long wings. The lapwing, shown opposite with similar-looking large waders, is also a plover

Winter

GREY PLOVER p207
Large; small white patch on tops of wings, black patch beneath

LITTLE RINGED PLOVER p154
Small; plain brown wings; black eye-stripe

RINGED PLOVER p221
Small; white wing-bar; black eye-stripe

Summer

GOLDEN PLOVER p104
Pointed wings, short tail; belly black in summer

Skuas

Powerful, broad wings enable skuas to spend a long time airborne. They manoeuvre well when pursuing other seabirds to rob them of food

GREAT SKUA p239
Very large and dark; heavy bill; prominent white wing-flashes; dives to attack intruders

Light phase

Dark phase

ARCTIC SKUA p240
Plumage varies from dark with light underparts to entirely dark brown; short tail-streamers

Gulls

In the air, gulls are versatile performers. They fly strongly, with slow wing-beats, often soaring and gliding, and sometimes floating on up-currents of warm air. Their wings are long and pointed

COMMON GULL p225
Grey back, yellow-green legs, yellow bill; immatures brown and white

KITTIWAKE p243
Black wing-tips, black legs, yellow bill; immatures' wings striped

Summer

BLACK-HEADED GULL p32
Wings white with black tips; red legs and bill; immatures brown and white

HERRING GULL p224
Pink legs, yellow bill, grey back; immatures brown and white

GREAT BLACK-BACKED GULL p242
Black back, white body, pink legs; immatures brown above, pale beneath

LESSER BLACK-BACKED GULL p241
Dark grey back, yellow legs; bill less stout than great black-backed's bill

Terns

Graceful flight marks out the terns from other coastal birds. They have slender bodies and long wings, and their plumage is usually pale grey and white

Summer

COMMON TERN p226
Pale grey back, white body; bill red, black tip; immatures brown and white

Summer

SANDWICH TERN p228
Large; slightly forked tail, black legs; small crest; bill black, yellow tip

LITTLE TERN p229
Small; slightly forked tail; white forehead; bill yellow, black tip

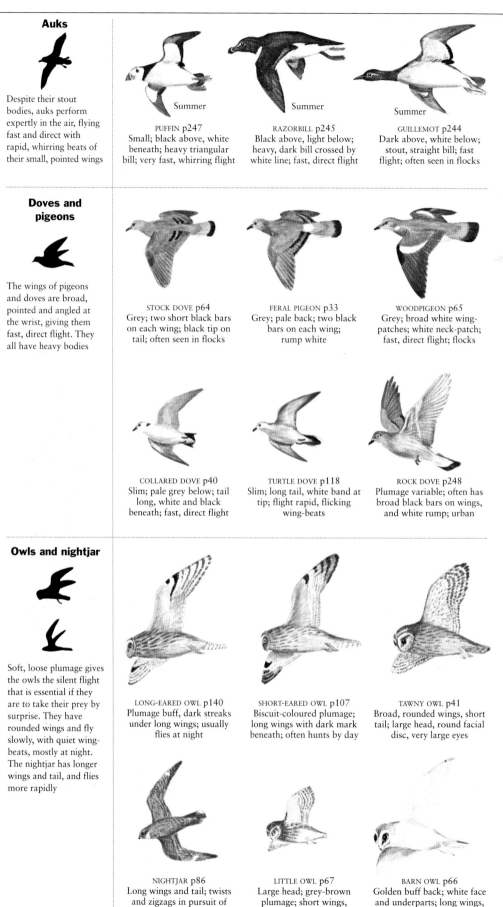

Auks

Despite their stout bodies, auks perform expertly in the air, flying fast and direct with rapid, whirring beats of their small, pointed wings

Summer

PUFFIN p247
Small; black above, white beneath; heavy triangular bill; very fast, whirring flight

Summer

RAZORBILL p245
Black above, light below; heavy, dark bill crossed by white line; fast, direct flight

Summer

GUILLEMOT p244
Dark above, white below; stout, straight bill; fast flight; often seen in flocks

Doves and pigeons

The wings of pigeons and doves are broad, pointed and angled at the wrist, giving them fast, direct flight. They all have heavy bodies

STOCK DOVE p64
Grey; two short black bars on each wing; black tip on tail; often seen in flocks

FERAL PIGEON p33
Grey; pale back; two black bars on each wing; rump white

WOODPIGEON p65
Grey; broad white wing-patches; white neck-patch; fast, direct flight; flocks

COLLARED DOVE p40
Slim; pale grey below; tail long, white and black beneath; fast, direct flight

TURTLE DOVE p118
Slim; long tail, white band at tip; flight rapid, flicking wing-beats

ROCK DOVE p248
Plumage variable; often has broad black bars on wings, and white rump; urban

Owls and nightjar

Soft, loose plumage gives the owls the silent flight that is essential if they are to take their prey by surprise. They have rounded wings and fly slowly, with quiet wing-beats, mostly at night. The nightjar has longer wings and tail, and flies more rapidly

LONG-EARED OWL p140
Plumage buff, dark streaks under long wings; usually flies at night

SHORT-EARED OWL p107
Biscuit-coloured plumage; long wings with dark mark beneath; often hunts by day

TAWNY OWL p41
Broad, rounded wings, short tail; large head, round facial disc, very large eyes

NIGHTJAR p86
Long wings and tail; twists and zigzags in pursuit of insects; often hovers

LITTLE OWL p67
Large head; grey-brown plumage; short wings, bounding flight; flies by day

BARN OWL p66
Golden buff back; white face and underparts; long wings, slow, wavering flight

Woodpeckers

The woodpeckers' broad wings give them a deeply undulating flight. Patterns on the back or face often prove a useful method of identification

GREEN WOODPECKER
p122
Large; bright green above; crimson crown, yellow rump

LESSER SPOTTED WOODPECKER
p121
Small; black and white, barred wings and back

GREAT SPOTTED WOODPECKER
p120
Barred wings; white patches on back; crimson under tail

Larks

Open countryside is the larks' natural home. They have streaked brown plumage and long wings, and their flight is either bounding or direct

WOODLARK p87
Small; very short tail; black and white patches on the 'elbow' of each wing

SKYLARK p69
Larger; white at sides of tail, white trailing edges to wings; hovers and soars

Swallows and swift

These birds spend most of their lives in the air, feeding on the wing by catching small insects. They have long, pointed wings, and fast, direct flight

SWIFT p34
Very long, scythe-like wings; fast flight, rapid wing-beats; often glides

SWALLOW p72
Steel-blue upper parts, white beneath; adults have long tail-streamers

HOUSE MARTIN p35
Small; blue-black above, white beneath; white rump, forked tail

SAND MARTIN p164
Small; white below with brown breast-band; long wings, forked tail

Pipits and wagtails

More at home on the ground than in the air, these birds tend to be slim and to have long tails and undulating flight. Their flight calls are often distinctive

MEADOW PIPIT p108
Small; olive-brown above, buff below; prominent white tail-sides; 'pheet' flight call

YELLOW WAGTAIL

PIED WAGTAIL p165
Black and white; very long tail; undulating flight; 'tschizzik' flight call

GREY WAGTAIL

YELLOW AND GREY WAGTAILS
pp166 and 167
Yellow breasts; male grey wagtail has longer tail and black throat

Thrushes and starling

Most birds in this group are plump-looking and spend much of their time on the ground, but they also fly well

RING OUZEL p109
Black, with white crescent on breast; pale wing-patch; flight usually fast and direct

BLACKBIRD p47
Male black with yellow bill; female dark brown with lighter throat; flight direct

STARLING p37
Pointed wings; fast, direct flight; sometimes glides; often seen in large flocks

MISTLE THRUSH p48
Large; long tail and light under wings; flight undulating

SONG THRUSH p49
Buff under wings; streaked breast; brown back; flight mainly direct

REDWING p71
Streaked breast; reddish under wings; white eye-stripe; undulating flight

FIELDFARE p70
Large; long tail; grey rump; chestnut wings and shoulders

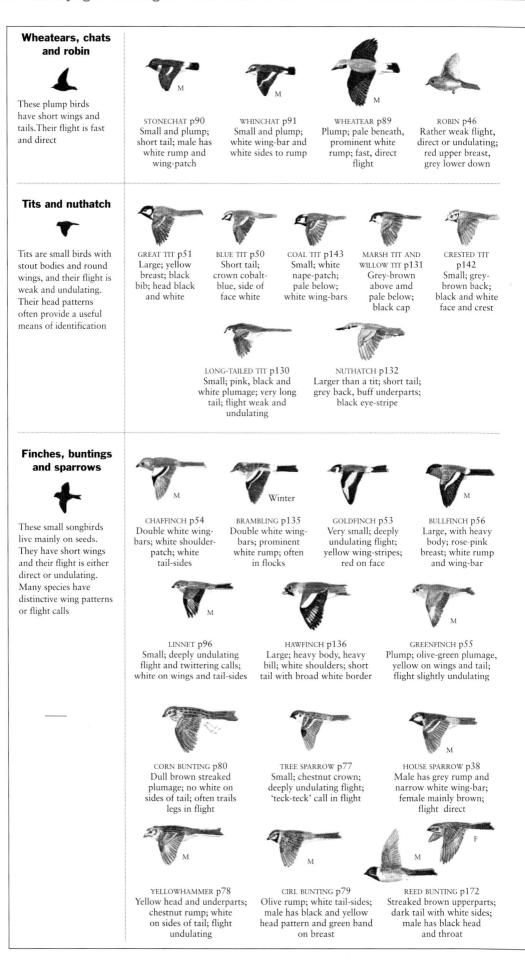

Wheatears, chats and robin

These plump birds have short wings and tails. Their flight is fast and direct

STONECHAT p90
Small and plump; short tail; male has white rump and wing-patch

WHINCHAT p91
Small and plump; white wing-bar and white sides to rump

WHEATEAR p89
Plump; pale beneath, prominent white rump; fast, direct flight

ROBIN p46
Rather weak flight, direct or undulating; red upper breast, grey lower down

Tits and nuthatch

Tits are small birds with stout bodies and round wings, and their flight is weak and undulating. Their head patterns often provide a useful means of identification

GREAT TIT p51
Large; yellow breast; black bib; head black and white

BLUE TIT p50
Short tail; crown cobalt-blue, side of face white

COAL TIT p143
Small; white nape-patch; pale below; white wing-bars

MARSH TIT AND WILLOW TIT p131
Grey-brown above amd pale below; black cap

CRESTED TIT p142
Small; grey-brown back; black and white face and crest

LONG-TAILED TIT p130
Small; pink, black and white plumage; very long tail; flight weak and undulating

NUTHATCH p132
Larger than a tit; short tail; grey back, buff underparts; black eye-stripe

Finches, buntings and sparrows

These small songbirds live mainly on seeds. They have short wings and their flight is either direct or undulating. Many species have distinctive wing patterns or flight calls

CHAFFINCH p54
Double white wing-bars; white shoulder-patch; white tail-sides

BRAMBLING p135
Double white wing-bars; prominent white rump; often in flocks

GOLDFINCH p53
Very small; deeply undulating flight; yellow wing-stripes; red on face

BULLFINCH p56
Large, with heavy body; rose-pink breast; white rump and wing-bar

LINNET p96
Small; deeply undulating flight and twittering calls; white on wings and tail-sides

HAWFINCH p136
Large; heavy body, heavy bill; white shoulders; short tail with broad white border

GREENFINCH p55
Plump; olive-green plumage, yellow on wings and tail; flight slightly undulating

CORN BUNTING p80
Dull brown streaked plumage; no white on sides of tail; often trails legs in flight

TREE SPARROW p77
Small; chestnut crown; deeply undulating flight; 'teck-teck' call in flight

HOUSE SPARROW p38
Male has grey rump and narrow white wing-bar; female mainly brown; flight direct

YELLOWHAMMER p78
Yellow head and underparts; chestnut rump; white on sides of tail; flight undulating

CIRL BUNTING p79
Olive rump; white tail-sides; male has black and yellow head pattern and green band on breast

REED BUNTING p172
Streaked brown upperparts; dark tail with white sides; male has black head and throat

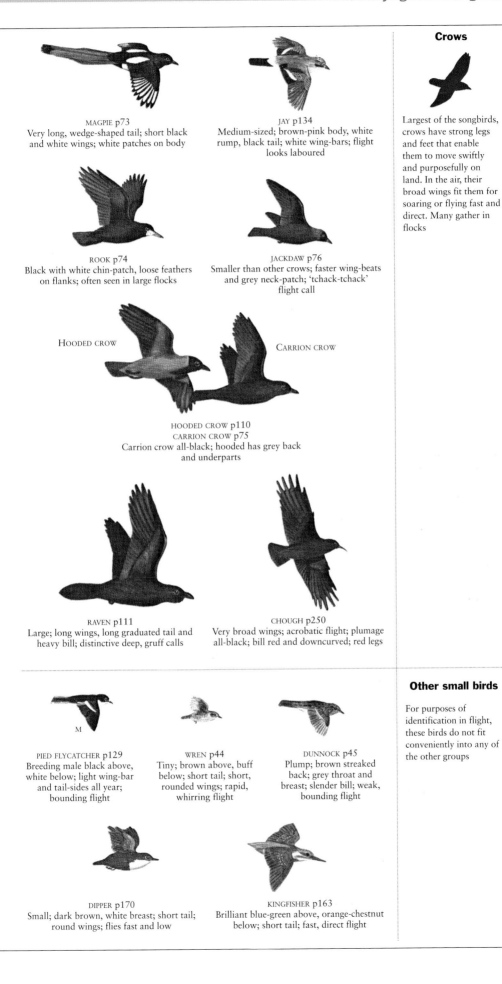

Crows

Largest of the songbirds, crows have strong legs and feet that enable them to move swiftly and purposefully on land. In the air, their broad wings fit them for soaring or flying fast and direct. Many gather in flocks

MAGPIE p73
Very long, wedge-shaped tail; short black and white wings; white patches on body

JAY p134
Medium-sized; brown-pink body, white rump, black tail; white wing-bars; flight looks laboured

ROOK p74
Black with white chin-patch, loose feathers on flanks; often seen in large flocks

JACKDAW p76
Smaller than other crows; faster wing-beats and grey neck-patch; 'tchack-tchack' flight call

HOODED CROW

CARRION CROW

HOODED CROW p110
CARRION CROW p75
Carrion crow all-black; hooded has grey back and underparts

RAVEN p111
Large; long wings, long graduated tail and heavy bill; distinctive deep, gruff calls

CHOUGH p250
Very broad wings; acrobatic flight; plumage all-black; bill red and downcurved; red legs

Other small birds

For purposes of identification in flight, these birds do not fit conveniently into any of the other groups

PIED FLYCATCHER p129
Breeding male black above, white below; light wing-bar and tail-sides all year; bounding flight

WREN p44
Tiny; brown above, buff below; short tail; short, rounded wings; rapid, whirring flight

DUNNOCK p45
Plump; brown streaked back; grey throat and breast; slender bill; weak, bounding flight

DIPPER p170
Small; dark brown, white breast; short tail; round wings; flies fast and low

KINGFISHER p163
Brilliant blue-green above, orange-chestnut below; short tail; fast, direct flight

British Birds

Britain is blessed with a remarkable variety of birds. Many travel vast distances to be here in spring and summer, or from autumn to spring; others remain all year; still others simply pass through on their remarkable migratory journeys. The following pages contain 216 bird profiles, grouped according to their habitats – the kind of places in which they are most often seen.

HABITATS

Towns

Built-up areas, with little vegetation beyond trees in the streets, weeds on waste ground and the lawns and borders of small gardens, are the most artificial of the habitats to which birds have had to adapt. The most successful species in this environment are those that originally nested where vegetation was scarce. The bridges, walls and office blocks of towns and cities provide them with a substitute for cliffs and ledges.

In winter the black-headed gull loses its chocolate brown hood

SUMMER

J F M A M J
J A S O N D

Black-headed gull Chroicocephalus ridibundus

RECOGNITION

Chocolate brown hood (lost in winter); pale grey back and wings; white forewing flash, black tips; rest of plumage white; red feet and bill; young are brown and white, with black band on tail; sexes alike.

NESTING

Nests in colonies; both sexes build substantial pile of dried vegetation on tuft of rushes or grass; lays mid April–July; usually 3 eggs, varying in colour from pale buff to deep brown, or blue-green; incubation about 23 days, by both parents; young, fed by both parents, leave nest in a few days, fly after 5–6 weeks.

FEEDING

Scraps and offal in towns; elsewhere crabs, sand-eels, moths, snails, earthworms and insects.

SIZE

38cm (15in)

During the past 100 years, this gull has become a familiar bird in towns, even in London where it survives as a scavenger. Black-headed gulls moved up from the Thames estuary during hard winters at the end of the 19th century, and found food plentiful around docks, in parks and along embankments where people threw scraps.

The birds are common in winter along the coast, on estuaries, and on farmland where they follow the plough and eat lots of worms and insects. They have learnt to live partly by 'piracy' on lapwings. The gull stands by, ready to pounce and snatch as the lapwing patters forward to take a worm or insect; or it will often give chase until the lapwing drops the food.

Thousands of gulls roost on reservoirs in the winter. They stream from the fields in the late afternoon, sometimes flying in a loose V-formation, sometimes in a wavering stream that may stretch for miles.

Although a few gulls breed on gravel pits near towns, most of them go to coastal sandhills and salt-marshes, to hills and moors where they nest in colonies in bogs and marshes, or beside upland lakes, even far inland.

Despite the fact that the black-headed gull is so common inland in winter, many people do not realise what it is; for its winter plumage does not include a dark head.

Feral pigeons nest and roost on large buildings in city centres

Feral pigeon Columba livia

This pigeon is the most urban bird of all; it lives in city squares and town gutters, docks, railway stations and open-air cafés – where it will even snatch scraps from people's plates. Notices in Trafalgar Square in London and in many other public places threaten a heavy fine for feeding the pigeons, but they are unlikely ever to go hungry, for with such sharp wits and alert enterprise they have no trouble finding food for themselves.

The original ancestor of the town pigeon is the wild rock dove of the sea cliffs. However the forerunners of the city birds were domestic pigeons that escaped from medieval dovecotes. Records show that there were pigeons on Old St Paul's Cathedral 600 years ago, for the Dean was then complaining that boys broke cathedral windows by throwing stones at the birds.

A study of feral pigeons in Leeds showed that in winter they lived almost entirely on bread, cake and bird-seed offered by the public. In March they went to the country to feed on freshly sown grain and weed-seeds. In summer they ate more weed-seeds and vegetable matter, and in autumn they fed on farmland stubble-fields.

The cooing voice of the feral pigeon is a familiar sound in cities. Familiar too are its courtship display, in which a puffed-out male bows repeatedly to an apparently uninterested female, and its habit of roosting on ledges, hunched up against the cold.

RECOGNITION

Plumage very variable; may be blue-grey, cinnamon-brown, black or white, or any combination of these colours; rock dove ancestry is often shown by double black wing-bars or white rump; sexes alike.

NESTING

Both sexes build nest of grass and twigs in hollow in building, often under the eaves; lays mainly March–September; usually 2 eggs, white; incubation 17–19 days, by both parents; young, fed by both parents, fly after 35–37 days; usually two to four broods.

FEEDING

Often bread and scraps, but includes chocolate, apples and bacon rind; also grain, weed-seeds and small snails.

SIZE

33cm (13in)

Swifts fly screeching round houses on late spring and summer evenings

Swift Apus apus

No birds are more aerial in their habits than swifts. Their legs have become so weak, because they are so seldom used, that the birds are helpless and easily caught once on the ground; but swifts never alight on the ground except by accident, and never perch on wires. They feed on the wing, sometimes mate on the wing, and even sleep on the wing. At dusk, swifts circle higher and higher until they disappear from sight. It used to be thought that they returned after dark to roost at their nests, but it is now known that those not incubating eggs or brooding young remain aloft until sunrise, probably cat-napping on currents of rising air between short spells of flapping to gain height.

To countrymen, the swift was once known as the 'devil bird', because of its habit of flying screaming round houses during late spring and early summer evenings. It is one of the latest migrants to arrive and one of the earliest to go. Only a few can be seen before the last few days of April or after the middle of August.

Swifts appear to pair for life. They have two courtship displays. On the nest, mating occurs after mutual crooning and preening, while in the air there is a spectacular chase before the birds mate on the wing.

If a strange swift intrudes on an occupied nest, fierce fighting may occur. One such battle, watched in a tower in Oxford, lasted 5¾ hours. There are two records of swifts being found alive and interlocked on the ground beneath their nests.

House martins build their mud nests under the eaves of houses and barns

House martin Delichon urbicum

A conspicuous white rump makes the house martin the easiest of the swallow family to distinguish in flight. Its nesting habits are distinctive, too, and the birds' mud nests are familiar under the eaves of houses. Surveys suggest that house martins may be slowly decreasing in Britain, but the evidence is conflicting. Certainly there are local fluctuations in their numbers. In 1966 they returned to inner London as a nesting species for the first time since 1889.

A famous colony under the arches of Clifton Hampden bridge, near Oxford, reached 513 nests in 1952, but today it is largely deserted. Few colonies now exceed a few tens of pairs at best and most house martins nest in small groups of up to five or so. They seem equally at home on new houses. A few still nest on cliffs in north and west Britain. Although they feed on the wing, they come to the ground to collect mud for nest-building and must have access to wet mud in spring.

Nesting begins three or four weeks after their arrival in April, and young birds of early broods often continue to roost in the nest until they migrate. Late in the season as many as 13 birds have been counted, crammed into a single nest.

RECOGNITION

Blue-black above, white beneath, with white rump; tail less forked than swallow's; sexes alike.

NESTING

Both sexes build rounded nest of gobbets of mud, grass and roots, under eaves of house, sometimes under bridge, in caves, or on cliff; nest thickly lined with feathers; lays May–August; usually 4 or 5 eggs, white; incubation 14 or 15 days, by both parents; nestlings, fed by both parents, fly after 19–22 days; two broods, sometimes three.

FEEDING

Almost entirely insects caught on the wing, especially flies and small beetles.

SIZE

12.75cm (5in)

J F M A M J
J A S O N D

MALE

*Black redstarts often sing
from buildings, perched
on a high ledge*

Black redstart Phoenicurus ochruros

RECOGNITION

Male mainly black in summer, grey-black in winter, with white wing-patch; female grey-brown; both sexes have chestnut-red rump and tail.

NESTING

Female builds nest of grass, moss and roots on ledge or in crevice of building, inside shed or under rafters; lays April–July; usually 4–6 eggs, glossy white; incubation 12 or 13 days, by female only; young, fed by both parents, leave nest after 16–18 days; two broods, often three.

FEEDING

Mainly insects; also spiders and millipedes; berries at times.

SIZE

14cm (5½in)

The black redstart used to be a rare and irregular nester in Britain, appearing mainly as a rather uncommon passage migrant and winter visitor, chiefly on southern coasts. One pair bred on the south coast in 1923, another in 1924, and two pairs in 1925. Since then, at least one pair has bred in England every year, increasingly since the Second World War, reaching 50-100 pairs, but with a sharp recent decline.

Although originally it nested on sea cliffs, the black redstart is today very much a town bird. It feeds on rubble-strewn waste ground – the kind of land that was once provided in abundance by bomb sites – and during and immediately after the Second World War it was established in the City of London. As numbers there have dwindled because of rebuilding, the bird has found other nest-sites in docks and other industrial areas in London and its suburbs, and on the east and south coasts, from Norfolk to Sussex – even on the nuclear power station at Dungeness in Kent. Much of its food is caught on the wing, and it is capable of hovering to catch flying insects.

Its call-notes are a short 'tsip' and a 'tucc-tucc' of alarm. The song, a grating warble, is usually given from a building, often at a considerable height. Migrating birds often sing in April and May, and occasionally in the autumn. They appear to sing as a means of defending territory, even though they may not breed.

J F M A M J
J A S O N D

MALE IN
SUMMER

*Hungry young starlings
chase their parents, urgently
demanding food*

Starling Sturnus vulgaris

Starlings, swarming in tens of thousands to their roost sites just before dusk, used to be a spectacular, noisy and inescapable part of life in many cities. Their high-pitched calls rose above the din of traffic and their droppings fouled streets and buildings. Many methods were used to drive them away, but it was the effects of intensive agriculture that eventually reduced them to much smaller numbers. Most town roosts have gone, but some exciting spectacles remain, as on Brighton pier, but it is in reedbeds and dense woods that huge roosts sometimes still appear in winter.

These birds, which create magnificent swirling performances in flocks sometimes hundreds of thousands strong, are largely winter visitors from Europe. Numbers of breeding birds in summer have been reduced by two-thirds since about 1970. A reduction in holes for nest-sites may have had some effect in places, but it is largely lack of food that is to blame, as old pastures and meadows, full of insects, have been replaced by dense, tall grass, cut early and squeezed into plastic bags for silage. There is little there for any insect-eating bird to find, still less for a starling to feed to hungry chicks.

Their vocabulary includes many clipped notes, and they are good mimics of other birds' voices, and sometimes pick up other sounds, even a human whistle.

RECOGNITION

Iridescent purple, green and blue plumage, handsomely spangled with white or buff in winter; spangling more marked in female than male; jerky walk; swift, direct flight, sometimes varied by gliding.

NESTING

Usually nests in loose colonies; male builds untidy nest of dried grass and straw in tree hole, on cliff or building; female lines it with feathers or moss; lays April–May; 5–7 eggs, pale blue; incubation about 13 days, by both parents; nestlings, fed by both parents, fly after about 21 days; usually two broods.

FEEDING

Insects (especially leatherjackets), earthworms, spiders, snails, slugs; fruit, seeds, roots and berries.

SIZE

21.5cm (8½in)

J F M A M J
J A S O N D

MALE

FEMALE

In courtship several cock sparrows surround the hen, chirping loudly

House sparrow Passer domesticus

RECOGNITION

Brown upper parts, streaked with black; grey crown and rump, red-brown shoulders and black bib; white wing-bar; more heavily built than tree sparrow; female brown, with streaked back and plain underside.

NESTING

Both sexes build untidy nest of dry grass in hole in building or tree, sometimes in open in thick hedgerow, when nest is domed; usually lays April–August; normally 3–5 eggs, white with grey and brown blotches; incubation 12–14 days, chiefly by hen; young, fed by both parents, fly after about 15 days; up to three broods.

FEEDING

Grain and weed-seeds; insects and their larvae; almost entirely bread and scraps in built-up areas.

SIZE

14.5cm (5¾in)

The house sparrow is so familiar that townspeople often suppose it to be the most numerous bird in Britain while, in fact, it is largely confined to the neighbourhood of human settlements, and is surpassed in numbers by both the chaffinch and the blackbird. Of all birds suffering severe declines in numbers, this one is perhaps the most unexpected, but a lack of insect food in summer, seeds in winter and holes for nest-sites is responsible for a dramatic reduction.

There were probably no house sparrows in Britain before the arrival of man. They are believed to have come with Neolithic men, our first farming ancestors, spreading across Europe from their original home in Africa. Like starlings they have been introduced into North America and have spread widely.

Only in autumn does the house sparrow break its close ties with buildings and move to farmland to feed on ripening corn. Its habit of tearing garden primulas and crocuses – especially the yellow ones – may be connected with its diet, for at least part of the petal is eaten.

The bird utters a wide variety of 'chirps' and 'cheeps' and has a double note, 'chissik', all of which are strung together to form a rudimentary song. The most important element of its courtship display is the 'sparrow party', which usually begins with a single cock displaying to a hen and bowing to her. Then others join in, all chirping loudly until the hen flies off, pursued by the whole flock.

Parks and Gardens

Birds and people have nowhere achieved a happier relationship than in parks and gardens. All the common garden birds were originally woodland species, but in living alongside people they have found security and a regular food supply, which more than compensates them for leaving their old surroundings. In return, they eat many harmful garden insects – and they add to the stock of human pleasure simply by being there.

J F M A M J
J A S O N D

In flight the collared dove shows its distinctive white tail-tip

Collared dove Streptopelia decaocto

RECOGNITION

Grey-brown above, pale grey below; long tail, black and white beneath; black and white half-collar on back of neck; distinctive 'cu-coo-cuk' song; sexes alike.

NESTING

Both sexes build flat nest of twigs and stems, generally well up in tree, sometimes on ledge of building; lays March–September; 2 eggs, white; incubation about 14 days, by both parents; young, fed by both parents, fly after about 18 days, finally leave the nest a few days later; usually two broods, but up to five may be attempted.

FEEDING

Mostly grain and weed-seeds; some fruit such as elderberries.

SIZE

31.75cm (12½in)

The collared dove, easily the most recent arrival among our common breeding birds (although the little egret is now spreading quickly), has also rapidly become one of the most widespread. Its headlong advance across Europe and Britain reads like the story of a well-planned military campaign.

At the end of the 19th century the bird had only a tenuous bridge-head in Europe, in the Balkans. Seventy years ago the nearest collared dove to our shores was on the far side of the Danube in what was then Yugoslavia. Then, early in the 1930s, came a population explosion among the birds, and collared doves began their advance towards the Atlantic seaboard. By 1947 they were in the Netherlands; by 1948 they had reached Denmark and, a year later, it was the turn of Sweden. They reached Belgium in 1952 and in that same year the first collared dove was seen in Britain – at Manton in Lincolnshire. Three years later the first British nest was discovered, at Cromer in Norfolk; and by 1957 a pair had a nest as far north as Moray, in Scotland. Today, collared doves have reached the remote corners of the British Isles, and they are now to be found in almost every town, suburb and village in the land.

They are grain-eaters, taking food from bird tables and horse paddocks since grain for poultry is less readily available than it once was. The song, a triple 'cu-coo-cuk', with a marked accent on the second syllable, has become a familiar sound, especially in parks and gardens.

In the daytime, a roosting tawny owl may be mobbed by smaller birds

J F M A M J
J A S O N D

Tawny owl Strix aluco

When Shakespeare wrote down the call of the tawny owl as 'tu-whit, tu-whoo – a merry note' he was, for once, being a poor naturalist. What he did was to combine two notes, the beautiful, breathy hoot, 'hooo: hoo, hu, hoooo-oo-oo', which is the song, and a loud, nasal, sharp 'kee-wick', which is used by both sexes at dusk, as a means of keeping in contact in the dark. Young birds in late summer have a more vibrant, or whining version of the 'kee-wick' call.

The tawny owl, a bird of copses and well-wooded parks and gardens, is the most common owl over much of Britain, though absent from Ireland. Like most owls, it hunts by night and roosts by day, but if hard-pressed for food at nesting time, it will hunt in broad daylight. At other times, a roosting owl can often be located by following up noisy parties of smaller birds, especially jays, blackbirds and chaffinches, which seek out the predator and mob it. The owl may not be dislodged by their clamour, though, and will not be disturbed easily even at the sight of a human. Its astonishingly flexible neck allows it to turn its head almost full-circle, so that its face can be kept towards an observer moving round it.

The nest is usually in a tree hole, but a pair may take over a burrow in the ground, a cliff ledge, a sparrow-hawk's nest or a squirrel's drey. The birds' diet can be studied fairly accurately, for tawny owls bring up pellets of undigested fur, bones and beetle wing cases.

RECOGNITION

Mottled brown, with round facial disc and dark brown eyes; distinctive 'kee-wick' call and hooting song; sexes alike.

NESTING

No nest built; lays in old tree hole, squirrel's drey, occasionally an old building, rock crevice or on ground; lays March–May, sometimes earlier; usually 2–4 eggs, round and white; incubation 28–30 days, by female only; young, fed mainly by male, fly after 30–37 days.

FEEDING

Small mammals, especially mice, voles, young rats and shrews; some birds; at times fish, frogs, molluscs, worms and insects.

SIZE

38cm (15in)

J F M **A M J**
J A S O N D

Hoopoe in flight – like a large black and white moth

Hoopoe Upupa epops

Pink-brown plumage; very broad black and white wings and tail in flight; pink crest, black-tipped long curved bill; sexes alike.

NESTING

Seldom nests in Britain; breeds in southern Europe, in hole in tree or wall, or uses nest-boxes; usually no nesting material but droppings accumulate; lays May–June; 5–8 eggs, light grey to cream; incubation 18 days, by hen only; nestlings, fed by both parents, leave after 3–4 weeks.

FEEDING

Mainly beetle grubs, locusts, grasshoppers, moths, ants, earwigs, flies, some spiders, centipedes, woodlice, worms.

SIZE

29.25cm (11½in)

With its pink-brown plumage, a crest like a Native American's head-dress and boldly barred black and white wings, the hoopoe is one of the most exotic birds to be seen in Britain. Sadly, however, for most people a sighting of the bird is likely to remain little more than a dream because the hoopoe is rare and unpredictable. Small numbers arrive each April or May as vagrants from the Continent, although others may turn up at any time of the year.

Hoopoes breed regularly across the Channel, and when they do come to Britain, they usually seek places with scattered trees, nesting in a hole in an old willow or a cranny in a farm building. The site may soon become insanitary, for hoopoes do not keep their nests sweet. They are sometimes perceived as filthy birds because of their feeding and breeding habits.

The call-note, a rapid, far-carrying, clipped 'hoo-hoo-hoo', of the same pitch as the cuckoo's, gives the bird its name. It also has a harsh, starling-like 'errrr'. Fluttering before its nest, it looks like a gigantic black and white barred moth, but the flight is by no means as feeble as it seems and a hoopoe can out-manoeuvre a falcon.

Courtship leads to much display with the crest as the male, the tip of its bill pressed against a branch, bows to the female. During incubation, the male provides all the food for both birds.

J F M A M J
J A S O N D

Waxwings often eat ornamental berries in surburban gardens

Waxwing Bombycilla garrulus

Every few years, and sometimes for several years in succession, there are mass irruptions of waxwings from their breeding grounds in northern Europe. There may have been a failure in the crop of rowan berries, their favourite food; or there may have been a population explosion among the waxwings after a particularly good rowan year. Britain gets a share of the larger dispersals, and although the invasions are erratic, they have been going on for centuries. A 'waxwing winter' was recorded as long ago as 1679–80.

There were four successive invasions in 1956–60, a series that beat all records. A massive irruption came in 1965–66, with the arrival of more than 11,000 birds recorded in two weeks, and numbers in the 1990s and since the turn of the century have sometimes been much higher.

By the time waxwings arrive, other birds have usually stripped the rowan bushes, so the waxwings may turn up in parks and gardens to gorge on the berries of ornamental trees and shrubs. In Norfolk, in February 1957, in two days a party of seven stripped the berries on 9.25sq m (100sq ft) of a cotoneaster growing on a cottage. One bird ate 390 berries, roughly its own weight, in 2½ hours.

Waxwings are highly sociable and call frequently, usually with a soft trilling 'sirrr'. They were once known as Bohemian chatterers. In courtship, the handsome male displays its colourful wing feathers.

RECOGNITION

Waxy red, white and yellow markings on wing; bright yellow tip to tail; prominent crest; black throat; chestnut and grey above, pink-brown below; looks like large plump finch at first glance; sexes alike.

NESTING

Does not nest in Britain; many that 'invade' Britain probably breed in Finland; cup-shaped nest of twigs and moss built in conifer; lays May–July; 4–6 eggs, grey with dark spots; incubation about 2 weeks, chiefly by hen; nestlings, fed by both parents, leave after about 2 weeks.

FEEDING

Berries, including rowan, cotoneaster, pyracantha, viburnum, juniper, hips and haws.

SIZE

19cm (7½in)

J F M A M J
J A S O N D

The wren packs a surprising number of nestlings into its small domed nest

Wren Troglodytes troglodytes

RECOGNITION

Red-brown, with barring on wings, tail and flanks; small tail, often cocked up; loud shrill song; loud 'churring' alarm call; sexes alike.

NESTING

Male builds several domed nests of moss, leaves and grass, in bush, creeper, woodstack or hollow in wall; female lines one with feathers; lays late April onwards; eggs, white with fine red-brown spots; incubation about 14 days, by female only; nestlings, fed by both parents, fly after about 15 days; usually two broods.

FEEDING

Small insects and their larvae; a few spiders and small seeds.

SIZE

9.5cm (3¾in)

This second smallest of our regular breeding birds (it is only marginally larger than the goldcrest) has long been a national favourite; and considering its piercing, trilling song and perky stance with cocked-up tail, it is easy to understand why.

The Jenny Wren – a nickname applied to the male as well as the female – has an absorbing life history. The male often builds several nests and entices its mate to select one. Two broods are normal and the male may take the first brood to roost in one of the 'rejected' nests while the female is incubating the second clutch. In surroundings where the food supply is poor, wrens are monogamous, but in richer habitats, males will set up more than one mate in the nests that they build.

Despite the affection in which they are held, wrens were the victims of a cruel ritual that is still carried on in some parts of the British Isles, although the birds are seldom actually caught these days. In the past, on St Stephen's Day (December 26), groups of youths in motley dress would beat the hedgerows, singing and trying to kill any wren they saw. The origin of the wren hunt is obscure, but it has been linked with New Year ceremonies of Bronze Age megalith builders.

Ten or more wrens have been found huddling inside a single coconut shell – keeping warm is a problem for them and they suffer heavy losses in cold winters.

J F M A M J
J A S O N D

The dunnock sings its tuneless ditty almost all the year round

Dunnock Prunella modularis

For many years this bird was called the hedge sparrow, 'sparrow' being a name given to any small bird in past times. A glance at its bill is sufficient to tell that it is not, in fact, related to the house and tree sparrows, both of them thick-billed seed-crunchers. Sharp and thin, its bill is typical of insect-eaters, although from autumn until spring it does, for the most part, eat small seeds. To end the confusion, the old country word 'dunnock' has been revived as the common name of the species.

The dunnock is probably the cuckoo's most common victim in the south of England. It is not clear why this should be so, since there is rarely any resemblance between the eggs of the cuckoo and the light blue eggs of the dunnock. Cuckoos using meadow pipits' nests have evolved eggs looking like those of the host species, so that they will not be thrown out of the nest, but blue cuckoos' eggs have been found just once or twice in Britain.

The dunnock almost always feeds on the ground, moving in a series of hops. Its high, piping song can be heard almost all the year round, although it is generally silent in late summer. Occasional snatches are heard at night, for the bird breaks into song if startled awake. It is an inconspicuous bird, although it is often given away by a shrill, insistent 'tseep' call. The dunnock's social life is complex, with variations on polygamy frequent.

RECOGNITION

Grey eye-stripe, throat and breast; brown back with dark streaks; thin bill; squeaking call; sexes alike.

NESTING

Both sexes build bulky cup of moss and grass, lined with wool and hair, low in bush, hedgerow or woodpile; lays late March–early July 3–5 eggs, light blue; incubation usually about 13 days, by female only; nestlings, fed by both parents, fly after about 12 days; usually two broods, sometimes three.

FEEDING

Mostly insects and larvae in spring and summer; sometime spiders and small earthworms; chiefly small seeds in winter.

SIZE

14.5cm (5¾in)

J F M A M J
J A S O N D

Asserting territorial rights, the robin puffs out its red breast and sings

Robin Erithacus rubecula

RECOGNITION

Olive-brown above; orange-red breast, throat and forehead; whitish belly; sexes alike.

NESTING

Female builds domed nest of grass, dead leaves and moss in hollow in bank, tree hole, wall or ledge in shed; lays March–June; 3–6 eggs, white, usually with red-brown spots and blotches; incubation 13 or 14 days, by female only; young, fed by both parents, leave after 12–14 days; two broods, occasionally three.

FEEDING

Insects and larvae; fruit and seeds; earthworms.

SIZE

14cm (5½in)

In 1961, the British Section of the International Council for Bird Preservation was set the task of choosing Britain's national bird. After a long correspondence in *The Times* they chose the robin, that chest-puffing individualist whose tameness, according to the late David Lack, the world authority on robins, is a tribute to the British character. On the Continent robins are shy birds, keeping to deep woodland, but in Britain they are bold enough to dog the footsteps of a gardener who might turn over a worm or two for them.

The defence of territory is a robin's life – the main reason for the plaintive warbling song, which is heard all year round, except for a brief moulting period in July. Pauses of a few seconds between snatches of the song allow rival cock robins to get in their own songs, and so help to establish a pattern of robin territories. In winter the females sing, too, and hold territories of their own. Only when the cold is so severe that finding food takes precedence over every other activity do robins allow others of their species to intrude on their winter territories.

In late summer, when the young birds have put on adult plumage, there is a great deal of disputing as territories and borders are established. About midwinter the female goes mate-hunting. She does the choosing. While the cock sings from his tree, she unobtrusively enters the undergrowth, and if she is tolerated for a few weeks, she begins to accompany him.

MALE

Young blackbirds are still fed by their parents after leaving the nest

Blackbird Turdus merula

A dynamic expansion into man-made habitats in the past 100 years has made the blackbird the most common resident breeding bird in Britain. Its rivals for that title include the wren and the dunnock, and in much of the north and west, the chaffinch. The blackbird used to be confined to woodland, but it has moved out into gardens, fields, parks, squares, commons, heaths and, in hill districts, to cloughs and combes.

It has taken over the main singing role in the dawn chorus all over the country, and its mellow fluting is one of the most beautiful bird-songs heard in Britain – rated by some people even higher than that of the nightingale. There is also a sweet, muted sub-song, hummed through a closed bill and sounding like a distant echo. Other sounds made by the blackbird are harsher. Its nervous, scolding chatter gives notice of a prowling cat, a fox or a human being. At other times its tail-flicking 'chook-chook' shows a mild anxiety, and at dusk it carries on a persistent 'pink-pink'.

The blackbird is the only one of our three common breeding thrushes (the others are the song thrush and the mistle thrush) in which the plumage of the male and female is different. The handsome cock is jet black with a yellow bill while the hen is browner and more thrush-like. There are often a few partly white cocks about, some looking as if they have flakes of snow on their backs, and they become well known in their areas.

RECOGNITION

Male jet black with yellow bill; female dark brown, lighter below, slightly mottled, with brown bill.

NESTING

Female builds neat cup of dry grass, dead leaves and mud in hedge, low tree or on ledge of building; lays late March–July; usually 3–5 eggs, light blue-green with brown spots; incubation about 13 days, by female only; nestlings, fed by both parents, fly after 13 or 14 days; usually two or three broods, occasionally one, four or five.

FEEDING

Insects and their larvae, earthworms; fruit and seeds.

SIZE

25.5cm (10in)

J F M A M J
J A S O N D

White patches under the mistle thrush's wings flash as it flies

Mistle thrush Turdus viscivorus

Grey-brown above, very pale beneath, with round chestnut spots; white outer tail feathers; distinguished from song thrush by bolder spots, larger size and often by more upright stance; sexes alike.

Both sexes build bulky cup-nest of grass, twigs, earth and moss, usually high in tree; lays late February–June; usually 4 eggs, pale blue to buff, with red-brown spots and blotches; incubation 13 or 14 days, by female only; young, fed by both parents, fly after 14–16 days; usually two broods.

Fruit and berries; insects and their larvae, earthworms, snails.

26.75cm (10½in)

This largest of our native thrushes is named after its fondness for the sticky berries of the mistletoe. It has another name, too – the storm cock – which pays tribute to the way it will sing from a treetop in all weathers, even in a raging winter gale. The loud ringing song does not have the mellowness of a blackbird's fluting, or the elegantly repeated phrases of a song thrush, but it is often the finest bird music to be heard on a gusty January day.

The mistle thrush is an early breeder, and its bulky nest in an exposed position high in a tree may contain eggs in late February – long before there are any leaves to give it shelter. At this season the mistle thrush, always wary and suspicious, is at its most aggressive. It may attack a man or bird venturing too near the nest, or swoop down to threaten a cat.

After the breeding season, mistle thrushes take to open country, such as downs, moors and marshes. They move about in small family parties, eating mistletoe and other berries, including yew and hawthorn.

They frequently attract attention by the grating 'churr' of their flight-call and alarm note, a sound like a comb being scraped on a piece of wood. At other times, they sing on the wing. In flight their wings close at regular intervals for a perceptible time, and the white under-wing appears to flash on and off.

A song thrush uses a stone as an anvil for smashing snail shells

Song thrush Turdus philomelos

When a song thrush hops across the lawn and cocks its head intently to one side, it is not listening for the stirring of worms in the ground, although it is certainly fond of earthworms. It is looking for food, tilting its head because its eyes are at the sides.

The clutch of sky-blue eggs in a song thrush's cup-nest seems symbolic of spring itself. Robert Browning, nostalgic for April in England, gave a useful tip for identifying the bird's song: 'That's the wise thrush; he sings each song twice over.' The repetition of each loud, clear phrase – often more than twice – prevents confusion with either the mistle thrush or the blackbird.

The song can be heard in almost any month of the year. The thrush starts singing in January, unless the weather is very severe, and continues steadily until July. Late in September it starts up again, and on fine days in October and November it sings almost as strongly as in spring.

Snails and earthworms are favourite foods. They smash snails against a stone or 'anvil' to break the shells. Although the song thrush has a highly successful relationship with man, taking a wide variety of fruit, berries and insects in gardens, its numbers have decreased dramatically. Dry summers make life hard for the thrush where snails are scarce, and it is apparently badly hit by hard winters.

RECOGNITION

Brown above; breast buff, heavily streaked with chestnut and shading into white; smaller than mistle thrush, with no white on tail feathers; sexes alike.

NESTING

Both sexes build bulky cup-nest of dry grass and dead leaves, with lining of mud, in bush or hedge, low in tree or on ledge; lays March–July; 3–6 eggs, light blue with black spots; incubation 13 or 14 days, by female only; young, fed by both parents, fly after 13 or 14 days; usually two or three broods.

FEEDING

Snails, earthworms; insects and larvae; fruit and seeds.

SIZE

23cm (9in)

The blue tit is the most common of tits taking food hung in gardens

J F M A M J
J A S O N D

Blue tit Cyanistes caeruleus

RECOGNITION

Wings, tail and crown of head blue; cheeks white; back green and underparts yellow; sexes alike.

NESTING

Nests in tree hole, nest-box or crevice in wall; both sexes collect moss, grass, hair and wool as nesting material; lays late April–May; 8–15 eggs, white with red-brown spots; incubation about 14 days, by female only; young, fed by both sexes, fly after about 19 days.

FEEDING

Mainly aphids, caterpillars and other insects; some fruit, grain and seeds.

SIZE

11.5cm (4½in)

Brisk, bold and agile, the blue tit is one of Britain's favourite garden birds, whether scrambling for food at the bird table or hanging upside-down to get at a suspended coconut. When it comes to problem-solving, the blue tit has few rivals. Faced with 'intelligence test' apparatus, blue tits have learnt to pull out a series of pegs or open matchbox drawers to get at food. Some years ago, blue tits solved a less artificial problem – they learnt how to get at the milk left on suburban doorsteps, by pecking at the foil of the bottle tops.

Sometimes they take part in an even odder activity. Blue tits, if they get inside a house, may have a mania for tearing paper. Strips are torn from wallpaper and from books, newspapers and labels. Putty and other objects may be attacked. No one really knows why they do this, but it may be what is known as a 'dissociated' hunting activity, as tits commonly pull bark off trees when they are seeking insects.

Originally, blue tits were woodland birds, and in winter they often join other species of tits, and the occasional nuthatch or treecreeper, in large, loose flocks that move through the woods. An insect stirred up but missed by one bird will be picked up by the next.

The blue tit's trilling song often starts on a sunny day in January. Nest-boxes are used readily, but they should be put up by the end of February, because blue tits start prospecting for nest-holes early in the year.

The great tit is one of the most frequent users of garden nest-boxes

Great tit Parus major

The acrobatics of tits are matched by a mental agility in solving problems and tackling unusual situations. If a great tit, largest of the family, wants to get at a nut dangling from a string, it will pull up the string with its beak, and hold down loop after loop with one foot until the nut is reached.

The liveliness that makes the birds amusing to watch can turn them into clever nuisances at times. Great tits and blue tits were the chief culprits in sporadic outbreaks of milk-stealing when deliveries of milk bottles were more common. A few birds would prise off or peck through the tops of milk bottles to get at the cream, and the rest imitated them. On one occasion 57 out of 300 bottles left at a school in Merstham, Surrey, were opened in a single morning. However, these acts are more than offset by the birds' value to the gardener. The young are brought up largely on the caterpillars of moths, especially the winter moth, and it has been estimated that in the three weeks of feeding their brood, a pair can destroy 7,000–8,000 caterpillars and other insects. Wise gardeners put up nest-boxes.

The great tit has perhaps the most extensive vocabulary of any British bird. The most frequent spring song, if it can be called one, sounds like, 'tea-cher, tea-cher'. There is a 'pink' call, and another note suggests the sound of a saw being sharpened. When disturbed on the nest, the hen will make a snake-like hiss.

RECOGNITION

Head and neck glossy black; cheeks white; black band on yellow breast; back green; sexes alike.

NESTING

Often nests in hole in tree or wall, but readily uses nest-box; both sexes collect nesting material, mostly moss, with hair or down for lining; lays late April–May; 8–12 eggs, white, thickly spotted with red-brown; incubation 13 or 14 days, by hen only; young, fed by both sexes, fly at about 20 days.

FEEDING

Largely insects, including caterpillars, aphids, scale-insects; some buds, fruit, peas and seeds; occasionally young birds.

SIZE

14cm (5½in)

Spotted flycatcher pounces from its perch to catch a flying insect

Spotted flycatcher Muscicapa striata

RECOGNITION

Mouse-grey; white below; adults unspotted, but with dark streaks on head and breast; juvenile birds have inconspicuous dark spots on breast; sexes alike.

NESTING

Both sexes build untidy nest of moss, wool and hair, held together with cobwebs, on ledge, in creeper on wall, in tree, old bird's nest or in cavity; lays late May–June; 4 or 5 eggs, shades of green or blue, heavily freckled with red-brown; incubation about 13 days, mainly by female; young, fed by both parents, fly after 12 or 13 days; sometimes two broods.

FEEDING

Almost entirely flying insects – chiefly flies but also craneflies, butterflies and wasps; very occasionally earthworms and rowan berries.

SIZE

14cm (5½in)

So quiet and unobtrusive is the spotted flycatcher that many people do not know when they have one in the garden. Sadly, the opportunity to appreciate them may have gone because this little bird has dramatically reduced in numbers. Only the juveniles have spots, dark on the breast and pale cream on the crown and back. Adults are just softly, obscurely streaked.

A far better way of recognising a spotted flycatcher than looking at its plumage, is to observe whether it feeds by sitting bolt upright on a fence, spray or branch beside an open space, then darting out at a passing fly. It may have to twist and turn in flight, but it seldom misses, and its bill closes with an audible snap. Usually the bird returns to the same observation-post or one nearby. Warblers and other small song-birds sometimes use the same technique, but flycatchers alone have made it a way of life.

The spotted flycatcher is one of our latest summer visitors to arrive, usually reaching Britain in mid or late May and staying until September. It is a creature of habit, and will return year after year to a favourite nest-site – often a creepered house or a trellis. Its usual call is a shrill, robin-like 'tzee'; and the alarm note, 'whee-tucc-tucc' recalls that of the stonechat. What passes for a song is some half-dozen high-pitched rather squeaky notes, which sound at first as though uttered by several birds in a spasmodic exchange.

J F M A M J
J A S O N D

*In flight the goldfinch shows
its white rump and yellow
wing-bars*

Goldfinch Carduelis carduelis

Towards the end of the 19th century, the number of goldfinches in Britain had been brought dangerously low by intensive trapping for the cage-bird trade. In 1860 it was reported that 132,000 a year were being caught near Worthing in Sussex. A few years later, a House of Commons committee was told of a boy who took 480 in a single morning. The Society for the Protection of Birds (later Royal) made the saving of the goldfinch from the trapper one of its first tasks, and today small flocks and family parties, aptly known as 'charms' of goldfinches, are a familiar sight, feeding on the heads of thistles and other tall weeds in the late summer and early autumn.

The song for which the bird was caged in Victorian times is a tinkling variation of the most frequently heard flight-note, a liquid 'tswitt-witt-witt'. It is given when the male is establishing its territory in large gardens and orchards, and sometimes in thick hedgerows or open woodland. Changes in agriculture have reduced the thistle beds among which it feeds but, at the same time, the reservation of areas for quarries and other development has provided it with new foraging grounds.

In courtship, which always takes place near the nest, the male droops and partly opens its wings, sways from side to side and exhibits its bright yellow wing-flashes.

RECOGNITION

Brown back; black and white tail; wings mainly black, with broad band of yellow; red face, rest of head black and white; sexes alike.

NESTING

Female builds neat nest of roots, grass, moss and lichen, lined with wool and vegetable down, usually in spreading tree; lays early May–August; usually 5 or 6 eggs, pale blue, lightly spotted with brown; incubation 12 or 13 days, by female only; nestlings, fed by both parents, fly after 13 or 14 days; normally two broods, sometimes three.

FEEDING

Seeds of thistle, burdock, dandelion, knapweed and other weeds; fruit of birch, alder and other trees; some insects, especially for young.

SIZE

12cm (4¾in)

MALE

In autumn and winter chaffinches flock to feed on stubble-fields

J F M A M J
J A S O N D

Chaffinch Fringilla coelebs

Blue-grey head and neck; pink breast and cheeks; chestnut back; white on wings, tail and shoulders; female yellow-brown above, paler below, with white wing-bar and white tail-sides.

Both sexes build neat cup-nest of moss and lichen lined with wool, hair and feathers, in hedge, bush or tree-fork; lays April–early June; usually 3–6 eggs, off-white with red-brown blotches; incubation 12–14 days, by female only; nestlings, fed by both parents, fly after 12–15 days; sometimes two broods.

Seeds, beech-mast and sometimes grain.

15.25cm (6in)

Most people asked to name the most common bird in Britain would probably choose the house sparrow. In fact, the first place for sheer numbers must go to the blackbird or wren, with the chaffinch until recently running it close. Blackbirds have increased, while there seems to have been a decline in chaffinch numbers in some areas due to the disappearance of hedgerows.

Chaffinches breed almost wherever there are trees and bushes, but they are less suburban than blackbirds or robins. In winter they join other finches, buntings and sparrows in large flocks to feed on arable land and stubble-fields. Sometimes, though, they form vast chaffinch flocks, all of one sex.

Chaffinches start singing in February, but not all sing in the same way. Striking regional dialects have been recorded, especially among birds that winter here from the Continent. Despite this, the song is easy to identify, for it always ends with an emphatic flourish, 'tissi-cheweeo'. The main flight-note is 'tsup', but the most common call is a loud 'pink-pink'.

The male shares with several other birds the habit of attacking its own reflection in a window, and a female has been seen unsuccessfully trying to imitate great tits pulling up a string of nuts. The bird reached down to peck the string but could not hold on to it, or keep its balance on the branch.

MALE

In flight the greenfinch shows a pale flash on its wings

Greenfinch Carduelis chloris

So completely have greenfinches adapted to life in a man-dominated countryside that they are hardly ever found far from human settlements. In the breeding season, especially, they keep to suburban gardens, shrubberies and bushy places near villages.

In recent years these stout-billed seed-eaters have been well rewarded for their age-old attachment to man. Their numbers have increased with the growing popularity of feeding birds in gardens – they have a liking for peanuts and sunflower seeds – but, in the countryside, have declined with the huge reduction in natural weed seeds. Greenfinches are sociable birds at all times, tending to nest in loose colonies, using adjacent bushes. They usually have two broods in a season, and some even rear a third, so that it is not unusual to find young birds in the nest in August or even early September.

In winter, they may be tempted to leave the shelter of the garden to feed on stubble-fields or waste land with flocks of other finches or buntings. A disturbed feeding group rises with a sudden whirring of wings, and the birds have an up-and-down bounding flight as their wings momentarily close.

As befits a bird so fond of company, the greenfinch has an extensive vocabulary. Its calls include a nasal 'tsweee', a canary-like 'tsooeet' and a 'chi-chi-chi-chi-chit' flight-call. For its song it strings together a number of calls in a twittering medley.

RECOGNITION

Olive-green with heavy, pale bill; dark 'mask' effect; yellow wing-bar and tail-sides; female duller.

NESTING

Both sexes build untidy cup of grass, moss and roots, with lining of roots, in bush, tree or hedge; lays late April–August; 4–6 eggs, white to pale blue, with red-brown spots and streaks; incubation about 13 days, by female only; young, fed by both parents, fly after 12–16 days; usually two broods, occasionally three.

FEEDING

Almost entirely seeds, wild fruit and berries.

SIZE

14.5cm (5¾in)

MALE

J F M A M J
J A S O N D

Bullfinches are unpopular because of their liking for fruit-tree buds

Bullfinch Pyrrhula pyrrhula

RECOGNITION
Black cap; rose-pink breast; grey back; white rump; female much drabber than male.

NESTING
Female builds nest of twigs, moss and lichen in thick hedge, bramble, brake or other deep cover; lays late April–July; usually 4 or 5 eggs, green-blue, sparsely streaked and spotted with purple-brown; incubation 12–14 days, mainly by female; nestlings, fed by both parents, fly after about 14 days; two broods, sometimes three.

FEEDING
Tree-seeds, weeds and berries; buds of fruit trees in late winter and early spring; caterpillars fed to young.

SIZE
14.5cm (5¾in)

Handsome though it is, the bullfinch has made enemies in many parts of the country because in late winter and early spring it literally nips fruit trees in the bud. A single bird has been seen to eat the buds on a plum tree at the rate of 30 a minute, and fruit growers complained about their depredations. However, although the birds' numbers were on the increase after the 1950s, since the 1970s they have declined dramatically with the loss of orchards and a great reduction in the availability of winter seeds.

Attacks on fruit trees and ornamental shrubs occur mainly when the bird's natural food source is scarce, from January to April. Its short, rounded bill, with especially sharp cutting edges, is an excellent adaptation for this purpose. But even in fruit-growing districts it also takes many weeds and tree-seeds.

Many ornithologists believe, although positive evidence is hard to come by, that bullfinches mate for life. Certainly, once two have formed a bond, they do not seem to split up for the winter, as do most small birds. Whenever a glimpse is caught of the black-capped, pink-breasted male, its mate will be flitting a little way behind, looking like a toned-down copy with the colours filtered out. They are shy birds and retire quickly from human presence. Only a soft, indrawn whistle, usually written down as 'deu', indicates where they have gone.

Farmland

The character of farmland has changed dramatically in the past 50 years. Crops once sown in spring are now sown in autumn, and are too tall and dense for nesting birds in summer; traditional mixed farms that supported a variety of birds have been replaced by monocultures; hedges have been grubbed out; cut stubbles no longer provide seeds for flocks in winter. Farmland birds have suffered greatly and most are still in decline.

Red-legged partridge shows its strongly barred flanks as it flies

J F M A M J
J A S O N D

Red-legged partridge Alectoris rufa

Brown plumage; easily distinguished from smaller common partridge by black and white eye-stripes, rich chestnut barring on grey flanks, and lack of dark horseshoe mark on breast; sexes alike.

Cock makes scrape, sparsely lined with dried grass and other local materials, in ground in thick vegetation; lays late April–May; usually 10–15 eggs, yellow or yellow-brown with thin brown and ash-grey spots; incubation usually 25 days, by either or both parents; chicks, tended by either or both parents, leave nest and run almost as soon as hatched, fly after about 2 weeks; often two broods.

Predominantly vegetable, like that of native partridge.

34.25cm (13½in)

The red-leg, as farmers sometimes call it, is also known as the French partridge because ancestors of the British stock were introduced from France some 200 years ago. For a time, genetically inferior hybrids between this species and the chukar, an Asian relative, were also released, but the practice has now been banned.

Its habitat – heaths, farmland, coastal shingle and chalk downs – is similar to, although often drier than, that of the common partridge, and the red-leg flies and runs with the same action as its relative. But the two birds are distinctive in appearance – the red-leg's black-and-white eye stripes and strongly barred flanks make it easy to identify. Its voice is distinctive, too – a loud, challenging 'chucka-chucka'.

In courtship the cock holds its head up and slightly to one side, erecting the feathers of its white face and throat. The barred feathers on the flanks are also fluffed up and then prominently displayed.

The hen lays a large clutch of up to 15 eggs, in a lined scrape in the ground. She often lays two clutches in separate nests, incubating one herself and leaving the cock to incubate the other. This high rate of egg production is offset by a high rate of loss. The eggs are never covered when the incubating bird leaves them, and many are taken by stoats, rats and other predators.

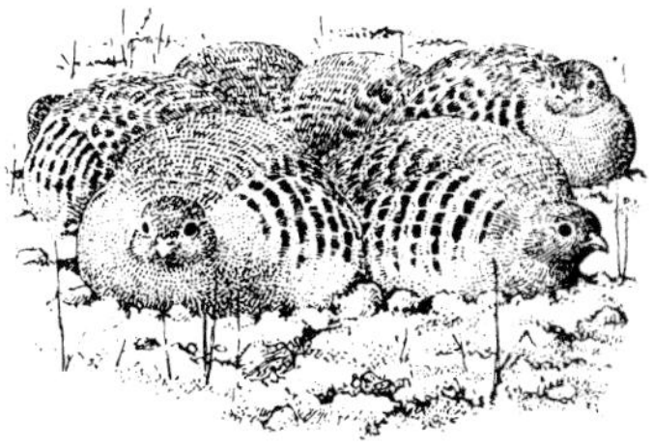

Partridges roost together, facing outwards to watch for predators

J F M A M J
J A S O N D

Grey partridge **Perdix perdix**

The loss of weeds and insects from the fields has also meant a widespread disappearance of grey partridges from the countryside. In many areas they have disappeared altogether.

In autumn, partridges gather into family parties, known as coveys. They break up into breeding pairs in late January and early February, and at this time the cock birds become aggressive in defence of their territories. In courtship, pairs of birds often spring into the air and chase one another. In one recorded case, a number of birds formed a circle before pairing off.

For nesting and feeding, partridges prefer farmland, either grass or arable, especially with good cover from hedges, bushes, rough-grass banks or ditches. They also nest on rough grassland, moorland edges and heaths. A widespread decline throughout the past 40–50 years has been caused by a pesticide-induced reduction in suitable insect food for the chicks.

Partridges have a whirring flight, alternating with gliding on down-curved wings. Their most frequently heard call-note is a loud, high-pitched, creaky 'keev-it', often degenerating into a rapid cackle, 'it-it-it' when flushed.

RECOGNITION

Brown plumage, barred with chestnut on flanks and chestnut tail; neck and under parts grey with dark horseshoe on breast; hen less boldly marked than cock.

NESTING

Hen makes scrape in ground lined with dried grass and leaves, often approached by runway, and usually in thick vegetation; lays late April–May; usually 12–18 eggs, pale olive; incubation about 24 days, by hen only; chicks, tended by both parents, leave after a few hours, fly after about 2 weeks.

FEEDING

Mainly grain and buds, flowers, leaves and seeds of low-growing plants; animal matter includes insects, spiders, small snails and slugs.

SIZE

30.5cm (12in)

Usually only dogs can force the shy quail into flight

MALE

Quail Coturnix coturnix

Sandy-brown above, paler below; light streaks on flanks; liable to be confused with young partridge, but is distinguished by buff streaks on head and absence of chestnut on tail; cock has long pale stripe over eye; hen drabber than cock, with black spots on breast.

NESTING

Hen makes scrape in ground among crops or grass, thinly lined with grass or leaves; lays late May–June; usually 7–12 eggs, pale cream, marbled with shades of brown; incubation 18–21 days, by hen only; chicks, tended by hen, leave after a few hours, begin to fly after about 11 days.

FEEDING

Mainly seeds of grasses and weeds; also snails, caterpillars.

SIZE

17.75cm (7in)

So shy and secretive are quails that they would hardly ever be detected were it not for their repeated, simple, liquid calls in summer. The call, although loud and far-carrying, is hard to pin down to a particular spot among the crops where it hides. Birdwatchers say that it can 'throw' its voice, with the effect produced by a ventriloquist.

In the breeding season, the cock bird 'advertises' with a persistent 'quic-ic-ic', a call that is sometimes given as 'wet-my-lips'. The hen calls a soft 'bru-bru' until contact is made. Then the cock bird runs up and circles round her, puffing up his neck and breast feathers, stretching his neck and dragging his wings along the ground.

The quail's normal habitat is farmland, especially light chalk and limestone soils, where the call can be heard in fields of clover, lucerne and young corn, and also in hayfields, fields of root crops and tussocky grassland. A great deal remains to be discovered about its feeding habits, but the seeds of weeds and grasses apparently form the main part of its diet.

Hunters have always taken their toll of quail, but in the early part of the 20th century the birds were netted live, too. London was one of the main exporting centres for this trade, which was halted by law in 1937.

FEMALE

MALE

J F M A M J
J A S O N D

Pheasant Phasianus colchicus

No firm evidence can be found to support the theory that the Romans first brought the pheasant to Britain. It was first definitely recorded a few years before the Norman Conquest, in 1059.

The bird's true home is in Asia, from the Caucasus across to China, and it was birds from the western part of this range, the Caucasus, that were originally introduced to Britain. This form became known as the Old English pheasant, but from the 18th century onwards there were repeated introductions, from eastern Asia, of forms with a white neck-ring. As a result, present-day stocks are an amalgam of forms – those with and those without the white neck-ring in roughly equal proportions.

Every year, gamekeepers release millions of reared pheasants into woods in preparation for the shooting season, starting on October 1. The bird is also well established as a wild breeding species in copses, heaths and commons, and beds of reeds and sedges. It has increased in almost all areas during the past 25 years.

The pheasant has the typical whirring flight of a game-bird, alternating with gliding on down-turned wings, and it can rocket explosively upwards when disturbed. The cock crows with a loud, hard 'korr-kok', and often responds to a shot or distant explosion by crowing.

RECOGNITION

Cock has mainly copper plumage; hen is browner and shorter-tailed; green, grey and black-barred forms of the cock are common.

NESTING

Hen scrapes hollow in ground, often under thick vegetation, lines it scantily with leaves and grass; occasionally nests in old bird's nest in tree; lays late April–June; usually 8–15 eggs, pale olive; incubation 22–27 days, by hen only; chicks, tended by hen, leave nest when a few hours old, fly after 12–14 days.

FEEDING

Wide variety of animal and vegetable food, from fruits and seeds to wireworms, caterpillars, grasshoppers and other insects; occasionally lizards, field voles and small birds.

SIZE

Male: 83.75cm (33in) including 45.75cm (18in) tail
Female: 58.5cm (23in) including 23cm (9in) tail

A hovering kestrel watches for movement that might indicate prey

J F M A M J
J A S O N D

MALE

Kestrel Falco tinnunculus

Like all birds of prey, the kestrel is protected by law throughout the year, but unlike many of the others, it is not in desperate need of this protection. Farmers recognise the bird as a useful ally against mice, rats, voles and harmful insects, and enlightened gamekeepers are prepared to overlook the occasional game-chick it takes, because of its value as a destroyer of pests.

Partly because it does not have to face persecution, and partly because it can adapt to many different kinds of country, the kestrel has become by far the commonest of Britain's day-flying birds of prey, although it is much less common than it used to be. It is equally at home in farmland, moorland and along sea cliffs. In recent years, the kestrel has become more of an urban bird, and is renowned as a hunter along motorway verges. It hovers with flickering wings and fanned tail, watching the ground for voles and mice. It also watches from perches on poles and wires.

The main call-note is a shrill 'kee-kee-kee-kee', but it is not often given unless birds are 'playing' together, or the male is chasing the female in courtship. In another courtship ceremony that has been recorded, the male was seen to beat upwind, then fly down fast at the female. She was sitting in a bush, and just when he seemed about to strike her, he shot up in the air. This performance was repeated several times.

*In flight, the corncrake trails
its legs behind its body*

Corncrake Crex crex

The rasping voice of the corncrake, like a piece of wood repeatedly drawn against the teeth of a comb, was once a familiar sound in the English countryside. But during the last 100 years the bird has become virtually extinct as a breeding species over much of Britain. Only in western Ireland, where they are decreasing, and the islands of Scotland, where numbers have increased again with conservation measures, are any numbers left.

The reason for the decline lies in early cutting of grass for silage, rather than hay, and mechanised cutting methods that proved lethal to corncrakes. In the 19th century, many hay meadows were either scythed or at least mown later in the year than today, giving corncrakes time to rear their young in the long grass. Modern mechanical haymaking and grass-cutting for silage leads to the destruction of both the nest and the sitting bird.

The corncrake is a relative of the coot and the moorhen and is sometimes called the landrail. Like many of the rails, it is shy and skulking, more often heard than seen. Its insistent, rasping voice – which gave rise to its curious scientific name, *Crex crex* – serves as a song with which to announce its territorial claims. The bird used to winter in small numbers in Britain, but is now reduced to the status of a summer visitor, when it feeds in fields of long grass and sometimes in damp, sedgy meadows or along hedges.

RECOGNITION

Brown, streaked darker above, with chestnut on wings; paler below, with dark bars on flanks; sexes alike.

NESTING

Nest of dried grasses is always on ground well hidden in thick vegetation, and may sometimes be domed; lays May–June; usually 8–12 eggs, pale cream, heavily spotted with red-brown and grey; incubation about 16 days, mainly by female; chicks, tended by both parents, leave nest a few hours after hatching, fly after about 5 weeks.

FEEDING

Grasshoppers, earwigs, beetles, crane-flies and other insects; slugs, small snails, earthworms and millipedes; some vegetable food, such as rush seeds.

SIZE

26.75cm (10½in)

In flight, the stock dove shows two black bars on each wing

Stock dove Columba oenas

RECOGNITION

Grey plumage; distinguished from rock dove by having no white rump; two short black bars on each wing; smaller than woodpigeon and lacks its conspicuous white markings on wings; sexes alike.

NESTING

Usually nests in hole in tree, on building, cliff or sandpit, or in nest-box or rabbit burrow; no nesting material in holes; lays late March–September; usually 2 eggs, white; incubation about 17 days, by both sexes; nestlings, fed by both sexes, fly after about 4 weeks; usually two broods, often three.

FEEDING

Mainly seeds of weeds and grain; some animal food, especially cocoons of earthworms.

SIZE

33cm (13in)

A bird as adaptable as the stock dove, which can breed in any kind of country from farmland, woods and parks to rocks, cliffs, old buildings and sand-dunes, might be expected to thrive in modern Britain. Its numbers declined in the 1960s – perhaps the result of poisoning from agricultural chemicals, particularly seed-dressing – but have recovered since.

Whatever its breeding habitat may be, the stock dove relies heavily on farmland to provide it with food throughout the year. In winter it feeds on stubble-fields, often with flocks of woodpigeons, concentrating on the seeds of fat-hen, knot-grass and other weeds. In spring it turns to chickweed, charlock and other early flowering weeds, continuing in summer with charlock even in preference to cultivated grains. In autumn it returns to the stubble-fields, and knot-grass.

Its gruff voice, a coughing or double grunting note with the accent on the second syllable, is different from the woodpigeon's cooing. The stock dove's display flight is also distinctive. Male and female fly round in circles, sometimes gliding on raised wings.

Stock doves are social birds, and tend to breed in loose colonies in suitable places, but territorial disputes still break out between males. They threaten one another on the ground, striking out with their wings.

In flight, the woodpigeon shows its handsome wing markings

| J | F | M | A | M | J |
| J | A | S | O | N | D |

Woodpigeon Columba palumbus

It may be that the woodpigeon is, or soon will be, the commonest bird in Britain. A beautiful, gentle-looking bird, the largest of our pigeons and doves, it is a serious problem for farmers. From January to March it settles on fields of clover and sainfoin, moving in on green crops in hard weather. In early spring it feeds on arable fields, taking newly sown grain, peas, charlock and wild mustard. In summer it takes ripe and ripening grain, and in autumn it stays in the fields, feeding among stubble. By laying its eggs usually in August and September, it is raising its young just when the year's harvest is ripening.

In spite of having so many enemies among farmers, the woodpigeon's numbers have increased fairly rapidly in recent years. Destruction of nests has proved the most effective method of control.

Although it feeds so widely on farmland, the woodpigeon has readily adapted itself to town parks and large gardens, where it can become tame enough to feed out of the hand.

The song is the well-known cooing phrase, usually made up of five notes: 'coooo-coo, coo-coo, coo'.

In courtship the male has an up-and-down flight, with wings clapping as it flies up. Displays on the ground include bowing, mutual caressing with the bill, and courtship feeding.

RECOGNITION
Head, neck and tail grey, with black tip on tail and green, purple and white patch at side of adult's neck; back and wings grey-brown, with white wing-patch; breast pale purple-grey; sexes alike.

NESTING
Female builds flat platform of twigs, usually in tree but sometimes in bush, ivy, on ledge of building or even on ground; may lay in any month, but mainly August–September; usually 2 eggs, white; incubation 17 days, by both sexes; young, fed by both sexes with 'pigeon's milk' from crop, leave after 16–20 days; usually at least two broods.

FEEDING
Mainly cereals and clover, but also wild fruit and seeds; at times bread and scraps, brassicas and a little animal food.

SIZE
40.5cm (16in)

J F M A M J
J A S O N D

MALE

In their silent flight, barn owls show white undersides of wings

Barn owl Tyto alba

Golden buff with white face and underparts; female slightly greyer.

No nest material; eggs laid on disgorged pellets; sites include old barns, ruined buildings, church towers, hollow trees, quarry faces, corn-ricks and nest-boxes; laying recorded in every month except January, but main period is April–early May; 4–6 eggs, white; incubation about 33 days, by female only; nestlings, fed by both parents, fly after 9–12 weeks; often two broods.

Shrews, mice, field voles, bank voles, water voles, brown rats, moles; small birds; beetles, moths; frogs, sometimes bats and fish.

34.25cm (13½in)

The ghostly form of a barn owl looks white when it is caught in a car's headlights at night, but towards the end of winter when food is so scarce that the bird is forced to hunt by day, its true colour can be seen – a golden buff, with white underparts.

When hunting, it does not rely on sight alone. Experiments have shown that the barn owl can locate its prey in pitch darkness by its sense of hearing. Its ears are placed asymmetrically on its head, so that there is a fractional interval between the sounds picked up by each ear, and this gives it unusually precise powers of pinpointing the slightest sound made by the small mammals that it hunts. Hardly any noise is made by the bird as it swoops on a victim, but there is nothing muffled about the owl's cry – a prolonged, strangled shriek.

Barn owls were once much more common and their decline is something of a mystery. It began long before some other birds of prey were affected by the build-up of pesticides in their bodies. The loss of their main feeding habitat – permanent grassland – has had an effect. Also, as the countryside becomes more efficient, there are fewer abandoned buildings and hollow trees for them to use as nesting sites. They do not build nests but lay their eggs on a heap of pellets made up of the indigestible fur, feathers and bones of their prey.

Little owls often sit on
telephone poles or wires
in daylight*

Little owl Athene noctua

Soon after it was introduced to Northamptonshire and Kent
from the Continent, towards the end of the 19th century, the
little owl became one of Britain's most controversial birds. It
spread rapidly, and as it spread it fell foul of ever greater
numbers of gamekeepers. They accused the little owl of every
crime in their calendar, until it seemed as if, in their eyes, the
bird existed entirely on a diet of pheasant and partridge chicks.

However, one of the earliest investigations launched by the
British Trust for Ornithology proved that the charges were
unfounded. About half the bird's diet is made up of insects,
especially cockchafers and other beetles, earwigs and crane-flies.
Leatherjackets, the larvae of crane-flies, are among the farmer's
most serious pests, and little owls are now protected by law,
along with native owls. While there is no doubt that game-
chicks are taken, they form only a minute part of the diet.

The little owl, our smallest and most common day-flying owl,
is a bird of the open countryside. It flies by night, too, and
hunts mainly at dusk and dawn. The flight is conspicuously
bounding or undulating, with occasional hovering. The little
owl can often be seen perched near its nest, on a post, telephone
pole or haybale, bobbing its body and wagging its tail when
anyone approaches it. The commonest call-note of the little owl
is a low, plaintive 'kiew-kiew'. Its song is infrequent and closely
resembles the opening sequence of the curlew's song.

RECOGNITION

Grey-brown plumage,
barred and mottled with
white; rounded wings, short
tail and bounding flight;
sexes alike.

NESTING

No nest material; nest in
hole, usually in tree but also
in walls, buildings, cliffs,
quarries, sandpits or
burrows in the ground;
lays late April–early May;
usually 3–5 eggs, white;
incubation about 28 days,
by female only; nestlings,
fed by both parents, fly
after about 5 weeks.

FEEDING

Insects, including beetles,
earwigs and crane-flies;
voles, mice, young rats
and other small mammals;
some small birds, frogs
and lizards.

SIZE

21.5cm (8½in)

*Lapwing tumbles earthwards
in spring display flight*

J F M A M J
J A S O N D

Lapwing Vanellus vanellus

Our only medium-sized black
and white bird with rounded
wings and short tail,
conspicuous in flight; at
rest, the only one with crest
and long legs; in bright
sunshine can look brilliant
green above; sexes alike.

NESTING

Female selects one of
several scrapes made by
male in ground, often on
slight rise, lines it with dried
grasses; usually lays late
March–May; usually 4 eggs,
olive-buff or olive-green,
heavily marked with black;
incubation about 27 days,
mostly by female; chicks,
usually tended by female
only, leave in a few hours,
fly after about 5 weeks.

FEEDING

Mainly insects,
especially wireworms
and leatherjackets;
also earthworms,
sometimes brought up
by stamping feet.

SIZE

30.5cm (12in)

Like so many farmland birds, the lapwing has undergone a
dramatic and widespread decline as a breeding bird, although
winter flocks coming from Europe remain widespread. Drainage
and the increased monotony of autumn-sown cereals, which are
far too long and thick for nesting lapwings by spring, are the
main culprits.

The lapwing, or peewit, derives both of its names from the
sounds it makes. In spring it performs a striking aerobatic
display, climbing steadily with its wings making a throbbing or
'lapping' sound while it utters its wild song 'p'weet-p'weet,
peewit-peewit'. Then it plunges down, over its territory, rolling
and twisting apparently out of control. Its call-notes are
variations on the 'peewit' theme.

Besides aerial display, the courting male makes scrapes in the
ground, rocking forward on to its breast.

Like other plovers, lapwings are highly gregarious, and
often flock with golden plovers in winter. At all seasons they
feed over farmland, both arable and grass, but when breeding
they are also fairly common in damp, rushy fields, coastal
marshes and moorland. In winter many join other waders on
freshwater margins and sometimes on sands and mud-flats
along the coasts.

Skylark hovers high in the sky in full-throated song

Skylark Alauda arvensis

For Wordsworth, the skylark was an ethereal minstrel, a pilgrim of the sky. For Shelley, it was a blithe spirit, showering the earth with a rain of melody, and lesser poets before and since have added their praises until it has become one of Britain's best-loved birds. Its sustained warbling song, which can last for five minutes without a pause, is usually delivered when the bird is flying high in the air, often nearly out of sight. The skylark is the only British bird that habitually sings while ascending almost vertically, keeps singing while hovering and goes on singing while descending.

A spring day when the air was full of skylark song was an unforgettable experience, but now much harder to find as changed farming techniques, especially the predominance of autumn-sown crops that become tall and dense in spring, have brought about widespread declines.

In the breeding season, skylarks nest in any kind of open country, from sand-dunes at sea level to peat bogs and moors on the mountains. Their singing has the twin objectives of defending territory and attracting females, and is heard from late January to early July. At other times of the year, particularly in August and September, they are fairly silent. After the breeding season they are often gregarious, gathering in flocks to feed and to migrate. Home-bred birds are joined by winter visitors and passage migrants from Europe.

RECOGNITION

Streaky brown; white outer tail feathers show in flight; characteristic soaring song-flight; small crest and white line along trailing edge of the wing; sexes alike.

NESTING

Hen builds cup nest of grass, sometimes lined with hair, on ground; lays April–August; usually 3 or 4 eggs, white, thickly speckled with brown; incubation about 11 days, by hen only; nestlings, fed by both parents, leave nest after 8 days, fly after 16 days; two or three broods.

FEEDING

Seeds of charlock, chickweed, sow thistle, sorrel and other weeds; leaves of clover and other plants; earthworms, caterpillars, beetles and their larvae, spiders and other small ground animals; some grain.

SIZE

17.75cm (7in)

J F M A M J
J A S O N D

J F M A M J
J A S O N D

In winter, flocks of fieldfares are often seen feeding in the fields

Fieldfare Turdus pilaris

RECOGNITION

Blue-grey head, nape and rump; chestnut back, dark tail and speckled brown breast; sexes alike.

NESTING

Very rarely nests in Britain; nest of mud, roots and grass built chiefly by hen, usually in tree or bush; lays April or May–July; usually 5 or 6 eggs, green or blue-green with red-brown spots; incubation about 14 days, chiefly by hen; nestlings, fed by both parents, leave after about 14 days.

FEEDING

Wild fruit; garden berries, such as those of pyracantha and cotoneaster; also insects, such as earthworms, snails, beetles, leatherjackets and caterpillars.

SIZE

25.5cm (10in)

Flocks of fieldfares, sometimes hundreds strong, flying overhead in loose formation, can be identified by the clamouring, chattering 'chack-chack' calls. These are sometimes varied by a higher-pitched 'week' from a bird that has lost touch with the others and wants to regain contact. They migrate to Britain in the autumn from their breeding grounds in northern Europe, and range over all kinds of rough, open country, including open woodland. They rest or feed on farmland, playing-fields, marshes and, in hard weather, in parks and large gardens.

It was not until 1967 that a pair of fieldfares nested in Britain, in Orkney. Since then, up to a dozen pairs have bred annually, mainly in northern Britain. Previous to 1967, 'sightings' were of mistle thrushes, although the two species should not be mistaken for each other. They are about the same size, and both show white flashes under their wings in flight, but the fieldfare is easily identified by its blue-grey head and rump – features that have given rise to one of its country names, 'blue-back'.

This large thrush is unusually aggressive at its breeding grounds. Combined attacks by members of the colony can rout animal intruders and this possibly explains the colonial nesting habit, which is unusual in thrushes.

In flight, redwings utter a plaintive, high-pitched call-note

J F M A M J
J A S O N D

Redwing Turdus iliacus

This smallest of our thrushes is, like the fieldfare, a winter visitor from northern Europe. But it has progressed further than the fieldfare towards establishing itself as a breeding bird as well as a visitor. The redwing was first proved to breed in Britain when a nest was found in Sutherland in 1925, and it has nested there and in other parts of northern Scotland regularly since 1953. Numbers reached about 50 pairs, but have since declined considerably again.

Redwings often feed alongside fieldfares in farmland, parks, playing-fields and other open grassland. They perish in large numbers during severe winters when the earth is frozen too deep for them to dig up food.

The most frequently heard call-note is a thin, high-pitched 'seeeee', often given by flocks migrating overhead at night. Other notes include a soft 'chup' and a harsher 'chittuck' or 'chittick'. The true song is rarely heard in Britain, but a few stilted, fluting phrases from it sometimes occur in the communal warbling sub-song, with which flocks often greet the approach of spring.

Redwings that breed in Scotland usually build their nests in birchwoods or areas of scrub, but in Scandinavia they often rest in town parks and gardens, too, and this pattern could be repeated in Britain if their colonisation really gets under way.

RECOGNITION

Rather smaller than song-thrush, from which it can be told by prominent white eye-stripe and red patches on flanks and under wing; sexes alike.

NESTING

Grass cup, on foundation of twigs and earth, is built in tree, bush or on ground, probably by female only, and sometimes decorated with moss or lichen; lays mid-May–July; usually 4–6 eggs, blue-green with red-brown markings; incubation about 13 days, probably by both parents; nestlings, fed by both parents, leave after about 14 days.

FEEDING

Earthworms, snails, caterpillars, beetles and their larvae; haws and other wild fruit; occasionally apples.

SIZE

21cm (8¼in)

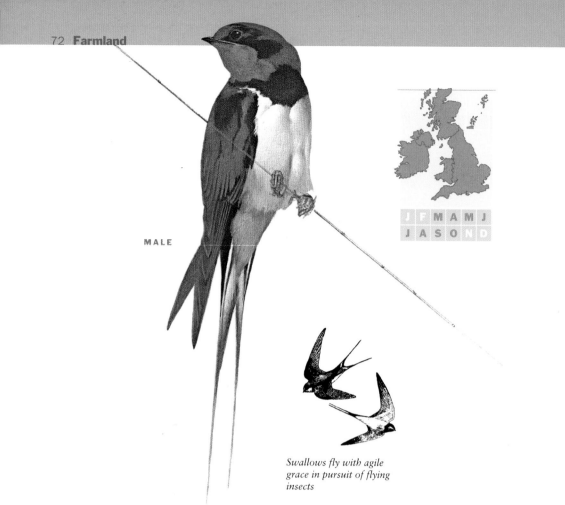

MALE

Swallows fly with agile grace in pursuit of flying insects

Swallow Hirundo rustica

RECOGNITION

Steel-blue upper parts; chestnut forehead and breast; long streamers on forked tail; female's tail is slightly shorter than male's.

NESTING

Both sexes build saucer-shaped nest of mud and dried grasses lined with feathers, usually on ledge or rafter in building; lays May–August; usually 3–6 eggs, white, heavily speckled with red-brown; incubation about 15 days, by hen; nestlings, fed by both parents, leave after 18–21 days.

FEEDING

Flying insects, sometimes including dragonflies and butterflies.

SIZE

19cm (7½in)

The saying 'One swallow does not make a summer' is based on accurate observation of the birds. When swallows begin to return from their winter quarters in Africa at the end of March or early April, they arrive at first in ones and twos. It is not until mid or late April that they are here in force, and summer is on the way.

They must have been familiar birds for centuries to have been drawn on for a folk proverb, but today there is evidence that swallows are decreasing. From many areas there are reports of declines, with more intensive and hygienic farming causing a reduction in large flying insects. Most swallows in Britain nest in farm buildings, and improvements in milking parlours and barns have hit their food supplies by reducing the numbers of insects. Ringing has proved that swallows often return year after year to the same nest. They often nest in loose colonies, and gather with martins on migration or when feeding. Their most common call-note is a twittering 'tswit, tswit, tswit' and the alarm note 'tsink, tsink'. The twittering song is given from a perch or on the wing.

Swallows, martins and swifts look somewhat alike, because what scientists call convergent evolution has made swifts develop a build similar to that of the other two species, with all three adapted to a life spent in catching flying insects. Swallows and martins are closely related but swifts belong to a quite distinct Order of birds.

Short wings and long tail make magpies distinctive in flight

Magpie Pica pica

Some of the magpie's feeding habits make it highly unpopular as a garden bird, but it has become widespread and often common in most lowland habitats. In the past 50 years, the magpie has moved into many towns and cities, and has successfully colonised even the central parks of London.

The magpie robs other birds' nests, including those of partridge and pheasant, of eggs and young, and this is what upsets people who see such depredations, natural as they are, in their gardens. The greater part of its food, however, consists of insects and grain.

Magpies usually go about alone or in pairs, but late in winter or early in spring as many as 100 or more may be seen in ceremonial gatherings, the purpose of which is not understood. They chatter, jump about in branches and chase each other. The hoarding instinct, common to all crows, is highly developed in magpies. They hide a great deal of surplus food and return to it later, but there is little evidence for the fanciful assertion that they steal shiny or precious objects.

The courtship displays of this common but shy bird are complicated and little understood. On some occasions male birds have been seen hovering a foot or so above their mates.

RECOGNITION

Boldly contrasting iridescent black and white plumage; long, wedge-shaped tail; sexes alike.

NESTING

Both sexes build domed structure of twigs in bush or tree, with lining of mud covered with rootlets; usually lays April–May; usually 4–7 eggs, light green closely speckled with grey-brown; incubation about 21 days, by female only; nestlings, fed by both parents, leave after about 27 days.

FEEDING

Insects and their larvae; grain, wild fruit and seeds; eggs and young of other birds, small animals and carrion; at times frogs, snails and bread.

SIZE

45.75cm (18in) including 20.25–25.5cm (8–10in) tail

*Rooks start revisiting their
rookeries in late autumn*

Rook Corvus frugilegus

Black with purple gloss;
bare, grey-white patches
on face and base of bill;
thick thigh feathers give
'baggy breeches' effect;
young do not have face
patch; sexes alike.

NESTING

Nests in colonies, normally
in trees; both sexes build
untidy nest of sticks, lined
with dry grass, leaves and
roots, and often added to
each year; lays late March–
April; usually 3–6 eggs, pale
green to grey or pale blue,
heavily flecked with grey and
brown; incubation about
18 days, by female only;
nestlings, fed by both
parents, fly after about
30 days.

FEEDING

Wireworms, leatherjackets
and other insects and
larvae; earthworms, snails,
grain and weed seeds,
fruit; sometimes carrion,
shellfish.

SIZE

45.75cm (18in)

Rooks are among the most sociable of birds, with a communal
life so well developed that it has given rise to fanciful stories of
'rook parliaments'. Although they nest in colonies and feed in
flocks, rooks have a strong sense of territory. Pairs defend a
small area around their nests, threatening and driving off
intruders. Sometimes they steal sticks from the nests of
neighbouring pairs while the rightful owners are away collecting
more nesting material. Misinterpretations of aggressive
behaviour in the defence of territory have led some observers to
claim that they have seen a circle of rooks sitting in judgment
on 'criminal' birds.

The treetop rookeries, loud with hoarse cawing, are often
near buildings and may even be in cities. They are usually
permanent communities. Pairs of rooks use the same nest
each year, repairing it for each new breeding season. Rookeries
vary considerably in size. Many contain just a few dozen nests,
but one colony in northeast Scotland once held as many as
9,000 pairs.

In courtship the male feeds the female – as he does again
when she is incubating – and the male bows and caws to
the female in the tree tops. The spectacular aerial displays
that rooks put on in the autumn, when they tumble, twist
and dive headlong through the air, seem to have no connection
with courtship.

J F M A M J
J A S O N D

Carrion, nestling birds and eggs are eaten by carrion crows

Carrion crow Corvus corone

Notorious as an egg-thief, the carrion crow has for long been on the black lists of gamekeepers and those responsible for looking after ornamental waterfowl in parks. However, the breathing space allowed by two world wars, when gamekeeping was relaxed to free men for more pressing duties, gave the bird all the opportunity it needed to expand.

Today, its hoarse cry can be heard even above the grinding of London traffic. One of its call-notes sounds oddly like a car horn, but the chief call is a hoarse 'kaaah', usually uttered three times in succession.

Like some of the gulls, the carrion crow has found a way of smashing open shells, such as those of mussels, crabs and walnuts, by dropping them from a height. This habit suggests that the carrion crow is quicker to learn than most birds – as are all of the crow family.

There are a good many exceptions to the rule that rooks are gregarious birds and crows are solitary, or seen only in pairs, although family parties of carrion crows are common in summer, and in autumn and winter they sometimes gather in flocks to roost in trees.

Courtship consists mainly of bowing by the male, with wings spread and tail fanned. Once the birds are paired, they stay together for life. Their bulky nests of twigs and dry grass are usually high in trees.

RECOGNITION

Black plumage; distinguished from adult rook by fully feathered base of bill (rook has bare face-patch, though young rooks start with faces feathered); sexes alike.

NESTING

Both sexes build bulky nest of twigs lined with dried grass, dead leaves and sheep's wool, usually in tree or on cliff ledge; lays April–May; usually 3–5 eggs, light blue or green, spotted with dark grey-brown; incubation about 19 days, by female only; nestlings, fed by both parents, fly after 30–35 days.

FEEDING

Grain, insects and their larvae, worms; eggs and carrion; also wild fruit and seeds, snails, frogs and sometimes small mammals.

SIZE

47cm (18½in)

*Jackdaws sometimes pluck
wool from backs of sheep*

J F M A M J
J A S O N D

Jackdaw Corvus monedula

RECOGNITION

Black, with grey nape;
flies with fast wing-beats;
sexes alike.

NESTING

Both sexes make untidy pile
of sticks, lined with wool or
hair, nearly always in hole or
crevice in tree, cliff or
building and often in a
chimney; lays April–May;
3–6 eggs, light blue with
black spots and blotches;
incubation about 18 days,
by female only; nestlings,
fed by both parents, fly after
30 days.

FEEDING

Insects and their larvae;
grain, weed seeds, wild and
cultivated fruit; sometimes
small animals, eggs and
young of other birds,
potatoes and carrion.

SIZE

33cm (13in)

Jackdaws feed mostly on insects, earthworms and grain, but they also eat a good many eggs of other birds, including seabirds nesting on cliffs. A jackdaw will perch on horses or sheep and pluck out tufts of hair to line its nest. Occasionally, it steals a home, making a cranny for itself in the base of the pile of sticks forming a rook's nest.

Jackdaws – once simply called 'daws' – regularly feed alongside rooks or starlings in the fields, although they may also be seen on their own, especially on sea cliffs, around cathedrals and other craggy buildings, and in parkland with old trees. They will eat almost anything that comes their way, but there is a heavy emphasis on animal food and grain in their diet. Often, flocks of them roost in their old nesting-sites, where they set up a clamour with their clipped, metallic calls of 'kow' or 'kyow'. There is also a softer 'tchack'.

Their numbers greatly increased during the 20th century. The reason is unknown, but is perhaps connected with changes in cultivation.

Courtship is elaborate. The male bows, with wings and tail outspread, and sometimes it displays its grey nape by raising the crown feathers while pressing its bill against its breast.

Tree sparrows make their nests in tree holes or sometimes nest-boxes

J F M A M J
J A S O N D

Tree sparrow Passer montanus

During the first half of the last century the tree sparrow was in retreat, to the point where it almost disappeared from Ireland and many parts of Scotland. Then in the 1960s its numbers increased again, with the bird returning to nest in some remote western and northern coastal areas. In the 1990s it was in retreat again, and is now scarce even in former strongholds in eastern England. Its fluctuations may be linked to periodic but increasingly erratic irruptions from the Continent.

Tree sparrows are gregarious birds, breeding in small, loose colonies and often flocking in winter with house sparrows, finches and buntings. In the breeding season they prefer areas with old trees, such as parks, derelict orchards, river banks and even large gardens, especially those with nest-boxes. Less commonly, they nest in old buildings, quarries and the rocky cliffs of windswept islands. In autumn and winter they feed over stubble-fields and rick-yards.

The tree sparrow chirrups like a house sparrow, but its voice is shriller and its 'chip, chip' and 'teck, teck' notes are distinctive. The simple, chirruping song is delivered from a tree-perch and is sometimes sung in chorus. The male's courtship displays include bowing, spreading the wings and raising the crown feathers.

RECOGNITION

Brown back; grey underparts; can be told from house sparrow by smaller size, and combination of chestnut crown, smaller black bib and black spot on each cheek; sexes alike.

NESTING

Both sexes build nest of dried grass, straw and similar materials, lined with feathers, usually in hole, but domed when built in open; nest-boxes sometimes used; normally lays late April–July; usually 3–5 eggs, white, often with heavy blotches of brown or chestnut; incubation about 11 days, by both parents; nestlings, fed by both parents, leave after 13–15 days; two broods, sometimes three.

FEEDING

Mainly seeds of weeds, some grain; also insects and larvae.

SIZE

14cm (5½in)

MALE

J F M A M J
J A S O N D

Yellowhammer perches by the roadside, singing

Yellowhammer Emberiza citrinella

RECOGNITION

Cock has bright yellow and chestnut plumage; hen duller, more streaked with brown; bright chestnut rump and white sides to tail.

NESTING

Hen builds nest of dried grasses, lined with finer grass and hair, well hidden, on ground, bank, hedge, ivy or on wall; rarely more than about 1m (4ft) up; lays April–August; usually 2–5 eggs, white or pale pink with brown or purple-brown squiggles; incubation about 13 days; by hen only; young, fed by both sexes, fly after 11–13 days; two broods, sometimes three.

FEEDING

Largely seeds of weeds, with some grain and wild fruit; also insects and small ground animals.

SIZE

16.5cm (6½in)

Like most other buntings – all of them seed-eating birds, with short sharp-pointed beaks – the yellowhammer avoids areas of human settlement. It rarely enters a garden, even in the countryside, yet it is not particularly shy of people. Its song, the traditional 'little-bit-of-bread-and-no-cheese' (a Scottish version is 'deil-deil-deil-tak ye') may be heard from almost any roadside hedge from late February until the middle of August, and in some years through to early November. The yellowhammer's song is a familiar sound, too, on bushy heaths and commons, and sometimes on farmland where there are few hedges but only dykes or field banks. It is often given from a favourite song-post.

Courtship, when a mate has been attracted, includes a chase in which cock pursues hen in twisting flight, at the end of which they may fall to the ground and mate. The cock may also parade around the hen, wings and tail spread and crest erect.

In winter, yellowhammers become gregarious, and often flock with other seed-eaters to feed over stubble-fields and rick-yards. Their call-notes are a sibilant, liquid 'twit-up' and a somewhat grunting 'twink' or 'twit'. Some yellowhammers from Europe come to Britain in winter, but there is no evidence that our native birds leave for warmer countries, or even that within these islands there is much drift southwards.

MALE

J F M A M J
J A S O N D

Cirl bunting perches on a bramble – it sometimes feeds in flocks with other seed-eaters

Cirl bunting Emberiza cirlus

Primarily, the cirl bunting is a Mediterranean species, and its remnant distribution in southwest England suggests that it is not well able to withstand our winter climate. This close relative of the yellowhammer is now one of our rarest breeding birds, its range shrinking from one that once took in much of Wales and southern England, to one restricted to a tiny area of south Devon, where numbers have recovered to around 700 pairs. The bird has recently been reintroduced to Cornwall, where the climate is good for cirl buntings. However, they depend on farming techniques that allow for old pastures, full of grasshoppers, hedgerows with trees and winter stubble-fields. Unlike other buntings, cirls will visit and even nest in large gardens.

Its normal song, often given from a song-post in the tree tops, is a brief, trilling rattle, quite distinct from the yellowhammer's song. But a rare variant is like the yellowhammer's 'little-bit-of-bread-and-no-cheese' without the terminal 'cheese'. The call-note is a sharp 'zit', with a wren-like 'chur' when the bird is alarmed.

The cirl bunting is extremely secretive and retiring, but it has been recorded luring predators away from its young by fluttering along the ground as if injured.

RECOGNITION

Brown back, yellow underparts; cock distinguished from cock yellowhammer by black throat, grey crown and grey-green band across breast; hen distinguished by olive rump.

NESTING

Hen builds bulky, untidy nest of grass and roots on foundation of moss, in bush or hedge, sometimes in tree or on ground; lays May–August; usually 3 or 4 eggs, light blue or light green with bold dark streaks and scribbling; incubation about 12 days, by hen only; nestlings, normally fed by hen, fly after 11–13 days; two broods, sometimes three.

FEEDING

Predominantly weed and grass seeds, with corn or wild fruit; also insects, such as beetles, grasshoppers and caterpillars.

SIZE

16cm (6¼in)

JFMAMJ
JASOND

Hour after hour the corn bunting sings its monotonous, jangling song from a bush, post or stem

Corn bunting Emberiza calandra

RECOGNITION

Streaked, dull brown plumage; heavy head and pale bill; 'jangling keys' song identifies male in summer; sexes alike.

NESTING

Hen builds untidy nest of dried grass, well hidden among coarse vegetation on or near ground; lays late May–July; normally 3–5 eggs, pale grey or pale brown with heavy black-brown streaks and lines; incubation 12 or 13 days, by hen only; nestlings, usually fed by hen only, start to fly after 9–11 days; usually two broods in south, one in Scotland.

FEEDING

Weed seeds, leaves and grasses and occasionally a little grain; also insects and small ground animals.

SIZE

17.75cm (7in)

Some birds are monogamous and some are polygamous, but the corn bunting may be either. There are records of individual males with up to seven mates, each with their own nests, and breeding in the same area as single-mated birds. The cock selects a song-perch, at any height from a clod of earth to 12m (40ft) up a tree, from which it can keep an eye on its nest, or at least on the route used by the incubating female when she leaves the nest to feed. The song it gives from its perch sounds like the jangling of a bunch of keys.

To look at, the corn bunting is an undistinguished brown bird, and its lack of glamour in the eyes of many birdwatchers may help to explain why it was not until the 1930s that its polygamous habits were suspected.

It is a bird of the open country, ranging over treeless farmland, downland and areas of rough grazing, but despite being able to live in many different environments, corn buntings are distributed in a curious way. It is possible to travel for miles in country apparently suitable for the birds, but to see or hear no evidence of them, and then, as though crossing some invisible boundary, to find suddenly that they are common.

Corn buntings have declined seriously since the mid 1970s, possibly due to changes in agricultural practices.

Heathland

Heaths and commons, semi-wild places where for centuries birds were little disturbed by man, are today a shrinking habitat. Land reclamation, military use of 'waste' land, road-building and the advance of suburbia have all made encroachments. A major decline in bird populations seldom has a single cause, but there is no doubt that heathland birds have suffered greatly from the whittling away of their breeding grounds.

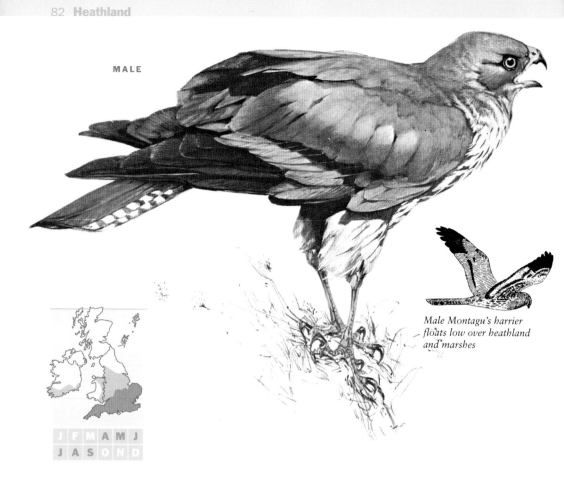

MALE

Male Montagu's harrier floats low over heathland and marshes

J F M A M J
J A S O N D

Montagu's harrier Circus pygargus

RECOGNITION

Male has grey upper parts, is distinguished from hen harrier by dark bars on wings and grey, not white, rump; female slimmer than hen harrier with less white on rump.

NESTING

Female builds nest of weeds, reeds or grass on ground in rough open country – heaths, downs, sand-dunes, marshes, young plantations, sometimes farmland; lays late May–early June; usually 4 or 5 eggs, white or pale blue; incubation about 30 days, by female only; male does all the hunting during incubation; nestlings, tended by both parents, fly after 4–5 weeks.

FEEDING

Small mammals, birds and frogs; some insects and earthworms.

SIZE

Male: 39.5cm (15½in)
Female: 43cm (17in)

Although this is a rare bird in Britain, flocks more than 70 strong have been seen in North Africa during the long autumn migration flight between their breeding grounds in Europe and winter quarters, which are often as far south as the Cape of Good Hope.

The birds usually nest on heaths, in marshland or among farm crops. They are confined to southern England and even there they have declined so seriously that they are now among the rarest breeding birds, with fewer than 12 nests observed each year.

Montagu's harrier – named after an early 19th century Devon naturalist, Colonel George Montagu – has the same graceful, buoyant way of flying as our two other breeding harriers, the marsh harrier and the hen harrier. It is the smallest of the three – the male is not much bigger than a woodpigeon. The female is like a small female hen harrier, with less white on the rump.

A safe way of telling them apart in southern England is by the time of year they are seen. Hen harriers, which breed further north, are winter visitors in the south. Montagu's harriers arrive in April and leave in autumn, so that the two birds usually overlap for only a few weeks in spring and autumn. The courtship display consists of spectacular dives, somersaults and loops by the male.

Hobby flies down its prey – often swallows, martins or swifts

J	F	M	A	M	J
J	A	S	O	N	D

Hobby Falco subbuteo

The scythe-shaped wings of the hobby carry it so rapidly on its hunting flights over downs or heaths that it can fly down a swift, or even catch a bat in flight. This handsome falcon is agile enough to twist and turn after a dragonfly, snatch the insect in its claws and hold it to its beak to eat, without pausing in flight. Hobbies sometimes pluck small birds on the wing, although with bigger prey it is more usual to take the victim to a branch or to the ground before plucking it.

Hobbies seem to fly for sheer joy, tumbling, gliding and soaring, with marked changes of pace and direction, especially when hunting insects, such as chafers and dragonflies. Their mastery of the air plays an important part in courtship, when male and female circle together in long, soaring flights, during which the male 'stoops' at the female, as if preparing to attack her. After snatching a small bird, the male climbs high to dive on the female and pass the prey to her in the air at full speed.

The birds usually breed in open country with scattered trees in which they may find the old nests of crows and sometimes sparrowhawks, or even squirrels' dreys. The hobbies take over, and may remove some lining from the abandoned nest. Their eggs are laid in June, and the hatching of the young hobbies a month later coincides with an abundance of swallows on which they can be fed. Although thinly dispersed, several hundred pairs breed in England and Wales.

RECOGNITION

Slate-grey back; black 'moustache', white breast and underparts streaked with black; red thighs; female similar to male, but slightly larger; in flight, scythe-like wings make it look like a large swift.

NESTING

Takes over abandoned nest high in tree, often a conifer; lays June; usually 3 eggs, white, heavily mottled with red-brown or yellow-brown; incubation about 28 days, chiefly by female; nestlings, fed by both parents, leave after 28–32 days.

FEEDING

Grasshoppers, dragonflies and other winged insects; small birds; occasionally bats and larger birds.

SIZE

33cm (13in)

In flight, the stone-curlew shows the white bars on its wings

Stone-curlew Burhinus oedicnemus

Large yellow eyes; broad whitish band across head; pale yellow legs, round head and short bill; sexes alike.

Both sexes make scrapes in ground, near vegetation but not normally among plants; scrape lined with white stones or rabbit droppings; lays late April–July; 2 eggs, buff, usually with heavy brown blotches; incubation about 26 days, by both parents; chicks, tended by both parents, leave soon after hatching, begin to fly after about 40 days; sometimes two broods.

Snails, slugs, ground insects and their larvae and earthworms; sometimes mice, voles, frogs, and chicks of partridge and pheasant.

40.5cm (16in)

To judge by its appearance, the stone-curlew could be a wader, and its shrill night-time call of 'coo-lee' is like the sound of the curlew. But in fact this rare bird is only distantly related to the curlew. Its closest relative could be the oystercatcher. Its favoured habitats in England are the dry sandy heaths of Breckland and east Suffolk, and the chalk downland of the southern counties. Much of this habitat has been converted from grass to crops in the past 70 years, and the survival of the species now largely depends on its ability to fit in its breeding between the farmer's cultivation and harvest.

Stone-curlews are believed to mate for life, and they may return to the same nesting territory each year. Their courtship displays include bowing and touching bills, and the birds have been seen running about excitedly, picking up straws, flints and other small objects and tossing them over their shoulders.

The birds are gregarious, even in the breeding season, calling to one another in the evenings and at night. They form flocks when migration time comes in October. But for all their sociability they are wary, bobbing their heads when suspicious and 'freezing' when taken by surprise. Both adults and chicks in the nest crouch low, stretching out their heads and necks and remaining immobile in this pose.

Young cuckoo; unguided by adults, the young make their way south to Africa in September

Cuckoo Cuculus canorus

No sound in nature is awaited more eagerly in these islands than the loud, ringing, repeated song of the cuckoo. The male's song, with its promise that summer is not far off, is a national institution, important enough in Britain's country calendar to be dignified by letters to *The Times*. The first cuckoos of the year usually arrive in the second or third week of April from their winter quarters in Africa. March cuckoos are not unknown, but more often, such early birds prove to be schoolboys hoaxing over-eager listeners, or singing collared doves.

When it is seen on the wing, a cuckoo can easily be mistaken for a male sparrowhawk, but it can be identified by its heavier appearance, pointed wings and long, graduated tail, spotted and tipped with white.

After their arrival, cuckoos spread out over almost the whole of the British Isles into any kind of country where they can find foster-parents for their young. The double-noted 'cuckoo', heard over woods and thickets, heaths, sand-dunes, moorland and hills, is the male's courtship song. The female has a bubbling trill.

When mating is over, the adult birds leave Britain, flying south in July and early August. Some newly fledged young linger until September after leaving their foster-parents. Then they migrate, finding their way unaided to their winter quarters – a remarkable example of a bird's inborn ability to navigate.

RECOGNITION

Grey head and back, barred underparts; distinguished from sparrowhawk by slender bill, pointed wings and graduated, spotted tail; sexes alike, though in a rare variety female is chestnut-coloured and barred above and below; juveniles are brown and barred, with white spots on the head.

NESTING

Female fosters young on other birds, replacing an egg from host's nest with one of her own; lays 12 or 13 eggs in different nests, similar in colour to host's eggs; incubation 12–13 days; nestlings fed by host birds, fly after 14–21 days.

FEEDING

Insects, chiefly large caterpillars; also spiders, centipedes and earthworms; nestlings share host bird's diet, usually insects.

SIZE

33cm (13in)

Nightjar feeds mainly at night, catching moths as it flies

MALE

Nightjar Caprimulgus europaeus

J F M A M J
J A S O N D

RECOGNITION

Night-flying bird with long, falcon-like wings and tail; grey-brown 'camouflage' plumage; mouth fringed with bristles; male has white spots near wing-tips, absent in female; distinctive 'churring' song.

NESTING

Nests in unlined scrape in the ground, often near dead wood; lays late May–July; 2 eggs, white, marbled with brown or grey; incubation about 18 days, chiefly by female; nestlings, fed by both parents, leave nest after about a week but stay nearby, fly after about 17 days; usually two broods.

FEEDING

Insects, chiefly those caught in flight.

SIZE

26.75cm (10½in)

At dusk the nightjar leaves its daytime hiding place and takes to the air silently on long, soft-feathered wings, twisting and turning through the twilight as it follows flying insects and traps them in its gaping bill.

It is after sunset, too, that the bird produces its song – the 'churring' sound that gives the nightjar its name. There are abrupt changes of pitch in the otherwise unvarying, prolonged 'churr' when the bird turns its head from side to side as it perches along, rarely across, a branch. In flight, the nightjar's call is a soft but insistent 'coo-ic', and it makes a sound like a whip-crack with its wings.

During the day, nightjars are almost invisible. They lie motionless on the ground and, at a distance, the delicate marking on their feathers make them look like dead leaves. There are often pieces of wood near the nightjar's nest – an unlined scrape in the ground, to the vicinity of which a pair of birds returns, season after season – and these make the sitting bird even harder to see. Nightjars arrive from Africa in mid-May to breed on heaths, commons and other places with bracken or gorse, as well as on the borders of woodland. Their numbers have been decreasing in Britain for more than 50 years. On its evening flights to catch insects, the nightjar visits pastures where farm animals graze – a habit that has earned the bird its name of 'goatsucker' from a false belief that it milks goats with its huge mouth.

Flying round in circles, the woodlark sings its mellow song

Woodlark Lullula arborea

The fluting song of the woodlark is not as spirited as the skylark's, but it makes up in sweetness for what it lacks in power, and the woodlark's song-flight is just as spectacular as the other lark's. It begins to sing when it is a metre or so off the ground, at first repeating one or two notes six times or so. Then it pauses, as if to get its breath for a series of liquid phrases. As it sings, the bird sometimes spirals high in the air above its territory, circles down until it is about 30m (100ft) from the ground, then drops to earth. The woodlark also sings from the ground or from a song-post overlooking its territory. The song, sometimes given at night, is heard mainly from early March to the middle of June.

Woodlarks will nest in almost any kind of grassy country with a few shrubs and some scattered trees. They prefer sandy heathlands, especially in their East Anglian stronghold, limestone slopes, parkland and the borders of woods. In winter they sometimes join up in wandering flocks to feed.

A series of severe winters since the early 1950s hit the birds hard. They used to be widespread in southern England, and bred regularly as far north as Yorkshire and North Wales, but now they are almost entirely limited to East Anglia and southern England. The species is rarely seen in Wales, and no longer breeds there.

RECOGNITION

Streaked brown plumage with white eye-stripes meeting across nape; small black and white mark on forewing; distinguished from skylark by smaller size, very short tail without white sides, lower crest and different song; sexes alike.

NESTING

Both sexes build nest of grass and moss, lined with grass, in depression in the ground; lays late March–July; usually 3 or 4 eggs, pale grey with fine red-brown or olive mottling; incubation 13–15 days, by female only; nestlings, fed by both sexes, leave after 11 or 12 days, fly some days later; usually two broods, sometimes three.

FEEDING

Mainly insects; some spiders; seeds in autumn.

SIZE

15.25cm (6in)

Tree pipit descends on uplifted wings during its song-flight

Tree pipit Anthus trivialis

Upper parts brown; breast buff with heavy stripes; best distinguished from meadow pipit by call and song-flight; sexes alike.

Builds nest on ground with dried grass on foundation of moss, lined with grass and hair; lays May–June; usually 4–6 eggs, variable, often red-brown or grey with darker blotches or marbling; incubation 13 or 14 days, by female only; nestlings, fed by both parents, leave after 12 or 13 days; often two broods.

Insects and their larvae, including beetles, flies and sometimes grasshoppers; also spiders.

15.25cm (6in)

A spectacular song-flight makes up for the inconspicuous plumage of this visitor from tropical Africa. The male chooses a high perch and launches into the air, climbing steeply. It begins to sing as it nears the peak of its climb, and continues as it descends, on uplifted wings, to end with a crescendo of 'see-er, see-er, see-er' notes.

Usually the male returns to the same perch or to one nearby, and only rarely to the ground. This is one way of telling tree pipits from the closely similar meadow pipits, which normally start their song-flights from the ground and return to it. Another way is by the sounds they make. The meadow pipit has no 'see-er' climax to its song, and the shrill 'pheet' of its call-note is quite different from the tree pipit's loud, high 'teez' call.

Sometimes the tree pipit will deliver a shortened version of its song from a perch. It breeds on commons, heaths or railway embankments – in fact in any rough country near woods or with scattered trees or telegraph poles that the male can use as song-posts, or even in open woodland.

Courtship consists mainly of a sexual chase, with both birds using a jerky flight action. After they have paired, the birds build a well-hidden nest on the ground, sometimes under a tussock of grass and sometimes in a bank, often with a 'mouse-hole' entrance.

Wheatear in flight – the bird was a favourite delicacy on Victorian dinner-tables

MALE IN SUMMER

| J | F | M | A | M | J |
| J | A | S | O | N | D |

Wheatear Oenanthe oenanthe

Early in March, wheatears begin to fly in from their winter quarters in Africa, spreading out mainly to northern and western Britain. When they reach their nesting grounds, the birds begin a curious dancing courtship display. A male and a female face one another in a shallow hollow and the male starts leaping into the air with puffed-out feathers, jumping out of the hollow onto the bank, or from one bank to the other, in rapid rhythm. Then it throws itself down in front of its mate, with wings and tail spread out and head stretched along the ground.

The wheatear sings its squeaky, warbling song, sometimes from a low perch, sometimes in a dancing flight after a display on the ground, and at other times in a hovering flight. When feeding, it chases insects on the ground, bobbing its head and hopping. It has also been observed hovering like a hawk and diving to the ground.

While breeding wheatears are building their nests on bare hillsides, heaths or sand-dunes, and raising their young, bigger and more brightly coloured wheatears pass through Britain, on their way to breed in Iceland and Greenland. Thousands of wheatears used to be trapped each year as they rested on the south coast on migration, and were served up as delicacies on Victorian dinner-tables.

RECOGNITION

Both sexes have white rump; male in summer has blue-grey back, black mask and wings, buff underparts; in winter has brown back, mask and wings; female at all seasons similar to male in winter plumage.

NESTING

Nests on rough open waste land, in rock crevice, rabbit burrow or even tin can; nest of grass and moss, lined with hair and feathers, built chiefly by female; lays late April–June; usually 6 eggs, pale blue, sometimes with red-brown spots; incubation about 14 days, chiefly by female; nestlings, fed by both parents, leave after about 14 days; sometimes two broods.

FEEDING

Chiefly insects and larvae; some spiders, centipedes and snails.

SIZE

14.5cm (5¾in)

MALE IN
SUMMER

J F M A M J
J A S O N D

Stonechat at its nest, built at the foot of a gorse bush

Stonechat Saxicola torquata

RECOGNITION

Plump, round-headed bird; male in summer has black head and back, white patches on neck, wings and rump, chestnut breast; browner and duller in winter; female in summer has streaky brown upper parts, no rump-patch; darker in winter.

NESTING

Female builds nest on or close to ground, mainly of moss, grass and hair; lays late March–June; usually 5 or 6 eggs, light blue, finely freckled with red-brown; incubation 14 or 15 days, by female only; nestlings, fed by both parents, leave after about 13 days, fly a few days later; usually two broods, sometimes three in south.

FEEDING

Mainly insects and their larvae, some worms and spiders.

SIZE

12.75cm (5in)

Low over its heathland territory, the handsome male stonechat 'dances' up and down in the air as it gives its squeaky song; or it chases the female in a darting courtship display. The song lasts only a few seconds when the stonechat settles on one of its song-posts on top of a bush or on a telegraph wire. As it sings from a perch, the bird repeatedly flirts its tail, and in the intervals between singing often gives its loud call-note, a harsh, grating 'tsak-tsak' or 'hwee-tsak-tsak'.

Stonechats, which move about in pairs all the year round, often breed in the same kind of habitat as whinchats, although it seems that in districts where one species is numerous, the other is uncommon. Stonechats prefer uncultivated land, usually appearing on farmland only in winter, when they also turn up on building sites and railway embankments.

Once they were common birds throughout Britain, but their distribution is now local, except in the coastal areas of south and west England and Wales. They breed inland mainly after a series of mild winters, but retreat to the coast after harsh ones. Their decline may be due to the steady destruction of their breeding habitat, and to the effects of hard weather. After each bad winter in recent years, they have taken a little longer to recover their numbers, and each time some small, isolated population seems to have been wiped out.

MALE IN
SUMMER

Female whinchat at its nest,
usually hidden in rough
vegetation

Whinchat Saxicola rubetra

Whinchats are among the earliest of Britain's summer
visitors, starting to arrive in ones and twos early in April, after
a journey across the Sahara from tropical Africa. They often
arrive with wheatears and yellow wagtails, but numbers have
declined everywhere and they are now absent as breeding
birds from many eastern and southern counties. They nest in
rough grassland and bracken on heaths, commons, hillsides
and farmland.

They appear on farmland more often than the related
stonechats, and are not so closely associated with gorse,
although in some districts both birds are known as 'furze-chats'.
Whinchats also breed in districts without bushes, provided that
there are tall plants, such as thistles or bracken, where they can
perch to sing. The song is a brief warbling, which sometimes
includes imitations of other birds, and the call-note is a sharp
'tic-tic' or 'u-tic'.

In its courtship display the male has been seen singing in
front of the female, with wings lowered and quivering, tail
fanned out and slightly raised, and head thrown back. The male
sings, too, as it keeps watch close to the nest while its mate is
sitting on the eggs.

Whinchats fly low and jerkily, with quickly beating wings,
from one tall plant to another, where they perch to watch for
insects. They catch the insects with a fluttering sally into the air,
but feed chiefly on the ground.

RECOGNITION

Streaky brown upper parts;
male has white eye-stripe,
female's is duller; both
sexes have white patches at
sides of tail; male duller in
winter, more like female.

NESTING

Female builds nest of
grass and moss, lined with
fine grass, on ground in
rough vegetation; covered
runway may lead to nest;
lays May–July; usually 5 or
6 eggs, green-blue with
red-brown speckles;
incubation 13 days, by
female only; nestlings,
fed by both parents, leave
after 14 days; sometimes
two broods.

FEEDING

Insects and their larvae;
some spiders and worms.

SIZE

12.75cm (5in)

MALE IN
SUMMER

*The whitethroat has a
vertical song-flight, so
that it seems to dance
like a puppet*

<table>
<tr><td>J</td><td>F</td><td>M</td><td>A</td><td>M</td><td>J</td></tr>
<tr><td>J</td><td>A</td><td>S</td><td>O</td><td>N</td><td>D</td></tr>
</table>

Whitethroat Sylvia communis

RECOGNITION

Male has grey cap in
summer, grey-brown cap
in winter; white throat
distinguished from lesser
whitethroat by absence
of dark 'mask' on cheeks
and pale legs; both sexes
have chestnut wings;
female duller.

NESTING

Male builds 'trial' nests,
female may use one, or
both may build another;
deep cup-nest, close to
ground in cover, is made
from grasses, often lined
with horse-hair and down;
lays May–July; usually
4 or 5 eggs, often pale
green or pale buff with
grey markings; incubation
about 12 days, by both
parents; nestlings, fed by
both parents, leave after
about 11 days; usually
two broods.

FEEDING

Insects and their larvae;
spiders; fruit in autumn.

SIZE

14cm (5½in)

Whitethroats are not such skulking, secretive birds as some of
the other warblers. The male will perch in full view on top of a
bush to sing its brief but sweet song. The bird may mate with
the first female whitethroat to cross the territory it stakes out as
soon as it arrives in Britain. The courtship display can be
violent, on both sides. The male follows the female closely with
a piece of grass in his bill, and then dashes at her with short
bursts of singing, as if attacking her. The female responds by
spreading her wings and tail and springing at the male as if to
drive him away. At the last moment he turns aside. About the
same time of year, the male starts to build 'trial' nests. He may
work on as many as three, none of which is usually completed.
Call-notes include a harsh 'churr', a hard 'tacc' and a softer
'wheet' or 'whit'.

Whitethroats live in a broad range of habitats – commons,
country lanes, wood borders and clearings, and any kind of
land with brambles, briers, osiers, bushes and overgrown
hedges. Their numbers crashed in the late 1960s, due to drought
in their African winter quarters, and have taken many years to
recover. After the breeding season, whitethroats will sometimes
visit gardens to raid soft-fruit crops. In August and September
they fly back to Africa.

Lesser whitethroat is a shy bird, usually seen as it flits rapidly from bush to bush

J	F	M	A	M	J
J	A	S	O	N	D

Lesser whitethroat Sylvia curruca

A tuneless, rattling, repetitive 'chikka-chikka-chikka-chikka' from deep inside an overgrown hedge or some other thick cover is one of the few ways in which the lesser whitethroat gives away its presence. This loud, far-carrying song is often preceded, and sometimes followed by, a more musical sound, a low-pitched warble. When the male is defending its territory, its song may be given from a song-post near the nest.

It is a much shyer bird than its relative, the whitethroat, and is much less abundant in Britain. It breeds on commons, open woods, shrubberies, large gardens and hedge-lined lanes. Only occasionally has it nested in Scotland, and it has bred in Ireland just once.

Its courtship follows the typical warbler pattern, with the male following the female as she walks or runs through thick vegetation, and posturing before her with breast and crown feathers fluffed out. Occasionally, the male takes off and flutters into a tree, singing. Often the bird gathers grass in its bill; this may be for a 'trial' nest or it may be to give to the female in a ritual presentation of nesting material. A noisy 'tacc-tacc' of alarm is often heard in late summer, when both parents are looking after their fledglings. There is also a well-developed distraction display in which a parent bird runs along the ground, behaving as if injured.

RECOGNITION

Grey upper parts, dark 'mask' on cheeks; distinguished from whitethroat by dull wings, dark legs, distinctive song; sexes alike.

NESTING

Male builds 'trial' nests, female lines chosen one; nest, in bush, hedgerow or evergreen shrub, made from stalks, roots and hair, sometimes decorated with cobwebs; lays May–July; usually 4–6 eggs, pale cream, with a few bold sepia and grey markings; incubation usually 11 days, mainly by female; nestlings, fed by both parents, leave after about 11 days; often two broods.

FEEDING

Mainly insects and their larvae; some berries in autumn.

SIZE

13.25cm (5¼in)

Grasshopper warbler at its nest; this species is among the shyest of British birds

Grasshopper warbler Locustella naevia

No grasshopper heard in Britain ever made a sound like the song of the grasshopper warbler, but the chirping of some Continental grasshoppers is close enough to justify the bird's name. The song, known as 'reeling', sounds like an angler's reel being wound in, or like a free-wheeling bicycle. After the birds arrive in Britain in April or May, reeling goes on every morning and evening, with occasional bursts during the night.

Grasshopper warblers are shy birds, and spend most of their time feeding in thick bushes or low cover, but sometimes a male perches on an exposed spray to sing, with its body quivering and head turning from side to side. The far-carrying song is a poor guide to the bird's whereabouts, since it seems to have the ability to 'throw' its voice.

The spread of dense young plantations in Britain has helped to increase the number of grasshopper warblers breeding here, although more recently they have declined quite severely in a 'tidier' countryside. Their chief winter home is in West Africa, south of the Sahara.

Courtship usually takes the form of a chase through the undergrowth. The female leads the way, pecking as she steps through the grass or through the branches of a bush. The male follows with wings flapping slowly, carrying a piece of grass or a dead leaf in his bill.

MALE IN SUMMER

Female Dartford warbler at its nest – its eggs were once much prized by egg-collectors

Dartford warbler Sylvia undata

Because it remains in Britain all year round, the Dartford warbler became one of our rarest breeding birds after the 1963 winter. Other warblers migrate, but this small, red-breasted bird stays on, to face what can sometimes be harsh winters ... and pays the penalty.

Each spring the survivors set about repopulating their habitat, but the gorsy heathland that Dartford warblers prefer is being swallowed up by farmland and by the advance of suburbia. There are now fewer areas that can serve as a refuge.

At the beginning of the 19th century, Dartford warblers bred widely throughout southern England, and they were still found in most counties south of the Thames until just before the Second World War. Then came a succession of hard winters. The worst, 1962–3, cut down the entire British population to a mere ten pairs, but by 1966 this population had doubled. A further series of mild winters enabled the population to increase to about 500 pairs by 1970, to 950 pairs by 1991 and 1,700 pairs by 1994. Now there are almost 2,000, including 70 pairs in Wales and others in East Anglia and even the West Midlands.

All that can usually be seen of the handsome but secretive Dartford warbler is its long tail vanishing rapidly into a gorse bush, but in winter some Dartford warblers become nomadic and may be seen foraging on rough ground. The birds may pair for life.

RECOGNITION

Both sexes have a long tail, often cocked; male in winter has dark brown upper parts and slate-grey head, with dark, wine-coloured underparts; head greyer in summer; female slightly browner than male.

NESTING

Male builds 'trial' nests; final nest built mainly by female, in gorse or long heather, of grass, roots and stalks decorated with spiders' webs; lays April–June; 3 or 4 eggs, dirty white speckled with grey, sometimes tinged with green; incubation about 12 days, chiefly by female; nestlings, fed by both parents, leave after about 13 days; normally two broods, occasionally three.

FEEDING

Insects and their larvae; some spiders.

SIZE

12.75cm (5in)

J F M A M J
J A S O N D

MALE IN
SUMMER

*Linnets have the typical
dancing flight of the smaller
finches*

Linnet Carduelis cannabina

Its persistent, twittering song helped to make the cock linnet one of the favourite cage-birds of Victorian and Edwardian England. Today the fashion for putting linnets in cages has long passed, and the handsome red-breasted male pours out its medley of notes in the wild. Usually it finds a song-post on a bush or a fence, but sometimes a linnet will sing as it flies, bounding up and down through the air. The usual flight-note is a high-pitched chittering and there is also a 'tsoo-eet' anxiety note. The cock sings again in its courtship ceremony, uttering a series of low, sweet notes as it droops its wings, spreads its tail and rapidly shakes its feathers.

Linnets even sing 'in chorus'. They are gregarious birds, often nesting in loose colonies. They mix with other finches in winter feeding flocks, sometimes hundreds strong, which roam the countryside on foraging trips to stubble-fields and other farmland, waste ground, and rough country near the coast.

In the breeding season, linnets prefer places with plenty of low bushes, which provide nest-sites. They frequent gorse-covered commons and heaths and scrub-covered downland, but sometimes move into big gardens. Cuckoos occasionally lay their eggs in linnets' nests, but the young cuckoos usually starve because of the specialised diet – chiefly seeds – on which linnet nestlings are fed.

Mountain and Moorland

Life is a constant battle for upland birds, requiring special qualities of hardiness – ptarmigan cannot be driven down the slopes by any weather short of a blizzard and red grouse are undeterred by drifting snow – but their future has been put in doubt by a rapidly warming climate.

MALE IN
WINTER

*Ptarmigan in summer
plumage – only the wings
remain white*

J F M A M J
J A S O N D

Ptarmigan Lagopus mutus

RECOGNITION

White wings and dark body
in summer; female tawnier
than male; pure white in
winter except for black tail;
male has black mark
through eye.

NESTING

Female makes scrape near
rocks; lays May or June;
usually 5–9 eggs, creamy
with dark markings;
incubation about 25 days,
by female only; chicks,
tended by both parents,
leave soon after hatching,
fly after 10 days.

FEEDING

Mainly fruit, shoots and
leaves of crowberry,
bilberry, heather and other
mountain plants; a few
insects, mainly crane-flies.

SIZE

35.5cm (14in)

Ptarmigan are birds of the high barren mountain tops, seldom seen below 610m (2,000ft) and for the most part spending their lives at least another 150m (500ft) higher. Early in the morning they move down the mountainsides to feed on the green shoots and fruits of the sparse vegetation above the tree line, but apart from hunger, the only force that can drive these hardy birds down into the sheltered corries is a full-scale blizzard.

The bird's colour change, from mottled brown in summer to nearly all white in winter, helps it in the struggle for survival – a struggle that begins even before the chicks hatch out in a nest that is sometimes scantily lined with grass, and often protected from the upland gales only by a boulder. Hen ptarmigan have been observed using an injury-feigning display, crawling along the ground and thrashing their wings to distract predators from their eggs and chicks.

When ski-lifts were first built in the Cairngorms, fears were voiced for the future of the ptarmigan, but these have proved to be largely unfounded. More likely to cause ptarmigan to disappear entirely from Britain is the seemingly unstoppable effect of a warming climate.

Male ptarmigan stake a claim to territory in March, flying up with croaking cries. They chase females in flight and on the ground, fanning their tails and drooping their wings.

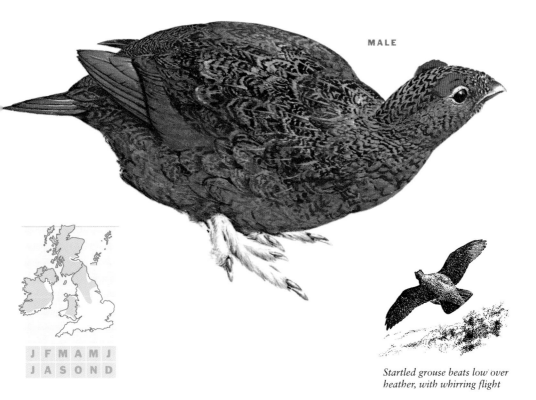

MALE

J F M A M J
J A S O N D

Startled grouse beats low over heather, with whirring flight

Red grouse Lagopus lagopus

Red grouse, as native birds, are unique to Britain and Ireland, but they are closely related to the willow grouse of Norway and are regarded as a race of the same species. They are hardy birds, restricted to a challenging habitat, the quality of which has declined in recent decades. The lack of good moorland management combined with wet summers has reduced grouse populations. Unlike other gamebirds, they are not reared and released for shooting, but wild populations are encouraged by intensive keepering. They rely for food almost entirely on ling heather, eating different parts of the plant from winter until its seeds fall in autumn.

The cock birds mark out their territory in a dramatic display, leaping into the air with spread wings and descending steeply again while extending their necks and feet and fanning their tails. They challenge rival cocks with their barking call: 'go-bak, go-bak-bak-bak-bak'. Birds that cannot establish a well-heathered territory often fall victim to disease or predators.

In winter on the high, bleak moors, grouse may have to keep treading with their feet for long spells to avoid being buried in drifting snow. Snowstorms are still common in April, when the female is laying, but even if the eggs are badly frosted, grouse chicks rarely fail to hatch – as long as their parents stay on guard against that moorland egg-thief, the hooded crow. The adults sometimes feign injury to distract intruders.

RECOGNITION

Dark wings and tail; male's body dark red-brown; female's browner, more barred.

NESTING

Female makes scrape in the ground, lines it with grass or heather; usually lays April or May; usually 4–9 eggs, creamy-white, almost obscured by dark chocolate blotches; incubation about 23 days, by female only; chicks, tended by both parents for about 6 weeks, leave soon after hatching, fly after about 13 days.

FEEDING

Mostly ling heather; also fruits and shoots of cranberry.

SIZE

Male: 38cm (15in)
Female: 34.25cm (13½in)

FEMALE

*Hen harrier beats the air lazily
in low-level hunting flight*

Hen harrier Circus cyaneus

RECOGNITION

Male grey; female brown, with streaked underparts and black bars on wings; male distinguished from Montagu's harrier by white, not grey, rump and absence of black bars on wings.

NESTING

Female builds nest on ground, often in heather; lays late May–June; usually 4 eggs, white or pale blue; incubation about 28 days, by female only; nestlings, tended by both parents, leave after 6 weeks.

FEEDING

Small ground-living animals; a few small birds caught on the wing.

SIZE

Male: 43cm (17in)
Female: 51cm (20in)

The hen harrier increased in numbers significantly in Scotland after the Second World War, and returned as a breeding bird to Wales. There are now more than 500 breeding pairs in Britain, but the increase has stalled and numbers remain tiny in England, despite suitable habitat being available to support many more pairs. Numbers are lower than they should be on many areas of moorland managed for grouse shooting.

Most hen harriers spend the breeding season on the moors and in moorland valleys, but the birds are beginning to spread to heaths and sand-dunes, and in winter they regularly visit coastal areas.

In its low-level hunting flight, the hen harrier is like other harriers – it lazily beats its wings four or five times, glides with them half-raised, and then pounces to seize a mouse, a frog, a lapwing chick or the egg of some other ground-nesting bird. Hen harriers will also chase small birds through the air but, in spite of their name, they are not much of a threat to hens.

In its spectacular courtship display, the bird flies steeply upwards, turns a somersault at the top of its climb, then plummets down with closed wings. While the female is on the nest, the male will call to her after making a kill and pass the prey to her in mid-air, either directly from foot to foot, or by dropping it for her to catch.

Young eagle in soaring flight shows black bar at end of tail

J F M A M J
J A S O N D

Golden eagle Aquila chrysaëtos

For sheer majesty there is no bird to compare with the golden eagle. This huge bird of prey soars above Highland peaks, primary feathers splayed at the tips of wings spanning 2m (7ft), as it scans the sky and ground below for quarry. Then it accelerates towards the target at a breathtaking speed of up to 145km/h (90mph) and thumps down to nail a red grouse, ptarmigan or blue hare to the ground.

Eagles may take lambs occasionally, although these are usually weaklings on overstocked pasture. They also eat carrion – a habit that, at one time, cut back the bird's range. In regions where sheep-dips based on dieldrin pesticides were used, eagles were poisoned if they ate dead sheep. Dieldrin has now been banned throughout the EU.

Eagles pair for life, and usually have two or three eyries, pitched between roughly 450m and 600m (1,500ft and 2,000ft) high, which they use in rotation. In courtship, the pair soar in spirals over their territory and plunge earthwards with half-closed wings, sometimes rolling over in mid-air so close that their talons appear to link.

The chosen nest, an immense basket of sticks on a mountain crag, tall pine or sea cliff, is added to year by year – repaired before the breeding season and often decorated with fresh greenery. As the downy eaglets grow up, the nest becomes fouled with a litter of bones, the remains of food brought by their parents.

RECOGNITION

Almost uniformly dark, with golden tinge on head; heavy, powerful bill; exceptionally long wings; female larger than male.

NESTING

Both sexes build or repair nests in November or December; lays March or April; usually 2 eggs, white, often with red-brown markings; incubation about 40 days, mainly by female; nestlings, fed by both parents, leave after about 12 weeks.

FEEDING

Blue hares, grouse, ptarmigan, lambs and carrion.

SIZE

Male: 76.25cm (30in)
Female: 89cm (35in)

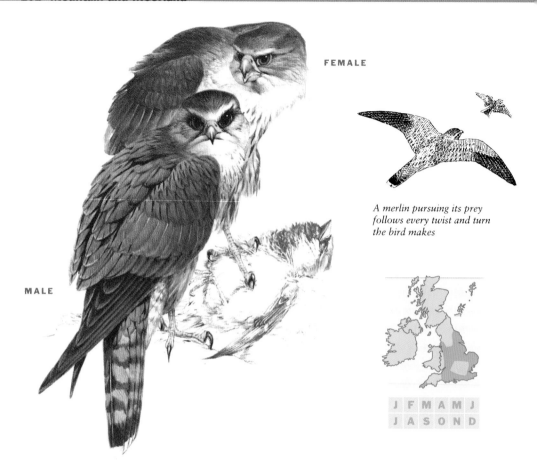

FEMALE

MALE

A merlin pursuing its prey follows every twist and turn the bird makes

JFMAMJ
JASOND

Merlin Falco columbarius

Slate-blue back and tail; female larger than male with dark brown back and banded tail; both have heavily streaked underparts.

Nests on ground or in old crow's nest; lays May–June; usually 4 eggs, cream, with heavy red-brown freckles; incubation about 30 days, by both parents; nestlings, tended by both parents, leave at 26 days.

Small birds, usually meadow pipits; some small mammals and lizards; a few insects; occasionally game-chicks.

Male: 26.75cm (10½in)
Female: 33cm (13in)

The merlin dashes along close to the heather, following every twist and turn of its quarry's flight as it chases one of the small birds – meadow pipits, twites or skylarks – that are its chief prey. The male, or jack, is little bigger than a blackbird, weighing a mere 160g (5½oz), yet it does most of the hunting throughout the breeding season, sometimes flying down birds as big as itself through sheer persistence.

With its prey safely clutched in its talons, the male flies towards its nest, uttering a shrill, chattering 'quik-ik-ik' call. At one of its plucking posts close to the nest, it often tears off the prey's head and then brings the body to the female, or occasionally signals to her to take it in mid-air.

Merlins vary their diet with small mammals, lizards and insects during their winter wanderings, which can take them to lowland pastures, marshes or the sand and shingle of the coast. On upland moors they occasionally kill a few game-chicks, although not enough to justify the persecution they have suffered from gamekeepers.

Merlins have declined over most of Britain in the last 80 years or so. The process appears to be continuing, but the reasons for it are unclear. Habitat loss, persecution and pesticide contamination may all be involved.

The merlin's name has no connection with the magician of King Arthur legends. It comes from an old French name for the species, *émerillon*.

FEMALE IN SUMMER

Migrant dotterels have traditional resting sites

Dotterel Eudromias morinellus

The tameness of the dotterel, and its need for a specialised upland habitat, make this member of the plover family a rarity in Britain. Around 100 years ago, dotterels were widespread on the higher hills from Highland south to the Pennines. Migrants, flying in small parties known as a 'trips', used to visit a few places each spring in eastern and southern England – and often they were promptly shot and eaten. Trips of dotterels still spend a day or two at their traditional resting sites before moving northwards.

Today about 950 pairs are believed to be in Britain. Many of them breed on the Cairngorms and nearby summits, nesting among the rocks on tussocks or mossy ground above 762m (2,500ft), but they are threatened by a changing climate.

Dotterels play a curious game of hide-and-seek as part of their courtship. The male hides among the stones of the barren mountain tops and the female, when she finds him, pecks at his neck feathers. In display flights, the female takes the initiative, chasing the male and then leading him to a scrape where the nest will be built.

The duties of hatching the eggs and tending the young are left to the male, which has an elaborate distraction display to protect the chicks. It runs along the ground in a crouch, looking like a small mammal, flies aggressively towards the intruder, then flops back to the ground as though on broken wings.

RECOGNITION

White eye-stripes, meeting in a V at nape of neck; white breast band; chestnut underparts; faint bar on wing visible in flight; female brighter than male.

NESTING

Nests on ground in scrape lined with lichen and moss; lays May–June; usually 3 eggs, buff, stone or red-brown, thickly blotched and streaked with dark brown; incubation about 27 days, by male only; chicks, tended by male, leave within 24 hours, fly after about 28 days.

FEEDING

Mainly insects; also spiders and crowberries; occasionally snails and earthworms.

SIZE

21.5cm (8½in)

SUMMER

WINTER

Feeding flock in February.
The bird on the left is
assuming summer plumage

J F M A M J
J A S O N D

Golden plover Pluvialis apricarius

RECOGNITION

Black face and underparts,
with spangled black and
gold upper parts in summer;
in winter black disappears
and underparts are white,
with golden mottling;
sexes alike.

NESTING

Both sexes make scrapes,
then female chooses one to
line with twigs, lichen and
grass; lays late April–June;
usually 4 eggs, creamy,
green-tinged or buff,
spotted and blotched with
dark brown; incubation
about 30 days, by both
parents; young, tended by
both parents, leave after
1 or 2 days, fly after about
30 days.

FEEDING

Mostly insects and their
larvae; snails, worms
and small shellfish; also
spiders, weed-seeds,
algae and moss.

SIZE

28cm (11in)

The mournful call-note and liquid song of the golden plover are
common summer sounds on the open moorland where it breeds.
However, these birds are not as common as they once were,
because their breeding range contracted steadily during the
20th century. Golden plovers no longer breed on any of the
Somerset moors, and there has been a sudden and dramatic
decline in numbers in Wales, due to a combination of habitat
loss, disturbance and climate change.

When these handsome birds arrive at their breeding areas,
they take part in communal courtship ceremonies. The males
skirmish, running at each other with raised wings, and
leapfrogging. Several males will chase one female. Later, when
the eggs are being incubated, the off-duty parent will keep
watch from a hummock near the nest, ready to launch itself
at an animal or bird intruder, or perhaps to start a distraction
display, which may at its highest intensity include lying on the
ground with thrashing wings.

In autumn and winter the birds form flocks as they move
south to farmland and estuaries. There they will feed on insects,
worms and small shellfish as well as grass and weed-seeds,
which form the vegetable part of their diet. They often join
feeding flocks of lapwings, but when disturbed the mixed flock
splits up in the air into two separate flights, one of each species.

*Male curlew planes
over breeding grounds
in display flight*

J F M A M J
J A S O N D

Curlew Numenius arquata

A loud, melancholy 'coor-li', the cry that gives the curlew its name, is the clearest sign of the bird's presence for most of the year. In spring, it is often accompanied by a bubbling song, which announces that the breeding season is beginning. The males trill the song as they fly in wide circles and glide down on extended wings to claim territories in the breeding area.

The curlew, Britain's biggest wader, was once confined to moorland, but it extended its range to low-lying farmland and lower heaths and bogs early in the 20th century. This trend has since been reversed and numbers in Wales, for example, have declined by four-fifths in just 30 years, leading to fears of an inevitable disappearance there before long.

In winter, curlews often feed in flocks, wading over coastal marshes and mudflats.

When female curlews arrive at the breeding place, sometimes as early as February, the males follow them in a crouching walk, circling them when they stop.

The customary caution of the birds is especially pronounced in the early stages of incubation, when male and female will change places on the nest in wary silence. But later, when the eggs have hatched, the parents become aggressive, running towards intruders and sometimes taking off to sweep down on them.

RECOGNITION

Grey-brown with long legs and downward-curved bill; white rump; larger than whimbrel and without stripes on crown; distinctive 'coor-li' cry; sexes alike.

NESTING

Nests in hollow, lined with grass or heather, among low vegetation; lays April–May; 4 eggs, buff, brown or olive, spotted with darker brown; incubation about 30 days, by both parents; chicks, tended by both parents, leave a few hours after hatching, fly after 28 days.

FEEDING

On coast, small molluscs, crustaceans, worms, small fish and sometimes seaweed; inland, insects and their larvae, worms, molluscs and at times berries and weed-seeds; occasionally grain.

SIZE

56cm (22in)

SUMMER

The greenshank – once a tempting target for egg-collectors

Greenshank Tringa nebularia

RECOGNITION

Long green legs; long grey-blue bill, slightly upturned; rump white, wings unmarked; upper parts ash-grey with dark markings; underparts white, with dark spots and bars in summer; sexes alike.

NESTING

Female makes scrape in ground, lines it with vegetation and sometimes hare droppings; lays early May–June; usually 4 eggs, buff, with dark blotches and spots; incubation about 24 days, by both parents; nestlings, tended by both parents, leave in a few hours, begin to fly after about 27 days.

FEEDING

Water insects and their larvae; worms and small fish; occasionally small frogs, more commonly tadpoles.

SIZE

30.5cm (12in)

The greenshank was badly harried in the past by egg-collectors, who seemed to find a challenge in the task of tracking down the inconspicuous nest made by the female in a shallow scrape, with often only a boulder or a fallen branch as a landmark. But egg-collecting is illegal now, and the bird is comparatively safe from people who intrude on the desolate expanses of moorland in the Highlands, Skye and Outer Hebrides where it breeds.

At dawn and dusk, greenshanks leave their breeding grounds and move to the shores of lochs to feed, mainly on water insects. In late summer and autumn, as they move south on migration, they feed in marsh pools, estuaries and reservoirs. In autumn, greenshanks are widespread in the south but only a few remain in Britain over winter.

Greenshanks have a fast flight with rapid wing-beats. Pairs climb high in display flights, swerving close together and diving steeply to zigzag in a low-level chase. In courtship, the male bows to the female on the ground, clicks his bill and sometimes leapfrogs over her.

The song, a repeated 'ru-tu', may be delivered either during a territorial display flight or from a perch. There are excited 'chip-chip-chip' calls when the sexes change places on the eggs, and a loud, ringing 'chu-chu-chu' call when the bird is alarmed.

J F M A M J
J A S O N D

*The short-eared owl hunts
regularly in broad daylight*

Short-eared owl Asio flammeus

A good supply of field voles is the main factor controlling the
distribution of short-eared owls. Voles are the owl's favourite
prey, and it has been calculated that a single bird may eat as
many as 2,000 of them in four months. Periodically, vole
plagues break out in hilly districts – sometimes with devastating
effects on grass crops – and then short-eared owls rapidly
move in to breed. If there are enough voles, the owls will
raise two broods.

The spread of plantations of conifers, an ideal habitat for
voles, helped the short-eared owl to increase and extend its
range southward to moorland in Yorkshire and North Wales,
but this process seems to have gone into reverse. The owl breeds
regularly in East Anglia. It hunts over open, treeless country in
broad daylight as well as at dusk, quartering the ground in
slow-flapping flight.

At sunset and dusk in April and May, the short-eared owl
patrols high over its territory in a display flight. It circles and
hovers, giving its low, booming song, and glides on outspread
wings. Then it suddenly twists its wings under its body so that
their tips meet behind its tail, and rapidly claps them together a
number of times. As it claps its wings, the bird plunges like a
stone, dropping a few metres before resuming its slow flight.

The 'ears' that give the owl its name are, in fact, merely small
tufts of feathers, with no function as organs of hearing.

RECOGNITION

Buff-brown plumage with
streaked breast; black
patches under long,
rounded wings; sexes alike.

NESTING

Nest is a depression
in the ground, lined with
vegetation; lays April;
usually 4–8 eggs, white,
almost spherical;
incubation about 26 days,
by female only; nestlings,
fed by female on food
brought by male, leave
after about 15 days, fly
about 11 days later;
sometimes two broods.

FEEDING

Chiefly field voles and other
small mammals; small
birds; insects.

SIZE

Male: 35.5cm (14in)
Female: 42cm (16½in)

J F M A M J
J A S O N D

Meadow pipit glides earthwards in territorial song-flight

Meadow pipit Anthus pratensis

RECOGNITION

Upper parts olive-brown with dark brown markings; breast streaked with white; best distinguished from tree pipit by 'pheet-pheet-pheet' call-note; sexes alike.

NESTING

Grass nest on ground, lined with finer grass or hair; lays late April–June; usually 3–5 eggs, very variable, usually brown or grey, mottled or marbled, but sometimes pale grey with fine streaks or pale blue without markings; incubation about 13 days, by female only; nestlings, tended by both parents, leave after 14 days.

FEEDING

Chiefly insects – beetles, crane-flies, blowflies, caterpillars and occasionally grasshoppers; spiders; earthworms; seeds.

SIZE

14.5cm (5¾in)

If there are such things as born victims among birds, then the meadow pipit is one of them. This small brown bird is the basic prey of the merlin, and a favourite host for the cuckoo. A young cuckoo quickly fills up the pipit's nest among the grass or rush tussocks, and the pipit sometimes stands on the back of its huge foster-child to feed it with insects and spiders, which form the diet of both parasite and host.

Ramblers on northern or western moors often flush meadow pipits, which are easily recognised by their sharp call-note, 'pit', 'pit-it' or a triple 'pheet-pheet-pheet'. But moorland is not the meadow pipit's only habitat. It will breed in most kinds of rough open country, including bogs, lowland heaths, downs and sand-dunes over most of Britain except parts of the extreme southeast. In winter, and when migrating to France or Spain, meadow pipits gather in damp places, such as marshes, sewage farms, lake shores and estuaries.

In spring and summer meadow pipits leave the ground in a fluttering territorial song-flight, singing a rather tuneless series of notes as they climb into the air and continuing more musically as they glide down to earth again. Their courtship display consists mainly of a sexual chase. They have the dipping flight characteristic of pipits and their relatives, the wagtails.

The ring ouzel's favourite song-post is a rock or boulder

J F M A M J
J A S O N D

MALE

Ring ouzel Turdus torquatus

Apart from the white crescent on its breast, and the fact that its wings when closed are paler than its body, this summer visitor to Britain looks like a mountain version of the garden blackbird. However, although they look alike, the two species are quite different in character. Blackbirds are often tame, but ring ouzels are shy and difficult to approach. They are most often seen perching on distant rocks or flying away. The contact call is a clear, piping 'pee-u', and their alarm call a harsh 'tac-tac-tac'.

There may be some difficulty in distinguishing a ring ouzel from a part-albino blackbird, but there is little danger of confusing them during the breeding season, because nesting ouzels are rare below 300m (1,000ft). The overlap between the two species comes when ouzels arrive in the south to rest and feed on migration. British ring ouzels winter in North Africa. Numbers have recently declined almost everywhere, probably as a result of a changing climate.

Like other thrushes, ring ouzels eat animal and vegetable food in roughly equal quantities. In spring and summer they find a plentiful supply of insects, small snails and earthworms. In autumn they turn to wild fruit, especially when on migration.

The nest is built on or close to the ground, often near a moorland stream or track.

RECOGNITION

Male sooty black with broad white crescent on breast; pale wing-patch; female browner, with smaller, duller half-collar.

NESTING

Both sexes build untidy grass cup nest on ground or on crag, building or bush, often with a base of heather stems; lays mid April–June; usually 4 eggs, pale blue-green with blotches of red-brown; incubation 14 days, mostly by female; nestlings, tended by both parents, leave after 14 days.

FEEDING

Insects and their larvae; earthworms; occasionally snails and small lizards in summer; wild fruit – bilberries, crowberries, rowan berries, haws, sloes – in autumn.

SIZE

24cm (9½in)

J F M A M J
J A S O N D

*Grey body distinguishes
'hoodie' from carrion crow*

Hooded crow Corvus cornix

RECOGNITION

Black, with grey back and underparts; sexes alike.

NESTING

Both sexes build bulky cup of twigs or heather roots in tree, on cliff ledge or among tall heather; lays April–June; usually 3–5 eggs, pale green-blue with dark brown blotches; incubation about 19 days, by female only; nestlings, fed by both parents, leave after about 33 days.

FEEDING

Mainly insects and their larvae, grain, other birds' eggs and nestlings, carrion; sometimes root crops, fish or fruit.

SIZE

47cm (18½in)

The hooded crow is the northern and western counterpart of the carrion crow. In England, it was once known as the grey crow, or the Royston crow from its regular appearances on the downs around Royston in Hertfordshire, but it is a much less frequent winter visitor to England than it used to be.

Until recently, the hooded crow was considered to be a race of carrion crow, but the maintenance of both pure black carrion crows and grey-and-black hooded crows over time, in well-defined areas, is one of several reasons for regarding the two as separate species. In the Highlands, there is a narrow line of hybridisation, where birds may be seen with intermediate plumage. However, those birds have not spread to breed outside that band.

The hoodie's harsh, rasping call – 'kaak', repeated three or four times – is like the carrion crow's call, sometimes thought to be a little higher or sharper.

Hooded crows are detested on keepered moors, because they eat eggs and chicks, but studies have shown that the vast majority of their diet comprises insects and worms. Exceptionally, they may kill small or medium-sized birds.

Hoodies fly strongly, and walk along the ground, hopping occasionally. Courtship includes bowing with outspread wings and tail. Eye-witnesses have seen Scottish birds performing a curious display, consisting of repeated jumps about 3–5m (12–15ft) into the air.

Male raven flies upside-down in aerobatic spring display

J F M A M J
J A S O N D

Raven Corvus corax

Ravens are the vultures of sheep country, patrolling in pairs or family groups in search of carrion – or a sickly sheep or deer, waiting to die. They will eat almost anything, from insects and shellfish to grain and acorns. Once they were common scavengers in the streets of London, but they have gradually been driven northward and westward to the hills and sea cliffs.

The big black bird, Britain's largest crow, is sometimes ponderous as it flies along, giving a deep croaking 'pruk-pruk-pruk' call, but it can also glide and soar freely, and put on a remarkable aerobatic show. In spring particularly, pairs of ravens tumble high in the air, half closing their wings, rolling over sideways and nose-diving. They also have a trick of flying upside-down for short distances. These antics are perhaps part of the raven's courtship display, although sometimes they seem to be performed from sheer high spirits. Ceremonies on the ground between male and female, who mate for life, include bowing, neck-stretching and ruffling the throat feathers. In the mating display, the male spreads its wings and tail and crouches with neck stretched up but bill pointed down. Sometimes it jumps into the air, or preens the female's face with its bill.

The nest, a substantial cup of sticks and other local materials, lined with sheep's wool or hair, is usually built on an inaccessible ledge, but in some districts ravens nest in trees.

RECOGNITION

Glossy black plumage; massive bill; end of tail wedge-shaped; sexes alike.

NESTING

Both sexes build nest of sticks cemented with mud and moss, on ledge or in crevice; lays February–April; usually 4–6 eggs, pale green or blue with dark markings; incubation about 19 days, by female only; nestlings, fed by both parents, leave after about 6 weeks.

FEEDING

Chiefly carrion and small animals; also seeds, fruit, grain, fish; eggs and young of other birds.

SIZE

63.5cm (25in)

MALE IN SUMMER

The twite – its range has contracted in recent years

Twite Acanthis flavirostris

Dull buff above, with black and brown streaks; lighter below; male has yellow bill in winter and pink rump feathers, distinctive 'twa-it' call-note.

Small cup of dried grass, lined with wool and built by female on or near ground; lays late May–June; usually 5 or 6 eggs, blue-tinged, with dark red-brown spots and streaks; incubation about 13 days, by female only; nestlings, fed by both parents, leave after 15 days; often two broods.

Chiefly seeds of rushes, grasses and salt-marsh plants; insects fed to nestlings.

13.25cm (5¼in)

The streaky brown twite – the name comes from its distinctive nasal 'twa-it' call-note – is the upland counterpart of the linnet. Its twittering song, delivered from a low perch or in flight, is reminiscent of the linnet's, and the bird closely resembles a streaky young linnet. Unlike the adult linnet, though, the male twite has no red on its breast or forehead.

Twites breed on heather-covered moorland, in high country with bracken or grass and on other rough, open ground. Their breeding range includes Ireland, the western Highlands and the Pennines, with a few in North Wales, although in recent years numbers have plummeted over much of their territory. Most twites desert the higher land in winter, and join other seed-eating finches and buntings near the coast, feeding on salt-marshes, and in hard winters on stubble-fields. Twites eat the seeds of moorland grasses and rushes, weeds and salt-marsh plants, and in spring they may also eat some insects.

Twites have the bounding flight typical of the smaller finches, and hop along the ground. The only courtship display on record is by the male bird. He repeatedly opens and drops his wings to show his pink rump feathers. Nests, often in loose colonies, are usually built close to the ground in long heather, but sometimes in gorse bushes and crevices in dry-stone walls.

Broad-leaved Woodland

In spring and summer broad-leaved woods offer a host of secret places where birds can hide themselves and their nests. It is no coincidence that many of the woodlanders have distinctive songs, because against the advantages of concealment must be balanced the need for advertisement, to attract mates and warn off rivals. The nightingale, one of the most elusive of birds, has the sweetest, most compelling song of all.

MALE

The forked tail identifies this rare bird of prey

Red kite Milvus milvus

RECOGNITION

Rusty brown plumage with streaked, white head; slender body; narrow wings, sharply bent backwards in flight; deeply forked tail; female slightly duller.

NESTING

Both sexes build nest of sticks and earth in tree, often on an old nest of a crow; lays April or May; usually 2 or 3 eggs, white, with red-brown speckles; incubation about 30 days, by female only; nestlings, tended by both parents, leave after 50–55 days.

FEEDING

Small mammals, rabbits, sheep carrion, fledgling rooks and gulls; sometimes worms and frogs.

SIZE

Male: 56cm (22in)
Female: 61cm (24in)

Red kites were widespread over Britain until the 18th century, and were common scavengers on the filthy streets of medieval and Elizabethan London, but they gradually declined until they became one of Britain's rarest breeding birds. Careful protection by the RSPB has led to numbers very slowly increasing in Wales, so that now much larger numbers breed there, partly sustained by artificial feeding. Since 1992, kites have been reintroduced into several parts of England, Scotland and Northern Ireland, vastly expanding their numbers and range.

Kites are magnificent fliers, circling tirelessly for hours over wooded valleys on their long, slender wings, usually bent at the 'wrist', and steering with their long, forked tails as they scan the earth for small mammals, which they kill with a sudden pounce to the ground. Their effortless flight long ago added a word to the English language – children's kites get their name from the bird.

Pairs of kites perform aerobatics in their courtship ceremony, and they have a diving display flight, in common with many birds of prey. Their call is a shrill, mewing 'weeou-weeou-weeou'. Kites build a bulky nest of sticks, lined with wool, moss, hair and even paper or rags. Shakespeare acknowledged this when he warned in *The Winter's Tale*: 'When the kite builds, look to lesser linen.'

FEMALE

J F M A M J
J A S O N D

*Hunting sparrowhawk
pounces on small finches*

Sparrowhawk Accipiter nisus

The fast-flying sparrowhawk relies on surprise attack as a
hunting technique. It will dash quickly along one side of a
hedgerow, concealed by the vegetation, and suddenly dart up
and over it to burst on an unsuspecting cluster of finches, snatch
one of them and dash away again. If its prey escapes, the hawk
rarely tries to repeat the attack, but flies on until it sees another
chance to pounce. In search of prey, it will sometimes glide in a
circular, prospecting flight, or soar into the sky, to plunge with
folded wings.

The male sparrowhawk's main victims are small birds, but
the larger female will occasionally kill birds as big as a pigeon.
Sparrowhawks were once persecuted by gamekeepers, until they
were given legal protection, and are sometimes now unwelcome
in gardens, where they naturally take advantage of the large
numbers of small birds attracted to birdtables.

In the 1960s, the sparrowhawk suffered badly from farmers'
use of poisonous agricultural chemicals, becoming extinct
in eastern parts of England. Since the worst of the pesticides
were banned, sparrowhawk numbers have made a strong
comeback everywhere.

The male hunts single-handedly while the hen is brooding,
landing at one of its plucking posts with its prey and calling its
mate to feed with a harsh, chattering 'kek-kek-kek-kek'. Later,
both parents work hard to feed their young, which will eat two
or three sparrow-sized birds a day.

RECOGNITION

Short, rounded wings; long
tail; male has slate-grey
upper parts and reddish-
barred underparts; larger
female has browner upper
parts, dark brown bars on
underparts, white stripe
behind eye.

NESTING

Nest built of twigs in tree,
frequently by female alone,
lined with thin twigs; usually
lays May; usually 4–6 eggs,
white tinged with blue with
red-brown blotches;
incubation about 30 days,
by female only; nestlings,
tended by both parents,
leave after 24–30 days.

FEEDING

House sparrows, finches,
starlings, other small birds;
occasionally mice, voles
and young rabbits; insects.

SIZE

Male: 28cm (11in)
Female: 38cm (15in)

Buzzard in hunting flight soars in slow, wide circles

Buzzard Buteo buteo

RECOGNITION

Dark brown plumage above, pale with darker bars and streaks below; broad wings and wide, rounded tail show in flight; sexes alike.

NESTING

Both sexes build bulky nest of sticks, usually in trees, sometimes on cliff ledges; nest often decorated with leaves or seaweed; lays late April–early May; usually 2 or 3 eggs, white with chocolate or red-brown markings; incubation about 36 days, by both parents; nestlings, tended by both parents, leave at about 45–50 days.

FEEDING

Small mammals, especially rabbits; sheep carrion; sometimes birds, earthworms, caterpillars, lizards, beetles; occasionally berries.

SIZE

Male: 51cm (20in)
Female: 58.5cm (23in)

Sailing through the sky with slow flaps of its broad wings, and giving its plaintive 'peeiou' call, the buzzard looks almost lazy, but the big bird is anything but aimless. It is quartering grassland or moor in search of prey, which may be as small as a beetle. As soon as its sharp eyes spot a quarry, it will pounce.

A buzzard will hover with wings angled against a high wind. Sometimes it will fold its wings and plunge towards the earth before sailing upwards again. As part of its display ceremony it will roll and turn in the air. When the bird soars, circling with wing-tips splayed out, it can look like a small eagle.

Buzzards are found in all kinds of country in northern and western Britain – woods, moorlands, mountains, sea cliffs and farmland. Their numbers were increasing steadily until myxomatosis reduced the rabbit population. With better protection, they have now spread over almost the whole of England, and are the commonest birds of prey in Britain. In the 1950s buzzards began to breed again in Ireland, where gamekeepers had stamped them out.

If a buzzard is mobbed by crows or seagulls it usually flies on, unhurriedly flapping to outdistance its tormentors. But a determined attack will make the buzzard turn over in the air to meet its enemies with its talons.

A woodcock beats the bounds of its territory in 'roding' flight

J F M A M J
J A S O N D

Woodcock Scolopax rusticola

The woodcock is a wading bird that has taken to the land, especially to the kind of woodland that is opened up by clearings and rides. With eyes set high in its head, and well to the back, it has the all-round vision that enables it to look out for enemies even when it is probing in the ground for earthworms and insects.

At dawn and dusk in spring and summer, male woodcock meander slowly above the treetops in their erratic 'roding' flight. This is a territorial display that each male performs around the bounds of its woodland domain. As it flies, the woodcock gives two calls – an extraordinary frog-like croak, repeated several times, and a high-pitched, whistling 'twisick'. This leisurely flight is quite different from the woodcock's way of flying when it is flushed from its hiding place in the undergrowth. Then it leaps into the air to dodge rapidly through the trees, quickly disappearing into cover again.

Roding occurs mainly between March and early July, when the birds are raising their two broods. If danger threatens before the young have learnt to fly, the female may 'airlift' them to safety, clutching the chicks in her claws or with her legs.

Migrant birds arrive in winter, joining resident woodcock. They fly in across the North Sea, and often drop into the first piece of rough cover near the coast, moving inland later. They rest on dry ground by day, and at twilight fly to marshy or boggy ground to feed.

RECOGNITION

Stout; long bill; russet plumage with barred head and underparts; sexes alike.

NESTING

Nests in a scrape lined with dead leaves; lays mid-March–June; usually 4 eggs, grey-white to brown, thickly marked with chestnut and ash-grey blotches; incubation about 21 days, by female only; chicks, tended by both parents, leave after a few hours; two broods.

FEEDING

Earthworms, beetles, other insects and their larvae; small molluscs; some seeds and grass.

SIZE

34.25cm (13½in)

J F M A M J
J A S O N D

*Distinctive tail pattern
shows when turtle dove flies*

Turtle dove Streptopelia turtur

RECOGNITION

Slim with red-tinged upper parts and pink breast; black and white striped patch on neck; long tail with white tip; sexes alike.

NESTING

Female builds flimsy platform of fine twigs, sometimes lined with roots, in tree or shrub, about 1–3m (4–8ft) up; lays May–July; usually 2 eggs, glossy white; incubation about 14 days, by both parents; nestlings, tended by both parents, leave after 18 days, fly a few days later; usually two broods.

FEEDING

Seeds, mainly from common fumitory, chickweed, charlock and grass; sometimes small molluscs.

SIZE

28cm (11in)

The 'voice of the turtle', heard in the Song of Solomon, is a sleepy, romantic sound, evocative of a summer's day, but the deep, purring croon becomes more of a wheeze during the turtle dove's energetic territorial display. The bird climbs steeply, then glides down, often circling to perch again on the tree from which it launched itself. In courtship display, the male bows or bobs in front of the female half-a-dozen times in quick succession, with breast slightly puffed out and bill pointing downwards. Another kind of display involves parent birds, seemingly helpless, fluttering to distract predators from their young.

The turtle dove, the smallest and slimmest of Britain's five breeding pigeons, is a summer visitor. It avoids hills and prefers open woods, parkland and large gardens to dense woodland. It breeds commonly in the south and Midlands, and its numbers thin northwards and westwards, having declined dramatically in the past 20–30 years. In many areas where it was once frequent, it has entirely disappeared.

The bird's favourite food is the seed of a weed of arable fields, the common fumitory, but weed-seeds have been eliminated from huge areas of agricultural land. The turtle dove's late arrival in Britain – at the end of April or the beginning of May – is probably related to the short supply of the seeds early in the year.

Characteristic pose shows how the wryneck got its name

Wryneck Jynx torquilla

The wryneck, which was found over the whole of England except the extreme north and west at the beginning of the 20th century, has declined steadily and mysteriously until it has now ceased to breed in this country. Between 1958 and 1978 the breeding population fell catastrophically from 100–200 pairs to none. Surprisingly, a few wrynecks have occasionally been found since 1969, nesting in the Scottish Highlands. These apart, the bird is extinct as a breeding species in Britain, although migrants continue to turn up on the east and south coasts.

The bird's name comes from its habit of twisting its head right round on its neck. Its early arrival in Britain at the end of March earned it another name among country people – 'cuckoo's mate'. The male announces itself by perching high in a tree and giving a shrill 'quee-quee-quee' song at the top of its voice. In their courtship display, male and female wrynecks often perch opposite each other, shaking their heads about, throwing them back on their shoulders and revealing the pink inside to their mouths.

Wrynecks, although they belong to the woodpecker family, do not bore into trees, either to get food or to make nests. Instead, they use their long, fast-moving tongues to pick up insects from bark or from the ground. They are fond of orchards and gardens where holes in old fruit trees serve as nests. They will also make use of holes in walls or banks, or nest-boxes.

RECOGNITION

Slim; grey-brown plumage, mottled above and barred below; distinguished from treecreeper by larger size, longer tail and straight bill; sexes alike.

NESTING

Nests in ready-made hole, without lining material; lays late May; usually 7–10 eggs, dull white; incubation about 12 days, chiefly by female; nestlings, fed by both sexes, leave at about 20 days.

FEEDING

Chiefly ants and their pupae; also beetles, moths and spiders.

SIZE

21.5cm (8½in)

*White-spotted wings
make this woodpecker
unmistakable*

MALE

J F M A M J
J A S O N D

Great spotted woodpecker *Dendrocopos major*

RECOGNITION

Black, with white patches and blotches; male has crimson on head; young birds have red crown; both sexes and all ages have red under tail; easily distinguished from lesser spotted by larger size.

NESTING

Both sexes excavate hole in tree, usually at least 3m (10ft) up; no nest material except few chips of wood; often dispossessed by starlings; sometimes uses nest-box; lays May; 4–7 eggs, glossy white; incubation about 16 days, mainly by female; nestlings, fed by both sexes, leave after 19 or 20 days.

FEEDING

Chiefly larvae of beetles, wood wasps and moths; some spiders; occasionally young birds snatched from nests; small vegetarian element.

SIZE

23cm (9in)

After becoming extinct in Scotland and northern England in the first half of the 19th century, the great spotted woodpecker has made a come-back during the past 130 years. Today it is the most widespread of the British woodpeckers, breeding in almost every mainland county, and numbers have increased dramatically everywhere.

Great spotted woodpeckers nest in all kinds of well-timbered country. Unlike green woodpeckers, they are as much at home in coniferous woods as in broad-leaved woodlands, and they tend to feed rather more in trees and less on the ground. In recent years they have spread to parks in central London, and in some districts regularly visit garden birdtables.

They are unpopular with bee-keepers because they sometimes raid hives in search of grubs. In the same quest, they will drill holes in telegraph poles.

Their flight is undulating, with wings folded against the body at the bottom of each bound. The call-note is a sharp 'tchich', and they also make a harsh churring note similar to that of the mistle thrush. But great spotted woodpeckers have no song. Instead, they produce a drumming noise by sharp taps of the bill on a resonant dead bough, making a sound far louder than when they are feeding. At one time naturalists believed that this sound was created vocally, but this has been disproved.

Parent bird feeds hungry nestling in tree-hole nest

J F M A M J
J A S O N D

MALE

Lesser spotted woodpecker *Dendrocopos minor*

The lesser spotted woodpecker, a bird little bigger than a sparrow, is far from easy to pick out as it walks up the small branches high in deciduous trees. It keeps to well-timbered country and avoids conifers. Nowhere in Britain were lesser spotted woodpeckers ever common and now they are declining substantially – they are hardly known north of Lancashire and Yorkshire – so there is something of a challenge in tracking them down. The crimson-crowned male may sometimes be sighted as it flits from branch to branch, searching for insect larvae, or from tree to tree in a slow courtship display flight. Sometimes a pair can be seen side by side after a courtship display, perched stock-still on a branch.

The lesser spotted woodpecker's flight is slow and hesitant, with typical woodpecker 'bounds'. Its calls are a 'tchick' note, weaker and more sibilant than that of the great spotted woodpecker, and more often, a 'pee-pee-pee' call like the wryneck's, but lacking its ringing quality. The bird also makes a mechanical drumming sound with its bill, more prolonged than the great spotted's drumming but softer.

The shrill calls of the nestlings often draw attention to the nest-hole, which the parents bore in decaying tree trunks or branches at almost any height up to about 21m (70ft) from the ground. A shaft about 18–25cm (7–10in) long leads from the entrance to the nest chamber, which is bare except for a few wood chips.

RECOGNITION

Black and white plumage; wings and lower back barred; male has crimson crown, female's is white.

NESTING

Both sexes bore nest-hole in decayed wood; lays late April–June; usually 4–6 eggs, glossy white; incubation about 14 days, by both parents; nestlings, tended by both parents, leave after about 21 days.

FEEDING

Mainly grubs of wood-boring beetles and moths; also grubs of gall-wasps, flies and spiders; some fruit, mainly currants and raspberries.

SIZE

14.5cm (5¾in)

J F M A M J
J A S O N D

MALE

*Green woodpecker scoops
up ants with its long sticky
tongue*

Green woodpecker Picus viridis

RECOGNITION

Largest and most brightly
coloured of British
woodpeckers; crimson
crown; bright green
upper parts; grey-green
underparts; yellow rump;
stripe under eye is red in
male, black in female.

NESTING

Both sexes bore hole in
tree; chips left scattered
on ground; lays April–May;
5–7 eggs, white; incubation
about 19 days, by both
sexes; nestlings, tended
by both sexes, fly after
18–21 days.

FEEDING

Wood-boring larvae of
beetles, moths and other
insects, mainly ants;
occasionally grain, acorns,
apples, cherries and
other fruit.

SIZE

31.75cm (12½in)

In country districts, this largest British woodpecker is sometimes
called the yaffle, because its loud ringing call can sound almost
like laughter. Its other country name, 'rain bird', probably arose
through its call being heard more clearly in the atmospheric
conditions before rain. The bird also has yelping and squealing
cries, but these are most often heard from its young.

The green woodpecker is found in all kinds of well-timbered
country, from open woodland, heaths, commons and farmland
to parks and large gardens. Its numbers have risen in northern
England and southern Scotland in recent years, but the reason
for this has not been established. It has been suggested that the
widespread planting of conifers has led to an increase in the
wood ant, one of its favourite foods, yet the birds usually prefer
broad-leaved woods to conifers.

A green woodpecker on the garden lawn is probably
performing a useful service by ridding it of ants or other insects,
but the birds can be troublesome. Very occasionally they take
fruit, and they have been known to damage beehives while
trying to get at the grubs.

Male birds challenging other green woodpeckers for territory
will sway their heads from side to side, and usually spread their
wings, fan their tails and raise their crown feathers. In courtship
they tend to droop their wings and raise the spread tail.
Sometimes the male and female chase each other round a tree.

Nightingale's nest is well hidden in thick undergrowth

Nightingale Luscinia megarhynchos

In spite of their name, and contrary to popular belief, nightingales are as likely to be heard singing by day as by night. But their virtuoso performances are best heard in the stillness of a warm evening in late spring, when the males compete to attract females arriving from wintering grounds in tropical Africa. The females arrive ten days or so after the males. When the birds sing by day, it is partly to warn other males to keep off their territory.

In volume, in variety of notes, and in the vigour with which it is poured out, the song is unforgettable. It consists of a rapid succession of repeated notes – some harsh, some liquid – including a very loud 'chooc-chooc-chooc' and a fluting, pleading 'pioo', building up slowly into a crescendo. As well as this, there are also call-notes – a soft, chiffchaff-like 'hweet' and a harsh 'tacc-tacc' – and the bird has two alarm notes, which are a scolding 'krrrr' and a grating 'tchaaaa'.

For every ten people who have heard a nightingale sing there can hardly be one who has actually set eyes on this shy bird. When they do come into the open, they are inconspicuous. Only their song draws attention to them. The nightingale hides its nest as carefully as it conceals itself, building close to the ground among thick undergrowth. In its courtship display, the male spreads his tail and moves it up and down, fluttering his wings and bowing to pull his bill down below the level of the perch.

Brown plumage; rather like a large warbler, with red-brown tail and grey-brown underparts; whitish throat; sexes alike.

NESTING

Female builds nest of dead leaves lined with grass and hair, on or close to ground; lays May; usually 5 eggs, olive-green or dark olive; incubation about 14 days, by female only; nestlings, tended by both parents, leave at about 11 or 12 days.

FEEDING

Mainly ground insects; also earthworms, spiders, some berries.

SIZE

16.5cm (6½in)

Redstarts will nest wherever they can find a ready-made hole

J F M A M J
J A S O N D

MALE

Redstart Phoenicurus phoenicurus

Bright chestnut tail and rump; male distinguished from black redstart by chestnut breast and white forehead; female duller, with no white on forehead.

Female builds nest of grass, lined with hair, in natural hole or hollow in ground; may use nest-box; lays mid-May–June; usually 5–8 eggs, pale blue, very occasionally speckled; incubation about 13 days, by female only; nestlings, fed by both sexes, leave after about 16 days.

Mainly insects and their larvae; also spiders and small worms; some berries.

14cm (5½in)

The fiery chestnut tail of the redstart gives the bird its name – *steort* is an Old English word for tail. It helps to make the male, with its white forehead, black throat and grey mantle, one of the handsomest of Britain's smaller birds, and plays an important part in courtship display. The male bows, stretches out its neck, droops its wings and splays its tail feathers to show a blaze of flame-red, then chases the female from perch to perch. Both sexes quiver their tails all the while.

Redstarts breed in almost any habitat where they can find holes for nesting – woodland, parks, gardens and riversides with old trees, and they will breed in treeless districts if stone walls or quarries provide nesting sites. They are most common in old woodland, especially in hill country, but may turn up in open country on their migration flights between Africa and Britain. Over the past 130 years the redstart has declined as a breeding bird in eastern and southeastern England, and now breeds mainly in the north and west.

Redstarts repeatedly flutter from branch to branch or make hovering sallies into the air to catch flying insects, and they often collect food on the ground. The song begins strongly with a squeaky warble, then peters out in a twitter of feeble notes. Some male redstarts mimic notes from other species. The call is a long 'hooeet' and the alarm note a loud 'twee-tucc-tucc'.

J F M A M J
J A S O N D

The nest is built in thick cover, quite close to the ground

Garden warbler Sylvia borin

Only a large garden with extensive shrubberies is likely to make a home for garden warblers. The birds prefer deciduous woodland with widely spaced trees and plenty of bushes and briers. Sometimes they breed where there are no trees, in thick brier patches, osier beds and tangled hedges, or in conifer woods with deciduous undergrowth.

Garden warblers are secretive, spending most of their time in the shrubs, and when they do venture into the open they are not noticeable birds, with their nondescript plain brown plumage. But their song gives them away, even when it comes from a concealed perch deep inside a hawthorn bush. The song is less of a virtuoso performance than the blackcap's, but mellower – a sweet, even warble, low-pitched and well sustained. The calls are typical warbler notes – a 'churr' and a 'tacc-tacc' of alarm.

Garden warblers fly in from central and southern Africa from mid April to late May, spreading over most of England and Wales to breed. In the extreme west of Cornwall and Wales the birds are rare, and they seldom breed in Scotland outside the Lowlands. The male's courtship display consists of spreading its tail and fluttering its wings in front of its mate. The same behaviour from either sex serves as a distraction display to protect the young. Several 'trial' nests are built by the male before a site is finally chosen.

RECOGNITION

Plump; brown with pale buff underparts; low-pitched warbling song, well sustained; sexes alike.

NESTING

Both sexes build nest from dry grass, lined with hair and rootlets, in thick cover usually less than 1m (3ft) from ground; lays late May–early June; usually 4 or 5 eggs, white or pale green, with olive freckles; incubation about 12 days, mainly by female; nestlings, fed by both sexes, leave after about 10 days.

FEEDING

Chiefly insects, with spiders in spring and summer; fruit and berries in autumn.

SIZE

14cm (5½in)

FEMALE

MALE

Male blackcap flaps wings vigorously in aggressive display

Blackcap Sylvia atricapilla

RECOGNITION

Grey-brown upper parts; male has glossy black cap; female's cap is red-brown.

NESTING

Slight nest, built chiefly by hen, of dried grass lined with hair and rootlets, in bushes or other coarse vegetation; lays May–July; usually 4 or 5 eggs, white tinged with green and marbled with brown; incubation about 12 days, by both parents; nestlings, fed by both parents, leave after about 10 days.

FEEDING

Flies, caterpillars and other insects; fruit and berries in autumn.

SIZE

14cm (5½in)

Its cap – glossy black in the male and red-brown in the female – makes the blackcap the easiest to identify of Britain's 13 breeding warblers. A further aid to identification is its rich and melodious song, which has won it a reputation as the 'northern nightingale'.

The male, usually perched in deep cover near the nest-site, pours out a clear, powerful warbling, varied with phrases mimicked from other birds' songs, and ending abruptly. The song is higher pitched and less sustained than that of the garden warbler. The blackcap's call-notes are a harsh 'churr' and an excited 'tau-tau', rapidly repeated when the bird is alarmed.

Most blackcaps are summer visitors, arriving in late March to breed over most of England and Wales, with a sparse population in Scotland and Ireland, but small numbers remain all winter. They nest in woods, heaths and gardens with a plentiful undergrowth of brambles and rose briers or evergreen shrubs, particularly rhododendrons. In this coarse vegetation they build their frail nests, attached to the surrounding plants with 'basket handles'. They usually keep hidden among the bushes as they feed and their flights from one patch of cover to the next are short and jerky.

The male has a variety of courtship postures. Sometimes it raises its cap feathers and fluffs out its body feathers; sometimes it droops its wings and at other times it flaps them; and it may spread and raise its tail.

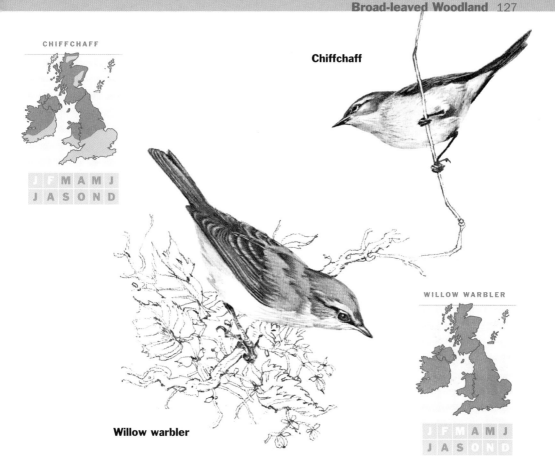

CHIFFCHAFF

J F M A M J J A S O N D

Chiffchaff

WILLOW WARBLER

J F M A M J J A S O N D

Willow warbler

Willow warbler Phylloscopus trochilus

The willow warbler and chiffchaff (*Phylloscopus collybita*) are so alike that only an expert can tell them apart by their appearance, but the chiffchaff's frequent downward bob of the tail is a good clue. The willow warbler has a fluent, wistful song, a gentle series of descending notes, hanging over the woods from April to June, and even over suburban gardens where they adjoin woodland. The chiffchaff's song is a monotonous, high-pitched 'chiff-chaff' or 'zip-zap', interspersed with a quiet churring. Both willow warbler and chiffchaff have a call-note, 'hoo-eet', but the chiffchaff pronounces it as a single syllable, 'hweet'.

The habitat favoured by both these summer migrants is almost identical – woods and bushy places, such as heaths, commons, shrubberies and large gardens. The chiffchaff shows a preference for places with plenty of trees, because it needs a song-post at least 5m (15ft) high. It is one of the earliest migrants to arrive, appearing from mid March and often staying into October, although small numbers remain in winter in southern Britain. The willow warbler usually arrives about a fortnight later and leaves a fortnight or three weeks earlier. While chiffchaffs thrive, willow warblers are declining.

Courtship in both species consists largely of a slow-motion display flight. The willow warbler normally builds a well-hidden nest on the ground, and the chiffchaff nearly always seeks a site in a low bush.

RECOGNITION

Both have green to olive-brown plumage; flesh-coloured legs of some – but not all – willow warblers distinguish them from chiffchaffs; different songs of the two species are best guide to telling them apart.

NESTING

Hens build domed nest of moss and dried grass, lined with feathers; lay late April–early May; usually 6 or 7 eggs, white with red-brown spots or blotches (willow warbler) or purple-brown spots (chiffchaff); incubation about 13 days, by hen only; nestlings, fed by both sexes (willow warbler) and hen only (chiffchaff), fly after about 13 days; willow warbler often has a second brood.

FEEDING

Mainly small insects, such as caterpillars, gnats and midges.

SIZE

Both species: 10.75cm (4¼in)

SUMMER

In display flight, the wood warbler quivers its wings like a dragonfly

Wood warbler Phylloscopus sibilatrix

RECOGNITION

Yellow breast; white belly; yellow-green above; yellow streak above eye; colouring duller in autumn; larger and more brightly coloured than chiffchaff or willow warbler; distinctive song; sexes alike.

NESTING

Female builds domed nest of grass, leaves and fibres, lined with grass and hair, in natural hollow; lays May–June, usually 5–7 eggs, white, thickly spotted with dark red-brown; incubation about 13 days, by female only; nestlings, fed by both sexes, fly after about 12 days.

FEEDING

Insects, mainly small caterpillars, beetles, flies and aphids; some wild berries in autumn.

SIZE

12.75cm (5in)

Wood warblers are rarely seen or heard in Britain outside a clearly defined habitat of mature woodland with a closely knit canopy of leaves and sparse undergrowth. Here they find the insect life on which they feed throughout the summer. The birds hover to pick up insects from the underside of leaves, or sally from their perches to snap up food on the wing.

Their preference for a particular type of woodland means they are less common in the south and east than in the north and west. Nevertheless, fair numbers are attracted to the beechwoods of the southern chalk and limestone districts, as well as to the valley oakwoods and birchwoods of Wales and western Scotland, although numbers have declined by at least two-thirds in recent years, in common with several other woodland birds. Even outside the breeding season, wood warblers keep to the trees, and before they migrate back to Africa, they eke out their diet with wild berries.

The 'warbler' part of the bird's name is a tribute to its song, or rather to both of them, for the wood warbler has two distinct songs. The first is a repeated single note, speeding up into a whistling trill, while the second is a mellow, liquid 'dee-ur', which is also the bird's anxiety note, plaintively repeated seven or more times.

In courtship, the male has two styles of flying. It quivers its wings rapidly or flaps them slowly. The nest is built in a hollow in the ground, and the dome shows above ground level.

Although numbers fluctuate the pied flycatcher has been in decline for the past 100 years

MALE IN SUMMER

Pied flycatcher Ficedula hypoleuca

Over the past 50 or 60 years, pied flycatchers have extended their breeding range from Wales into the bordering English counties, and from there into Yorkshire and southern Scotland, with outposts in the Pennines, the Highlands and the West Country. This advance seems to have been helped in a few districts by the large-scale provision of nest-boxes – pied flycatchers have to compete with redstarts and tits for the nesting-holes available in woodland, and suitable holes are often scarce in the hilly districts where they prefer to breed. In recent years, however, a major decline has been noted. On autumn migration, they often appear on the coast.

Pied flycatchers are retiring birds, usually keeping to the upper branches of trees. They live on insects, usually snapped up on the wing, but they will also feed on the ground and sometimes cling to tree trunks, like tits. In its feeding flight, the bird launches out from a branch to swerve and twist quickly after an insect, then lands again to watch for another one, flicking its wings and tail as it settles. Unlike the spotted flycatcher, it rarely returns to the same perch.

The song has a rhythm, which is echoed in the countryman's version: 'Tree, tree, tree, once more I come to thee.' The call-notes are a swallow-like 'whit' and a short 'tu', sometimes repeated, and these sounds often draw attention to migrants resting on the coast.

RECOGNITION

Male black above, with white forehead; white below, with white bar on wing; female and autumn-plumaged male olive-brown with buff-white bar on wings and sides of tail.

NESTING

Female builds nest of oak leaves, lined with grass, in a ready-made hole 1–12m (3–40ft) above ground; lays mid May; usually 5–8 eggs, pale green-blue; incubation about 13 days, by female only; nestlings, fed by both parents, leave after about 14 days.

FEEDING

Flies, flying beetles, sometimes butterflies and moths; occasionally earthworms and grubs.

SIZE

12.75cm (5in)

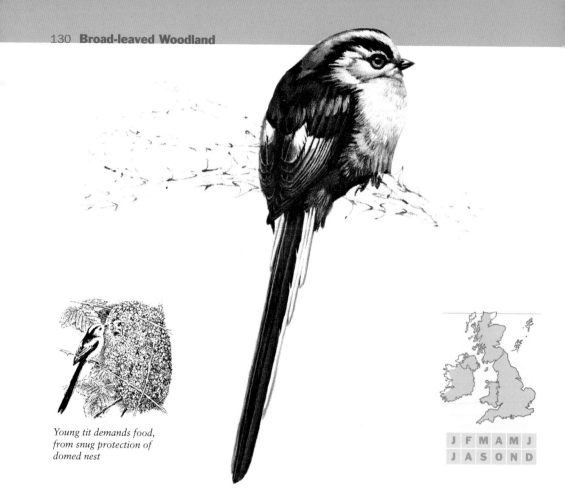

Young tit demands food, from snug protection of domed nest

J F M A M J
J A S O N D

Long-tailed tit Aegithalos caudatus

RECOGNITION

Distinctive black and white tail, longer than body; pink, black and white plumage; sexes alike.

NESTING

Intricate domed nest, covered with lichen and cobwebs, built by both sexes in tree or bush; lays late March–early May; usually 8–12 eggs, white with red-brown freckles; incubation about 16 days, mainly by female; nestlings, fed by both parents, leave after about 14 days; parents often helped to feed young by neighbours with failed brood.

FEEDING

Mainly insects and spiders; occasionally seeds. May visit hanging seed feeders.

SIZE

14cm (5½in) including 7.5cm (3in) tail

Pairs of long-tailed tits start building their elaborate nests in late February or early March. In the fork of a tree or bush, at almost any height from around 1–20m (4–70ft) from the ground, they piece together lichen, cobwebs and animal hair to form an unmistakable oval-shaped domed nest. This has an entrance hole near the top, and has earned them the country name of 'bottle tits'. They work from inside the nest, and when the basic structure is finished, they add a lining of up to 2,000 feathers, and camouflage the outside with cobwebs. The nest is finished in time for egg-laying, which takes place sometime between late March and early May, and the fit is so snug that the parent birds have to fold their long tails over the back of their heads when they go inside.

In the breeding season, long-tailed tits are found on the outskirts of woods and in woodland clearings. Some spread out to hedgerows and thickets but, unlike great tits and blue tits, they rarely visit suburban gardens. When winter comes, they usually keep to the woods, and at night they roost in groups, huddling together on branches.

There are two types of special courtship flight – a fast sexual chase through the leaves and a slower solo flight by the male. Long-tailed tits have nothing corresponding to a song, but the bird has a variety of call-notes. These are a spluttering 'tsirrup', a soft 'tupp' and a thin 'si-si-si'.

Marsh tit uses ready-made hole as its nesting site

J F M A M J
J A S O N D

MARSH TIT

J F M A M J
J A S O N D

Marsh tit

Marsh tit Poecile palustris

Virtually the only way of telling a marsh tit from a willow tit (*Poecile montana*) is by listening to the birds' calls and songs. In appearance they are almost twins, although a long, close scrutiny will reveal that the marsh tit has a glossy black cap rather than a sooty one, and no pale patch on its wing, as the willow tit has.

The calls of the marsh tit are a scolding 'chickabee-bee-bee-bee', a harsh 'tchay' and a characteristic bright 'pitchew', which the willow tit never gives. The willow tit has a grating, nasal 'tchair tchair' often following a 'chickit' note. The marsh tit's song is a high-pitched, rattling 'schuppi schuppi schuppi' while the willow tit has two songs. One is a series of full-throated 'piu-piu' notes, rather like the wood warbler's call. The other consists of liquid notes interspersed with higher-pitched notes in a fluent warble.

The marsh tit is not especially associated with marshes, nor the willow tit with willows, although both live in woodland, often in damp surroundings. They share a courtship display with other tits. The male parades in front of the female with feathers puffed out, wings drooped and tail held erect. Both nest in holes, but marsh tits use natural holes in trees or walls, whereas willow tits excavate holes in rotten wood. Willow tits have disappeared from much of England in recent years.

RECOGNITION

Black cap, glossy in marsh tit, sooty in willow; willow has pale wing-patch; both have grey-brown upper parts, dull buff-white underparts; best told from each other by calls and song; sexes alike.

NESTING

Marsh tit builds in natural hole with foundation of moss and pad of hair and down; willow tit digs hole in decaying wood, builds nest mainly of wood chips and fibres with pad of hair; both lay April or early May; usually 6–8 eggs, white with red-brown speckles; incubation about 14 days, by female only; nestlings, fed by both sexes, leave after about 16 days.

FEEDING

Insects; also seeds and wild fruit.

SIZE

Both species: 11.5cm (4½in)

J F M A M J
J A S O N D

Nuthatch wedges nut in tree bark and cracks it open with 'hatchet' bill

Nuthatch Sitta europaea

RECOGNITION

Black eye-stripe; white throat; slate-grey upper parts; buff underparts; often climbs down trees head first; sexes alike.

NESTING

Builds nest of bark flakes (often pine) or dead leaves, usually in tree hole; often reduces entrance with mud to keep out larger birds; lays late April–May; 6–10 eggs, white, spotted with red-brown; incubation about 14 days, by female only; nestlings, fed by both parents, fly after about 24 days.

FEEDING

Mainly hazel nuts, beech mast, acorns; also beetles, earwigs and small caterpillars.

SIZE

14cm (5½in)

The nuthatch gets its name from its habit of wedging nuts in the bark of a tree and splitting them open with vigorous blows from its 'hatchet' bill. It often attacks the nut from above, and is the only British bird that regularly climbs down trees head first.

In the past few years, nuthatches have spread north and west. When they disappeared from central London parks in the late 19th century (they returned in 1958), it was suggested that atmospheric pollution, covering the trees with soot, had driven them out. This may be the reason why nuthatches are not usually seen near industrial centres.

The bird has a remarkable range of call-notes, mostly ringing or piping calls, such as 'chwit-chwit' or more frequently 'chwit-it-it'. Other notes in the range are a tit-like 'tsit'; a sibilant 'tsirrp' reminiscent of the long-tailed tit; and in the breeding season two or three loud repetitions of 'twee', as well as a note that sounds like a boy's whistling. Yet another call-note sounds like the shrill chatter of the kestrel.

In its courtship display the male often flies slowly, or postures with feathers fluffed out and wings and tail spread. The nest is always in a hole, and the birds generally choose a site more than 2m (6ft) up a tree, but nuthatches will use nest-boxes, too, and occasionally they build in a wall or a haystack.

Treecreeper spirals its way up bark in search of insects

J F M A M J
J A S O N D

Treecreeper Certhia familiaris

Many woodland birds are more likely to be heard than seen, and the treecreeper is one of the more elusive of this group. It spends most of its time in trees, well camouflaged as it crawls up the bark like a feathered mouse. Its nest is tucked away behind a tiny entrance hole that is easily overlooked, although tell-tale pieces of nesting material may stick out through cracks. The song, always delivered from a tree, is a high-pitched 'tee-tee-tee-titit-dooee'. The most frequent call-notes are a high-pitched and rather prolonged 'tseeee' and a tit-like 'tsit'.

In a leafless winter, the treecreeper may sometimes be seen probing tree trunks with its curved needle beak. The bird will work its way up a trunk in short jerks, sometimes spirally, occasionally moving quickly sideways or bracing itself against its stiff tail as it tugs at some stubborn insect. When it moves to another trunk it starts at the foot of the bole again. It is equally agile searching upside-down on the underside of a bough.

Hard winters punish this small bird, but when Wellingtonia trees were introduced from California, treecreepers learned to make hollows in the soft bark to use as snug roosting places.

Courtship includes chases, a bat-like display flight, wing-shivering and feeding.

RECOGNITION

Brown above, silvery white beneath; only small British land-bird with a curved beak; sexes alike.

NESTING

Probably both sexes build nest of dried grass and rootlets, lined with feathers, wool and bits of bark, behind loose bark or ivy roots or in other tree cavities, occasionally in nest-boxes, exceptionally in wall crevice or old shed; lays April–June; usually 6 eggs, white, with red-brown spots at blunt end; incubation about 15 days, probably mainly by hen; nestlings, fed by both parents, leave after about 14 or 15 days; sometimes two broods.

FEEDING

Invertebrates, such as spiders, woodlice, weevils and other small beetles, earwigs, small caterpillars; grain and weed-seeds.

SIZE

12.75cm (5in)

J F M A M J
J A S O N D

*In autumn, jays fly off with
acorns to bury and eat later*

Jay Garrulus glandarius

RECOGNITION

Brown-pink plumage; blue
wing-coverts barred with
black; black and white
crown feathers; white rump
seen in flight; sexes alike.

NESTING

Both sexes build nest of
twigs lined with rootlets and
hair in bush or tree, usually
1–6m (4–20ft) from ground;
lays April–June; usually 3–6
eggs, green-tinged with
olive-brown freckles;
incubation about 16 days,
by female only; nestlings,
fed by both parents, leave
after 20 days.

FEEDING

Acorns; eggs and young
birds; insects and larvae
in spring and summer;
occasionally worms, mice
and lizards.

SIZE

34.25cm (13½in)

Its exotically coloured plumage and screeching 'skaak-skaak'
cry make the jay a conspicuous bird at most times of the year.
In the nesting season, however, the jay is more silent, and is
hard to see as it slips from branch to branch under a thick
cover of leaves.

Jays keep to the woods far more than any of the other British
crows. They also visit hedgerows, town parks and gardens, but
they are seldom far from trees. They prefer open woodland with
tall undergrowth in summer while in winter they seem to
depend largely on oak trees to see them through the weeks
when food is scarce. In autumn, the jays pluck acorns and
fly off to bury them in the ground. Later, in hard weather,
they return to their hidden stores to feed. Any forgotten acorns
take root, so jays are important in spreading oaks to new areas
of woodland.

In early spring, jays become social birds, gathering for
ceremonies in which they chase one another on slowly flapping
wings. At other times, outside the breeding season, they move
about in pairs or small parties. Courtship consists chiefly of
posturing and spreading the wings and tail.

As well as its characteristic screech, the jay has a wide
vocabulary, including a loud, ringing 'kiew' note, and a sound
like a chuckle, which may be mimicked from the magpie. In
common with some other crows, the jay occasionally gives a
low, crooning warble.

J F M A M J
J A S O N D

MALE IN
SPRING

*Male in winter plumage has
dark mottling on head and
upper parts*

Brambling Fringilla montifringilla

From late September, bramblings flock into Britain, travelling across the North Sea from their breeding grounds north of the Baltic. They spread out over the eastern part of the country, often joining other finches to form mixed flocks, which feed in beechwoods and on farmland throughout the winter. Beech mast is an important item in the birds' winter diet, but bramblings also visit stubble-fields in search of grain and weeds.

The cock bird's handsome breeding plumage is seen only briefly in Britain before the bramblings return to Scandinavia and Siberia in March and April.

Its spring song – rather like the 'dzwee' of the greenfinch – is rarely heard in Britain, and even rarer is the melodic, fluting song that is given in the breeding season. Until 30 years ago there was only one known case of bramblings having nested in Britain – in Sutherland in 1920 – but since 1979 they have bred in Scotland and eastern England on several occasions. In winter the best way of identifying a brambling is by its call-note, a rather grating 'tsweek', or by the 'chucc-chucc-chucc' cry it gives in flight.

Bramblings often turn up in pinewoods before migrating back to their breeding grounds, where they move into conifers and birchwoods to build their nests.

RECOGNITION

White rump; orange-buff breast and shoulder patch in male; male's head and upper parts glossy black in summer, mottled brown in winter; female has dull brown upper parts.

NESTING

Nests in Scandinavia and Siberia; builds deep cup nest in tree; lays mid May–July; usually 6 or 7 eggs, green-blue to olive-brown with dark spots and streaks, incubation probably about 12 days, by female only; nestlings, fed by both parents, leave after about 14 days.

FEEDING

Seeds of weeds, beech mast, grain; sometimes berries; insects in spring.

SIZE

14.5cm (5¾in)

J F M A M J
J A S O N D

MALE IN SUMMER

Outsize bill makes the hawfinch unmistakable even as it flies

Hawfinch Coccothraustes coccothraustes

RECOGNITION

Upper parts red-brown, underparts peach; black bib and wings with white shoulders; white on wings and tail conspicuous in flight; massive bill is grey-blue in summer, yellow in winter; female duller.

NESTING

Female builds cup of roots and grass founded on twigs and moss, usually on a high branch; sometimes lined with hair or fibres; lays late April–May; usually 4–6 eggs, pale blue-green or grey-green with dark brown marks; incubation about 12 days, by female only; nestlings, fed by both parents, leave at about 11 days; sometimes two broods.

FEEDING

Mainly fruit stones and large seeds; sometimes peas, haws and beech mast; occasionally insects.

SIZE

17.75cm (7in)

The powerful bill of the hawfinch, operated by highly developed muscles, allows the bird to bring to bear a crushing force of 27–43kg (60–95lb) to crack open the cherry stones that are one of its favourite foods in autumn and winter. Hawfinches ignore the flesh of cherries, choosing to wait until the ripe fruit has fallen from the tree and then to feed on the stones. They crack open the stones of sloes and damsons in the same way. Haws, hips and holly berries also form part of their diet.

The hawfinch, Britain's largest finch, started nesting here around 170 years ago. It breeds in deciduous woodland and in orchards, large gardens and bushy places with scattered trees. Hawfinches are shy birds, preferring to perch in the topmost branches of tall trees. In foraging visits to the ground they hop rather heavily. In winter they often move into more open country, forming small feeding flocks. Hawfinches have declined or even disappeared in many areas where they were once found.

The song of the hawfinch is feeble, halting and seldom heard, but in flight it has a loud and distinctive clipped 'tick'. The male's courtship display includes puffing out the head and breast feathers, bowing and drooping the wing-tips. Sometimes the pair touch their bills in what looks like a kiss but is in fact courtship feeding.

Coniferous Woodland

Forests of tall conifers, where full daylight rarely penetrates the dark green roof and the ground is softly carpeted with needles, once covered large areas of these islands. As the pinewood retreated, in the face of a changing climate and the woodman's axe, life became precarious for those conifer-dwelling birds that were too specialised to change their habits. Today, extensive plantations provide vital opportunities for a range of birds.

MALE

FEMALE

Blackcocks threaten one another at a lek, or courtship, arena

J F M A M J
J A S O N D

Black grouse Tetrao tetrix

RECOGNITION

Male has lyre-shaped tail with white underfeathers; glossy blue-black plumage with white wing-bar; female smaller, with chestnut and buff plumage and forked tail.

NESTING

Female makes scrape in ground, often among rushes; lays May–June; 6–10 eggs, buff with sparse red-brown spots; incubation about 27 days, by female only; young, tended by female only, fly after 2–3 weeks, but are not fully grown until much later.

FEEDING

Conifer shoots and birch buds; some beetles and other insects.

SIZE

Male: 53.25cm (21in)
Female: 35.5cm (14in)

Black grouse are polygamous, with the males, or blackcocks, taking no part in nesting duties. Their remarkable courtship ceremonies take place at communal display grounds known as leks. Blackcocks arrive there in March, about a month before the hens. At the lek, cocks joust with cocks and, to a lesser extent, hens with hens. The fighting is mostly mock, with opponents hopping up and down, their tails fully spread. Battles occasionally become more serious as the birds try to force their way towards the centre of the lek, which is the best place for securing matings. Sometimes old blackcocks resume their lek displays in the autumn.

Black grouse were once widespread on the heaths and moors of southern England. The last few pairs on Dartmoor and Exmoor have disappeared and the present most southerly populations – in Wales and the Peak district – are declining alarmingly. In northern Britain, despite local, temporary increases due to new forestry planting, there has also been a general decline over the past 100 years.

The blackcock is easily recognised by its lyre-shaped tail, which is white underneath. The female, confusingly known as the greyhen, is brown, smaller and has a forked tail.

The bird's diet is almost entirely vegetarian, although it will take insects occasionally. Birch buds are its favourite food, and it also has a taste for young conifer shoots, which has made it unpopular with foresters.

MALE

FEMALE

Wet summers are disasterous for capercaillie chicks

J F M A M J
J A S O N D

Capercaillie Tetrao urogallus

Towards the end of the 18th century, the capercaillie, the largest British gamebird, became extinct in these islands – a victim of the disappearance of many natural pine forests, and of the guns and snares of huntsmen. Then in the late 1830s a collection of 55 birds was brought from Sweden to the Marquis of Breadalbane's estate in Perthshire, and the capercaillie quickly re-established itself in the pine forests there and in the surrounding areas. Today it occurs in the greater part of its former range in the Scottish Highlands, although for largely unknown reasons, its numbers have declined over the past 20 years. Previous attempts to establish it in other parts of the British Isles have failed.

The cock capercaillie is much the largest bird likely to be seen in a pinewood, and could be mistaken for an escaped and unexpectedly airborne turkey. It can weigh up to 7.75kg (17lb). In the spring it performs an extraordinary courtship display on a special ground. The ceremonies include mock battles in which the males leap into the air and fan their tails. The song of the male is one of the weirdest in the world of birds. It begins with a resonant rattle, continues with a noise like the drawing of a cork and pouring liquid out of a narrow-necked bottle, and ends with a knife-grinding sound.

Some males defend the boundaries of their territories exceptionally boldly, attacking dogs and humans as well as other birds.

RECOGNITION

Fan tail; plumage grey-black with dark green breast and brown tinge on wings; female smaller, ruddy brown and mottled.

NESTING

Hen makes scrape in the ground lined with vegetation, often at foot of pine tree; lays late April–May; 5–8 eggs, pale yellow speckled with brown; incubation about 4 weeks, by hen; young, tended by hen only, can flutter after 2–3 weeks, but are not fully grown until much later.

FEEDING

Conifer shoots; fruit and berries in summer; occasionally insects.

SIZE

Male: 83.75cm (33in)
Female: 63.5cm (25in)

'Ear tufts' have no connection with the bird's true ears

J F M A M J
J A S O N D

Long-eared owl Asio otus

The 'ears' of the long-eared owl have nothing to do with hearing. They are simply elongated head feathers, useful in species recognition when they are held erect. The bird breeds in many parts of the British Isles, although it is not common in Wales, the Midlands or the south. Normally, it chooses pinewoods, and its low, moaning hoot is one of the most eerie sounds of the woodland night. It also nests on heathland, dunes and marshes, and sometimes it searches for prey over open country.

The long-eared owl hunts by night and roosts by day, flattening itself against a tree trunk. If smaller birds, which often make up part of its prey, find one hiding in a tree, they will mob it mercilessly. At other times, its presence may be given away by pellets lying on the ground beneath a favourite roosting tree. A recent study of the diet of long-eared owls in Northern Ireland showed that the long-tailed field mouse, or wood mouse, was easily its favourite food, supplemented by house mice, brown rats, pigmy shrews and various small birds.

The male has a special courtship display flight. It claps its wings together, then jumps up in the air. When angry, it threatens with outspread wings, hissing and snapping. As well as hooting, it has a barking call at breeding times, and the young have a hunger cry that sounds like the squeaking of an unoiled hinge.

Goldcrest's nest is usually slung under the branch of a conifer

MALE

J F M A M J
J A S O N D

Goldcrest Regulus regulus

Lively and fearless, the goldcrest is Britain's smallest bird, and it makes up in pugnacity for what it lacks in size. Cock birds have been known to fight to the death over a hen in the breeding season, and the hen will defend its nest by flying out to peck at any animal intruder, or keep watchful guard from a short distance away against a human.

The nest is often built in a conifer, even in areas of mixed woodland. Goldcrests look for sites from which they can sling an intricate structure of moss, spiders' webs and feathers, suspending it by 'basket handles' at any height up to about 15m (50ft) or more. After the breeding season is over, they are likely to be seen on heaths, commons and other open places as well as in conifers and deciduous woods.

In courtship, the cock spreads and raises the black-bordered orange crest that gives the bird its name. Its call-note is a thin 'zi-zi', higher pitched than the cries of a coal tit or treecreeper, and its high-pitched song is distinctive – 'cedar-cedar-cedar-cedar-sissa-pee'.

Goldcrests have benefited as a species from the planting of conifer trees, but their numbers are always severely reduced by a cold winter. In some exceptionally hard winters they have been almost wiped out. After a few years, however, they always manage to re-establish their numbers.

RECOGNITION

Yellow-green plumage with double wing-bar; male's crest is orange, female's more yellow; both have black border at base.

NESTING

Nests usually in conifer, but sometimes in deciduous tree, bush or creepers, 1–15m (3–50ft) high, or more; both sexes build elaborate nest of spiders' webs, moss and feathers, suspended by 'basket handles'; lays April–June; usually 7–10 eggs, white or pale yellow, freckled with brown; incubation about 15 days, by hen only; young, fed by both parents, fly after about 20 days; usually two broods.

FEEDING

Flies and other insects; spiders.

SIZE

9cm (3½in)

Crested tit – its pointed crest distinguishes it from other tits

Crested tit Lophophanes cristatus

RECOGNITION

Black crest feathers edged with white; black semicircle behind the eye; grey-brown back; sexes alike.

NESTING

Uses natural hole, or hole excavated by the female, usually in rotten pine stump; male may help to gather deer hair, feathers and wool for nest-building; lays late April–May; usually 5 or 6 eggs, white with red-brown spots; incubation about 14 days, by female only; nestlings, fed by both sexes, fly after about 18 days.

FEEDING

Aphids, caterpillars and other insects; sometimes conifer seeds and juniper berries.

SIZE

11.5cm (4½ in)

Extensive felling of woodland in Scotland during the 17th and 18th centuries drove the crested tit into a small area of the Highlands, but now, because of re-afforestation, the species is moving back into areas from which it was once lost. The advance is a slow one. The crested tit, which lives mainly on insects picked from pines, and sometimes by taking the seeds of conifers and juniper berries, has never been recorded as breeding outside Scotland. Even there, its nesting areas are limited to pinewoods in Highland, with a spread in recent years to Moray and Aberdeenshire.

The crested tit is the second smallest of the tits found in Britain, being just marginally longer than the coal tit. It is easily identified by its distinctive crest of long black feathers with white tips, and by its white cheeks with a curve of black round the eye. Its vocabulary is mostly restricted to a soft 'tsi-tsi-tsi' contact note and a soft churring sound.

Courtship consists of a special fluttering flight by the male. He goes on to chase the female through the high conifer branches, and feeds her during incubation. There is also a posture in which the male raises its crest and flutters its wings. The female may excavate a nest-hole, usually in a rotten pine stump, but natural holes in trees and fence-posts are also used. The male sometimes helps to gather nesting material.

J F M A M J
J A S O N D

Coal tit on cedar cone
shows distinctive white
patch on nape

Coal tit Periparus ater

This smallest of the seven British breeding tits is easily
recognised by the white spot on its nape. It is less bold than
most other tits and not so brightly coloured, but it constantly
draws attention to itself with its clear, high-pitched song. The
most characteristic notes of this song, a piping version of
the so-called 'saw-sharpening' sound produced by the great
tit, are 'teechu-teechu-teechu' and a triple 'tchuee', followed
by a trill. Its calls include a plaintive 'tsui-tsui' and a thin,
high-pitched 'tsee'.

Coal tits are often seen in town parks and gardens, but their
shyness makes them less frequent visitors to birdtables than
great tits or blue tits. Their favourite haunts are woods and any
place where there are scattered trees, particularly pines, firs,
spruce and other conifers. They nest in any convenient hole in
a tree, bank or wall, and will often make use of nest-boxes.
The male feeds the female during incubation, and if a potential
enemy approaches, she sits tight on the eggs until the last
possible moment, when she starts hissing angrily.

In winter, coal tits often join other tits, treecreepers and
goldcrests in foraging parties through the woods. Two different
courtship displays have been observed. In one, the male parades
up and down with tail erect, wings drooping and feathers
puffed out. In the other, it leans forward with tail outspread
and wings fluttering.

RECOGNITION

Glossy blue-black head
and white 'flash' on nape;
drab olive-buff back, pale
underparts apart from
black bib; sexes alike.

NESTING

Nest, in tree hole, bank or
wall, built by both sexes,
with thick pad of animal hair
and feathers on moss
foundation; usually lays
April–early May; usually
6–10 eggs, white with red-
brown speckles; incubation
about 14 days, usually
by female; nestlings, fed by
both parents, fly after about
16 days.

FEEDING

Insects, including beetles,
flies and their grubs, and
caterpillars; spiders; seeds
of thistles and other weeds;
sometimes wild nuts.

SIZE

10.75cm (4¼ in)

Siskin often mixes with other small birds to feed in woods

MALE

J F M A M J
J A S O N D

Siskin Carduelis spinus

RECOGNITION

Yellow-green plumage, with dark streaks on back and flanks; bounding flight typical of finches; male has black bib and crown, female is more drab.

NESTING

Both sexes build neat and compact nest, high in conifer, of twigs, lichen, moss and wool, lined with roots, hair, feathers and down; lays April–June; 3–5 eggs, pale blue, spotted and streaked with purple-red; incubation usually 11 or 12 days, by female only; nestlings, fed at first by female only, fly at about 15 days; usually two broods.

FEEDING

Mainly seeds of trees and weeds; insects during breeding season.

SIZE

12cm (4¾in)

This small yellow-green finch, once much admired as a cage-bird under the name of 'aberdevine', is another species on the advance because of the spread of conifer plantations. It is widespread as a winter visitor, when it often joins feeding flocks of redpolls on birches and alders, but as a breeding species it was almost confined to northern Scotland and the pine plantation areas of Ireland until quite recently. Now it is breeding regularly in newly afforested areas where it was formerly unknown – in East Anglia, Wales, Northumberland, Devon and Hampshire. In the past 30 years, it has become a common feeder on peanuts in gardens.

The cock siskin is much yellower than any other British finch except the male greenfinch, and is the only one, apart from the greenfinch, to have yellow patches at the base of its tail.

In the breeding season, siskins live in coniferous woods, but they will also nest in large gardens if there are pine trees present. The males put on a display flight over the nesting territory, and their song, a sweet, twittering succession of notes ending with a creaking sound, is mainly heard from the middle of February to the end of May. In courtship, the male chases the female and postures before her with feathers fluffed out and wings spread. Both sexes build the nest, usually towards the end of a branch and at least 5m (15ft) from the ground.

MALE IN
SUMMER

| J | F | M | A | M | J |
| J | A | S | O | N | D |

*Black chin distinguishes
lesser redpoll from other
small brown finches*

Lesser redpoll Carduelis cabaret

With the spread of conifer plantations, lesser redpoll numbers in Britain increased rapidly to reach a peak in about 1970. Since then, although remaining common locally, the trend has been reversed. The lesser redpoll usually breeds in loose colonies, mainly on heaths and in copses where there are conifers, birch trees and alders, but it will also nest in large gardens and shrubberies. It is slightly smaller and darker than the common, or mealy, redpoll, a visitor from Europe, and the very rare Arctic redpoll.

It builds its nest in a bush or tree at any height over about 60cm (2ft). From the outside the nest appears rather untidy, but inside it is neat and compact, with a lining of willow down, and sometimes hair and feathers.

Lesser redpolls are lively, sociable birds, often flocking with siskins in autumn and winter to feed on alder and birch seeds, or sometimes joining other finches and buntings to pick up food as they hop over stubble-fields and salt-marshes. When the birds are feeding, they have a habit of suddenly flying up in a mass, wheeling in the air and returning to their feeding place. Their flight is bounding, and the flight-note, 'chuch-uch-uch-uch-errrr', which also forms the basis of their somewhat primitive song, often enables them to be identified at a distance. The song is a long series of trilling notes, usually given in flight.

RECOGNITION

Plumage brown and streaked; adult has red forehead, black chin; male in summer has pink breast and rump.

NESTING

Female builds flimsy cup nest lined with down on foundation of thin twigs; lays May–June; 4–6 eggs, blue, spotted and streaked with pale brown; incubation about 11 days, by female only; nestlings, fed by both parents, leave at about 12 days; sometimes two broods.

FEEDING

Mainly seeds of birch and alder, weed-seeds, conifer and willow seeds; young are fed on insects at first.

SIZE

12.75cm (5in)

Crossbill extracts seeds from a pine cone

CROSSBILL

FEMALE

MALE

Crossbill Loxia curvirostra

RECOGNITION

Crossed bill; adult male crimson with orange tint, young male duller; female yellow-green; both have dark brown wings and tail.

NESTING

Female builds substantial nest of twigs lined with grasses in conifer; usually lays February–March; 3 or 4 eggs, green tinged with purple-red marks at blunt end; incubation about 13 days, by female; nestlings, fed by both parents, leave after 18 days.

FEEDING

Seeds of pine, larch, spruce and other conifers; very occasionally fruit, weed-seeds and insects.

SIZE

16.5cm (6½ in)

Variation in bill shapes to suit a special kind of diet is marked in the finch family, and the crossbill is a specialist among finches. It is the only British bird that has the tips of its bill crossed – an adaptation that enables it to pick seeds out of cones as it moves sideways along branches, parrot-fashion. Conifer seeds form the major part of the bird's diet, although occasionally it will take wild fruit and insects.

This reliance on conifers may cause irregular 'invasions' of crossbills across the North Sea into Britain. Mass irruptions of the birds every few years are believed to be triggered off by a failure in the supply of spruce cones in Scandinavia. Crossbills start to arrive on the east coast of Britain in late June or early July, and later spread to any part of the country where conifers have been planted. Some stay to breed in southern England, but unless they are reinforced by fresh arrivals from the Continent, these breeding stocks tend to die out. In the Highlands, though, a distinct breeding population survives independently of fresh arrivals. These Scottish crossbills (*Loxia scotia*) are slightly bigger at 17cm (6¾in) and have larger bills. They are the only bird species unique to Britain, but their status is complicated by the presence of a few breeding parrot crossbills.

The song of the crossbill is rather like that of the greenfinch, but its flight-note, a metallic 'jip-jip', is unmistakable. Its courtship displays include a sexual chase and courtship feeding. The birds nest in conifers, often in loose colonies.

Freshwater Margins and Marshes

Intensive reclamation of marshland had a punishing effect on bird life, but a change in public attitude encouraged a reversal in fortune for some species. The return of birds such as the osprey and avocet after decades of absence are spectacular conservation triumphs.

Bittern, pointing its bill to the sky, merges into the reeds

Bittern Botaurus stellaris

RECOGNITION

Buff plumage is mottled, streaked and barred with dark brown and black; green feet and legs; sexes alike.

NESTING

Female builds untidy pile of sedges and other material, usually in water or on thick water vegetation; lays April–May; 4–6 eggs, olive; incubation about 25 days, by female; nestlings, fed by female, leave in 2–3 weeks, fly after about 8 weeks.

FEEDING

Frogs and small fish; water-voles, water-beetles, water-boatmen, dragonfly nymphs; some small birds and nestlings; water-weed at times.

SIZE

76.25cm (30in)

The boom of the bittern, resembling something between a lowing cow and a distant foghorn, is a sound that has returned to the Norfolk Broads, and now and then is to be heard in other parts of the country. Two hundred years ago, nesting bitterns were not uncommon, but with the draining of marshes they were gradually pressed back into the fens, and even there they were extinct by 1850. Fifty years later, the foghorn 'song' of bitterns was heard again on the Broads, with increasing frequency, but not until 1911 was breeding actually proved, at Sutton Broad. They had started to spread out when a renewed decline brought the population of boooming males down to 11. Then, early in the 21st century, extensive conservation efforts brought another recovery and numbers are back up to more than 75 booming males.

When unaware of being seen, the bittern may look rather like a large domestic hen, hunched up with its long neck drawn in. But if the bird suspects danger, it may freeze, with neck and beak stretched vertically. The streaked plumage provides excellent camouflage among the dried reeds.

Bitterns are almost entirely confined to extensive swamps, fens and reed-beds. In the breeding season they perform collective aerial displays. Booming is not their only sound. At dusk they produce a harsh flight-call, 'kow' or 'kwah'.

J F M A M J
J A S O N D

Grey heron flies with head drawn back and legs trailing behind

J F M A M J
J A S O N D

Grey heron Ardea cinerea

Like a tall grey sentinel, the heron stands in the shallows, poised to wade forward and strike with its pick-axe bill at a fish, frog or water-vole. Small fish are swallowed whole, head first, and larger ones are stabbed repeatedly, then taken to the bank to have the flesh picked from their bones.

Grey herons will range more than 12 miles for food. Sometimes they raid garden ponds for goldfish, and they may visit rick-yards and cornfields, searching for small rodents. Occasionally, they nest in parks. A small heronry has become established in Regent's Park, London, since 1968.

The common breeding heron of Britain is the grey heron, as distinct from the purple heron, which is a rare visitor from the near Continent. The breeding population is fairly stable at 14,000 pairs, with a temporary drop after severe weather.

Once a heronry has been established, birds will return to the same site, year after year. They have a wide and raucous vocabulary, with the common call a loud, harsh 'krornk'. Courtship is preceded by a dance ceremony in which the male stretches its neck up and then lowers it over its back, with the bill pointing upwards. When there are eggs or nestlings to care for, one parent stays on guard against predators while the other is away feeding.

RECOGNITION

Grey upper parts; dark grey flight feathers; black crest; bushy breastplate and stout yellow bill; usually flies with legs trailing and neck drawn in; sexes alike.

NESTING

Nests in colonies, usually in trees, but also locally in reed-beds or on sea cliffs; female arranges platform of sticks or reeds brought by male; lays February–May; 3–5 eggs, light blue; incubation about 25 days, by both parents; young, fed by both parents, leave after 7–8 weeks.

FEEDING

Fish, water-voles, beetles, frogs, moles and rats.

SIZE

91.5cm (36in)

Osprey plunges towards the water to snatch a fish near the surface

Osprey Pandion haliaetus

RECOGNITION

Upper parts dark brown, contrasting with white underparts speckled with brown; dark brown band on side of head; long wings distinctly angled in flight; sexes alike.

NESTING

Both sexes build bulky pile of sticks, in tree or on ground near loch; lays late April–early May; usually 3 eggs, white, heavily blotched with red-brown; incubation about 35 days, mainly by female; young, fed by female, fly in 7–8 weeks.

FEEDING

Almost entirely fish, mainly pike and trout.

SIZE

56cm (22in)

In the mid 1950s a pair of large, brown-and-white birds set up their nest in a tree near Loch Garten, Highland – ospreys were back in Britain after an absence of almost 50 years. Their return captured the public's imagination, and more than a million people have visited the Loch Garten site to see the birds – through a telescope at a discreet distance. The nesting area, now a bird reserve, is guarded by the RSPB. The need for a close guard was underlined in 1958, when the nest was robbed. Numbers in Scotland have increased to more than 100 pairs, and recently a few pairs have nested in England and Wales.

The osprey, also known as the fish hawk, is normally seen near lakes, broads and estuaries outside the breeding season. It lives almost entirely on fish, and one reason that it was harried out of the country is that it competes with fishermen for trout. Fish remains found at Loch Garten have all proved to be pike or trout but Welsh nesters also take grey mullet. A hunting osprey has a rather slow, flapping flight, but it also soars, hovers and drops from a height on its prey, feet first. Its shrill, cheeping cry is like the call of a young gamebird.

In early spring, before the female arrives at the eyrie, the male performs spectacular flights, climbing as high as 300m (1,000ft), hovering briefly with tail outspread and then plunging earthwards.

Marsh harrier searching for prey beats low over the ground

FEMALE

Marsh harrier Circus aeruginosus

This long-winged hawk quarters its hunting grounds from just a few metres above the reeds, looking for the ripple that will betray a water-vole below, or sending a party of coots scuttling for cover. For all the panic it causes, the marsh harrier is highly sensitive to disturbances at its own nesting sites. The RSPB's nature reserve at Minsmere in Suffolk was for many years its only nesting place. Most of the birds in England are summer visitors. As a breeder, the marsh harrier is one of Britain's rarest species.

Although once widespread, marsh harriers stopped nesting in Britain regularly around 100 years ago, mainly because of the draining of the fens. They returned to Norfolk in the late 1920s, and slowly spread until by 1958 there were 15 nests. After that there was a serious decline – due perhaps to the side-effects of pesticides – to a low point of only one pair in 1971. A resurgence followed, and the number of nests had reached more than 200 by the early 21st century.

In courtship, the male performs a spectacular soaring flight, diving and somersaulting in descent for as much as 61m (200ft). Their call is a shrill 'kwee-a'. The female may call loudly for food when she is incubating, and sometimes flies up to take it from the male in a spectacular aerial pass.

RECOGNITION

Mainly dark brown; male has tawny, brown-streaked breast, large blue-grey wing-patches and grey tail; female has pale crown and throat; male in flight shows broad grey band on wings.

NESTING

Female builds substantial pile of aquatic vegetation, lined with grass, always on the ground among thick growth of marsh plants; lays late April–June; 4 or 5 eggs, very pale blue; incubation about 38 days, mainly by female; young, fed mainly by female, leave nest in 35–40 days, fly a week or two later.

FEEDING

Water-voles; moorhens, coots, starlings and other birds; eggs and young; frogs and grass snakes.

SIZE

53.25cm (21in)

MALE

J F M A M J
J A S O N D

Startled water rail flies off weakly, with trailing legs

Water rail Rallus aquaticus

RECOGNITION

Long red bill; slate-grey breast, face and throat; flanks barred, upper parts dark brown with black streaks; white under tail; distinctive voice; female duller than male.

NESTING

Both sexes build nest of dead reeds near lake or river or in marshy ground; nest raised above water level and hidden from above; lays April–July; usually 6–11 eggs, buff with grey or brown blotches; incubation about 20 days, by both parents; nestlings, tended by both parents, leave soon after hatching, fly after about 7 weeks; two broods.

FEEDING

Insects, spiders, freshwater shrimps, earthworms; perhaps small fish; roots of grasses and watercress, seeds and berries.

SIZE

28cm (11in)

The discordant voice of the water rail often betrays this secretive bird as it moves through the cover of reeds and sedges. The call most often heard starts as a grunt and ends as a piercing squeal, like a pig's. The water rail's other notes are a variety of grunts, groans, whistles, squeaks, hisses and a sharp 'kik-kik-kik' call.

In the marshes, fens and swamps where it breeds, the water rail darts from one piece of cover to another in the thick reeds, with its long red bill lowered. It is small and slender enough to move unnoticed through the vegetation, using a high-stepping walk. As it walks it sometimes jerks up its tail, showing the white feathers underneath. Its flights often last for just a few seconds – the bird flutters feebly with its long legs dangling. In hard weather water rails move into the open to feed in unfrozen spots, and if alarmed will stand motionless, allowing time for a close look at them.

Courtship includes the feeding of the female by the male. The female has been seen to get up from nest and eggs to walk round the male, rubbing her bill against his and crooning softly.

Water rails, which breed in wet districts, particularly in East Anglia and Ireland, remain in Britain throughout the year. The population grows in September, when birds fly in from the Continent and Iceland.

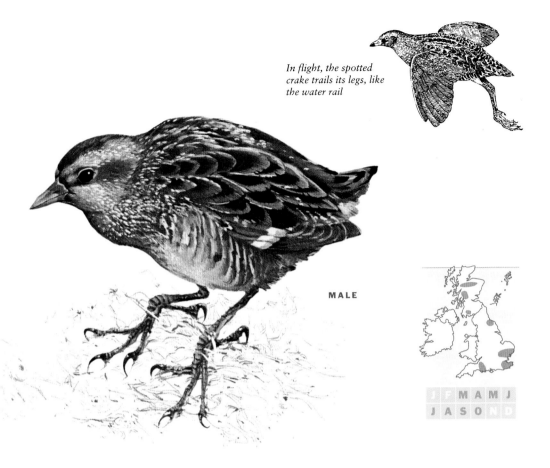

In flight, the spotted crake trails its legs, like the water rail

MALE

Spotted crake Porzana porzana

A great deal remains to be found out about the spotted crake, a shy, secretive bird that skulks among water plants in swampy places, and creeps deeper into cover far more readily than it flies out. Naturalists are not certain whether it raises two broods in Britain, as it does on the Continent. For that matter, it has not even been established whether the spotted crake is a regular breeding species in the country. A total of 10–20 pairs probably nest annually in Britain, but proof of breeding is difficult to obtain, and the birds are best left to their own devices.

Its nesting sites in fens, bogs and mosses are almost inaccessible to humans because of the spongy nature of the ground. If it were not for the bird's distinctive call-notes, one of them a loud 'hwit-hwit-hwit', like the crack of a whip, and another a rhythmic 'tic-toc', its presence would hardly be noticed at all. On migration it may turn up in reed-beds and ditches, the margins of lakes and other damp places with thick cover.

When the spotted crake takes to the air it flies weakly, with legs dangling. For all its unobtrusiveness, the bird has its moment of self-parade. The displaying male struts in front of the female with long, rather exaggerated steps, and later in the courtship may pursue her on land, on water or in the air.

RECOGNITION

Streaked and speckled olive-brown above; dark brown wings; grey breast with white spots; barred flanks and buff under tail; green legs; red at base of bill; female duller than male.

NESTING

Both sexes build nest of sedges and grasses, usually in tussock; 8–12 eggs, olive-buff, well speckled with purple-grey and ash-grey; lays May–June; incubation 18–21 days, apparently shared by both parents; young, tended by both parents, leave soon after hatching, fly after about 7½ weeks.

FEEDING

Beetles, dragonfly nymphs, caddis larvae, caterpillars, slugs, small water-snails; seeds of water plants.

SIZE

23cm (9in)

Little ringed plover lacks pale wing-bars of ringed plover

Little ringed plover Charadrius dubius

RECOGNITION

Brown back; white below, with thick black neck-band; black band behind eye and on white forehead; no white wing-bar; sexes alike.

NESTING

Female selects one of several scrapes, usually in gravel or shingle, sometimes lines it with a few pebbles or stalks; lays late April–June; 4 eggs, pear-shaped, pale buff with black spots; incubation about 25 days, by both parents; chicks, tended by both parents, leave nest almost at once, fly after about 3½ weeks.

FEEDING

Mainly insects; also spiders, small molluscs and worms.

SIZE

15.25cm (6in)

The still rare little ringed plover is one of the half-dozen birds to have colonised the British Isles since the first recorded nesting at Tring in 1938. There are now around 1,000 nesting pairs, occasionally as far north as southern Scotland, but suitable habitat tends to be short-lived.

Gravel pits, before the banks become overgrown, provide the bird's favourite nesting sites, and its distribution therefore tends to follow river valleys where deposits of gravel are being exploited. Lately, it has also been nesting in shingle banks along rivers. In spring and autumn, migrating birds may turn up at the edges of lakes or any other stretch of fresh water.

On the ground it looks like a smaller version of its relative, the ringed plover, but in flight, the little ringed plover has no white wing-bar. It also has distinctive call-notes, mainly 'pee-oo' and a continuous 'pip-pip-pip'. The courtship song, a trilling of the call-notes, is usually delivered during a bat-like flight in the air. The showpiece of the display is a performance in which the male flies round erratically with slow wing-beats. Like many other ground-nesters, the little ringed plover uses a show of injury-feigning to distract intruders from its nest or brood.

J F M A M J
J A S O N D

Two males in
breeding plumage
display to female

MALE IN
SUMMER

Ruff Philomachus pugnax

The courtship displays of the ruff are violent and colourful.
Males rush at one another with ruffs fluffed out, threatening
and sometimes coming to blows as they compete for mating
territories. After a fight, they crouch with bills on the ground,
ruffs spread out and ear-tufts raised, waiting for the females,
or reeves, to arrive. The reeves pick their way between the
crouched ruffs and select one for mating by preening its ruff.
Mating may take place on the display ground, or the paired
birds may fly off together. Both sexes are promiscuous, and
males take no part in raising the young.

Certain ruffs, known as 'satellite' males, do not fight over
territory but often secure matings while the established males
are threatening one another. They are tolerated probably
because, in their conspicuous white plumage, they attract more
reeves to the display ground. In breeding plumage, the exotic
ruff feathers and ear-tufts may be shades of purple-brown,
black, chestnut, yellow or white.

Ruffs were once quite common as breeding birds, but their
popularity as table delicacies and the draining of the marshlands
had almost entirely stopped their breeding in Britain before the
middle of the 19th century. They come to Britain now mainly as
passage migrants in autumn and spring, but since 1963 small
numbers have bred in East Anglia and occasionally elsewhere.

RECOGNITION

Male in summer has huge
ruff around neck, and ear-
tufts; smaller reeve is
generally grey with boldly
patterned back; in winter
sexes are similar, with oval
white patches on each side
of dark tail.

NESTING

Reeve alone builds nest,
usually hidden in a hollow,
and lines it with dried grass;
lays May; usually 4 eggs,
variable in colour from pale
brown to pale blue with dark
blotches; incubation about
21 days, by reeve only;
chicks, tended by reeve
only, leave soon after
hatching and become
independent in a few days.

FEEDING

Chiefly insects, with some
worms, molluscs and plant
seeds.

SIZE

Male: 28cm (11in)
Female: 23cm (9in)

Snipe nests in hollow on ground, often near water

| J | F | M | A | M | J |
| J | A | S | O | N | D |

Snipe Gallinago gallinago

RECOGNITION

Brown streaked and patterned plumage; long straight bill; boldly striped head; zigzag flight; sexes alike.

NESTING

Nests in hollow lined with grasses, in tussock of rushes, grass or sedge, usually near water; lays April–August; 4 eggs, pear-shaped, olive-grey or olive-brown, heavily marked with dark sepia; incubation about 20 days, by female only; chicks, tended by both parents, leave the nest in a few hours, fly after about 21 days.

FEEDING

Chiefly worms, also water-beetles, beetles, caddis larvae, grubs of flies, snails, woodlice; some seeds of marsh plants.

SIZE

26.75cm (10½in)

The 'song' of the snipe – a resonant, quavering humming, which has earned it the country name of 'heather bleater' – has nothing to do with its voice. As the male plunges through the air at an angle of 45°, with tail outspread, the two outer tail feathers vibrate in the wind to produce the sound mechanically. Almost exactly the same sound has been reproduced by fixing tail-feathers from a snipe on either side of a cork and whirling them round on a string.

The sound may be produced at any time of year, but is usually part of the bird's courtship behaviour, and heard regularly from late March to the middle of June. A courtship display takes place on the ground.

The snipe's long straight bill has a flexible tip and is used for probing in the mud for worms. Its bill makes up a quarter of the bird's total length. Sometimes a snipe may be spotted feeding quietly at the edge of a pool, but often the bird is not seen until it has been flushed and dashes up zigzagging with a loud harsh 'creech'.

The resident population of snipe has declined dramatically – residents have gone from most of the lowlands – but numbers are swollen by visitors in autumn and winter. In hard winters they sometimes move from their damp inland haunts to feed along the shore. Parties of snipe, called 'wisps', carry out manoeuvres in the air, and parent birds have been seen carrying their young, but this is rare.

J F M A M J
J A S O N D

Jack snipe probes the mud for earthworms and molluscs

Jack snipe Lymnocryptes minimus

Except in the breeding season, when it performs a low-key version of the common snipe's display flight, the jack snipe is a self-effacing bird. It crouches when alarmed, and may not fly up until almost trodden on. Shooting people have reported that it will even allow a dog to pick it up.

Jack snipe may, at a distance, be confused with common snipe, but their flight is less erratic, and they rise from the ground silently or with a low weak call, move a little slower and alight again sooner. They are also smaller – which is why they have been given the diminutive name 'jack' – and have much shorter bills. A close look will reveal a distinctive head pattern with two narrow pale streaks in the centre of the crown instead of the common snipe's one broad streak.

Both birds prefer damp regions but the jack snipe, which is exclusively a winter visitor to Britain, may also be found on drier ground. It is sometimes seen in 'wisps' or small flocks.

The display, to be seen on its continental breeding grounds and not in Britain, is less spectacular than the common snipe's. The bird descends at a shallower angle, and the wings make a whirring rather than a humming sound. Then it checks, glides silently for a short way, and finally hangs suspended and flies up and down as if jerked by an unseen puppet-master.

RECOGNITION
Streaked brown plumage; stripes on crown; two bold stripes down back; flight slower than common snipe's; sexes alike.

NESTING
Nests in Scandinavia, north Russia, Siberia; makes scrape, lined with dried grasses, in ground, hummock of grass or moss in swamps; usually 4 eggs, olive-buff or olive-brown, with darker markings; incubation about 24 days, apparently by hen only; chicks leave in a few hours.

FEEDING
Earthworms, small land and freshwater snails, beetles, grubs of flies; also seeds of grasses, rushes and other waterside plants.

SIZE
19cm (7½in)

SUMMER

J F M A M J
J A S O N D

Black-tailed godwit in flight shows broad white bars on its wings

Black-tailed godwit Limosa limosa

RECOGNITION

In winter, brown-grey above, light below; in summer, head and breast red or chestnut; broad black band on end of pure white tail; long legs; straight bill; broad white wing-bar shows in flight; sexes alike.

NESTING

Both sexes make scrape in ground, usually well hidden in thick grass, padded with dead grass and lined with leaves; lays May; 4 eggs, light green to brown, blotched and spotted with brown; incubation 24 days, by both parents; chicks, tended by both parents, leave nest after a few hours, fly after about 4 weeks.

FEEDING

Insects, including beetles, grasshoppers, dragonflies, mayflies; shellfish, snails, slugs and earthworms.

SIZE

40.5cm (16in)

Early in the 19th century, the black-tailed godwit was lost to Britain as a breeding bird. Large numbers were netted to be served up as table delicacies, and the remaining birds were driven away by the draining of the fens, so that by the 1830s they had ceased to nest here. Today, because of protection, the black-tail's prospects are promising. It has become a frequent passage migrant and winter visitor but remains a very rare breeding bird, because of its need for a particular habitat.

Since 1952 black-tails have become established at protected sites on the Ouse and Nene Washes, East Anglia, and pairs have nested in recent years in several other parts of Britain, including Orkney and Shetland.

They nest in damp, grassy and marshy districts and at other times appear on estuaries, mudflats and sandy shores, and to a lesser extent near fresh water. The flight call is a loud 'wicka-wicka-wicka', but over the breeding grounds two other calls may be heard, 'pee-oo-ee' and a greenshank-like 'wik-ik-ik.

The song, which sounds like a repeated 'crweetuu', is most often heard as part of the display performance over the breeding grounds. The male first rises steeply with rapid wing-beats, then flies in slow motion with tail spread out, calling loudly, before gliding silently downwards and finally side-slipping to the ground.

SUMMER

Startled redshank flies off
swiftly with noisy yelps

J F M A M J
J A S O N D

Redshank Tringa totanus

For most of the year, redshanks are sociable birds, mingling
with other waders on muddy, open shores and often collecting
in substantial flocks. When the time comes to raise a brood,
however, pairs prefer to nest on their own, in some damp grassy
corner or marsh.

A ringing 'tu-tu-tu' is the redshank's cry. It sets up a clamour
when startled, and has a range of loud, yelping, but fairly
musical calls, including a scolding 'teuk-teuk-teuk' and a 'chip-
chip-chip' of alarm. A yodelling 'tu-udle' song, based on the
more musical of its call-notes, is given in the breeding season.
The displaying male chases the female with his tail fanned out
and head stretched forward. When she stops, he raises his wings
above his back, flutters them and advances slowly.

The white on the wings identifies the redshank as it flies or
stretches itself while at rest. No other wader of similar size has
such a broad white wing-bar. The bird makes a bobbing
movement when suspicious, and has a rather erratic flight.

In the late 19th and early 20th century, the redshank
increased rapidly in numbers and range, but this trend has been
put markedly into reverse since about 1940. Drainage and
intense cultivation are among the reasons, especially inland, and
coastal salt-marshes are both decreasing in size and threatened
by climate change.

RECOGNITION

Grey-brown with darker
markings, light below; long
orange-red legs; white rump
and white patch on back of
wings show in flight;
appears darker in summer
than in winter; sexes alike.

NESTING

Both sexes make scrapes in
marshy ground, usually well
hidden by tuft of grass;
female lines one with dried
grass; lays mid April–June;
usually 4 eggs, pear-
shaped, buff with dark
brown spots and blotches;
incubation about 23 days,
by both parents; chicks,
tended by both parents,
leave as soon as hatched,
fly after about 4 weeks.

FEEDING

Mainly insects, small
shellfish, worms and
lugworms; some vegetable
matter.

SIZE

28cm (11in)

Common sandpiper flies low over water with wings deeply bowed

J F M A M J
J A S O N D

Common sandpiper *Tringa hypoleucos*

RECOGNITION

Dark brown above, pure white below, with a light buff-grey area on sides of neck; white wing-bar shows in flight; sexes alike.

NESTING

Lines scrape or depression in ground with grass and dead leaves, often close to water; lays May–June; usually 4 eggs, pear-shaped, buff, sometimes grey with red-brown blotches; incubation about 22 days, by both parents; chicks, tended by both parents, leave nest within few hours, fly after about 4 weeks.

FEEDING

Mainly insects, such as water-beetles, flies, mayflies, water-bugs, caddis flies; snails, worms, a few tadpoles; a little vegetable matter.

SIZE

19.75cm (7¾in)

The head-bobbing sandpiper, about the same size as a starling, breeds in Europe and Asia, and winters in Africa, or even in Australia. (The similar spotted sandpiper replaces it in North America.) It comes to Britain in the summer to nest beside the streams and lochs of the north and west. The first few make their landfall in the last days of March and the main stream pours in at the end of April and early May. They are easily identified by their flight and call. A shrill 'twee-wee-wee' is uttered as the sandpipers fly in a half-circle low over the water, alternately flickering their wings and momentarily gliding.

The trilling song, given from the air, ground or perch, is mainly an elaboration of the call-note, and plays a prominent part in the male's circular courtship flight. Although they are birds of the north and west, odd pairs occasionally nest by rivers or flooded gravel-pits in the south. On their spring and autumn migrations, they may be seen by almost any stretch of water where the edge is shallow enough for wading. Individuals may winter in the south, but this is exceptional.

Common sandpipers are among the many birds that lure intruders away from their nests and eggs by the trick of trailing a 'broken' wing. When flushed they skim low over the water, then land on a convenient perch and start bobbing their heads.

Green sandpiper in flight shows distinctive white rump

Green sandpiper Tringa ochropus

It is something of a misnomer to call this bird 'green'. It has greenish legs and a dark greenish-brown back, but is usually seen as a dark bird. The green sandpiper rises from the water's edge with shrill cries, its conspicuous white rump making it look like a large house martin as it flies away. It almost always rises to a great height on being flushed, uttering a shrill 'weet-a-weet' or a variation on this call. Although it flies off high and fast, it will return to a favourite feeding spot.

Compared with most other waders, the green sandpiper is not a sociable bird, and usually probes the river margins alone. Flocks are met with on migration only, and even then are seldom large.

In courtship, green sandpipers have been observed leapfrogging one another on the ground, with a flutter of wings, but their displays are unlikely to be seen in Britain. They rarely nest in Britain although there were nestings at a couple of sites between 1999 and 2004.

Green sandpipers appear most often in spring and autumn as birds of passage, in marshes and near fresh water, even around small pools and flood puddles. They may investigate salt-marsh runnels but rarely go to the open shore, and keep more to rivers than most waders. A few birds may stay for the winter.

RECOGNITION

Dark brown-grey above, white below; breast slightly mottled; white rump and upper tail with black bars on tip of tail; wings black underneath; sexes alike.

NESTING

Very rarely breeds in Britain; nesting sites are in northern Europe and Asia, in old trees near water; may use old nests of other birds; lays mid April–June, later in north; usually 4 eggs, buff with deep brown and lighter markings; incubation about 21 days, chiefly by hen; young, tended by both parents, spend brief time in nest.

FEEDING

Mainly insects, small worms and molluscs; some vegetable matter.

SIZE

23cm (9in)

Phalarope in winter spins round on water to stir up insects

FEMALE IN SUMMER

J F M **A M J** J A S O N D

Red-necked phalarope Phalaropus lobatus

RECOGNITION

Head and upper parts slate-grey with buff streaks; white throat; white underparts; orange patch on sides of neck in summer; female more strongly marked; in winter plumage is white and grey, with head lighter; delicate, with needle-like bill.

NESTING

Both sexes make scrapes, lined with grass, in coastal or lochside areas; lays late May–early June; 4 eggs, pear-shaped, buff, heavily blotched with brown; incubation about 20 days, by male; chicks, tended by male, leave within a few hours, fly after 17 days.

FEEDING

Almost entirely insects found on the water or on waterside vegetation.

SIZE

17.75cm (7in)

Almost every rule about the roles of male and female birds in the breeding season is reversed in the case of the red-necked phalarope. The female moves into the breeding area first and establishes a territory, the female displays to attract the male and the female takes the initiative in courtship and mating. The male, once it has been led to the nesting site, sits on the eggs to incubate them and looks after the chicks until they are able to fly. Not surprisingly, the female is the brighter coloured of the two.

With its slightly webbed feet, the bird is a buoyant swimmer. It constantly bobs its head as it swims, and often spins in circles, stirring up water insects, which it picks off the surface. The phalarope is much the smallest bird likely to be seen swimming.

Red-necked phalaropes fly to the open sea in winter, moving well offshore, but they may be blown inland by storms, and turn up on almost any small pond.

This rare species has suffered more than any other from egg-collectors determined that, if it should become extinct, they would have the last clutch of eggs in their cabinet. Its numbers fell rapidly in the 19th century, but the RSPB has helped it to build up a stronghold in the Shetlands, where a few pairs nest on Mainland and Fetlar.

J F M A M J
J A S O N D

Kingfisher excavates its nest-hole in river banks or sand or gravel-pits

Kingfisher Alcedo atthis

A flash of sapphire is all that is needed to identify the kingfisher as it streaks downstream or bellyflops to snatch a minnow. This most brilliantly coloured of British birds is largely confined to the banks of rivers and streams because of its diet, but it also feeds on lakes and large ponds and – especially in hard weather – on the seashore. Its bright colouring is a defence adaptation – predators have learned to leave the bird alone, because its flesh is foul-tasting.

Kingfishers are liable to starve to death in hard winters, when their food supply is cut off by frozen waters. After the winter of 1962–3, their numbers fell drastically throughout the British Isles. Along upper reaches of the Thames in 1961 there was one pair of breeding kingfishers to every 1¾ miles, but in 1964 only one pair to every 20 miles. In Scotland, partly as a result of mild winters, but also in some areas because of improvements in water quality, kingfishers have recently increased and spread northwards.

The bird fishes with a shallow dive from a perch or from a hovering position, and beats its catch on a branch before bolting it down, head first. A fish swallowed tail first would choke the bird as its fins and scales opened, so the kingfisher carries a fish by its tail only when the fish is going to be presented to another bird.

RECOGNITION

Brilliant blue-green above, orange-chestnut below, with white throat and patch on each side of the neck; sexes alike.

NESTING

Both sexes dig out tunnel about 60–90cm (2–3ft) long, often in canal bank; lined thinly with fishbones; entrance often betrayed by 'whitewash' slime of disgorged fishbones running out after young have hatched; lays April–August; 6 or 7 eggs, glossy white, almost round; incubation 19–21 days, by both sexes; nestlings, fed by both sexes, fly after 23–27 days; two broods.

FEEDING

Mainly minnows, sticklebacks and gudgeon; also water-beetles, dragonfly nymphs and other water life.

SIZE

16.5cm (6½in)

J F M A M J
J A S O N D

*Young sand martins in a
nest-hole take insects from
a parent*

Sand martin Riparia riparia

Smallest swallow; plain
brown above, white below;
brown band across the
breast; tail short and
slightly forked; sexes alike.

Both sexes bore tunnel,
about 60–90cm (2–3ft)
long, in sandy banks, cliffs
or gravel-pits; grass and
feathers gathered in flight
for lining nest chamber; lays
May–August; 4 or 5 eggs,
white; incubation about
14 days, by both parents;
young, fed by both parents,
fly after about 19 days;
normally two broods.

Mosquitoes, other small
flies, beetles, mayflies and
other insects, usually
caught over water.

12cm (4¾in)

This is the smallest of Britain's three swallows, and the earliest
to arrive. Interweaving flocks fly in at the end of March,
gathering over lakes, rivers and reservoirs to feed on gnats.
Later, they seek the nesting sites of previous years in steep river
banks, cliffs, railway cuttings and old sand-pits.

Comings and goings at the colony are abrupt. At one moment
the spot seems almost deserted, with perhaps only a young bird,
showing its white chin, peering from a hole. The next moment
the air is clamorous with wings and chattering as birds dip and
swing up to their nest entrances. Birds clinging on to the steep
bank side or cliff face keep up a chatter at those flying up. Then
suddenly the main body takes off and disperses.

Both sexes drive a tunnel roughly 60–90cm (2–3ft) long in
the sandy soil at their nesting sites, scooping out a small
chamber at the end to be lined untidily with grass and feathers.

There should be little danger of confusing the bird with a
swallow or a house martin. The sand martin's brown breast
band is distinctive, its tail is the least forked of the three and it
lacks the house martin's white rump. It hardly ever comes to the
ground, except to roost in reed-beds and osiers, where large
flocks gather outside the nesting season. Communal roosting in
Britain does not last long. In September most sand martins leave
to winter in Africa.

MALE

Pied wagtail springs into the air to catch a passing insect

J F M A M J
J A S O N D

Pied wagtail Motacilla alba

In many parts of the country, modern agricultural techniques have robbed this bird of one of its most reliable sources of food. It is a specialist in catching winged insects, and until fairly recently found a plentiful supply in farmyards, but the traditional farmyard is on the way out. Hygienic cowsheds, the greatly increased use of piped water and efficient methods of insect control bring bleak prospects for the bird.

The pied wagtail's roosting habits have long drawn the attention of naturalists – or even of casual passers-by. Up to 1,000 wagtails at a time roost in trees in a busy Dublin street, and there was another mass roost on the glass roof of a post office in Leicester. Roosts in commercial greenhouses have been reported at more than 20 places, from Kent to Lancashire. The birds may be seeking warmth, shelter and protection from predators.

Nesting is usually in a cavity or ledge on a building, bank, cliff or pile of stones. A pair once built on a mudguard of a car that was regularly parked outside an Isle of Man school – they waited for its arrival each day to resume building.

The pied wagtail's flight is markedly undulating, and the bird often gives a high-pitched 'tschizzik' flight-call as it takes to the air. The same call is given in courtship, during which the male chases the female, then postures in front of her, head lowered, wings drooping and tail spread.

RECOGNITION
Black and white plumage, long tail, often wagged up and down; female's back greyer than male's.

NESTING
Female lines hole in wall, shed, bank or thatch, with hair, feathers and wool; sometimes re-lines old nest of another bird; lays April–June; 5 or 6 eggs, grey-white, marked with grey or brown; incubation about 14 days, chiefly by female; young, fed by both parents, fly after about 2 weeks; normally two broods, sometimes three.

FEEDING
Flies, beetles, small moths and other small insects.

SIZE
17.75cm (7in)

Yellow wagtail perches readily on fences, hedges and bushes

MALE IN
SUMMER

J F M A M J
J A S O N D

Yellow wagtail Motacilla flava

RECOGNITION

Predominantly yellow bird, with long tail; green-brown upper parts; distinctive 'tsweep' call-note; female duller than male, with olive back and paler yellow underparts.

NESTING

Female builds nest of dried grass and roots, lined with hair, always in hollow in ground, concealed in vegetation; lays May–July; usually 5 or 6 eggs, pale grey, heavily sprinkled with yellow-buff; incubation about 13 days, mainly by female; nestlings, fed by both parents, fly after about 13 days; two broods normal in south.

FEEDING

Flies, and other small insects and larvae; at times beetles and even caterpillars.

SIZE

16.5cm (6½in)

Any 'yellow wagtail' reported in Britain in winter is almost certain to be a grey wagtail, another small bird with yellow underparts. The yellow wagtail is a summer visitor, arriving in April and leaving in September and October to winter in West Africa.

Yellow wagtails breed in two distinct types of country – in damp river valleys, water meadows, sewage farms and fresh and salt-marshes, and also on dry heaths and commons, moorland and arable land under crops. They often feed among cattle and horses, snatching at insects stirred up by the animals' hoofs.

In recent years, the numbers of yellow wagtails have fallen drastically and they have disappeared entirely from some localities. Likely reasons include land drainage, a loss of mixed farming regimes in favour of autumn-sown crops with fewer cattle and the early cutting of dense grass for silage.

The male is one of Britain's brightest birds. The deep yellow of its plumage is approached only by the colouring of the cock yellowhammer. Its brief, warbling song, punctuated with 'tsweep' call-notes, is heard mainly in May and is given either from a perch or in bouncing song-flight.

In one of its courtship ceremonies the male runs round the female with feathers fluffed out and wings quivering.

Grey wagtail – an expert at snatching insects from the air

MALE IN SUMMER

J F M A M J
J A S O N D

Grey wagtail Motacilla cinerea

In spite of its name, this is one of the most colourful of the wagtails. Its bright yellow underparts contrast boldly with its blue-grey back and long black tail whatever the time of year. The bird has a marked preference for being near water – especially rushing water. It flits along mountain streams, pausing now and again to perch on a boulder or overhead branch and flicking a tail as long as its body as it waits to dart out at an insect. In hilly country it is often seen in company with dippers.

In winter, the grey wagtail moves to lowland streams and may be found around cress beds, sewage farms and even small pools, but again seldom far from a weir or some other tumbling water.

The usual call is very like the pied wagtail's double-noted 'tschizzik', but is more metallic and staccato, and sometimes only a single 'tit'. The song, a shrill 'tsee-tee-tee', is not often heard. The male has a variety of courtship displays. In one, a slow-motion flight, the tail is fanned. In another, the bird runs towards the female on the ground and takes up a posture presenting its black throat.

While still most common in the hilly areas of the north and west, the grey wagtail has for many years been increasing in eastern and southern England.

RECOGNITION

Blue-grey above, yellow below, including tail feathers; long black tail with white sides; male's throat is black in summer, white in winter; female's slightly more buff.

NESTING

Female builds nest of moss and grass, lined with hair, usually in hole close to water; sometimes uses the old nest of dipper or other bird; lays April–June; usually 5 eggs, buff, faintly speckled with grey-brown; incubation 12 or 13 days, chiefly by female; nestlings, fed by both parents, fly after 12 days; sometimes two broods.

FEEDING

Mostly insects, including flies, small beetles, dragonfly nymphs; on coast, sandhoppers and small molluscs.

SIZE

20.25cm (8in) including 10.25cm (4in) tail

Sedge warbler's song is heard most frequently from April to July

Sedge warbler Acrocephalus schoenobaenus

RECOGNITION

Dark brown above, distinctly streaked; tawny rump; pale stripe over eye; pale buff below; sexes alike.

NESTING

Female builds shallow nest of dead grass and stalks, lined with hair, grass heads and sometimes feathers, hidden in waterside vegetation; lays May–July; 5 or 6 eggs, pale green or olive, well speckled with light grey-brown; incubation about 13 days, chiefly by female; nestlings, fed by both parents, leave after about 14 days; sometimes two broods.

FEEDING

Mostly insects, including gnats, crane-flies and other flies, beetles, aphids, spiders, caterpillars, small dragonflies.

SIZE

12.75cm (5in)

The rule that small, drab brown birds advertise themselves with the most melodious songs has to be stretched a little for the sedge warbler. Its song is a vigorous jumble of mixed-up notes, some sweet, but most of them harsh and grating. The few clear sweet notes, though, are well up to the standard expected of dull-coloured birds – when heard at night, they have been mistaken for the notes of a nightingale.

The sedge warbler is a good mimic, and often introduces snatches of other birds' songs in its hurried medley. All this may issue from deep inside a tangle of bushes, from an exposed perch, or during flight. In the excitement of courtship, the cock birds sometimes sing while performing an up-and-down flight with quivering wings and outspread tail. The bird also has a harsh churring and a scolding 'tuc' call.

The sedge warbler shows no special preference for sedge, but creeps in and out of any thick cover. It may be found wherever coarse vegetation grows up over bushes and hedgerows fairly near water, and more rarely in bushy places away from water.

Several nests may be located near one another, usually low among nettles or waterside plants, and seldom more than about 1m (4ft) from the ground. The female cuckoo finds the sedge warbler one of the more accessible of birds on which to impose its offspring.

Reed warbler weaves its nest around stiff reed stems

REED WARBLER

J F M **A M J**
J A S O N D

Reed warbler Acrocephalus scirpaceus

Without hearing their songs, the most expert ornithologist might hesitate before distinguishing a reed warbler from a marsh warbler (*Acrocephalus palustris*), but this is now no longer a serious consideration, because the marsh warbler has been almost lost as a breeding bird in Britain. The reed warbler's song, with a flow of 'churr-churr-churr … chirruc-chirruc-chirruc' notes, sounds rather like two pebbles being chinked together, and sometimes is varied with mimicry of other birds. The marsh warbler, an even better mimic, has a much louder, more musical song, with liquid canary-like notes, which the reed warbler rarely approaches.

As its name suggests, the reed warbler keeps almost entirely to reed-beds. It has a way of sidling restlessly up and down the stems and hopping from one to another. The marsh warbler, which has recently disappeared from its old stronghold in Worcestershire and is no more than an erratic breeder in the southeast of England, is at home in most waterside habitats, with a strong preference for osier beds.

Both are summer visitors, the first of the reed warblers beginning to arrive at the end of April, and the marsh warblers arriving nearly a month later. The reed warbler attaches a deep cup nest to the reeds, and this often attracts cuckoos. The marsh warbler makes a shallower structure, sometimes in a bed of nettles.

RECOGNITION

Brown above, light buff below, with whitish throat; brown of marsh warbler slightly less 'warm'; reed warbler's legs usually dark, marsh warbler's flesh pink; sexes alike in both cases.

NESTING

Female does most building in both cases; reed warbler's nest is deep cup of dried grasses usually in reed-bed; marsh warbler attaches shallow cup nest of grass, lined with finer grass and hair, to plant stems by 'basket handles'; lays May–July (reed) and June (marsh); usually 4 or 5 eggs, green-white with grey marks; incubation about 12 days, by both parents; young, fed by both parents, fly in about 11 or 12 days.

FEEDING

Marsh insects – flies, moths and larvae; berries in autumn.

SIZE

Both species: 12.75cm (5in)

J F M A M J
J A S O N D

Dipper stands in the middle of a stream, watching for food

Dipper Cinclus cinclus

RECOGNITION

Dark brown plumage with white breast; highly characteristic bobbing or dipping action; sexes alike.

NESTING

Both sexes build substantial domed nest, mainly of moss, lined with dead leaves; nest nearly always on ledge or in cavity close to water; frequently on bridges, sometimes under a waterfall; lays March–early May; 4 or 5 eggs, white; incubation about 17 days, by female only; nestlings, fed by both parents, fly after about 23 days; two broods.

FEEDING

Water-beetles, water-boatmen, caddis larvae and nymphs of dragonflies and mayflies; worms and tadpoles; minnows and other small fish.

SIZE

17.75cm (7in)

The idea that the dipper can defy the laws of specific gravity and walk along the river bottom was once ridiculed by some respected naturalists, but those who had seen it happen and stuck to the evidence of their eyes have been proved right. Experiments have demonstrated that when the bird walks upstream with its head down looking for food, the force of a fast current against its slanting back keeps it on the bottom.

However, a bird-watcher is far more likely to see the dipper's plump form simply entering the water either by wading or diving, or swimming buoyantly on the surface. Often it will perch for some time on a rock or stone in midstream, dipping its head and curtseying, as if hinged on its legs, its wren-like lyric of a song mingling with the splash of tumbling water.

The dipper is usually confined to fast-running streams in hilly districts in the north and west, but can sometimes be seen on shores of lakes in the hills, and in winter, when some immigrants arrive from the Continent, also by sea lochs. It is rarely seen far from water.

Its most common call-note is 'zit-zit-zit', and there is also a metallic 'clink-clink'. Courtship display includes posturing to show off the white breast, bowing and wing-quivering. Its flight is rapid and direct with short wings whirring.

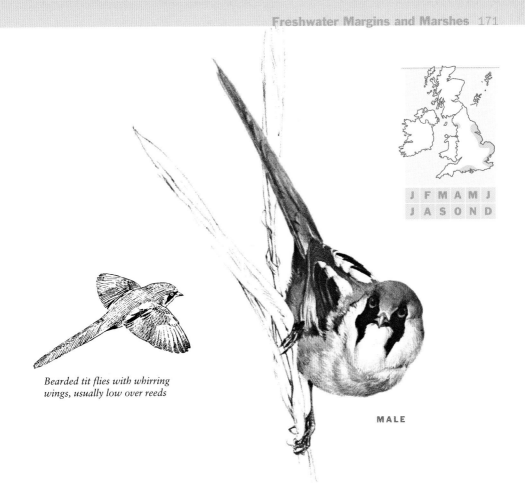

Bearded tit flies with whirring
wings, usually low over reeds

MALE

J F M A M J
J A S O N D

Bearded tit Panurus biarmicus

On cold days in the fens bearded tits snuggle together on the
same reed stem, the cock sheltering the hen under one wing so
that they form a single ball of feathers. Several observers have
recorded this, although the birds are often difficult to spot, deep
in the reed-beds.

Hard weather takes a heavy toll among these small birds. In
the winter of 1947 their numbers on the Norfolk Broads were
reduced almost to extinction point, and long before this their
future looked precarious, because of the reclamation of
marshlands, coupled with the demands of collectors who
offered high prices for their eggs. Fortunately, and with the help
of some protection, they have recovered from all these
misfortunes. At the RSPB reserve at Minsmere in Suffolk, their
population has built up to the point where there is a substantial
emigration almost every autumn.

The bearded tit is, in fact, misnamed. Its 'beard' is a
facial stripe that looks more like a moustache, and scientists
have decided that the bird is not related to the tits, but to
the thrushes.

In courtship, the male lifts its crown feathers, puffs out its
'beard', and fans out its tail. The hen responds with a kind of
dance, also spreading its tail, and sometimes the pair rise in a
slow flight together. They breed only in extensive reed and sedge
beds, and during winter they wander in small parties.

RECOGNITION

Tawny back, long tail;
male's black 'beard'
is more like a flowing
moustache; female has
no black on head or
tail coverts.

NESTING

Both sexes build nest of
sedge or reed blades, just
above water in beds of
reeds or sedge; nest lined
with reed flowers by male;
lays April–July; 5–7 eggs,
creamy-white, speckled and
finely lined with brown;
incubation about 13 days,
by both parents; nestlings,
fed by both parents, fly
after 9–12 days; two or
more broods.

FEEDING

Almost entirely insects,
their larvae and reed seeds
in winter; freshwater
molluscs and other small
animals at times.

SIZE

16.5cm (6½in) including
7.5cm (3in) tail

MALE IN
SUMMER

*Female reed bunting in
nest built close to ground*

J F M A M J
J A S O N D

Reed bunting Emberiza schoeniclus

RECOGNITION

Male in breeding season
has black head, black throat
and white collar, dark brown
streaked back, greyish
rump, grey-white below;
head pattern obscured in
winter; female is streaked
brown, lighter below with
black and white moustache
stripe.

NESTING

Female builds nest of dry
grass, lined with hair and
finer grass, usually in
tussock or on ground
among vegetation; lays
April–June; 3–5 eggs, olive-
buff or pale green, marked
with black; incubation about
14 days, mainly by hen;
nestlings, fed by both
parents, fly after about
12 days.

FEEDING

Mainly seeds of marsh
plants; some animal food,
including freshwater snails,
beetles, caterpillars and
other insects.

SIZE

15.25cm (6in)

Both the cock bird, conspicuous with its white collar against a
black head, and the drably coloured female, use a bluff that is
uncommon among small perching birds. If surprised, they may
divert attention from the nest by shuffling along the ground
with wings half spread as if broken.

The reed bunting is often seen bounding along in short jerky
flight or flicking its tail on a perch as it delivers its rather
indifferent song, a succession of squeaky 'tweek-tweek-tweek-
tititick' notes. Courtship consists mainly of fast pursuits, often
ending in squabbling rough-and-tumbles. The male also puffs
out its white collar for its mate's benefit. Not all form simple
pairs. A few males run a string of nests, each with its own
female and brood.

Many reed buntings stay in Britain all the year, although they
move south in the autumn. Others visit Britain in the summer,
and a number from northern Europe fly in for the winter, in the
same way as some British nesting birds head south. Marshy
places and riversides are their favourite nesting areas, but in
recent years, despite an overall decline, there has been an
expansion into drier places, such as chalk downs. Reed buntings
have even been seen feeding with chaffinches and sparrows at
some suburban birdtables.

Lakes, Rivers and Reservoirs

Britain's open inland waters are a haven for swimming and diving birds that are retreating before the onset of bitter northern European and Siberian winters. Attracted by the prospect of waters that are not regularly frozen over, they join resident populations in the day-long search for food.

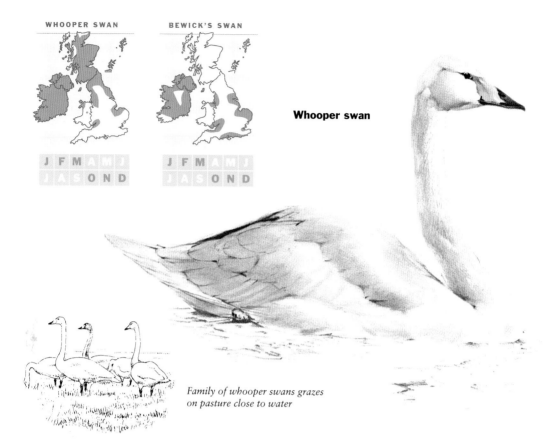

WHOOPER SWAN   BEWICK'S SWAN

J F M A M J
J A S O N D

J F M A M J
J A S O N D

Whooper swan

Family of whooper swans grazes
on pasture close to water

Whooper swan Cygnus cygnus

RECOGNITION

White; long bill, black at tip
with triangular yellow patch
at base; Bewick's smaller,
white, slightly concave bill,
with smaller, more rounded,
yellow patch; sexes alike in
both cases.

NESTING

On islets; build large
mound of moss and lichen
or dried plants, with
depression for eggs; lays
late May–early June; usually
5 or 6 eggs, creamy-white;
incubation 35–42 days, by
female; cygnets, tended
by both parents, fly after
about 8 weeks. Bewick's
lays June; 3–5 eggs,
creamy-white; no reliable
data on incubation; cygnets,
tended by both parents, fly
at about 6 weeks.

FEEDING

Seeds, water plants; insects
and molluscs (whooper).

SIZE

Whooper: 153cm (60in)
Bewick's: 122cm (48in)

A winter visitor to Britain, the whooper swan flies in from
northern Europe and Russia, in company with the smaller
Bewick's swan (*Cygnus columbianus*). The whooper was once
a British breeding bird, but became extinct in Orkney in the
18th century and has so far failed to re-establish itself,
although pairs have bred occasionally in Scotland. Some
15,000 spend the winter in Britain and Ireland, mostly in
Scotland and East Anglia. Around 9,000 Bewick's swans
winter in East Anglia, especially on fenland, and in decreasing
numbers at the Wildfowl & Wetlands Trust reserve in
Slimbridge, in Gloucestershire.

Both swans carry their necks stiffly erect, instead of in the
mute swan's gentle curve, and both are noisier. The voice of the
whooper is a powerful, trumpeting 'ahng-ha'. The Bewick's –
named after Thomas Bewick (1753–1828), a famous illustrator
of birds – has a softer, higher pitched voice. It usually gives a
'hoo' or 'ho' note, or makes a honking sound.

The whooper's courtship display consists of a sinuous
up-and-down movement of the head and neck with the wings
outspread. Similar behaviour is the preliminary to an attack on
another male – just before it attacks, the bird partly spreads its
wings and lowers its head, sometimes to the point where the
head is below water. After mating, the female starts to call and
the male joins in, spreading its wings as the two birds rise
breast-to-breast in the water.

MALE

J F M A M J
J A S O N D

*Pair of mute swans perform
pre-mating ceremony*

Mute swan Cygnus olor

Legend says that Richard the Lionheart brought the first mute
swans home from Cyprus after the Third Crusade, but they
were probably breeding wild in England long before this.
They gradually became semi-domesticated because of their
value as ornamental birds and as a luxury food. For centuries
the Crown controlled the ownership of swans through royal
swanherds and courts called 'swanmotes'. Privately owned
swans were pinioned to prevent them from flying away, and
branded or nicked in the skin of the upper bill as a mark of
ownership. In the reign of Elizabeth I, 900 distinct swanmarks
were recognised.

   Until recently the custom of marking was preserved in the
swan-upping ceremony on the Thames every summer, when
cygnets' bills were nicked by the bargemaster of the Dyers'
Company or the swanmarker of the Vintners' Company. One
nick meant that a bird was owned by the Dyers and two that it
was a Vintners' swan. An unmarked bird on the Thames
belongs to the Queen, as seigneur of the swans. There was a
similar ceremony on the rivers Yare and Wensum near Norwich.

   In the past 100 years, mute swans have been allowed to
escape from bondage and are now common wild breeding birds.
They are not as silent as their name suggests – mute swans snort
and hiss when annoyed, and some produce a weak trumpeting.
But the legendary 'swan song' – the music said to be made by a
dying swan – is a myth, with no foundation in fact.

RECOGNITION

White plumage; orange bill
with black base and knob
(less prominent in female);
long neck, usually carried in
a curve; sexes alike.

NESTING

On ground near water;
male brings sticks and
reeds, which female
arranges in a huge pile; lays
March–May; usually 5–7
eggs, grey-green; incubation
about 36 days, by both
parents; cygnets, tended
by both parents, leave after
1 or 2 days, fly after about
4 months.

FEEDING

Chiefly water vegetation;
some small frogs, fish and
insects.

SIZE

153cm (60in)

Canada goose flies heavily with slow, regular wing-beats

J F M A M J
J A S O N D

Canada goose Branta canadensis

Grey-brown plumage; black head and neck with white chin-patch extending upwards behind the eye; sexes alike.

Female lines ground depression, on lake islands or marshlands, with dead leaves, grass and down; nest usually well hidden in vegetation; lays April–May; usually 5 or 6 eggs, dirty white; incubation about 28 days, by female only; nestlings, tended by female, leave soon after they hatch, fly after about 6 weeks.

Almost completely vegetable, chiefly grass; some insects in summer.

96.5cm (38in)

The handsome appearance of the Canada goose, with its striking black head and neck and white chin-patch, led to its introduction as an ornamental bird from North America more than 300 years ago. A number of geese escaped from the lakes of Victorian collectors and established themselves as wild birds, particularly beside lakes, broads and meres in Norfolk, Cheshire, Shropshire and the Thames Valley. The Canada goose population in Britain has increased enormously, from about 3,000 birds in 1953 to as many as 82,000 adult birds today.

Canada geese are sociable birds. They form flocks of up to 2,000 outside the breeding season, and often whole colonies make their nests together near lowland lakes – close to marshes and pastures where they graze during the day. Courtship ceremonies include neck-stretching, with the head and neck held out parallel to the ground. When they are pairing in springtime, the birds are particularly noisy, trumpeting out their loud 'ker-honk' calls.

In winter some Canada geese leave the inland waterways and move out to the coast, feeding on estuaries and salt-marshes. They are heavy fliers, but fast and direct. For long journeys they travel in 'V' formations in the air, trailing each other in a head-to-tail file or spreading out across the sky in an oblique line.

*Duck (front) and two drake
wigeon rest on the water*

MALE

Wigeon Anas penelope

A piping 'whee-oo' call gives the drake wigeon away even in
fog or at a distance. A number of them often chorus the call as
they crowd around a duck, raising the crest feathers of their
chestnut and cream heads. The duck's answering call is a
purring sound. Later in courtship, the paired drake and duck
raise the tips of their wings and cross them almost vertically
over their backs.

About 70 years ago, wigeon were expanding as a British
breeding species, but this advance has now come to a halt,
and as far as is known there is no regular breeding south of
Yorkshire. Lochs, rivers and inland marshes, especially in
wooded country, are their favourite breeding habitat, although
they occasionally nest on coastal marshes. The nest is always
built on the ground, and several pairs may breed in the same
area, the drakes standing guard over the ducks during
incubation. Outside the breeding season, they gather mainly
on the coasts, flocking inland at dusk to crop the grass in fields
and meadows, but some winter inland, in flooded districts and
on large lakes and reservoirs.

Wigeon are highly gregarious. Flocks hundreds strong rest by
day on estuaries and mudflats, rising straight out of the water
together when disturbed and keeping in tight formation during
their rapid flights.

RECOGNITION

Drake has chestnut head
with creamy-buff forehead
and crown, white forewing,
grey upper parts, green
wing-patch; duck has grey-
green wing-patch, is
slimmer and has more
pointed tail than mallard
duck; in eclipse plumage
(June–October or November)
male looks like dark female,
but with white forewing.

NESTING

Duck makes nest on ground
among heather or bracken,
lined with grass and down;
lays May; usually 7 or 8
eggs, creamy-buff;
incubation about 25 days,
by duck only; ducklings,
tended by duck, leave soon
after hatching, fly after
about 40 days.

FEEDING

Mainly grasses; grain; also
eel-grass from mudflats.

SIZE

45.75cm (18in)

MALE

Feeding gadwall dabbles in the water for roots and plants

<table>
<tr><td>J</td><td>F</td><td>M</td><td>A</td><td>M</td><td>J</td></tr>
<tr><td>J</td><td>A</td><td>S</td><td>O</td><td>N</td><td>D</td></tr>
</table>

Gadwall **Anas strepera**

RECOGNITION

Both sexes grey-brown at distance; white patches on back of wings; duck like female mallard with white belly, yellower legs; in eclipse plumage (June–late August) drake browner, like duck.

NESTING

Duck lines hollow, in thick cover near water, with dead leaves, sedges and down; lays May; usually 8–12 eggs, yellow-buff; incubation about 28 days, by duck only; ducklings, tended by duck, leave soon after hatching, fly in about 7 weeks.

FEEDING

Leaves and roots of sedges and other water plants; some small snails and worms.

SIZE

51cm (20in)

The history of the gadwall as a British breeding species goes back little more than about a century and a half. In 1850 a pair of migrant birds caught in a decoy were introduced on the Breckland meres in East Anglia, and it seems likely that some of the English breeding colonies are descended from these two birds. Their advance was slow but has gathered pace since 1970, so that possibly around 1,000 pairs may now nest regularly in the British Isles.

From their main stronghold in East Anglia, they have spread to many other parts of England, especially flooded gravel pits. There are other gadwall concentrations in and around Lough Neagh in Northern Ireland, and Loch Leven in Kinross, and the ducks breed sporadically elsewhere in Scotland and Ireland. These Scottish and Irish birds probably represent a natural spread from the main breeding areas in eastern Europe, southern Scandinavia and Iceland. Migrating birds, which visit Britain in small numbers in winter, appear on the coasts and rest on estuaries and coastal waters during their journeys. However, gadwalls generally prefer quiet inland lakes and reservoirs, and slow-moving streams thickly surrounded by vegetation.

The drake has a deep nasal croak, 'whek', and the duck's quack is soft. Courtship displays include mock preening.

Duck (front) dabbles for food while drake upends

MALE

J F M A M J
J A S O N D

Mallard Anas platyrhynchos

Probably the best-known among British ducks are the green-headed drake mallard and its dark brown mate. They have learnt to live alongside humans in the ponds of town and city parks, and their courtship displays have become so familiar that they are sometimes overlooked. When several drakes chase a duck through the air in the autumn, this is an important part of mate selection. As the display develops, the drakes swim round the duck, sometimes with their necks stretched out along the surface of the water.

Late in the breeding season, bands of drakes chase ducks again, and try to mate with them by force, without going through the proper courtship routine. This is especially common in areas where nests are crowded together. Early in the year, pairs of mallard fly off to their breeding grounds, which are located near stretches of water or sea lochs. They usually nest close to the ground, but sometimes they use a hollow tree or the abandoned nest of another bird. The duck makes a loud quacking sound like a farmyard duck, while the drake mallard has a softer, higher-pitched call-note, 'quork' or 'quek'.

At dusk, regular flights of mallard take off for farmland – often well away from any stretch of water – to feed on grain and weeds. Some mallards that live in towns are reputed to drown and swallow sparrows.

RECOGNITION

Drake has glossy green head, white collar and purple-brown breast; duck is brown; both have purple wing-patch; in eclipse plumage (July–September) drake is almost identical to duck, but slightly darker; hybrids with domestic ducks are often black or white.

NESTING

Builds well-hidden nest, usually on ground, from leaves and grass, lined with down; lays February–May; usually 7–16 eggs, pale grey-green or olive-buff; incubation about 28 days, by duck only; ducklings, usually tended by female only, leave soon after hatching, fly at about, 6½ weeks.

FEEDING

Mainly seeds, buds and stems of water plants; some animal food.

SIZE

58.5cm (23in)

Drake garganey throws back its head in courtship display

FEMALE

MALE

Garganey Anas querquedula

J F M A M J
J A S O N D

RECOGNITION

Drake has white streak from eye to nape of neck, mottled brown breast, and grey flanks; duck mainly speckled brown, both sexes distinguished from teal by obscure wing-patch and pale grey forewing and bolder face stripes; in eclipse plumage (July–October) drake is much like duck.

NESTING

Duck lines space in rushes or long grass near water with grass and down; lays late April–May; usually 10 or 11 eggs, creamy-buff; incubation about 22 days, by duck only; ducklings, tended by duck, leave soon after hatching, fly after 30 days.

FEEDING

Buds and leaves of pond-weeds; some water-beetles, shellfish, young fish.

SIZE

38cm (15in)

On their migration flights of 3,000 miles and more from equatorial Africa to their breeding grounds in Europe, garganeys have to run the gauntlet of hunters with guns, especially in Latin countries, and despite their fast flight, many are shot. Some making for Scandinavia pass through Britain – where they used to be known as 'summer teal' in some areas – and small numbers stay to breed.

They are less gregarious than teal, and are rarely seen in large parties. In common with teal, breeding birds show a preference for thick cover, and nest near freshwater, particularly on marshes and fenland and in damp meadows. They nest regularly only where they can find this kind of environment – in Yorkshire, Somerset and southeastern England from Norfolk to Sussex – and are among the rarest of Britain's breeding birds. Fewer than 70 pairs nest here. They are early migrants, arriving towards the end of March, and the last stragglers fly south again at the end of October.

Another country name for the garganey is the 'cricket teal', because the drake's croaking courtship call sounds like a cricket's chirping. Drakes give this call as a number of them fly after a single duck. The duck will pair off with the last drake to keep up the pursuit. A wide range of courtship displays takes place on the water.

J F M A M J
J A S O N D

MALE

Teal often nest on moors or bogs, well away from open water

Teal Anas crecca

Compact flocks of teal perform rapid aerial manoeuvres outside the breeding season, wheeling together rather like waders. Their reactions to danger are also rapid – they catapult themselves almost vertically into the air and dash away in twisting, swerving flight. This quick response to any threat is a vital survival factor. Teal often live on sheltered, tree-fringed pools where cover is thick and there is little warning of a predator's approach.

Secluded rushy moorland, freshwater marshes, peat mosses and the edges of lakes are their favourite nesting sites, and they will often go some distance from water to find cover for their nests among gorse or bracken. In winter, teal leave their moorland breeding sites and fly to estuaries and mudflats on the coasts, or to sewage farms and flooded districts.

The handsome drake has a whistling 'crrick, crrick' call-note, and the duck has a short, high-pitched quack. In the courtship display, the drake dips its bill in the water, rises from the surface, then arches its neck to draw the bill in again.

Britain's smallest native duck, the teal is widely distributed in Scotland and Ireland, and breeds in most of the counties of north and east England, thinning out southwards and westwards.

RECOGNITION

Drake has grey upper parts and chestnut head with metallic green stripe around eye, running to nape of neck, and white stripe above wing; both sexes have green and black wing-patch; in eclipse plumage (July–October) drake is much like female, with browner upper parts.

NESTING

Duck lines hollow in ground, among thick undergrowth, with dead leaves, bracken and down; lays April–May; usually 8—10 eggs, pale buff, often with green tinge; incubation about 21 days, by duck only; ducklings, tended mainly by duck, leave soon after hatching, fly after about 23 days.

FEEDING

Water-weeds and their seeds; some insects, worms and molluscs.

SIZE

35.5cm (14in)

Pintail duck is greyer and more delicate than mallard duck

J F M A M J
J A S O N D

MALE

Pintail Anas acuta

The long, sharply pointed tail, from which this bird gets its name, is just one of the features that make the male unmistakable. Its chocolate-coloured head, pale grey back and white bib help to distinguish it as one of the most elegant of British ducks. The female is dowdy by comparison but, as with many ducks, this means she is inconspicuous to predators during the nesting season. The female also has an extended tail, but it is not as long as the male's, which can grow to a length of more than 20cm (8in).

Pintails walk easily, even gracefully for a duck, and fly rapidly, particularly when disturbed. In Britain their breeding tends to be sporadic and they rarely keep to the same sites for more than a few years. At present, they appear to nest in three places in England and three in Scotland. Fifty years ago they bred regularly in just three places in Britain, all of them in Scotland, and none in places where pintails nest today. This habit of deserting a site makes their numbers difficult to assess, but a general increase in the breeding population has come to a halt in recent years.

The male guards the nest during incubation, and a distraction display has been recorded in which the drake flies just above the ground, with legs dangling, as though in difficulties.

MALE

Shoveler collects food with its highly specialised bill

| J | F | M | A | M | J |
| J | A | S | O | N | D |

Shoveler Spatula clypeata

The enormous heavy bill that gives the shoveler its name is specially adapted for feeding on the surface of ponds and lakes. The duck paddles quickly through the shallows, holding its head low and thrusting its spoon-like bill forward in the water or thin mud. By this means, it scoops up tiny plants and animals, sieving out what it doesn't want. Unlike most surface-feeding ducks, shovelers rarely upend to pick up food under the water, but they may dive if alarmed.

They are clumsy on land, and their bills give them a top-heavy look, but they are active fliers, particularly in spring, when duck and drake circle their territory in a courtship flight. The drake chases its mate, issuing a throaty 'took-took' call-note. The duck has a double quack, but outside the breeding season shovelers are usually quiet birds.

Shovelers are found in varying numbers over most of Britain, most frequently in East Anglia, but their distribution is local. The main reason for this is probably a shortage of suitable breeding sites. For breeding, they prefer marshes, damp meadows and sewage farms with plenty of cover, although they breed sometimes beside more open lakes, provided that shallow muddy water is available, where they can feed. In winter they spread to almost any kind of inland shallow water.

RECOGNITION

Both sexes have huge bill and pale blue patch on forewings; drake has dark green head, white breast and chestnut sides; duck has speckled brown underparts; in eclipse plumage (May–December) drake is much like duck, but darker.

NESTING

Duck lines deep hollow in dry ground with grass and down; surrounding grass stems sometimes form a 'tent'; lays April–May; usually 8–12 eggs, buff or green; incubation about 24 days, by duck only; ducklings, tended by duck, leave soon after hatching, fly after 40 days.

FEEDING

Animal and vegetable food in equal amounts – freshwater insects and shellfish mixed with seeds, buds and leaves of water plants.

SIZE

51cm (20in)

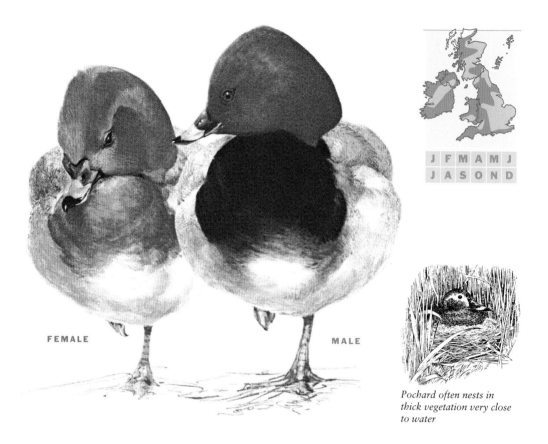

FEMALE   MALE

Pochard often nests in thick vegetation very close to water

Pochard Aythya ferina

RECOGNITION

Drake has chestnut-red head, black breast, grey body; distinguished from drake wigeon by absence of cream crown and white forewing; duck is brown with pale mark around bill, distinguished from tufted duck by absence of white wing-bar in flight; in eclipse plumage (July–September) drake looks like duck with greyer back.

NESTING

Nests in cover over or near water on a pile of vegetation, lined with down by duck; lays late April–early May; usually 6–11 eggs, green-grey; incubation about 28 days, by duck; ducklings, tended by duck, swim a few hours after hatching, fly after 7½ weeks.

FEEDING

Roots, leaves and buds of water-weeds; small water animals.

SIZE

45.75cm (18in)

In the lakes of many town parks, small parties of pochards may be seen swimming and diving in autumn and winter, when the chestnut-headed birds are among Britain's most common freshwater ducks. By the time the breeding season comes round, however, most pochards have vanished. They fly off to breed in eastern Europe and only about 400 pairs stay to nest in Britain, most of them in the southeast.

Pochards breed around inland lakes and slow-moving streams that have beds of iris or reeds where they can dive for food, although they sometimes upend like surface-feeding ducks. They build their nests close to the water, or even above it, in a thick clump of vegetation, and rarely venture on to land. The position of their legs, set well back for diving and underwater swimming, makes them front heavy and clumsy when they walk.

They are reluctant fliers, too, preferring to swim away from danger. To take off, pochards have to patter across the surface of the water in typical diving-duck manner. Once launched, they fly fast, often in tight formation, forming flocks sometimes hundreds strong.

Pochards are quiet except when courting. Then the drakes hold up their heads, puff out their necks and give a soft, wheezing whistle. The ducks reply with a harsh, growling 'kurr' sound.

*Tufted duck dives for food
in water usually about
60–180cm (2–6ft) deep*

MALE

FEMALE

J F M A M J
J A S O N D

Tufted duck Aythya fuligula

Unknown as a breeding species in Britain at the beginning of
the 19th century, the tufted duck is now the most common of
the country's diving ducks. About 10,000 pairs breed in Britain
and Ireland, and in winter visitors flock in from northern
Europe and Iceland, spreading out to reservoirs and other
stretches of inland freshwater. In the breeding season, tufted
ducks usually keep to lakes and ponds that are fringed with
rushes and other plants to provide cover. They nest in colonies,
generally close to the water and often on islands. Gregarious
birds, tufted ducks are usually seen in parties of a few dozen,
although sometimes in much bigger flocks, and they mix freely
with pochards and coots.

   Although they are wary in the wild, they become quite tame
wherever they are protected, and often set up their colonies in
lakes in city parks – in St James's Park, London, for example.

   When they dive, tufted ducks pick up both animal and
vegetable food before bobbing back to the surface, but they
seem to prefer weeds and grasses to the small freshwater
shellfish and insects that form the animal part of their diet.

   Courtship is simple. The drake tilts back his handsome head
and whistles very softly to the duck. She dips her bill repeatedly
into the water and gives a raucous, growling call.

RECOGNITION

Drake has long drooping
crest; white flanks contrast
boldly with rest of plumage,
which is dark; duck is
browner with smaller crest;
both have white wing-bar in
flight; in eclipse plumage
(July–October) drake looks
like duck, but is darker.

NESTING

Duck lays foundation of
grass and reeds on ground
near waterside, lines it with
down; lays late May–June;
usually 6–14 eggs, pale
grey-green; incubation
about 24 days, by duck
only; ducklings, tended by
duck, swim and dive in a
few hours, fly after about
6 weeks.

FEEDING

Water plants; also water
animals, including insects,
frogs, spawn and small fish.

SIZE

43cm (17in)

JFMAMJ
JASOND

MALE

Displaying drake goldeneye lays its head back and raises its bill

Goldeneye Bucephala clangula

RECOGNITION

Drake has black and white body, black head with green sheen and a white circle in front of the eye; duck is grey with brown head, white collar and wing-patches; in eclipse plumage (August–October or December) drake is like duck, but keeps some dark green head feathers.

NESTING

Duck lines hole in tree with wood chips, feathers and down; lays mid-April; usually 6–15 eggs, pale blue-green; incubation 26–30 days, by duck only; ducklings, tended by duck, leave after a day, scrambling out of nest and tumbling to ground, fly after 55 days.

FEEDING

Small water animals, mostly shellfish and insects.

SIZE

45.75cm (18in)

In the region of 30,000 goldeneyes are believed to visit the British Isles in winter, but only since 1970 has breeding been recorded. In each year since then, increasing numbers have nested in tree-holes or in nesting boxes specially provided for them in the Scottish Highlands. Currently, about 200 pairs nest annually.

The winter visitors arrive about the middle of September, settling to feed on estuaries and sheltered coastal waters, as well as inland lakes, reservoirs and rivers. They are tireless divers, often travelling underwater in preference to paddling along the surface. Their rapidly beating wings make a loud, whistling noise as the ducks take off, rising directly into the air instead of pattering along the water like other diving ducks. They usually form small parties, but flocks of 1,000 or more of the yellow-eyed birds can be seen regularly in some places, such as the Firth of Forth.

Goldeneyes may turn up on the Scottish lochs in summer, performing their complicated courtship ceremonies in which a drake swims round a duck, lifting his head and tail and occasionally kicking up water.

Generally, they are quiet birds, although the duck makes a gutteral grunting noise. When they are excited, they stretch up their necks and puff out the feathers on their triangular heads, making them look swollen.

Duck's white throat and cheeks contrast with its darker head

MALE

Smew Mergus albellus

Wildfowlers used to call this duck 'white nun' because of its black and white plumage, but the description fits the drake only. The female is smaller and greyer, and has a chestnut-brown patch on the top of head and nape. At rest, the drake smew looks mostly white, with just a few black markings, but when airborne it appears blacker.

The smew is the smallest of Britain's three saw-billed ducks, so called because their bills have serrated edges for keeping a grip on slippery fish. It is a winter visitor and has never bred in Britain. The nearest nesting sites are in northern Scandinavia, where the bird chooses a hole in a tree, usually near water, and lines it with down. In an average winter, the number of visitors is unlikely to be more than a hundred or so, and these are mostly confined to large reservoirs in Somerset, Essex and the London area, and flooded gravel pits in Kent.

Smews constantly dive after fish. They have a rather laboured take-off, like diving ducks, and walk with an ungainly waddle, but they fly strongly. They are silent birds on the water, although an occasional harsh 'karr' may be uttered. In flight they are also silent – their wings do not make the whistling sound associated with other saw-bills.

The smews' courtship ceremonies, which may be seen late in winter just before they migrate, include various crest-raising and head-bobbing movements.

RECOGNITION

Male white with black markings, looks more black with white foreparts in flight; female grey with bold white cheeks and red-brown cap and nape; large white wing-patches; short grey bill.

NESTING

Does not breed in Britain; nest, in tree-hole and usually near water, is lined with down; lays May; usually 6–9 eggs, creamy-buff; incubation, by female only, believed to be 4 weeks; ducklings, tended by female, fly after 5–6 weeks.

FEEDING

Large variety of small fish, shrimps, snails and water-beetles.

SIZE

43cm (17in)

MALE

J F M A M J
J A S O N D

*Red-breasted merganser's nest
is screened by vegetation*

Red-breasted merganser Mergus serrator

RECOGNITION

Drake has dark green head
with double crest, chestnut
breast, grey and white back;
duck browner than
goosander, with fuzzy crest,
blurred white throat,
brownish-grey body.

NESTING

Duck makes lining of leaves
and down in hollow in
ground, well screened by
thick vegetation; lays May–
early July; 7–12 eggs,
olive-buff, sometimes with
blue tinge; eggs covered
with down when duck leaves
nest; incubation about
28 days, by duck only;
ducklings, tended by duck,
leave shortly after hatching,
fly after about 5 weeks.

FEEDING

Small fish, eels, crabs,
shrimps; worms and
insects.

SIZE

58.5cm (23in)

Although this handsome duck is now a protected species throughout Britain, thanks to the Wildlife and Countryside Act 1981, licences to kill it are issued freely in Scotland under the same act, despite the fact that salmon and trout – the two fish that matter most to anglers in Scotland – do not form a large part of its diet.

Before 1981 mergansers were unprotected in Scotland, but even so they became widespread there. Breeding birds are found on many rivers and lochs and in low-lying coastal areas. They are also common in Ireland and in the past 30 years have colonised northwest England and north and central Wales. Given a chance, they may well spread farther south as breeders.

In winter, red-breasted mergansers prefer salt water to freshwater, and visit estuaries all round the coasts of the British Isles. Flocks several hundred strong occur regularly on some estuaries in Scotland.

The red-breasted merganser is a saw-billed duck, equipped with serrations on its bill, so that wriggling fish cannot slip away. The drake is easily recognised by the untidy double crest on its head, which is dark green but looks almost black from a distance.

Its courtship, displays include much bowing and gesturing with the head and bill, raising the crest, arching the wings and pattering along the water in a cloud of spray.

MALE

Goosander – one of the few ducks that nest in tree-holes

J F M A M J
J A S O N D

Goosander Mergus merganser

This largest of the British saw-billed ducks has been rather too efficient for its own good at the task of catching fish. Like the red-breasted merganser, it is unpopular with anglers. When the goosander began to colonise the Tweed Valley in the course of its steady upward spread, water bailiffs succeeded in temporarily exterminating it there. In fact, although the bird lives largely on fish, it takes relatively few salmon or trout. Despite this persecution, goosanders have spread to other parts of Scotland and northern England in the past 120 years, and more recently to Wales, the Peak district and south Devon. They are now protected by law.

Goosanders become more widespread in the winter and numbers may reach 100 or more on large English reservoirs – those close to London, for example. On land, they look ungainly, but on water they come into their own. Highly efficient underwater swimmers, they are able to stay down for longer than a minute. Often they are mistaken for divers or large grebes, but no grebe or diver has the drake's pattern of dark green head and neck, and white or pinkish body plumage, or the duck's chestnut head and white chin.

In courtship, the male stands up in the water, stretches its neck and raises its crest feathers. The courtship display also includes a sexual chase. The call of both sexes is restricted to a harsh 'krarr' or 'kraah'.

RECOGNITION

Straight, deep red bill; male has dark green glossy head and neck, and grey rump, with salmon-pink underparts; duck smaller, with red-brown head, shaggy crest, sharply defined white chin and clear grey back.

NESTING

Nests in a tree-hole, or cavity in a bank; duck lines cavity with rotten wood, leaves and feathers; lays April–June; 7–13 eggs, creamy-white; incubation about 5 weeks, by duck only; ducklings, tended by duck, leave after a few days, fly after about 5 weeks.

FEEDING

Small fish, shrimps and frogs; some caterpillars and other insects.

SIZE

66cm (26in)

The shape of a red-throated diver in flight, this one in winter

SUMMER

J F M A M J
J A S O N D

Red-throated diver Gavia stellata

Red patch on the throat in summer; rest of neck grey; back and wings brown with paler underparts; female smaller, but similar in plumage; both lose red patch in autumn; distinguished in winter from black-throat by more white on face, uptilted bill and white speckles on back.

Eggs laid on the ground or on a heap of water-weed; lays May; 2 eggs, olive-green, spotted with brown; incubation about 28 days, by both parents; chicks, tended by both parents, leave shortly after hatching, fly in about 8 weeks.

Char, dace, perch, gudgeon, herring, flounders, sprats, shrimps, mussels; some insects.

61cm (24in)

The courtship ceremonies of most ducks, bizarre though many of them are, have nothing to equal the displays of the red-throated diver. Up to four divers race across the water, with bodies half-submerged and heads and necks pointed forwards and upwards, looking like the long-extinct plesiosaur. As well as swimming, they sometimes patter along the surface, beating the water with their wings, and during these courtship displays they utter metallic-sounding cries, sometimes starting with a long, loud, mewing wail.

This wail – which is also the bird's cry at other times, along with a 'kwuk-kwuk-kwuk' given in flight – earned it the old country nickname of 'rain goose'. People believed that when they heard the cry, rain was on the way. Another country name, 'sprat loon', comes from its feeding habits, although the red-throated diver eats many other kinds of fish as well as sprats.

Red-throated divers nest in the Highlands and Scottish islands, and have established an outpost in County Donegal in northwestern Ireland, where a few pairs breed regularly. Attempts to colonise the mainland of southwest Scotland during the 1950s were not successful, but as visitors, the birds are widespread in British coastal waters, especially off East Anglia. Those found inland in winter are either storm-driven or sick.

SUMMER

Black-throated diver in winter is dark grey above and white below

Black-throated diver Gavia arctica

A black-throated diver has been known to swim for 400m (¹/4 mile) underwater before coming up for air. Part of the price these birds pay for being such good swimmers is that on land they are clumsy. In fact, they rarely visit land except to nest, and even then they choose somewhere very close to the waterside to lay their eggs. Black-throated divers have a superficial resemblance to cormorants and shags, but they can be identified by their manner of swimming – a black-throated diver holds its head and bill straight instead of tilted upwards.

About 170 breeding pairs of black-throated divers are to be found in Britain, and most of them are confined to the larger freshwater lochs of the Highlands and Scottish islands although, since the 1950s, they have also nested on Arran and occasionally elsewhere in southwestern Scotland. In winter they are much more widespread, although still not common. At this time of year, many appear on the east coast of England.

In their flight, which is direct and fast, black-throated divers give a barking 'kwuk-kwuk-kwuk' flight-note in the breeding season. Their other calls at this time include a loud hoot, a mournful-sounding wail, and a special cry given during courtship when paired birds fly off. Before pairing up there is a good deal of chasing about on the water, and the female may turn somersaults as she leads the male in this sexual chase.

RECOGNITION

Black throat and striped neck in summer; these become white in winter; distinguished from winter red-throated diver by straight bill, more extensive darker grey on head and neck and blacker back.

NESTING

No proper nest; eggs laid on the ground, very close to water, and exceptionally on a heap of water-weed; lays May–June; 2 eggs, pale green or brown, sparsely marked with black; incubation about 28 days, by one or both parents; chicks, tended by both parents, leave shortly after hatching, fly in about 9 weeks.

FEEDING

Trout, perch, roach, herrings, sprats, crabs, prawns, mussels.

SIZE

68.5cm (27in)

SUMMER

J F M A M J
J A S O N D

Little grebe in winter – its plumage is paler than in summer

Little grebe Tachybaptus ruficollis

RECOGNITION

In summer, dark brown with rusty-red face and black cap; in winter, pale buffy-brown with paler face; pale spot at base of beak. Plain brown wings.

NESTING

Both sexes build nest on a floating tangle of water-weeds, either grounded on or anchored by vegetation; lays April–July; 4–6 eggs, white, soon stained by damp weed; incubation about 24 days, by both parents; chicks, tended by both parents, able to swim almost at birth; two broods, sometimes three.

FEEDING

Small fish, especially sticklebacks; shrimps; dragonfly nymphs, water-beetles and other water insects, and water molluscs.

SIZE

23cm (9in)

The courtship of the little grebe centres around a strange love duet – the male and female face one another on the water and embark on a trilling song. There is some scuffling and chasing, and sometimes the male will give the female a symbolic present of weeds.

The little grebe, also called the dabchick, is the smallest of the British grebes, and is widespread on inland waters. It breeds on ponds, lakes, slow-moving rivers and sometimes in town parks. In summer, the pale patch on the bird's face is a good guide to identification. The male has black on its chin, and chestnut on its cheeks, neck and breast. In winter, the chin becomes white and the chestnut areas brown.

Like other grebes, the little grebe has a weak, direct flight, holding its stretched-out neck just below the level of its body while its legs trail behind after a pattering take-off. It swims and dives freely, and – ungainly out of water – avoids land as much as it can. The chicks, which are able to swim almost at hatching, will climb on to their parents' backs and hide there in response to the 'whit-whit' alarm note.

The birds' size does not allow them to swallow large fish, and their favourite food is often sticklebacks, although they also eat shrimps and water insects.

J F M A M J
J A S O N D

The wing pattern of a great crested grebe in winter

SUMMER

Great crested grebe Podiceps cristatus

During the 19th century, great crested grebes were all but exterminated in Britain, because their feathers were in demand by the fashion industry. Grebe feathers – sometimes the entire plumage – were used to decorate women's hats, and by around 1860 there were believed to be no more than 42 pairs left in the whole of England.

Their relative abundance nowadays – more than 12,000 adults are present in Britain and Ireland in the breeding season – is one of the triumphs of the bird protection movement. The increase in flooded gravel pits and other man-made water habitats in the south during the past 40 to 50 years has helped their recovery – grebes nest exclusively on inland stretches of freshwater, including slow-flowing rivers. In winter, they may also be seen on estuaries and coastal waters.

The great crested grebe's courtship ceremonies, famously including elaborate postures and gestures, were studied intensively by Sir Julian Huxley as long ago as 1914, and his writings on the subject are among the classics of bird-watching literature.

The parents change places on the nest every three hours or so, and after the chicks have hatched they are often carried on the back of one parent while the other brings food.

RECOGNITION

Double-horned crest and chestnut 'frills' about the head in breeding season; long white neck, but this may not show when bird is hunched up and resting; sexes alike.

NESTING

Both sexes build pile of weeds in water, either floating or grounded; floating nest is anchored to nearby plants; lays April–July; 3–5 eggs, white, but soon discoloured by water-weeds; incubation about 28 days, by both parents; chicks, tended by both parents, leave soon after hatching, dive at 6 weeks and are independent at 9–10 weeks; sometimes two broods.

FEEDING

Small fish; molluscs; algae, weed and other vegetable matter.

SIZE

48.25cm (19in)

Black-necked grebe in winter has dusky cheeks and neck

SUMMER

J F M A M J
J A S O N D

Black-necked grebe Podiceps nigricollis

In summer, black neck, copper-red flanks, drooping yellow fan on cheek; in winter, black and white with peaked crown, uptilted bill; white wing-patches.

NESTING

Frequently colonial; nest, built by both sexes, is a pile of water-weed in water, grounded on or anchored by vegetation; lays May–July; 3 or 4 eggs, white but soon stained because parents cover them with weeds before leaving nest; incubation about 21 days, by both parents; chicks, tended by both parents, leave soon after hatching but are occasionally carried on backs of adults for about 4 weeks.

FEEDING

Feeding: fish; freshwater insects.

SIZE

30.5cm (12in)

Black-necked grebes provide a perfect illustration of the way in which birds cope with a major change in their environment. In the 19th century there were none breeding in Britain. They were primarily birds of the steppe lakes in southern Russia. Then, in 1904, the first British breeding pair was recorded in Anglesey. The explanation was that the steppe lakes were gradually drying up due to climatic changes, and the grebes reacted by moving westwards. In the early 1930s, a colony of up to 250 breeding pairs gathered on a lake in County Roscommon, Ireland. Now, however, breeding in Britain is confined to a few sites in central Scotland, and occasionally elsewhere.

Shallow lochs with horsetail or some other vegetation growing in the water are the birds' favourite breeding environment. On migration and during hard winters they appear on inland stretches of freshwater, and regularly on estuaries and shallow coastal waters.

The bird is easily identified in breeding plumage by its black neck and face, and the golden-chestnut tuft of feathers fanning out behind its eyes. In winter, the head adornments are lost, but at all times the black-necked grebe can be picked out by its slightly up-tilted blue-grey bill.

Its most frequent call is a soft 'pee-eep'. Courtship ceremonies include head wagging and a 'penguin dance' like the great crested grebe's display.

J F M A M J
J A S O N D

SUMMER

Slavonian grebe in winter has black cap and white cheeks

Slavonian grebe Podiceps auritus

In North America this bird is known as the horned grebe, and the name is appropriate, since the most conspicuous feature of its breeding plumage is its set of golden ear-tufts, pointing upwards. The tufts vanish in winter and the grebe's neck, breast and cheeks turn white. At this time of year the easiest way to tell it from the black-necked grebe is by its bill, which is straight as opposed to being tilted upwards, and by its clean white cheeks.

Like black-necks, Slavonian grebes began nesting in Britain in the last century, and they are still rare as breeders. About 40 pairs breed regularly on lochs in the Inverness district and there are a few in neighbouring areas. The nest is a pile of weeds, usually anchored in shallow water, and the parent birds pull weeds over the eggs when they leave them unattended.

In winter, Slavonian grebes are more widespread than in the breeding season. They usually go down to estuaries, but in hard weather they will move to inland waters. Their breeding-season calls include a low rippling trill, and their courtship ceremonies are similar to those of the great crested grebe. They have their own version of that bird's famous 'penguin dance', in which male and female rise up in the water, breast to breast.

Slavonian grebes fly more readily than other grebes, but when suspicious they sometimes sink low in the water, almost disappearing from sight.

RECOGNITION

In summer, chestnut neck and sides, golden wedge on side of head; in winter, black and white with rounder crown, straighter edge to black cap and straighter bill than black-necked grebe.

NESTING

Both sexes build floating platform of weeds at loch side; lays late May–July; 3–5 eggs, white but soon stained by weeds; incubation about 24 days, by both parents; chicks, tended by both parents, leave in a few days, but are fed for over 4 weeks and often carried on parents' backs.

FEEDING

Small fish; water-snails and other water insects; some vegetable matter.

SIZE

33cm (13in)

Conspicuous white flash shows as a moorhen flicks its tail

Moorhen Gallinula chloropus

RECOGNITION

Red on forehead, extending into bill; white undertail coverts; tail constantly flicked while swimming; young birds olive-brown; sexes alike.

NESTING

Both sexes build platform of dried water plants, usually near water, but sometimes some distance away or in a tree or bush; lays late March–July; 5–11 eggs, buff, speckled with red-brown; incubation 19–22 days, by both parents; chicks, fed by both parents and sometimes by young of earlier brood, leave in 2 or 3 days, and can swim and dive at once; two broods, sometimes three.

FEEDING

Wild fruit and seeds, grain, water-weed; worms, slugs, snails, insects and larvae; sometimes eggs and chicks of other birds.

SIZE

33cm (13in)

The moorhen has no connection with moors. Its name is a form of 'merehen', or bird of the lakes. Possibly the most common of Britain's waterfowl, the moorhen can sink when alarmed and leave only its bill protruding from the water, like a periscope. It probably stays down by forcing air out of its plumage and air sacs and by treading water.

Moorhens defend their territory jealously. Males fight fiercely on the water, sometimes ending up with broken toes or dislocated thighs. There is even a record of a moorhen trying to drown a homing pigeon by holding it underwater.

The birds breed near freshwater among thick cover, and their favourite nesting sites are by the side of a pond, lake or river. They are often seen in town parks, and feed freely in marshes, sewage farms and meadows.

The moorhen's flight is weak, like that of many swimming birds, and its take-off from water is usually laboured and pattering. It swims with a jerky movement, constantly flicking the white flashes on the sides of its tail. The most frequent call-notes are two loud but rather liquid croaks, 'kurruk' and 'kittic', and a harsh 'kaak'. The male has a special courtship posture in which it tilts its body upwards, points its wing-tips almost vertically, spreads its tail to display the white undertail coverts and points its head downwards.

Coot threatens with lowered head and raised wings

J F M A M J
J A S O N D

Coot Fulica atra

The received wisdom that coots will fight off enemies by kicking up spray in their faces is not far from the truth. If a marsh harrier or some other bird of prey swoops down on a crowd of coots, they will paddle furiously towards the nearest reeds, and raise a cloud of spray as they crash-dive to safety.

Aggressive birds, coots have a highly developed territorial sense, and are much given to quarrelsome pursuits of one another, although they often nest in loose colonies. They prefer large, open stretches of water where there is good cover for their nests, and are particularly common on flooded gravel pits in southern England. They are easily recognisable by a white flash on the forehead, contrasting with the black of their plumage. In winter, they take to large reservoirs and lakes without much cover. Coots live on estuaries as well, and will feed along other stretches of the coast when inland waters are frozen.

The bird's name echoes its loud, high-pitched cry. It is completely at home on water and, like the moorhen, can submerge its body until only its bill shows above the surface. On land, it has a rather inelegant walk, and its flight, usually low over the water, is heavy and laboured. The main courtship display consists of stretching out the neck until it almost touches the water.

RECOGNITION

All black except for white on forehead and bill, and narrow white wing-bar seen in flight; sexes alike.

NESTING

Both sexes build substantial nest of reeds in shallow water; nest may be floating or stranded on a half-submerged bough; lays March–May; usually 6–9 eggs, buff with black spots; incubation 21–24 days, by both parents; nestlings, tended by both parents, leave after 3 or 4 days, are independent after about 8 weeks; two broods, sometimes three.

FEEDING

Shoots of reeds, roots of water plants; corn and seeds; some small fish, newts, tadpoles; dragonfly nymphs and other water insects; sometimes eggs and chicks of other birds.

SIZE

38cm (15in)

*The grey and white plumage
of a black tern in winter*

SPRING

Black tern Chlidonias niger

RECOGNITION

Black and smoky-grey in summer, white under tail; in autumn, lead-grey above, white below, with black cap and dark mark at side of breast; black beak.

NESTING

No longer nests regularly in Britain; both sexes build floating platform of weeds; nest is made of grass and rushes; lays May–June; 2–4 eggs, buff to brown, with darker markings; incubation about 14 days, by both parents; nestlings, tended by both parents, leave after about 14 days, fly after about 3 weeks.

FEEDING

Dragonflies and their nymphs, caddis flies and water-boatmen; occasionally minnows, small frogs and tadpoles.

SIZE

25.5cm (10in)

The draining of the fens and other marshes wiped out the black tern as a British breeding species, and since its wintering grounds are also outside Britain – in Africa – it is now among the small group of birds that are seen in these islands only during spring and autumn migrations.

Once the birds bred in large numbers in eastern England but in the past 100 years only occasional pairs have nested in East Anglia and Ireland, and there is no sign of any recolonisation in the near future.

In the spring, the black tern is easy to recognise because there is no other bird with its markings – a black head and underparts, and dark grey upper parts – that has the habit of hovering over water. In autumn, its plumage is grey and white, like that of most other terns, but its dipping flight is still distinctive as it plunges to collect a small fish or water insect.

The black tern is a quiet bird, although it has an occasional 'kik-kik' call, and flocks sometimes produce a reedy whistling sound. They often join feeding flocks of sea terns on estuaries, but are most common over inland waters. On the Continent, they usually breed in marshes and swamps, sometimes in huge colonies, choosing nesting sites where reeds grow in shallow water.

Salt-marsh and Estuary

Expanses of mudflats uncovered by the tide, and salt-marshes intersected by water channels, have a magnetic appeal for many birds. On these open, comparatively safe feeding grounds geese, ducks and waders can dabble and probe for marine organisms, while birds migrating from the far north find hospitable winter quarters on the margins of ice-free waters. Now many of these areas are threatened by development and climate change.

PINK-FOOTED GOOSE

J F M A M J
J A S O N D

Pink-footed goose

BEAN GOOSE

J F M A M J
J A S O N D

A formation of pink-footed geese in flight

Pink-footed goose Anser brachyrhynchus

RECOGNITION

Pale blue-grey forewings, upper parts grey-brown; dark head and neck, pink and black bill and pink legs; bean goose has dark head and neck, long black and orange-yellow bill; sexes alike in both cases.

NESTING

Breeds in Greenland, Iceland, Spitsbergen; nests, lined with down, on ground or cliff ledge; bean goose nests in northern Europe and Siberia, lines scrape in ground with leaves, moss and down; both lay late May—June; 4 or 5 eggs, creamy-white; incubation about 28 days, by female only; goslings, tended by both parents, leave nest soon after hatching, fly at about 8 weeks.

FEEDING

Grass, crops and roots.

SIZE

Pink-foot: 61–76.25cm (24–30in)
Bean goose: 71–89cm (28–35in)

The pink-footed goose looks much like the bean goose (*Anser fabalis*), and identification is further complicated by the fact that two races of the bean goose visit Britain, one longer-necked and longer-billed than the other. The pink-foot is the commonest grey goose in Britain in winter, especially in Scotland, Lancashire and Norfolk where numbers have grown remarkably. Bean geese are scarce with just two or three regular flocks, but ones and twos occasionally mingle with other geese and are a challenge to find. The pink-foot creates a chorus of deep 'ung-ung' calls, mixed with distinctive, high 'wink-wink' sounds, while the bean goose makes a deeper series of 'ahng-ank' notes.

At any distance, the dark head and neck distinguish both from other grey geese. The pink-foot has a less conspicuous pale grey forewing than the heavier greylag, and no other grey goose has pink legs and bill. The bean goose's bill is orange and black.

Pink-footed geese roost in marshes and estuaries, and move inland to feed on cultivated fields, eating grain, potatoes and other crops, as well as grass, wild shoots and roots. Both the pink-foot and bean goose share the flight habits of other grey geese, including the 'whiffling' spiral descent from a height, but the pink-foot is more buoyant in flight than the bean goose. Courtship, too, follows the general pattern of the greys, which suggests that these displays, with their characteristic 'triumph' calls, may have developed early in the evolutionary timescale.

J F M A M J
J A S O N D

Adult (top) and immature white-fronts feed in winter pasture

White-fronted goose *Anser albifrons*

Mixed parties of white-fronted and pink-footed geese often gather in flocks of hundreds, and fly in the typical grey goose 'V' formation. The white-front's flight is not so heavy as the greylag's, and these geese are masters of air manoeuvres. Sportsmen say they can 'reverse engines' and come to a dead stop when alarmed, or rise almost vertically from the ground. Like greylags, they will swoop from a height towards their feeding grounds in a 'whiffling' spiral dive, with wings half folded.

The white-fronted goose has become markedly scarcer in Britain in winter and most regular sites have been abandoned, although some pastures and marshes in Norfolk, Kent and at Slimbridge in Gloucestershire still have regular flocks. The extremely rare lesser white-fronted goose (*Anser erythropus*) occasionally appears with these. Both feed on flooded fields and similar wetland.

A characteristic gabble of 'kow-yow' or 'kow-lyow' sounds, harsher and louder than the pink-foot's call, has earned the white-front the name 'laughing goose' in some districts. The lesser white-front's 'ku-ku' or 'ku-yu-yu' is shriller sounding.

White-fronts are the easiest of the grey geese to recognise. The white forehead and black-barred plumage underneath show up both at rest and in flight, and the combination of pink or orange bill with orange legs is distinctive.

RECOGNITION

Grey-brown; black bars on belly; pink or orange bill; orange legs; white forehead; immatures have no white on forehead; sexes alike. Lesser white-front is smaller version but white extends higher on forehead and has yellow eye-ring.

NESTING

In Arctic, from Greenland to Siberia; nest of heather, grasses or lichen, lined with down, in hollow in ground; lays late May–June; 4–7 eggs, creamy-white, often stained; incubation 27 or 28 days, by female; goslings, tended by both parents, leave nest soon after hatching, fly after several months; both species.

FEEDING

Grass, clover and plant shoots; grain, sometimes potatoes.

SIZE

White-front: 66–76.25cm (26–30in)
Lesser white-front: 53.25–63.5cm (21–25in)

J F M A M J
J A S O N D

Wings of greylag in flight have pale leading edge

Greylag goose Anser anser

RECOGNITION

Pale brown; big head with large orange bill; legs pink; white around tail. In flight shows very pale grey forewings. Loud, clanging calls.

NESTING

Builds nest of heather, grass, moss and other local materials, on ground near water; female lines nest with down; lays late April–May; 4–7 eggs, white, often stained; incubation 27 or 28 days, by female only, male on watch at distance; goslings, tended by both parents, leave in a few hours, begin to fly after about 8 weeks.

FEEDING

Grass, crops and water-weed.

SIZE

76.25–89cm (30–35in)

Britain's one native breeding goose, the greylag, has a reputation for intelligence, devotion and lifelong fidelity to its mate. Year by year a pair cement and renew their bond with a 'triumph ceremony' – triumphant because, during the performance, the gander produces a resonant note like the one it uses after it has driven off an intruder and hastens back to reassure its mate.

The greylag is the ancestor of the farmyard goose, which it closely resembles – the alertness and nervous cackling from the farmyard's sharpest 'watchdog' comes from the wild bird.

Its nest, usually on loch-studded moorland or near lakes and reservoirs, is nearly always in a hollow in deep heather. The goose pulls the feather-and-down lining over the eggs on leaving. Left to itself, the greylag's breeding grounds would now be confined to the extreme north of Scotland and the Outer Hebrides, but wildfowlers and landowners have introduced wild breeding stock in many parts of the British Isles, and the birds have become established and are thriving.

Winter-visiting greylags from Iceland are more widespread than the native breeders, chiefly in Scotland. The flocks, when they arrive, are not always popular with farmers whose grazing land and crops are invaded.

Barnacle geese graze together on pasture close to shore

JFMAMJ
JASOND

Barnacle goose Branta leucopsis

The barnacle goose owes its name to a medieval myth. Its breeding grounds in the Arctic were unknown to our ancestors, and they believed that the goose did not come from an egg, like other birds, but was generated from the curiously shaped goose barnacles, which are still washed ashore in clusters, attached to driftwood. To a fanciful eye, some of these barnacles could resemble a goose. So persistent was the myth that less than 100 years ago barnacle geese were eaten during Lent in parts of Ireland, in the belief that they were more fish than fowl.

The barnacle is one of the three geese described as black, to distinguish them from the greys, and in size it comes between the other two – the brent and the Canada goose. The smaller brent has an all-black head and no wing-bars, and the Canada goose is browner than the barnacle, with less white on its face. The barnacle's striking black and white head makes it stand out from white-fronts and other grey geese.

In winter, barnacles visit the western isles of Scotland, the marshes of the Solway Firth and parts of Ireland. The island birds graze on improved grassland and machair, the short turf found behind sand-dunes in the Hebrides. Together with the Irish birds, numbering about 25,000 in all, they breed in Greenland. The Solway's 10,000 plus birds breed in Spitsbergen.

RECOGNITION

White face and black head; neck and upper breast black; lower breast and flanks whitish; back lavender-grey; wings strongly barred; black tail, bill and legs; sexes alike.

NESTING

Nests in colonies on rock ledges, and sometimes islands, in Spitsbergen, Novaya Zemlya and Greenland; nest depression is lined with down and lichen; lays late May–June; usually 3–5 eggs, grey-white and soon stained; incubation about 28 days, by female only; goslings, tended by both parents, leave nest after a few days, fly after several months.

FEEDING

Almost entirely grass.

SIZE

58.5–68.5cm (23–27in)

Brent geese fly swiftly in loose but well co-ordinated flocks

DARK-BREASTED RACE

Brent goose Branta bernicla

RECOGNITION

Black head, neck and upper breast; small white patch on neck; dark grey back and wings; white above and below the black tail. Two geographical races: dark-breasted (slate-grey underparts) and pale-breasted (whitish underparts); sexes alike.

NESTING

Nests in hollows between rocks, filled with moss and lined with down; lays June; 3–5 eggs, creamy-white; incubation about 28 days, by female only, male standing guard; goslings, tended by both parents, leave nest soon after hatching, fly after several months.

FEEDING

Eel-grass (Zostera) in winter; shoots of Arctic plants, seaweed and mussels in summer.

SIZE

56–61cm (22–24in)

Long, irregular lines of small, dark brent geese, feeding along east coast tidelines in winter, are a much more common sight than they were a few decades ago, except in Scotland. For winter diet, the brent relies almost exclusively on eel-grass, one of the few flowering plants to grow submerged in salt water – wherever the weed is abundant, brent geese gather. They have a habit of upending, like ducks, to get at the plant.

The decline of the large flocks in the 1930s was probably caused by a disease that devastated the eel-grass beds on both sides of the North Sea. Now, thanks to legal protection and to the brent's adaptation to feeding on farmland behind sea walls, numbers have increased enormously. About half the population of 200,000 dark-breasted brents wintering in Europe are to be found on the east and south coasts of England. They nest in Arctic Russia and Siberia.

Another race, the pale-breasted brent, comes from Greenland and winters mainly in Ireland. Small numbers, wintering in Northumberland, come from Spitsbergen.

The brent is a sea goose and has only recently taken to feeding on farmland. Huge flocks rest on the sea at high tide and roost there at night. The occasional straggler seen inland is likely to have escaped from a collection of ornamental fowl.

SUMMER

*Spoonbill sifts through mud
and salt water for food*

J F M A M J
J A S O N D

Spoonbill Platalea leucorodia

Spoonbills nested in East Anglia until the 17th century, while in the 16th century they bred in Sussex and Middlesex, and a colony existed just a few miles from the centre of London. In 1523, the Bishop of London, who had leased a part of his park at Fulham, brought an action to prevent herons and spoonbills – then known as 'shovelars' – being taken from their nests there.

Nowadays the nearest breeding colonies to Britain are in Holland, but spoonbills still turn up, singly or in small parties, with fair regularity on some east-coast marshes. One of their favourite spots is Breydon Water, near Great Yarmouth. In another development, a pair recently nested in Scotland.

They are usually silent birds, only occasionally raising a grunt or rattling their bills in excitement. However, their courtship routine is spectacular – a mixture of dancing, bill-clapping and fanning the crest.

The spoon that makes this white, heron-like bird remarkable is not just a decorative oddity. The bird wades through the shallow waters of lagoons and marshes, or along the shore, sweeping its bill from side to side to scoop up and filter a varied diet of water plants, small fish and water insects.

The bill is distinctive enough to identify the bird on a reasonably close view. At a distance, a flying spoonbill can be told from a heron by the way its neck is extended.

RECOGNITION

All white, apart from buff patch at base of neck in summer; long bill with yellow tip, widening into 'spoon' shape; adults crested in summer; sexes alike.

NESTING

Does not now breed in Britain; nearest colonies are in Holland; both sexes build substantial nest, among reeds or in bushes; lays late April–May; usually 4 eggs, white with sparse red-brown markings; incubation about 21 days, by both parents; nestlings, tended by both parents, leave at about 4 weeks, fly after 6 weeks.

FEEDING

Water plants; small fish, tadpoles, frog-spawn, water-snails, worms and insect larvae.

SIZE

86.25cm (34in)

The striking black-and-white pattern of an avocet in flight

J F M A M J
J A S O N D

Avocet Recurvirostra avosetta

RECOGNITION

Bold black and white plumage; long, slender, upcurved bill; long, leaden-blue legs project behind tail in flight; sexes alike.

NESTING

Nests in colonies near water, on tussocks or sandbanks; nest is often a substantial pile of dead vegetation; lays late April–May; usually 4 eggs, pale buff, spotted with grey and dark brown; incubation about 23 days, by both parents; chicks, tended by both parents, leave in few hours, fly after about 6 weeks.

FEEDING

Shrimps; water insects and their larvae.

SIZE

43cm (17in)

The return of avocets to nest in Britain is one of the success stories of bird protection. Two hundred years ago they were plentiful, but fen drainage reduced their numbers and the birds that were left were shot for feathers to make fishing flies, and their eggs were stolen to make puddings. The last breeding colony, at Salthouse in Norfolk, was wiped out by 1825.

Then, after the Second World War, a few pairs, probably dislodged from their Dutch breeding grounds by wartime flooding of the polders, began to nest on Minsmere and Havergate Island in Suffolk. The RSPB secured both sites as reserves, the colonies flourished and avocets began to spread elsewhere. Now more than 500 pairs breed at several colonies in East Anglia and southeast England, the odd pair nest inland and a few breed in northwest England.

The avocet is mainly a summer visitor to East Anglia. It winters on the Tamar and Exe estuaries in Devon, at Poole harbour in Dorset and Pagham harbour in Sussex. Like the spoonbill, it uses its curved, upturned beak in a side-to-side action to sweep the shallows for small sea creatures. One of its old names, 'yelper', seems inappropriate for so elegant a bird, but is understandable because the bird yelps loudly if an intruder approaches its nest or young. In calmer moments it calls 'klooit' and has a soft, grunting note in flight.

SUMMER

Grey plover flying in
winter shows black patch
under wing

WINTER

J F M A M J
J A S O N D

Grey plover Pluvialis squatarola

The grey plover, drab in its grey-brown winter plumage and
sometimes looking the picture of dejection as it waits on the
mud-banks for the tide to turn, is a vastly different bird on its
breeding grounds in northern Russia and Siberia. There, in
its handsome summer plumage – grey-spangled, white-edged
and black-breasted – it plunges and tumbles acrobatically in
the air and will boldly attack marauding skuas that come too
near its nest.

The grey plover's striking summer plumage sometimes lasts
until autumn, and from then until spring, fair numbers of the
birds inhabit Britain's coasts, especially in the east. They form
loose parties, rather than close flocks, and keep their distance
from other waders. Almost all of them return to the Arctic
when winter is over, but a few non-breeding birds sometimes
stay over summer.

The only bird with which it might be confused is the golden
plover, but the grey can always be told by the black mark under
each wing, and by white 'flashes' on its rump and on top of the
wings. When feeding, it has the regular plover habit of making a
short run, then pausing to look around. Its three-note call, 'tee-
oo-ee', with the middle syllable the low one, is quite distinct
from the golden plover's more musical double call, and sounds
rather like a boy's whistling.

RECOGNITION

Brown-grey upper parts,
lighter underparts in winter;
spangled grey upper parts,
black underparts in
summer; black patch under
wings; white on rump and
top of wings; sexes alike.

NESTING

Breeds on Siberian tundra;
nests in depression in peat,
lined with moss and lichen;
lays June–early July; 4 eggs,
buff to green, sometimes
with pink tinge, marked
with chestnut blotches;
incubation 23 days, by both
parents; chicks, tended by
both parents, fly after about
4 weeks.

FEEDING

Worms, molluscs, small
crabs and other crustacea
in winter; worms, slugs,
insects and spiders in
summer.

SIZE

28cm (11in)

WINTER

Knot Calidris canutus

Grey above, paler below in winter; mottled black and chestnut above, russet below in summer; grey tail; light rump and wing-bar show in flight; dumpy, short neck; sexes alike.

Nests in stony Arctic tundra, in hollow lined with lichen; lays June–July; usually 4 eggs, grey-green to olive-buff, with dark markings; incubation probably 3 weeks, by both parents; chicks, tended chiefly by male, leave nest when dry, fly after about 4 weeks.

Early naturalists were baffled by the knot – thousands of birds in tightly packed flocks, rippling over the mud-banks like a grey carpet, came from and returned to no one knew where. Even its name is old and obscure. One theory was that, in the middle of the 18th century, when the Swedish naturalist Linnaeus was classifying all the living creatures then known, the knot was thought of as a little King Cnut, the 11th century Viking monarch who stood on the shore to show that even a king cannot order the tide to go back, and this idea was reflected in the Latin name, *canutus*. However, that explanation is more fanciful than probable. The name may come from the birds' low-pitched cry 'knut, knut', which when uttered by a dense flock becomes a continuous low twitter. Knots also produce another, mellower note – a higher-pitched, whistle-like 'twit-twit'.

We now know that migrating knots sometimes make vast journeys, quitting their bare breeding grounds far north of the Arctic Circle to stream south in their hordes as far as southern Africa, Patagonia, New Zealand and Australia. They begin to

In winter, huge flocks of knots put on dazzling displays of co-ordinated flight.

arrive in Britain, chiefly on eastern and northwestern coasts and along the coasts of northern and eastern Ireland, in late summer and continue into October, the young coming first. The birds provide a great spectacle when they perform their elaborate, group aerobatics – spectacular co-ordinated displays during which dense clouds of birds wheel in perfect unison over the water, appearing white at first, darker as the birds tilt over and show their grey upper parts, then silvery as they turn exposing pale rumps and tails.

Although non-breeders may remain in Britain all year, the main groups start to return to their northern breeding grounds the following April and May, by which time many birds will be in full breeding plumage. On migration, the flocks keep up a collective chatter. Once they reach the Taimyr peninsula of northern Siberia, or islands still farther north, the male performs a circling song-flight and engages in courtship chases. Then, after a brief, energetic summer without night, the flocks gather for their trip south and the cycle begins again.

FEEDING

In winter – crustacea, such as small crabs; worms, small molluscs, insects; in summer – insects, spiders, molluscs, plant buds and other vegetable matter.

SIZE

25.5cm (10in)

Dunlins in winter lose their black belly markings

SUMMER

Dunlin Calidris alpina

RECOGNITION

Streaked brown-grey above, white below with grey breast in winter; chestnut, streaked with black above and black belly in summer; white wing-bar and sides of tail show in flight; slightly downcurved bill; sexes alike.

NESTING

Nest, on ground in scrape or tussock, is lined with grass or leaves; lays May; usually 4 eggs, buff to blue-green, well sprinkled with dark brown blotches; incubation 21 or 22 days, by both parents; chicks, tended by both parents, leave in few days, fly after about 3 weeks.

FEEDING

Insects and larvae, small, molluscs, small crustacea, earthworms, marine worms; occasionally grass or seed.

SIZE

17.75cm (7in)

Great flocks of dunlins, like wisps of smoke blown by the wind, make one of the most charming sights of the shore. They skim low over the water, sweep upwards in a bunch, spill out in a long wavering line, change course, dive and shower down again with a rushing of wings.

Dunlins were known to the old wildfowlers by a variety of names – 'ox-bird', 'ploverspage', 'sea snipe' and 'stint'. They are among the smallest of Britain's shore birds. Some stay around the estuaries all the year, and a small proportion nest in Britain, but sizable flocks come for the winter, and spectacular numbers build up with passage birds at migration times. They mingle with other small waders, probing the tidal runnels for animal life. In spring and summer they are easy to identify, because the dunlin is the only small shore bird with a black belly.

The dunlin's flight-note is a rather weak 'tweep' or 'teerp', and over its breeding grounds the main theme of its display is a lark-like ascent with hovering and trilling. Fast, twisting pursuit flights are also in evidence. Nesting pairs are not abundant in Britain, and are declining, especially in England and Wales. Very few nest in mid Wales and the Pennines but they are more widespread in Scotland.

WINTER

SUMMER

Distinctive tail markings of bar-tailed godwit in flight

Bar-tailed godwit Limosa lapponica

Flocks of bar-tailed godwits visit Britain from Scandinavia and northern Russia in winter, and large numbers, heading for destinations much farther south, use Britain as a staging post on their spring and autumn migrations. They gather with knots and oystercatchers at the edge of the sea, crowding on the rocks as the tide comes in. New arrivals drop into the thick of the crush, forcing others to leap into the air to find fresh spots. They are constantly moving. Then, when the tide uncovers their feeding banks, the birds take wing and often perform aerobatics together before settling down. They are rarely seen inland.

Godwits – nobody knows for certain how they got that name – look rather like small curlews during winter, except that their bills are straight or curved upwards. In summer the chestnut breeding plumage is distinctive. In flight, the bar-tail can be distinguished from the larger black-tailed godwit by its lack of a white wing-stripe.

The bar-tail, which has never bred in Britain, is common on passage migration from late April in East Anglia, southeast England and Lancashire. By June, most of them have left to nest in the Arctic. They return again in the autumn, some young birds arriving first.

Usually they are quiet birds, but the parents set up a clamour when a potential enemy approaches their nesting marsh. They also have a 'kirruc-kirruc' flight-note and a more anxious 'wik-wik-wik-wik' call.

RECOGNITION

Mottled grey-brown, whitish below in winter; chestnut breast, neck and face in summer; white rump; straight or slightly upcurved bill; barred tail; sexes alike.

NESTING

Nests in Arctic, making a scrape in wet bog, lined with birch leaves and lichen; lays late May–June; 4 eggs, olive-green or brown, with darker blotches; incubation about 21 days, by both parents.

FEEDING

In winter – sandhoppers, shrimps, lugworms, snails, small shellfish; in summer – insects and small ground animals.

SIZE

38cm (15in)

Whimbrels searching the shore for molluscs and worms

Whimbrel Numenius phaeopus

RECOGNITION

Streaky buff-brown; a smaller version of the curlew, distinguished by head markings – two dark stripes separated by pale streak; downcurving bill shorter than curlew's; female slightly larger than male.

NESTING

Scantily lined scrape in heather or rough grass on moorland; lays late May–June; usually 4 eggs, olive-green to buff-brown, heavily blotched; incubation 27 or 28 days, by both parents; chicks, tended by both parents, leave nest in few hours, fly after 5–6 weeks.

FEEDING

Inland – insects and larvae; spiders, earthworms, snails; bilberries, crowberries; coasts – small crustacea, molluscs, marine worms.

SIZE

40.5cm (16in)

It is no use looking for whimbrels in winter, but at migration times small passing flocks may turn up anywhere on the coast, often among the larger curlews, which they resemble. The whimbrel can be told from the curlew by its quicker wing-beats, shorter bill and entirely different call, and at close range by the bold striping on its head – a pale streak sandwiched between two streaks of dark brown.

Another difference is that it is not shy. Long after a curlew has put others on the alert to some fancied danger, the whimbrels, unconcerned, will continue probing for small shellfish or crabs among the shore pools, or catching sandhoppers. Most distinctive of all is the whimbrel's cry, a whinnying, rippling, tittering peal unlike any of the curlew's usual calls. Its song, on the other hand, which is given in courtship flight over its remote nesting grounds, is much like the curlew's bubbling. The whimbrel rises energetically to a great height, then planes in descending circles or tumbles acrobatically, nearly to the ground.

The whimbrel maintains its status as a British nesting species only in the Shetlands, with odd pairs occasionally on the Orkneys, Lewis and St Kilda in the Hebrides and the north Scottish mainland. The total population has declined dramatically to just 100–200 pairs.

Seashore

The tide is a dominant fact of life for shore birds, washing in a regular supply of food from the inexhaustible storehouse of the sea. Oystercatchers are expert at prising open stranded shellfish; gulls are scavengers and beachcombers; terns scoop up fish near the surface; and long-tailed ducks dive deep to mussel beds at the bottom of the sea. In these ways, birds exploit the shore habitat to the full.

Female shelduck attend young from several broods

MALE

Shelduck Tadorna tadorna

RECOGNITION

Both sexes have black, white and chestnut plumage; adults have red bill, drake's has a knob at base.

NESTING

Duck lines well-concealed nest with grass and down; lays May–June; 8–14 eggs, creamy-white; incubation about 30 days, by duck only; ducklings, tended by duck, usually leave nest immediately, fly at about 9 weeks; broods often join together.

FEEDING

Molluscs; small crabs and shrimps; insects; small quantities of vegetable matter.

SIZE

66cm (26in)

Every July almost the entire population of British shelduck makes for the Heligoland Bight, off northwest Germany, to moult. Juveniles stay behind with a few adult 'nurses', and small flocks of moulting shelduck remain in Bridgwater Bay, Somerset, and in large estuaries, such as the Wash.

Shelduck are the largest British ducks and are an exception to the rule that females are far more drably coloured and less conspicuous than drakes. Both sexes of shelduck have a boldly contrasting plumage pattern of black, white and chestnut. If the birds nested without cover, the duck would be an easy target for predators, so they use rabbit burrows, the shelter of boulders or bushes, or a hollow tree. Sand-dunes are an ideal habitat for breeding shelduck. They also nest on other rough ground by the sea, and occasionally even in woods and on farmland. They breed in almost every coastal county in the British Isles and increasingly in many inland ones in England.

A shelduck's life follows the ebb and flow of the tide. At high tide the bird rests on the sea or the shore, and when the tide retreats, it hurries down to search the tidal pools for mussels and crabs. It looks like a goose as it waddles along the shore, and it flies like a goose, too, with slow wing-beats, often in lines or in wedge formation.

Scaup diving for food usually stay down for 25–30 seconds

FEMALE

MALE

J F M A M J
J A S O N D

Scaup Aythya marila

A hard winter by British standards is fair weather for scaup. They flock down from the Arctic and sub-Arctic to gather off the coasts of Scotland and in bays and estuaries along the English coast, mainly on the east side, as far south as the Thames. Large flocks once concentrated in the Firth of Forth, attracted by waste grain discharged by breweries and distilleries.

Scaup are primarily diving birds, but they also have a fast and powerful flight. Webbed feet, on legs set to the rear of their bodies, drive them down to mussel beds on the sea floor. On land, their centre of gravity is too far back for ease of walking, and they can only waddle clumsily. In fact, few of them ever come to land, except in the breeding season. Small numbers feed in freshwater lakes close to the shore, but scaup rarely appear farther inland unless they have been driven there by storms.

By early May, most scaup have returned to their breeding grounds in Iceland, northern Europe and Siberia. The odd pairs sometimes breed in the north of Scotland, particularly in Orkney, Wester Ross and the Outer Hebrides. They are silent birds outside the breeding season, apart from the occasional harsh 'karr-karr-karr' call by the duck. During courtship, the drake swims towards the female with head and neck stretched fully upright, then he suddenly jerks them backwards. Sometimes the duck swims round, dipping her bill into the water and calling gently.

RECOGNITION

Drake has black head and breast, light grey back, white sides; duck is dark brown with large white face-patch; male's eclipse plumage (July–November) is duller. Long white stripe on wing.

NESTING

Rarely nests in Britain; uses down and local materials to line hollow in ground, sometimes sheltered by tussock; lays late May–June; 7–11 eggs, green or olive-green; incubation about 28 days, by female only; ducklings, tended by female, swim almost immediately, fly after 5–6 weeks.

FEEDING

Mussels and other molluscs; small crabs; eel-grass.

SIZE

48.25cm (19in)

FEMALE

MALE

J F M A M J
J A S O N D

*Duck incubates alone,
sitting for days without
moving*

Eider Somateria mollissima

RECOGNITION

Drake is white above, black below; duck is brown, except for white on wing; forehead has no bulge, joins bill almost in a straight line.

NESTING

Both sexes build nest of grass and seaweed, always on the ground; female lines nest with feathers and down; lays May–June; 4–6 eggs, light green; incubation about 30 days, by female only; ducklings, tended by female, leave immediately, fly after about 2 months.

FEEDING

Molluscs, including mussels, whelks, cockles; crustacea, including small crabs; very little vegetable matter.

SIZE

61cm (24in)

If a large black and white duck is seen paired with a brown one, they are almost certainly eiders – and if they slide off the rocks into the sea in the middle of a storm, bobbing up among waves that look big enough to crush them, there can be no doubt. Their whole life centres around the sea, in all its moods. They even fall asleep on rocks that are wet with spray.

The female plucks down from her breast to line the nest she and her mate build close to the line of high tide. She incubates alone and will sit for days without moving. When at last she leaves, she rearranges the down to cover the eggs. In parts of the Arctic and sub-Arctic, although not in Britain, this down forms the basis of an important industry – the eider's nesting colonies are 'farmed', and the nests are robbed of their fine dark lining to make into quilts.

Eiders breed on flat, rocky and sandy shores, from the Arctic to the British Isles. Their breeding range in Britain reaches Coquet Island off Northumberland on the east coast, Walney Island off Cumbria on the west coast, and parts of Ireland.

Large flocks of non-breeding birds, believed to come from Holland, are seen off the coasts of southern England at all seasons. Their calls, a crooning 'ah-oo' from the male and a harsher note from the female, may be heard on a calm day. Sometimes the birds fly in lines, low over the water.

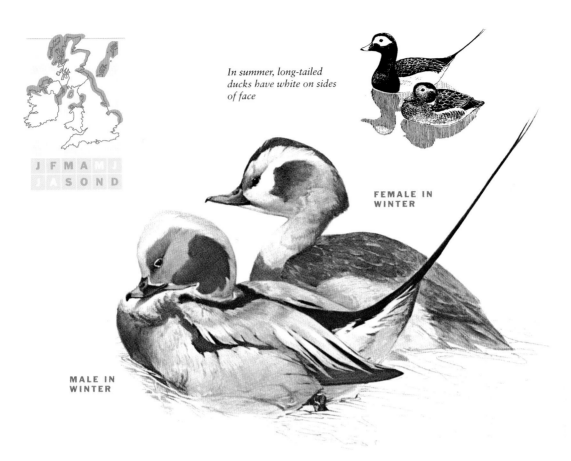

In summer, long-tailed ducks have white on sides of face

J F M A M J
J A S O N D

FEMALE IN WINTER

MALE IN WINTER

Long-tailed duck Clangula hyemalis

In Scotland, this bird is sometimes known as 'coal and candlelight', a name supposed to echo the cry it makes, but the pitfalls of translating a bird's call into human speech are nowhere better illustrated than in the case of the long-tailed duck. Its loud, ringing 'coal and candlelight' has also been written down as 'ow-ow-owdl-ow', 'cah-cah-coralwee', a simple 'calloo' and, probably nearest of all to the actual sound, 'ardelow-ar-ardelow'.

Flocks of these sea-going ducks start arriving around British coasts in September or October. Most are to be seen in Scotland, with the largest flocks – each numbering more than 1,000 birds – in the Moray Firth and Orkney. They keep well out to sea, diving 27m (90ft) deep or more, and staying down for at least a minute at a time. The bird was once known to wildfowlers as 'sea pheasant', because of its tail, which is not full-sized until the third year. It shared this name with the pintail, the only other long-tailed duck seen in British waters.

By May, most long-tailed ducks have left Britain for their breeding grounds, mainly on the lake islands of northern Scandinavia. Sometimes a few non-breeding birds will stay in the north of Scotland, and nesting there is not entirely unknown.

RECOGNITION

Drake has long pointed tail, dark brown upper parts and breast, white flanks and belly; head and neck, mainly white in winter, are brown in summer except for white on side of face; duck has short tail, sides of head white, brown upper parts and white underparts; both have short bill and dark wings without bars; moulting male loses tail feathers.

NESTING

Very rarely breeds in Britain; nests always in hollow in ground, near water; lays late May; 6–9 eggs, olive or buff; incubation about 3½ weeks, by duck; ducklings, tended by duck only, leave nest immediately, fly after about 5 weeks.

FEEDING

Small molluscs; crabs and shrimps; some vegetable matter.

SIZE

58.5cm (23in)

COMMON SCOTER

VELVET SCOTER

J F M A M J
J A S O N D

J F M A M J
J A S O N D

*Velvet scoters – sometimes
seen with flocks of common
scoters*

Common scoter

MALE

Common scoter Melanitta nigra

RECOGNITION

Drake is all black, apart
from distinctive orange mark
on bill; duck is dark brown,
with pale buff cheeks.

NESTING

Nests in hollow in ground,
usually well sheltered and
close to water; female lines
nest with moss, feathers
and down; lays late
May–June; usually 5–7
eggs, cream on buff;
incubation about 28 days,
by female only; ducklings,
tended by female, leave
soon after hatching, usually
fly after 6–7 weeks.

FEEDING

Mussels, shrimps and
crabs; sandhoppers; worms,
insects and vegetable
matter in breeding season.

SIZE

Common: 48.25cm (19in)
Velvet: 56cm (22in)

Between September and April, thousands of common scoters
visit Britain, arriving in the autumn from their breeding grounds
in the Arctic and northern Europe. The all-black drakes and
brown ducks can be seen diving for crabs or mussels in coastal
waters all around the British Isles. They avoid rough water and
stay close to the shore, but they rarely come to land unless gale-
blown or fouled by oil. The drakes often sit on the water with
their short tails cocked up. When disturbed, they rise heavily
and fly off in line astern, just above the waves.

Most common scoters return northwards in the spring,
although some non-breeders stay behind, especially along the
east coast of England, and small numbers nest in Scotland and
Ireland. During courtship the drake raises itself high out of the
water with tail cocked up, and sometimes calls with a high
piping note.

Occasionally, among the large flocks of common scoters, one
or two birds may appear larger than the rest. If the drakes have
a white spot near the eye, and the ducks have two white face-
patches, they are a related species, the velvet scoter (*Melanitta
fusca*). When they flap their wings they reveal a broad white
hindwing panel. These birds are seen around the coasts mainly
in winter. A few stay in Scottish waters for the summer, but it's
not known for sure if they have bred there.

SUMMER

Great northern diver in winter is dark above and white below

J F M A M
J A S O N D

Great northern diver Gavia immer

This bird's full courtship ritual is not often seen in the British Isles – its first recorded breeding here was in 1970 – but a curious 'speed-boating' display, in which the male and female birds plane through the water with their bodies half submerged, has been recorded off the Irish coast.

Great northern divers, as the name suggests, are strong underwater swimmers, and have been known to stay down for minutes on end. Nothing that swims in the sea and is small enough to be swallowed is safe from them – haddock, herring, sprats, sand-eels, gurnard, whiting, trout, prawns, shrimps and crabs have all been identified in the crops of the birds. With such a variety of food in the sea, they seldom need to go to land except to breed.

As winter visitors to Britain, they are most common off the coasts of Scotland and western England, and are seen inland infrequently, usually after coastal gales or oil spills. Non-breeding birds often spend the summer off northern Scotland.

Its size – it's the largest British diver – black head with green gloss, back covered in white spots and neck with a band of black and white stripes make this diver fairly easy to distinguish in summer. In winter it might be confused with the black-throated diver, which is a smaller bird. The most frequently heard call is a loud mournful wail.

RECOGNITION

Black head and neck, with green gloss and bands of white on neck, and white spots on black back in summer; dark above, white below in winter; black bill, heavier than bill of other two divers; sexes alike.

NESTING

Breeds in Iceland, Greenland and North America; nests on flattened tussock, by lakesides; lays June; usually 2 eggs, dark brown to olive, with a few dark spots; incubation about 30 days, by both parents; young, tended by both parents, probably fly after 6–10 weeks.

FEEDING

Many kinds of fish; prawns and crabs; some seaweed.

SIZE

Male: 83.75cm (33in)
Female: 76.25cm (30in)

Oystercatchers in flight utter a loud, shrill 'kleep-kleep'

J F M A M J
J A S O N D

Oystercatcher Haematopus ostralegus

RECOGNITION

Black and white; long orange bill, pink legs; sexes alike.

NESTING

Both sexes make scrape in the ground; female selects final scrape, lines it with shells, pebbles and sometimes vegetation; lays April–May; 2 or 3 eggs, pale buff with black spots and blotches; incubation about 27 days, by both parents; chicks, tended by both parents, leave within a few hours, fly at about 4 weeks.

FEEDING

Mussels, cockles, periwinkles and other molluscs; crustacea, including crabs and shrimps; inland, worms and insects.

SIZE

43cm (17in)

A shrill, penetrating 'kleep' often draws attention to two or three waders flying low over the sea or shore. These are oystercatchers, easily the most conspicuous of Britain's shore birds with their bold black and white plumage and long orange bills. They settle to feed along the edge of the sea, looking for shellfish, which they rap with their bills, then prise open.

During the past 60 years there has been a marked rise in the population of oystercatchers and there are now around 45,000 pairs breeding annually in the British Isles. The key to this increase is that they have expanded into new breeding habitats. Once they were confined to shores and cliff tops, but a habit of nesting inland began in the Scottish Highlands, and spread from there to the Lowlands and northern England, where now they breed on moorland, arable fields and on riverside shingle beds.

In spring and summer oystercatchers put on what is called a 'piping performance' at their breeding grounds. Groups of birds form circles and run up and down, pointing their bills to the ground and piping out their shrill call.

All through the nesting period, the off-duty parent stands guard, ready to give its 'klee-ee' alarm call at the first sign of an intruder. Oystercatchers from other nests in the area respond to the call by mobbing the outsider, and the young birds freeze, remaining motionless, camouflaged by their down.

J F M A M J
J A S O N D

*Ringed plover distracts enemy
by feigning a broken wing*

Ringed plover Charadrius hiaticula

Although ringed plovers are still among the most common of
Britain's shore birds, they are fighting a losing battle against
disturbance by humans in many areas. Bungalows and beach
huts have been built in seaside localities where they used to
breed, and once-remote beaches that supported large numbers
of the birds are now within the reach of cars and caravans. One
place where they have been reduced almost to extinction is the
Breckland of East Anglia. Some 400 pairs used to breed each
year on this wild heathland, but as the area has been
increasingly cultivated and afforested, the number of breeding
pairs has been reduced to barely ten. On the other hand, in
sanctuaries their numbers have risen in recent years.

Ringed plovers still breed all round the coast, and some nest
in arable fields near the sea. In Scotland, they breed far inland
and in the English midlands they nest beside flooded pits. In
winter they are widespread on shores and estuaries, and at
migration times they are common on freshwater margins inland.

Feeding parties of ringed plovers scatter along the shore,
running about energetically and stopping every now and again
to bob their heads or pick food from the sand. When disturbed,
they fly off in compact flocks, twisting and turning low over
the water.

RECOGNITION

Black collar; black and
white head pattern;
yellow legs; short bill;
distinguished from little
ringed plover by larger size
and, in flight, by prominent
wing-bar; sexes alike.

NESTING

Male makes scrape in bare
ground or short turf; female
adds lining of pebbles,
shells or grass; lays May–
July; 4 eggs, pear-shaped,
stone-buff, spotted and
blotched with brown-black
and ash grey; incubation
about 24 days, by both
parents; chicks, tended by
both parents, leave nest
within a few hours, fly
after about 25 days; two
broods normal.

FEEDING

Molluscs, crustacea and
insects of many types;
also worms and some
vegetable matter.

SIZE

19cm (7½in)

WINTER

SUMMER

Sanderling scurries along the tideline looking for food

Sanderling Calidris alba

Winter plumage is pale grey and white, with black shoulder spot; in summer, upper parts are brown with darker streaks; straight bill; can be told from ringed plover by longer bill, and from dunlin by more conspicuous white wing-bar; sexes alike.

Always makes nest in scrape in ground, usually unlined; lays late June; 4 eggs, pear-shaped, olive-green with dark brown spots and blotches; incubation about 24 days, by female only; chicks, tended by both parents, leave nest after a few hours.

Small crustacea, including shrimps; marine molluscs and worms; remains of fish or jellyfish.

20.25cm (8in)

Groups of sanderlings, mingling with other waders along the tideline, can be picked out at a distance by their restless manner of feeding. They hurry along with heads down, darting after shrimps and sandhoppers that have been uncovered by the waves, and stopping now and then to dab at the remains of a stranded fish or jellyfish. They are so tame – or so intent on feeding – that a human can get quite close before they run off, and even then they will not go far.

They seem reluctant to fly, but when they do, they rise with a hubbub of shrill 'twick-twick' calls, and their flight is swift, direct and generally low over the water. A white wing-bar, which shows as they fly, is more conspicuous than the dunlin's, and the tail is dark at the centre and white at the sides.

Sanderlings are rare in summer, when most fly to the Arctic to breed. A few non-breeding birds may stay all year, but they have never been recorded as breeding in the British Isles. In its display flight at the breeding grounds, the male rises in the air then descends steeply, giving a loud, rather harsh churring 'song'.

Sandy shores are the sanderling's usual winter habitat, but it occasionally feeds on mud-banks, and sometimes turns up on freshwater margins inland, especially on migration.

WINTER

SUMMER

J F M A M J
J A S O N D

*The bold wing pattern of an
adult turnstone in summer*

Turnstone Arenaria interpres

Stones are not the only objects moved about by turnstones as they search the shore for food – seaweed, pebbles, shells, driftwood, dead fish, anything that might conceal insects or small shellfish may be turned over or levered aside by their probing bills.

Turnstones are common winter visitors, and also appear in Britain as passage migrants in spring and autumn, when a few birds may turn up on freshwater inland. The greatest numbers gather on rocky and stony beaches, where seaweed covers a rich supply of food. They search along the tideline in small feeding parties, often in the company of other waders – dunlin, ringed plovers and purple sandpipers. On the shore, their mottled backs provide good camouflage against the stones, pebbles and seaweed. The first sight of a flock may be as they fly up, showing the black and white pattern of their wings. They are noisy birds for their size, twittering 'kit-kit-kit' when disturbed, or crying a clear 'kecoo-kecoo'.

In summer almost all of the turnstones return north to breed in the Arctic. They nest on rocky islands, often close to bigger birds, such as gulls and skuas, which would take their eggs if the turnstones did not keep a constant watch. A few non-breeders stay in Britain, especially on the north and west coasts.

RECOGNITION

In winter upper parts are black-brown, underparts white except for broad dark breast-band; in summer upper parts appear tortoiseshell, head is more white; bill short and black; legs orange; sexes alike.

NESTING

Does not breed in Britain; nest, either on bare rock or in tussock, is sometimes scantily lined with vegetation; lays May–June; 4 eggs, green with brown markings; incubation about 21 days, mainly by female; chicks, tended by both sexes, leave nest within a few hours.

FEEDING

Sandhoppers, shellfish, insects; young fish and remains of fish; bread and carrion have been recorded.

SIZE

23cm (9in)

The yelping wail of a herring gull is a common sound on the coast

HERRING GULL

JUVENILE

ADULT

J F M A M J
J A S O N D

Herring gull Larus argentatus

RECOGNITION

Grey back; white underparts; yellow bill with red spot; pink legs; young are brown-backed with dark tail band; sexes alike.

NESTING

Nests in colonies; both sexes build fairly bulky nest of local materials, on ground, cliff ledge or building; lays late April–June; usually 3 eggs, olive-brown with darker marks; incubation about 26 days, by both parents; chicks, tended by both parents, stay in or near nest for a week or two, then remain nearby, often hidden, until they can fly – after about 6 weeks.

FEEDING

Edible offal; shellfish; eggs and chicks; fish.

SIZE

Herring: 58.5cm (23in)
Yellow-legged: 61cm (24in)

The herring gull's ability to eat almost anything, from fish offal to the young of its own kind, has made it one of the most successful species in Britain. Numbers surged with increased amounts and ready availability of edible refuse, but the population then suffered a downturn, almost halving in the past 30 years. Its extended breeding range, however, still includes buildings in coastal towns and inland bogs and lakes, as well as its traditional nesting places on sea-cliffs and islands.

In winter the herring gull is abundant in fishing ports and harbours. It scavenges along the coastline and has developed a habit of cracking open shellfish by dropping them from the air. Inland, herring gulls feed over farmland and rubbish dumps, and roost at night on large reservoirs. Some birds feed in these districts all year round.

At breeding colonies, loud with wailing and yelping 'keeow' calls, one of the parent birds must stand guard against the depredations of neighbouring gulls from the moment the eggs are laid. Otherwise few of their chicks would get the chance to begin their four-year growth to full maturity.

The darker-backed yellow-legged gull (*Larus cachinnans*), previously regarded as a herring gull sub-species, is now known to visit southern Britain regularly. A few pairs have even begun to nest there.

JUVENILE

ADULT

J	F	M	A	M	J
J	A	S	O	N	D

Common gulls in winter often feed on fields far inland

Common gull Larus canus

Despite its name, this bird is not the commonest British gull – herring gulls and black-headed gulls are far more numerous, both inland and around the coast – but the common gull is by no means rare and it is thought to be slowly increasing. Like the herring gull, it is a scavenger, eating almost anything that comes its way. It also shares the herring gull's habit of dropping shellfish from the air, to burst them open upon the shore. A feeding habit of its own is that it will wait until a bolder, black-headed gull has taken food from a human's hand, then dart in to rob the other bird.

Common gulls are widespread in winter, following herring and black-headed gulls to their feeding places round the coast and in towns, but as breeding birds their range is more limited. They nest on moors, bogs, loch islands, coastal marshes and shingle beaches, usually in small colonies, but sometimes in pairs, apart from other birds. They breed in many parts of Scotland and Ireland. In England the only long-standing colony is a small one at Dungeness, in Kent.

The characteristic calls of the common gull are a mewing 'kak-kak-kak' and a screaming 'keeee-ya' – both like herring-gull calls, but not so piercing. It also looks like the herring gull, except that it is smaller, its legs are yellow-green and its bill has no red spot.

RECOGNITION

Grey back; white underparts; black wing-tips with white spots; yellow bill and yellow-green legs; young are dark brown above, with white underparts and broad dark band on end of tail; sexes alike.

NESTING

Usually nests in small colonies, on ground; nest built by both sexes, of local materials; lays late May–early June; usually 3 eggs, olive with dark markings; incubation about 26 days, by both parents; chicks, tended by both parents, leave in first week, fly after 4–5 weeks.

FEEDING

Any edible refuse; shellfish; earthworms and insects; seeds; small mammals, small birds and their eggs.

SIZE

43cm (17in)

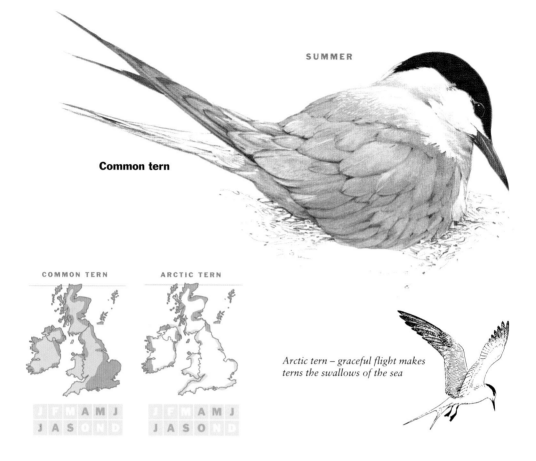

SUMMER

Common tern

COMMON TERN   ARCTIC TERN

Arctic tern – graceful flight makes
terns the swallows of the sea

| J | F | M | A | M | J |
| J | A | S | O | N | D |

| J | F | M | A | M | J |
| J | A | S | O | N | D |

Common tern Sterna hirundo

Intensely aggressive at its breeding colonies, the common tern dive-bombs intruders, screaming its anger with harsh cries of 'keeyah', and has been known to draw blood from a human's head. Exactly the same behaviour is displayed by the Arctic tern (*Sterna paradisaea*).

The two species are also alike in other ways. Both have shrill 'kik-kik-kik' and 'keerree' calls; both have the habit in courtship of presenting a fish to the female; and their plumages are so similar that it is hard to tell them apart. The Arctic tern has paler, semi-transparent, more sharply tapered wing-tips and shorter legs than the common tern. The common's wing-tips are marked with darker outer feathers.

Another guide is their distribution in the breeding season. The common tern is more likely to be seen in the south of Britain than is the Arctic tern. Both nest on sand or shingle beaches, rocky islands and salt-marshes but the Arctic tern does not regularly breed south of a diagonal line from Northumberland to Anglesey, and never breeds away from the coast. The common tern's breeding range extends farther south, and the bird has increasingly taken to nesting inland in recent years.

Twice yearly the Arctic tern sets out on an amazing journey, which carries it from one end of the globe to the other. It nests from Britain northwards to the Arctic, and winters 10,000 miles away in Antarctic seas.

Roseate tern hovers over water before diving for a fish

SUMMER

Roseate tern Sterna dougallii

The roseate tern is by far the rarest of Britain's terns, with very few regular colonies left after years of decline. Although more than 3,500 pairs nested in the early 1960s, now fewer than 100 is the norm, plus slightly better numbers in Ireland.

Long-established colonies in Wales have disappeared, and in England only one colony off the Northumberland coast remains. Even when more numerous, roseate terns were notorious for their habit of deserting a breeding site suddenly and for no apparent reason, and setting up a new colony elsewhere. In a less intense form of this mass desertion, pairs of roseates often set up their nests in the terneries of other species. They give away their presence by their cries, a long drawn-out 'aach-aach' and a softer 'tchu-ick' and 'chik-ik' note. They breed on sandy beaches or shingle, and their nests are scrapes in the ground, usually unlined.

When the bird is seen at a distance, its pink breast does not show up and it closely resembles the common and Arctic terns, but it can be identified by its black bill, which goes red at the base for a few weeks in midsummer, and by its longer tail streamers.

RECOGNITION

Whiter than common or Arctic, with black crown and nape, and pink flush on breast in summer; black bill, red at the base in midsummer; red legs, long white tail streamers; sexes alike.

NESTING

Nests in colonies; both sexes make scrapes in sand or shingle; final nest is only rarely lined, with vegetation or rabbit droppings; lays June–July; 1 or 2 eggs, creamy or buff, blotched and spotted with chestnut; incubation about 24 days, by both parents; chicks, tended by both parents, leave in a few days, fly after about 4 weeks.

FEEDING

Mainly small fish.

SIZE

38cm (15in)

SUMMER

J F M A M J
J A S O N D

Male displays with wings held out and neck stretched up

Sandwich tern Sterna sandvicensis

RECOGNITION

Very pale grey and white; black crest; black bill with yellow tip; wings and back pearly grey; forked tail; young brown and white; sexes alike.

NESTING

Nests in colonies; both sexes make scrapes in ground; chosen scrape sometimes lined with grass; lays May–June; usually 1 or 2 eggs, any colour from white to deep brown, usually spotted, blotched or smeared with darker brown; incubation about 23 days, by both sexes; chicks, tended by both sexes, leave within a few hours, fly after about 5 weeks.

FEEDING

Small fish – often sand-eels.

SIZE

40.5cm (16in)

Sandwich terns often set up their colonies on the same sites as more aggressive birds, relying on them to drive off intruders. There is a price to pay for this protection – whenever they leave their nests unattended, their chicks are at risk from the other species, which may inflict heavy losses.

About 11,000 breeding pairs of sandwich terns are scattered in about 30 colonies round the British Isles, from Orkney to the south coast of England. The bulk of them nest in a comparatively few colonies from the Firth of Forth down the east coast of England to East Anglia. Sometimes they switch sites from year to year, but in most years there is a large colony on the Farne Islands, off Northumberland.

The bird is the largest British tern, and one of the earliest summer visitors – the first migrants often arrive by the end of March. Sandwich terns prefer shingle beaches, sandy coasts and offshore islands for breeding, but in Ireland they occasionally nest on lake islands. Elsewhere they are rarely seen inland, even at migration times. A special gliding flight signifies courtship, and the male will feed fish to the female and lead her to a scrape in the ground. Once the birds have settled in, they make the air over their colonies loud with harsh 'kirrick' and 'kirwhit' calls.

The sandwich tern is named after the seaside town in Kent but has long since deserted the area.

Male presents female with a sand-eel – a courtship gift

Little tern Sterna albifrons

This is the smallest of Britain's breeding terns, and, after the roseate tern, the rarest. Its numbers have fallen seriously in the past 30 years because its breeding sites on sandy coasts, shingle beaches and islands have been disturbed by holidaymakers. A handful of colonies still exist – notably at Blakeney Point, Holkham and Great Yarmouth in Norfolk and at Langstone Harbour in Hampshire – but most are small, and barely more than 1,000 breeding pairs remain.

The nests are not as close together as in other terneries – they may be 9m (30ft) or more apart – but the birds are like most other terns in their way of dealing with intruders. They dive-bomb animals or gulls that approach their nests, and warn off interlopers with angry screams. Their chief call-notes are 'kik-kik' and 'pee-e-eer'.

The little tern is the only adult tern with a white patch on its forehead at all seasons. When its head is pointed away, it can be distinguished from the black tern, also a small bird, by its more deeply forked tail and less sharply defined shoulder patch. It is unusual to see little terns inland. Even on migration, they hug the coastline. Their courtship ceremonies follow the usual tern pattern, with a special display flight and the presentation of fish to the female.

RECOGNITION

White forehead all the year; yellow bill with black tip; bright orange feet; sexes alike.

NESTING

Breeds in small colonies on beaches; both sexes make scrape in ground and female sometimes lines chosen site with pebbles; lays May; 2 or 3 eggs, buff with dark spots; incubation about 22 days, by both parents; chicks, tended by both parents, leave after a few hours, fly after about 4 weeks.

FEEDING

Sand-eels and other small fish.

SIZE

23cm (9in)

J F M A M J
J A S O N D

Snow buntings show a flash of white wings as they fly in winter

MALE IN WINTER

Snow bunting Plectrophenax nivalis

RECOGNITION

In winter, both sexes are buff-brown above, white beneath; more white shows on male; in summer, male has black on back and centre of tail, rest of plumage pure white, bill orange.

NESTING

Female builds nest of dry grasses and moss, lined with hair and feathers; lays late May–June; 4–6 eggs, yellow-white, sometimes with green or blue tinge, with red-brown spots and blotches; incubation about 13 days, by female only; nestlings, tended by both parents, leave after about 11 days; sometimes two broods.

FEEDING

Seeds of grass, rushes and weeds; crane-flies and other flying insects in summer; occasionally grain, sandhoppers and beetles.

SIZE

16.5cm (6½in)

The flash of white wings when snow buntings are flushed in winter can come as a surprise to anybody who has been watching them feed, because their white markings are obscured by brown when they are on the ground.

Flocks of snow buntings can be seen all along the east coast from autumn until spring. They eat the seeds of coarse grass on sand-dunes and other rough open country near the coast. On the mainland they usually feed in small parties, but a flock some 2,000 strong has been recorded on Fair Isle. In their northern breeding grounds during summer, they often feed on insects carried on air currents and trapped in the snowfields.

A few snow buntings nest in Britain, but they are among the rarest breeding species, confined to mist-shrouded peaks in the Highlands. About 70 years ago they were more widespread in the region, but in recent years probably no more than 25 breeding pairs have been present in Britain at any one time, nearly all of them in the Cairngorms. Climate change may reduce numbers even more.

During the breeding season the male has a display flight in which it hovers almost like a skylark, singing vigorously.

Sea-cliffs and Rocky Islands

Nearly all birds of the open sea are suspicious of land, and at breeding times they tend to crowd into colonies on rocks, ledges and clifftops, often returning to traditional safe sites in vast numbers. Gannets have massed on the Bass Rock for centuries, making the air ring with their noisy cries.

Fulmar holds its wings stiffly as it wheels over the sea

J	F	M	A	M	J
J	A	S	O	N	D

Fulmar Fulmarus glacialis

RECOGNITION

Pale grey back, wings and tail; white head and underparts; tubular nostrils show at close range; stiff-winged flight; sexes alike.

NESTING

Nests on cliffs; scrape in turf or depression in rock; nest sometimes lined with a few pebbles; lays May; 1 egg, white; incubation about 52 or 53 days, by both parents; nestling, fed by both parents, leaves after about 53 days.

FEEDING

Fish, whale or seal offal; also fish and crustacea.

SIZE

47cm (18½in)

One hundred years ago, fulmars barely had a toehold in Britain. They bred on the most westerly of the Outer Hebrides, St Kilda. Then, at the beginning of the 20th century, they colonised Foula in the Shetlands, and so began a spectacular advance that has been restricted only by the coastline.

At least 500 colonies are inhabited by more than 600,000 pairs of breeding birds, on suitable cliffs all around the coast. There is some argument about the reason for this population explosion, but most ornithologists link it with an increase in the amount of offal being discarded by trawlers.

Like shearwaters and petrels, the fulmar is a bird of the open sea. It has the effortless gliding flight typical of shearwaters, but occasionally flaps its wings like a gull and rises higher than most of the shearwaters.

Colonies are occupied throughout the year except in September and October, although the attendance of individual pairs is sporadic outside the breeding season. In May, the female lays a single egg in a hollow in turf or on a bare rock. Fulmars will look over a possible site for several years before settling there. Any intruders at their colonies risk being hit by a foul-smelling fluid that the birds eject from their mouths.

Fulmars have an exceptionally long period of immaturity, and on average do not start breeding until they are nine years of age.

Shearwaters gliding over the sea almost touch the waves

F M A M J
J A S O N D

Manx shearwater Puffinus puffinus

A Manx shearwater, taken from its breeding site on the Welsh island of Skokholm and released in Massachusetts, well away from its normal range, found its way back to its mate and chick in 12 days. The experiment proved what ornithologists already suspected – that the birds have a phenomenal homing ability. Many of those seen around the coast of Britain in summer go halfway across the world in winter, to the South Atlantic. They cover vast distances in an almost effortless gliding flight, sometimes swooping so low that the tips of their long, narrow wings actually shear the waves. On land, by contrast, they are awkward birds, able to move only with an ungainly shuffle, but they never go ashore, except to breed.

Manx shearwaters breed on turfy islands along the western seaboard. The Skomer colony numbers some 95,000 pairs. At sea, the birds are normally silent, but at night on their breeding grounds they set up an extraordinary noise. They nest in burrows, often taking over rabbit warrens, and in the hour before midnight, particularly when there is no moon, the shearwaters produce an unearthly chorus as their mates fly in from fishing expeditions. The burrows, honeycombing the ground, throb with an eerie range of strangled cooing noises.

The Balearic shearwater (*Puffinus mauretanicus*), an endangered species from the Mediterranean, is larger and browner than the Manx and regularly visits British and Irish seas in the autumn.

RECOGNITION

Upper parts, crown and nape black; chin, throat and underparts white; sexes alike.

NESTING

Both sexes excavate burrow in turf, usually at least 1m (3ft) deep; often takes over rabbit burrow; lays April–May; 1 egg, white; incubation 47–55 days, by both parents; nestling, tended by both parents, fledges in 62–76 days.

FEEDING

Small fish, such as herring, sprats and pilchards.

SIZE

Manx: 35.5cm (14in)
Balearic: 38cm (15in)

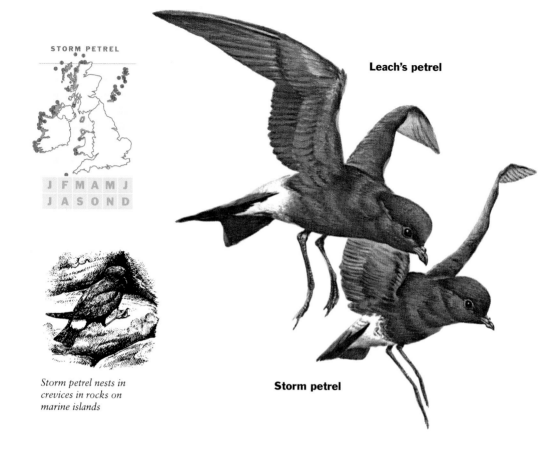

STORM PETREL

J F M A M J
J A S O N D

Leach's petrel

Storm petrel

Storm petrel nests in crevices in rocks on marine islands

Storm petrel Hydrobates pelagicus

RECOGNITION

Storm petrel has sooty plumage, white rump, long wings, square tail; weaving flight near water; follows ships; Leach's petrel, larger and browner with forked tail, has buoyant, erratic flight; sexes alike in both cases.

NESTING

Both dig burrow, or nest in abandoned rabbit burrow or crevice among stones; usually lays June (storm), May or June (Leach's); 1 egg, white with faint brown spots; incubation about 44 days (storm), 50 days (Leach's), by both parents; nestlings, fed by both parents, leave after 7–8½ weeks.

FEEDING

Chiefly plankton, fish and floating oil; also seaweed.

SIZE

Storm: 15.25cm (6in)
Leach's: 20.25cm (8in)

The oceans of the world are home to the petrels. They go ashore only to breed or when driven by storms, but it takes a storm of extraordinary fury to get the better of these birds. They shelter from Atlantic gales by keeping to the troughs of waves and avoiding the crests. On calm days they often patter over the surface of the water as if walking – the name 'petrel' is said to have been derived from the biblical episode in which St Peter walked on the water. The storm petrel, once known to sailors as 'Mother Carey's Chicken', follows ships, feeding on plankton, offal and oil churned up by the ship's passage.

When on land for the breeding season, petrels keep to their burrows on rocky islands, and only their nocturnal crooning or purring 'songs' indicate where they are. The storm petrel has colonies in the Scillies, on Skokholm and Skomer off the Pembroke coast, and on many islands off the west and north coasts of Scotland and the west and southwest coasts of Ireland.

Leach's petrel (*Oceanodroma leucorrhoa*), more widely distributed on a world scale, is less widespread as a British breeding species. It breeds mainly in four colonies on the most oceanic of the Scottish islands – the Flannans, North Rona, St Kilda and Sula Sgeir.

Adult gannet glides over the sea – its wings can span 2m (6ft)

Gannet Morus bassanus

Flying far across the North Atlantic, gannets wheel against the wind on barely moving wings, resting in the waves when they must, and seldom going to any shore except when instinct calls them to the lonely fortresses that are their breeding grounds. Two-thirds of the world's gannets are hatched on the cliff ledges of around 20 UK gannetries. One of the largest, after a huge increase, is on the Bass Rock in the Firth of Forth. A visitor noted in 1518: 'Near to Gleghornie, in the ocean, at a distance of two leagues, is the Bass Rock, wherein is an impregnable stronghold. Round about it is seen a multitude of great ducks that live on fish.' Now, more than 490 years later, the 'great ducks' are still there, 50,000 pairs of them, packed close together. So many huge webbed feet might seem a threat to the eggs but, in fact, gannets incubate with their feet, placing one over the other, and both over a single egg.

For most of the year, gannets are silent birds, but they make up for this in the breeding season. The screeching roar of a gannet colony – the biggest in the world is on St Kilda, most remote of the the Outer Hebrides – has few equals in nature.

The gannets' fishing technique is spectacular. They dive-bomb their catch from as high as 30m (100ft), with their wings – which can span 2m (6ft) – folded back to form a living arrowhead.

RECOGNITION

White plumage with black wing-tips; 2m (6ft) wing-span; pale blue bill; immatures, dark brown with white cheeks, resemble adults by fourth year; sexes alike.

NESTING

Both sexes gather pile of seaweed and flotsam, build on cliff ledge or flat ground; lays March–June; 1 egg, white; incubation about 44 days, by both parents; nestling, fed by both parents, flies and makes own way to sea after 90 days.

FEEDING

Fish, edible offal.

SIZE

91.5cm (36in)

SUMMER

Cormorant stands with spread wings, to dry out its feathers

Cormorant Phalacrocorax carbo

RECOGNITION

Black with green gloss and white face-patch; hooked beak; white patch on thighs in summer; upright stance when settled; sexes alike.

NESTING

Nests in colonies on cliff ledges, flat rocks, or grassy headlands, occasionally in trees inland; both sexes make mound of dried seaweed and sticks; lays April–June; usually 3 or 4 eggs, pale blue; incubation about 29 days, by both parents; nestlings, fed by both parents, leave after about 4 weeks, fly after about 8 weeks.

FEEDING

Chiefly flat-fish; also wrasse, sand-eels, sticklebacks, and occasionally crabs.

SIZE

91.5cm (36in)

These are among Britain's most pervasive breeding seabirds. In recent years their numbers have increased enormously, and cormorants have spread inland to form new colonies in the English midlands and southeast. During the breeding season they are most often seen on cliffs and marine islands, but at other times of year they can be found on sandy and muddy shores as well, and non-breeding birds are increasingly numerous on island reservoirs and lakes.

The cormorant eats about one-sixth of its body weight of fish in a day, which is a normal amount. It is a strong underwater swimmer, pressing its wings to its body and driving forward with powerful movements of its webbed feet. Back on the surface, the bird rises heavily from the sea and flaps low over the waves on the way back to its nest and young. The nestlings peck impatiently at the parent bird's bill until it regurgitates its catch. Then they jostle to get into position for poking their bills down its gullet.

In between diving after fish and feeding their young, cormorants often perch on posts and buoys, with their wings stretched out. They are the only web-footed birds that do not secrete a waterproofing oil for their feathers, and so they must dry out every time they come to land.

J F M A M J
J A S O N D

SUMMER

Shag flies faster than cormorant, and has no white face-patch

Shag Phalacrocorax aristotelis

With a show of instinctive courage, the parent shag sticks to its seaweed nest against all intruders, defying them by hissing, croaking and pecking menacingly at the air. It can also grunt, startlingly like a pig. The normally nervous shag maintains this vigil on rocks and cliff ledges throughout its breeding season.

The shag breeds all around the British coast, except between Flamborough Head and the Isle of Wight. Around the end of the First World War, the bird established itself on the Isle of May in the Firth of Forth, and that colony has now grown to more than 800 pairs. From there, shags moved into the Farne Islands off Northumberland in about 1930, and have built up to more than 350 pairs there, and at the end of the 1940s they began breeding at Flamborough Head, where there is now a thriving colony.

Unlike the cormorant, to which it is closely related, the shag is confined to cliffs, rocky coasts and offshore islands and is rarely seen on muddy or sandy shores or estuaries. It never goes far inland, unless driven by storms. The shag has a fast, direct flight, more rapid and graceful than that of the cormorant, with which it shares a habit of perching on rocks, sometimes with wings outspread.

RECOGNITION

Plumage black, with satin-green tinge; no white patches on face or thighs; distinct crest in spring and summer; sexes alike.

NESTING

Nests in colonies on rocks, cliff ledges or in a cavity among boulders; both sexes build nest of sticks and seaweed, lined with grass; usually lays March–May; usually 3 eggs, pale blue; incubation about 31 days, by both parents; nestlings, fed by both parents, fly after 48–58 days.

FEEDING

Fish, especially wrasse, blenny, goby, dragonet, garfish and sand-eels.

SIZE

76.25cm (30in)

J F M A M J
J A S O N D

MALE

*Peregrine, stooping head-
long from above, prepares
to strike*

Peregrine Falco peregrinus

RECOGNITION

Long wings, broad-based
tail; anchor shape when
gliding; grey above with
paler rump, white below
with dark bars; white throat
against black cheeks and
hood; juvenile streaked
beneath. Flies with
deep, rapid beats and
short glides.

NESTING

Nests in bare scrape on
rock ledge or in abandoned
nest of other species;
usually lays April; usually
3 or 4 eggs, red-brown;
incubation about 30 days,
chiefly by female; nestlings,
fed by both sexes, leave
after 30–40 days.

FEEDING

Birds on the wing; some
rabbits and other mammals.

SIZE

Male: 38cm (15in)
Female: 48.25cm (19in)

Soaring high above its hunting territory, the peregrine looks too
remote to be menacing, but once it has singled out its prey – a
gull, perhaps, or an unsuspecting feral pigeon – it arches
through the sky in a breathtaking 'stoop', which gives its quarry
little chance of escape. Speeds of up to 145km/h (90mph) have
been measured for the diving peregrine, and the bird's talons
strike the quarry with such shattering force that they may break
off its head. If the prey somehow manages to dodge the attack,
the peregrine often stoops again and again.

Falconers have always prized these spectacular, efficient
killers, but their reputation as hunters led to large numbers of
peregrines being shot during the Second World War, because it
was thought that they were a threat to carrier pigeons, used
when radio silence was imposed on submarine-spotting planes.
As the peregrine population began to recover from this setback,
it was hit by a worse one – the birds were either poisoned or
made infertile by ingesting pesticides used on crops and eaten
by their prey.

In 1956 there were more than 650 pairs of peregrines in the
British Isles. Six years later, only 68 breeding pairs were left, but
the peregrine has staged a remarkable recovery. Now 1,400
pairs nest in the UK and 350 in Ireland, and several cities have
been colonised by nesting pairs feeding largely on town pigeons.

Peregrines mate for life, and often return year after year to
the same eyrie.

Great skua in flight shows bold white patch on wing

Great skua Catharacta skua

In common with other skuas, the great skua is a pirate. It harries gulls and other seabirds until they choke up their last meal. Slow and heavy in normal flight, the great skua turns into a skilful flier when it hunts, twisting from side to side as it chases a gull as big as itself. A great skua will even tackle a gannet, sometimes hanging on to its tail or a wing-tip until it gives up the fish it has just swallowed.

In their journeys over the Atlantic, great skuas will follow fishing-boats to pick up offal flung overboard. They are capable of catching their own food by fishing, killing young birds or scavenging on the carcases of stranded sea animals, such as whales and seals.

Great skuas spend most of the year on the ocean, only coming to land to breed. Until 110 years ago, they were found in Britain on just two of the Shetland Islands, Unst and Foula. They have since increased in numbers and range, but now the colonies in the Scottish islands are in decline again as dwindling fish stocks affect the seabirds from which they prefer to steal their food.

In courtship, pairs soar in circles over the nesting site. On the ground they have a bowing ceremony. They are aggressive birds, fearlessly driving away people or animals from their colonies. They have been seen to cling to the head of an intruding sheep and batter it with their wings until the bruised animal is driven away.

RECOGNITION

Brown, heavily built, gull-like bird with short tail; white wing-patch; sexes alike.

NESTING

Both sexes make scrape in ground on heath or rough grass, sparsely lined with lichen and other plants; lays late May–June; usually 2 eggs, olive to green, with dark brown blotches; incubation 29 or 30 days, by both parents; nestlings, tended by both parents, leave nest after a few days and fly after 40–50 days.

FEEDING

Mainly fish stolen by forcing other birds to disgorge; some young birds, carrion and offal.

SIZE

58.5cm (23in)

Arctic skua in pursuit of
tern – it gives up only when
the tern drops its fish

Arctic skua Stercorarius parasiticus

RECOGNITION

Dark brown upper parts, underparts vary from light brown to dark brown, with intermediate forms; all mature birds have two central tail feathers which stick out in a distinctive point; sexes alike.

NESTING

Usually nests in colonies on moors and other rough land; both sexes make scrape, sparsely lined with dry grass or other local material; lays June; usually 2 eggs, olive-green to brown with dark markings; incubation 25–28 days, by both parents; chicks, tended by both parents, leave shortly after hatching, fly after about 5 weeks.

FEEDING

Fish disgorged by other birds; small mammals; eggs and chicks; insects and their larvae; carrion; berries.

SIZE

45.75cm (18in)

When a seabird is attacked it will often vomit up its last meal, so reducing its weight for a quick escape. Skuas take advantage of this behaviour, hurtling down on gulls, terns and kittiwakes and bullying them until they disgorge the fish they've just eaten. As well as finding food by this form of extortion, Arctic skuas are experienced nest robbers. Normally, they hunt singly – and they can terrorise birds far larger than themselves – but occasionally male and female go hunting together. They make an efficient team, with one bird matching itself against, say, a pair of common gulls while its mate robs their nest.

The Arctic skua is predominantly brown, but there are two main colour variants – a dark form and a light form – and intermediates between them are often seen. All adult Arctic skuas are easily recognisable by their two central tail feathers, which stick out in short, straight spikes beyond the rest of the tail.

Confined as a breeding bird to Scotland, the Arctic skua's numbers are falling due to lack of food. Like other skuas, it nests on moorlands often some distance inland, and not on sea-cliffs. It is boldly aggressive towards intruders at its colonies, where its wailing 'ka-aaow' and gruff 'tuk-tuk' are associated with a spectacular display flight.

Lesser black-back's nest is often concealed in vegetation

J F M A M J
J A S O N D

ADULT

JUVENILE

Lesser black-backed gull Larus fuscus

Like its close relative the herring gull, the lesser black-back is a scavenger. It sometimes follows ships for offal thrown into the sea, and often searches inland rubbish tips, on the look-out for anything that is edible. Its powerful, deliberate flight, with frequent soaring and gliding, is similar to the herring gull's. In fact, the two birds have so much in common that it is arguable whether they may be extreme forms of the same species. Their nests, eggs and young are alike; their vocabulary, with its wide range of keening, wailing, chuckling and yelping notes, is similar; both have a taste for carrion and are ruthless thieves of other birds' eggs and chicks.

Lesser black-backs breed round the Irish coasts, along the west side of Britain and down the east side to Yorkshire, and occasionally on parts of the south coast. Some colonies are to be found on moorland bogs and, nowadays, they also breed in towns well inland. The lesser black-back used to be a summer visitor, but for several decades many have remained in Britain throughout the winter. It is especially common in urban and industrial areas where it finds edible refuse on rubbish dumps.

RECOGNITION

Back usually more grey than great black-back's; bill much less stout; legs yellow (after third or fourth year); immatures have brown backs, pale underparts, broad band on end of tail; sexes alike.

NESTING

Nests in colonies, on ground or on cliff ledges, sometimes in deep cover, such as bracken or heather; both sexes build nest of grass, seaweed and feathers; lays May–June; usually 3 eggs, olive-brown or light green with brown marks; incubation about 27 days, by both parents; young, fed chiefly by female, fly after about 5 weeks.

FEEDING

Carrion and garbage; fish, shellfish, worms, insects, mice, voles, birds and eggs; also seaweed and grain.

SIZE

53.25cm (21in)

Great black-backed gull Larus marinus

Black back, white
underparts; dark markings
on head in winter;
immatures brown above,
pale below; sexes alike.

Nests in small groups, on
ground, rocky stack or cliff
ledge; both sexes build
substantial nest of heather,
seaweed and other local
materials; lays April–May;
usually 3 eggs, olive or light
brown with dark spots;
incubation about 27 days,
by both parents; young,
fed by both parents, leave
after 2–3 weeks, fly after
7–8 weeks.

Almost any kind of animal
food, including dead fish,
offal, carrion and other
birds; small vegetable
element.

68.5cm (27in)

With its great weight and formidable beak, this largest of
Britain's gulls is the likely victor in any fight for offal with other
gulls – and it can be a ferocious killer in seabird colonies,
tearing its prey inside out. Eider ducklings that stray from their
parents are among its favourite quarry. It can gulp them down
in a single mouthful. In defence of its own eggs and young it
swoops low over intruders.

Partly because it will eat almost any animal food, alive or
dead, partly because it is no longer a target for marksmen, as it
was at the end of the 19th century, and partly because there has
been an increase in the amount of edible offal left unburnt at
fish docks and other places, the great black-back is a species
on the advance. It breeds widely all round the British Isles,
except on the east coast of England and the southeast coasts
of both England and Scotland. However, unlike most of its
close relations, the great black-back does not breed far away
from the coast anywhere in the British Isles, although it has
become considerably more common inland than used to be
the case outside the breeding season.

Its voice is basically like the herring gull's 'kyow-kyow-
kyow', but deeper and more raucous. The great black-back also
has a chuckling 'uk-uk-uk' call, which it utters especially when
its breeding territory is being invaded by a human intruder.

JUVENILE

J F M A M J
J A S O N D

ADULT IN
SUMMER

Kittiwakes nest in close-packed colonies on cliff ledges

Kittiwake Rissa tridactyla

Alone among the gulls breeding in Britain, the kittiwake is faithful to the sea. Other gulls have taken advantage of man-made food supplies, flocking to rubbish dumps, sewage outfalls and food markets, but the kittiwake roams the sea for much of the year, following the movements of fish and ships, and rarely goes to land except to breed.

The kittiwake also differs from other British gulls in building a fairly elaborate cup-shaped nest. It uses mud to anchor the nest to narrow ledges, such as ridges on cliff-faces, projections on seaside piers or even window sills. The kittiwake's claws are longer and sharper than those of other gulls, giving it a more secure footing on its ledge. Its young, secure in their cup, stay in their nest for more than six weeks after hatching until they can fly – to leave earlier would mean falling to their deaths.

At its breeding colonies the air is filled with deafening cries of 'kitt-ee-wayke', from which the bird takes its name. This note features largely in the mutual bowing and bill-rubbing courtship ceremonies.

Kittiwake numbers increased substantially during the 20th century, but even some of the largest colonies have recently failed to produce any young. The reason is a reduction of their food supply, and the population is plummeting dramatically.

RECOGNITION

White with black wing-tips; uniform grey head and nape in winter; black legs and yellow bill; immatures have dark stripes on wings; dark markings on head in winter; sexes alike.

NESTING

Nests in colonies, usually on narrow cliff ledges or inside sea caves; both sexes build cup-shaped nest of seaweed and other local materials; lays May–June; 1–3 eggs, pale blue-grey to buff-brown with dark blotches and spots; incubation 26–28 days, by both parents; young, fed by both parents, leave after 40–45 days.

FEEDING

Almost entirely fish and fish offal.

SIZE

40.5cm (16in)

J F M A M J
J A S O N D

SUMMER

*Guillemot in winter has
black streak behind its eye*

Guillemot Uria aalge

Pointed bill; upper parts
dark brown in summer,
greyer in winter, though
birds in northern Britain are
darker; in less common
'bridled' variety, birds have
white ring around eye with
a white line running back
from it over sides of head;
sexes alike.

NESTING

Breeds on rock ledges,
without nesting material;
lays May–June; 1 egg, pear-
shaped, very variable in
colour – blue-green, brown,
buff, yellow or white, usually
with yellow, brown or black
blotches; incubation 32–36
days, by both parents;
chick, fed by both parents,
flutters down to sea
after about 16 days,
accompanied by a parent.

FEEDING

Fish, shellfish; worms;
some seaweed.

SIZE

42cm (16½in)

Late in January, after months spent at sea, guillemots gather
near the cliffs where they will nest. As more birds flock in they
begin complex ceremonies, in which groups 'dance' over the
water. Weaving and dodging, the birds patter over the waves
until, suddenly, the whole flock may dive at once and the dance
goes on underwater. Guillemots also take part in communal
display flights. Flocks hundreds strong wheel, soar and dive as if
controlled by one mind.

When they begin to move on to their cliff ledges in spring, the
guillemots at first leave plenty of space between one bird and
the next. The ledges quickly fill up with jostling birds, though,
their 'arrr' cries combining into a growling chorus as they
struggle for breeding sites.

Guillemots make no nest. The female lays her single egg on a
bare rock, but the egg is pear-shaped so that if it is knocked or
caught by the wind, it is less likely to roll off the ledge. By the
time the guillemots have laid their eggs, the ledges are filled
with rows of birds packed almost shoulder to shoulder, facing
inwards, with their eggs clutched between their legs. Usually, by
February, most of their number have arrived off the cliffs and
they normally leave in July, spending the rest of the year out at
sea. Many colonies have recently suffered massive declines in
breeding success.

Razorbill's throat and sides of neck are white in winter

SUMMER

J F M A M J
J A S O N D

Razorbill Alca torda

Like all members of the auk family, razorbills are expert divers and underwater swimmers. They use their wings as paddles, forcing their buoyant bodies down below the surface. The greatest depth recorded for a razorbill's dive is 7m (24ft), and one has been timed as staying down for as long as 52 seconds.

For much of the year razorbills keep well out to sea, but about the middle of winter they move to waters near cliffs and rock-strewn shores, where they will breed. Colonies of nesting razorbills are usually established close to the breeding grounds of the related guillemot, often on another part of the same cliff-face. They lay a single egg in a cavity towards the top of the cliff or under a boulder on the shore.

Pairs of courting birds often pose in what is known as the 'ecstatic' posture. One bird points its bill upwards, with the jaws slightly parted and vibrating with a castanet-like rattle, while its mate nibbles at its throat. Mated razorbills may also touch, rub and cross their bills – they get their name from the bill's similarity to a cut-throat razor.

At sea, where flocks of razorbills form 'rafts' on the waves, they take part in communal displays. Birds shake their heads from side to side and swim rapidly around within the group. Sometimes they make sudden dives, reappearing in the ecstatic pose.

RECOGNITION

Heavy bill; black upper parts; white wing-stripe; in summer, head and neck are black, with white line from bill to eye; in winter, throat and sides of neck are white; sexes alike.

NESTING

Nests in crevice of cliff or under boulder; no nesting material; lays May–June; 1 egg, wide colour variation including brown, cream, white and blue-green, with brown or black blotches; incubation about 35 days, by both parents; nestling, fed by both parents, flutters down to sea after 16–21 days.

FEEDING

Fish, shellfish, worms

SIZE

40.5cm (16in)

J F M A M J
J A S O N D

In winter, black guillemot's back is barred black and white

SUMMER

Black guillemot Cepphus grylle

Summer – plumage black, with conspicuous white wing-patch; winter – upper parts barred black and white, head and underparts white, wing-patch as in summer; sexes alike.

Builds no nest; eggs laid in crevices in cliffs or among boulders, in holes in walls, or sometimes in shallow burrows; lays May–June; usually 2 eggs, buff or blue-green with black, red-brown or grey blotches; incubation about 28 days, by both parents; nestlings, fed by both parents, leave and fly after about 35 days.

Small fish, small crabs, shrimps, prawns and shellfish; some seaweed and drowned insects.

34.25cm (13½in)

Whatever the time of year, the black guillemot is unlikely to be mistaken for any other seabird, because no other bird around British coasts is anything like it in plumage. In summer, the bird is all black apart from a broad white patch on its wings. In winter its back is barred black and white, with the head and underparts mainly white.

In courtship, too, the black guillemot is in a class of its own, its wide variety of displays usually involving several pairs of birds. In one, a bird swims around its mate, opening its bill to show its brilliant red gape and giving a squeaky cry while the other bird squeaks and nods its head in reply.

Parties of birds often swim in formation, although this is not a courtship display and is probably connected with feeding. The birds move with almost military precision over the water in a file, a rank or a staggered line.

Black guillemots are more sedentary than Britain's other breeding members of the auk family. Instead of making for the open sea, they spend the winter close to the rocky, cliff-lined coasts where they breed. Their main breeding grounds are in Shetland, the far northeast of the Scottish mainland and the islands and mainland of western Scotland. Small numbers breed in Ireland, the Isle of Man, Anglesey and Cumbria.

Puffin in winter – its triangular bill is always distinctive

SUMMER

J F M A M J
J A S O N D

Puffin Fratercula arctica

Its huge, brightly coloured bill – comical in the eyes of some observers – is for the puffin a weapon, a digging tool and an advertising medium. Puffins thrust their bills at neighbours as a threat, which may be the prelude to a fight. They toss their heads, hiding their bills, when they want to make peace, and pairs of birds put their bills together in courtship. On the turf-covered sea-cliffs, which are their main breeding sites, puffins hack into the soil – or even into soft rock – with their bills to make nesting burrows, shovelling away the loose earth with their webbed feet.

The puffin sometimes collects grass and feathers to line its nest, plucking pieces of vegetation until it has a heap of materials clasped in its bill. Then it shuffles back to its nest-hole with its finds.

The bill is at its brightest in summer, when puffins go ashore to breed. In winter, when they live on the sea, the bill changes, losing its horny sheath and exposing the duller colours beneath. Puffins usually winter in sea areas a little south of their breeding grounds, but they are sometimes seen on deeper water.

Puffins have declined in Britain, particularly in the south. Between the Scillies and the Isle of Wight, colonies of thousands once held sway, but no more than a few dozen puffins remain there now.

RECOGNITION

Huge bill, blue, yellow and red in summer; mainly yellow and horn-coloured in winter; black upper parts and white underparts; sexes alike.

NESTING

Both sexes dig burrow in turf or under boulders, or occupy old shearwater or rabbit burrow; nest may be lined with vegetation and feathers; lays May; 1 egg, white with faint brown markings; incubation about 6 weeks, mainly by female; nestling is fed by parents in burrow for about 6 weeks, then deserted and left hungry; after several days' fast, it crawls out and flutters down to the sea by night.

FEEDING

Marine organisms, including molluscs and small fish.

SIZE

30.5cm (12in)

J F M A M J
J A S O N D

Rock dove in flight shows black wing-bars and white rump

Rock dove Columba livia

RECOGNITION

Two black wing-bars, iridescent neck-patch of green and purple; distinguished from stock dove by white rump; sexes alike.

NESTING

Nests in colonies; builds untidy nest of twigs, roots, stems or seaweed in cliff hole or on ledge in cave; lays throughout the year, but mainly in spring and summer; usually 2 eggs, white; incubation 18 days, by both parents; nestlings, tended by both parents, leave after about 18 days; two broods, often three.

FEEDING

Mostly seeds and grain; peas, potatoes, shellfish and seaweed.

SIZE

33cm (13in)

Homing pigeons, and the feral pigeons that strut about urban pavements, are all descended from rock doves. In the days when an all-year-round supply of fresh meat was a rarity, rock doves were provided with dovecotes and kept for food in some places. When tame birds escaped, they interbred with birds from the ancestral stock, and hybrids have now replaced pure rock doves in many of their old breeding haunts. Most of the birds seen on cliffs, no matter how similar in appearance to the rock dove, are really descendants of pigeons that went wild.

The true rock dove is now largely confined to a few colonies in Scotland and Ireland, mainly on the north and west coasts. In other parts of the world, particularly in North Africa, rock doves live away from the sea on inland cliffs and in caves, but doves in these habitats in Britain are either domestic pigeons gone wild, stock doves or woodpigeons.

The rock dove's cooing voice is like that of the street pigeon. Its bowing courtship display is the same, too, but the bird is difficult to watch at breeding time because it builds in colonies inside dark sea-caves, slippery with spray, or in deep crevices in the cliffs.

In flight, the rock dove climbs for a short distance and then glides down on raised wings. It occasionally perches on trees, but prefers to land on rocks, on the ground or on buildings.

J F M A M J
J A S O N D

Rock pipit – this small song-bird stays by the sea all year round

Rock pipit Anthus spinoletta

This is the easiest of Britain's three breeding pipits to identify, not only because of its appearance but also because of its distinctive habitat. The rock pipit, somewhat larger and greyer than the tree pipit or the meadow pipit, never breeds anywhere but on coasts, and usually on wild, rocky shores. In winter it is still mainly a coastal bird, moving on to flat and muddy shores and salt-marshes. Just occasionally, it flies inland to feed beside reservoirs and other stretches of freshwater.

Another clue to recognition is the rock pipit's call-note, given in dipping flight – a single 'pheet' or 'fist' that is a little thicker and more slurred than the meadow pipit's nervy 'peet'. Its fluttering song-flight is similar to the meadow pipit's, though. The male rock pipit takes off from a rock or cliff ledge and launches into a song that gathers speed as the bird rises, culminating in a trill as it glides down.

In many parts of its range the rock pipit has adapted to a diet consisting mainly of very small sea snails, but on coasts with a good supply of seaweed it is chiefly an insect eater. A careful study of its diet on a stretch of coast in Cornwall showed that the most important item was kelp flies that bred on rotting seaweed. Sandhoppers and shorehoppers were also taken. In other parts of the country, rock pipits have eaten winged ants, beetles, slugs and even small fish.

RECOGNITION

Upper parts grey-brown; larger and greyer than meadow or tree pipit; tail has grey outer feathers; dark brown legs; sexes alike.

NESTING

Builds nest of dried grass in hole or crevice in cliff, often sheltered by vegetation, sometimes in a bank or wall; lays late April–June; usually 4 or 5 eggs, off-white with grey and brown speckles; incubation about 14 days, by female only; nestlings, fed by both sexes, leave after 16 days; usually two broods.

FEEDING

Chiefly small molluscs; also sandhoppers and other insects, many picked from rotting seaweed; some small fish, slugs and seeds.

SIZE

16.5cm (6½in)

Choughs often give spectacular and acrobatic aerial displays

JFMAMJ
JASOND

Chough Pyrrhocorax pyrrhocorax

RECOGNITION

Black plumage with green and blue gloss; curved red bill; red legs; sexes alike.

NESTING

Both sexes build nest of sticks, lined with wool and hair, in crevice or hole in cliff-face – often in sea-cave, sometimes inland in building or abandoned mineshaft; usually lays April–May; usually 3–6 eggs, white with green or cream tint and grey-brown blotches; incubation about 18 days, by female only; nestlings, fed by both sexes, leave after about 45 days.

FEEDING

Chiefly insects and larvae; worms, spiders and sometimes lizards.

SIZE

38cm (15in)

Nowadays the red-billed chough is a rare bird in the British Isles, breeding mainly on sea-cliffs in Wales, Ireland and, after a long absence, Cornwall. It was once much more widespread. The pioneering 18th-century naturalist, Gilbert White of Selborne, saw choughs on the Sussex cliffs. In Cornwall it was once so common that it was called the Cornish chough. Jackdaws have been blamed for invading the choughs' territory and driving them out, but it seems more likely that the jackdaws moved in after the choughs disappeared.

Choughs are sociable birds outside the breeding season, gathering in flocks of as many as 100 to roost on ledges, crevices and caves along the cliffs. They are often seen on coastal fields. A communal courtship ceremony, in which members of the flock strut and flap their wings together, has been recorded. In other courtship ceremonies, the male caresses the female's bill and preens her head feathers, often feeding her. The couple also have a display in the air.

In flight, choughs are spectacular performers, soaring in the updraught at the edge of cliffs and swooping from ledge to ledge, often diving acrobatically with wings almost closed, or turning over on their backs in the air. Their calls include distinctive, ringing 'chow' and 'chi-yaaa' notes.

A Guide to Rarer Birds

In spring and autumn, when great numbers of migrant birds are entering or leaving Britain, an unfamiliar silhouette flying along the shoreline or a strange bird feeding inland may defy quick identification. This could be one of the birds illustrated in the following pages – perhaps a rare passage migrant, resting in Britain before continuing its journey, or a storm-driven vagrant, hundreds of miles from its proper route.

Visitors from western Europe

The English Channel and the North Sea may not seem like much of a barrier to birds, but many species that breed on the western shores of the Continent do not breed in the British Isles, and a few, such as the pygmy owl and the middle spotted woodpecker, have never even been recorded on these shores. The tawny pipit and great reed warbler, both of which breed in the Netherlands, are remarkably rare in Britain.

A few of the visitors from western Europe once nested regularly in Britain, including the Kentish plover, which has been lost since the Second World War. Britain was always on the fringe of its range and probably some small change in climate or increase in human disturbance near its breeding quarters caused it to disappear. The goshawk was lost as a regular breeder long before the 20th century, although it now nests in various parts of England, Wales and Scotland, due mainly to falconers' introductions. Climatic reasons probably account for the fact that the golden oriole has never been firmly established, although it has bred in small numbers for the past 50 years.

Several more species have nested in Britain from time to time, often just once or twice. These include the white stork (which nested once on St Giles' Cathedral in Edinburgh as long ago as 1416), the red-crested pochard, little gull and Baillon's crake. The black woodpecker, woodchat shrike and tawny pipit were formerly believed to have bred here, but their breeding records are now generally discredited. In 1968 the bluethroat nested here for the very first time.

In autumn, regular passage migrants include the ortolan bunting and icterine warbler, which pass over eastern Britain almost every year. In winter, the great grey shrike and red-crested pochard are regular visitors to some parts of Britain.

Another group seems to visit these islands not as regular passage migrants on their way to winter quarters, but during their post-breeding dispersal before migration gets under way. These include the purple heron, which also occurs in spring, the ferruginous duck, which may also be seen in winter, and the melodious warbler.

Woodchat shrike
Lanius senator 17cm (6¾in)
Rare and irregular visitor, mainly in spring and autumn, to south and east England; may have bred in the Isle of Wight; breeds from North Sea to east of Mediterranean; winters in tropical Africa.

Great grey shrike
Lanius excubitor 24cm (9½in)
Regular winter visitor in very small numbers, especially to Scotland and eastern side of England; breeds across Europe north from central France; winters in southern Europe; grey and white body; black and white wings.

Firecrest
Regulus ignicapillus 9cm (3½in)
Small numbers have bred in England since 1961; also occurs as passage migrant in southern counties, and a few winter in southwest England; like a goldcrest, with black stripe through eye, white stripe above it.

Bluethroat
Luscinia svecica
14cm (5½in)
Scarce spring and autumn migrant, mostly on east coast; has bred in Scotland; often skulks on ground, among vegetation.

Tawny pipit
Anthus campestris
16.5cm (6½in)
Irregular visitor, mainly to coasts of southern England in autumn; breeds in Europe, Asia, northwest Africa; winters in Africa.

Golden oriole
Oriolus oriolus
24cm (9½in)
Breeds in tiny and decreasing numbers in East Anglia; otherwise rare, mainly spring visitor; winters mainly in tropical Africa.

Ortolan bunting
Emberiza hortulana
16.5cm (6½in)
Scarce spring and autumn passage migrant, especially on Fair Isle and along east coast, probably from Scandinavia.

Serin
Serinus serinus 11.5cm (4½in)
First bred in England in 1967 but only occasionally since; rare migrant. Spread northwest across Europe in last century; stumpy bill, bright yellow rump; male has yellow on head and breast.

Goshawk
Accipiter gentilis 53.25cm (21in)
Rare resident, breeding in several parts of Britain, some being introduced or falconers' escapes; resident in much of Europe; looks like a huge sparrowhawk with rounder tail, protruding head.

White stork
Ciconia ciconia 101.5cm (40in)
Rare vagrant, chiefly to East Anglia in spring and summer; bred once in Britain; decreasing as a breeding species in parts of Europe; also breeds in northwest Africa, Asia.

Night heron
Nycticorax nycticorax
61cm (24in)
Irregular visitor from the Netherlands and southern Europe, mainly to south and east coasts in spring and autumn; feral colony in Edinburgh; breeds in Europe, Asia, Africa.

Little bittern
Ixobrychus minutus 35.5cm (14in)
Irregular spring, early summer and autumn visitor, especially to southern England; has nested at least once in Britain; breeds in Europe, Asia, North Africa.

Purple heron
Ardea purpurea 78.75cm (31in)
Scarce visitor from the Netherlands, mainly to south and east coasts in spring and autumn; breeds in Europe, Asia, Africa; grey-brown appearance, with black and chestnut striped neck.

Baillon's crake
Porzana pusilla 17.75cm (7in)
Extremely rare spring and autumn vagrant to coastal counties; bred here occasionally until 1889; breeds in Europe, north to France, Holland and Germany; winters in North Africa; weak flight; heavily barred flanks.

Ferruginous duck
Aythya nyroca 40.5cm (16in)
Irregular visitor, mainly in autumn to East Anglia, from scattered breeding colonies in France, but chiefly in south and central Europe; breeds here in waterfowl collections; also breeds northwest Africa, Asia.

Red-crested pochard
Netta rufina 56cm (22in)
Rare winter visitor to eastern England from the Netherlands and central Europe; however, most are escapees from waterfowl collections, some now nesting in the wild; drake has orange-chestnut head, duck has pale cheeks.

Kentish plover
Charadrius alexandrinus
16cm (6¼in)
Now very rare migrant mainly on south and southeast coasts; nested in southeast England until 1950s; winters in Africa.

Gull-billed tern
Gelochelidon nilotica
38cm (15in)
Very rare visitor, mainly spring, on Channel and southeast coasts; winter range includes Red Sea and The Gulf.

Little gull
Hydrocoloeus minutus
28cm (11in)
Regular passage migrant and winter visitor in small numbers, chiefly on east coast and in Scotland; has nested in eastern England.

Savi's warbler
Locustella luscinioides
14cm (5½in)
Now very rare although it nested in East Anglia until mid 19th century; skulking; trilling song more buzzing than grasshopper warbler's.

Icterine warbler
Hippolais icterina
12.75cm (5in)
Scarce passage migrant on south and east coasts; winters in southern Africa.

Melodious warbler
Hippolais polyglotta
12.75cm (5in)
Scarce passage migrant in south; breeds in southwest Europe; winters in Africa.

Aquatic warbler
Acrocephalus paludicola
12.75cm (5in)
Annual autumn visitor in small numbers, especially to coastal counties in the south.

Great reed warbler
Acrocephalus arundi-naceus 19cm (7½in)
Rare visitor, to south coast in spring and autumn; winters in Africa; white eye-stripe.

Visitors from northern Europe

A belt of territory that stretches from Scandinavia eastwards across Russia to the Ural Mountains is the home of a substantial group of rarer visitors. They come to Britain when hard weather drives them further south than their usual winter range, or when they are blown off course on migration. Some of those that breed in Russia are often completely off any normal migration course but others, and especially the spotted redshank, are on their normal route and arrive in substantial numbers each year.

Other more frequently recorded visitors from northern Europe are the shore lark, rough-legged buzzard and Lapland bunting – all regular on parts of the east coast of Britain.

Most of the north European visitors are land birds, but a few – the crane, great snipe, broad-billed sandpiper and Caspian tern – are marsh or waterbirds. The crane performs one of the most remarkable known migrations, flying non-stop from its breeding grounds in Norway and Sweden to southern Spain. Occasionally, birds fail to make the journey in a single flight, perhaps because the wind and weather are against them, and they may then come down somewhere in the British Isles, usually in the eastern half of England. A small resident breeding population has established itself in Norfolk.

The land birds fall into two groups. One group breeds all the way from Scandinavia eastwards through Siberia. It includes the rough-legged buzzard, the white-tailed eagle, which has begun to breed again in northwest Scotland following a lengthy re-introduction programme, Tengmalm's owl, the shore lark, Lapland bunting, nutcracker and Arctic redpoll. The other group has a more easterly breeding range, normally within Russia, and includes the Arctic warbler, the rustic and little buntings, and the two-barred crossbill.

White-tailed eagle
Haliaetus albicilla
81.25cm (32in)
Rare winter visitor from Scandinavia or north Germany to eastern Britain; breeds west Scotland following re-introduction on Rhum; adult tail white, young dark brown.

Honey buzzard
Pernis apivorus
54.5cm (21½in)
A few pairs breed in England and Scotland; also scarce passage migrant, most often on east coast; feeds on wasps' nests; barred tail; holds wings flat, not raised in a 'V'.

Crane
Grus grus
114.25cm (45in)
Rare passage migrant from Scandinavia, with a small resident population breeding in Norfolk since 1981; tall grey bird with black, white and red head.

Rough-legged buzzard
Buteo lagopus 56cm (22in)
Annual winter visitor from Scandinavia to northern Scotland and eastern counties south to Kent; most winter in central Europe; tail white, with broad black band at end.

Tengmalm's owl
Aegolius funereus 25.5cm (10in)
Very rare and irregular winter visitor from Scandinavia, chiefly to Orkney and northeast England; moves south in winter if food is scarce; plumage warmer brown than little owl's.

Snowy owl
Nyctea scandiaca 61cm (24in)
Bred in Shetland 1967–75; now very rare in winter, mostly in the north. Breeds in northern Europe; buzzard-like flight and white plumage.

Caspian tern
Sterna caspia 53.25cm (21in)
Irregular summer visitor mainly to southern Britain; in northern Europe breeds only on coasts of the Baltic sea; black crown and heavy, orange-red bill.

Arctic warbler
Phylloscopus borealis
12cm (4³/₄in)
Rare passage migrant from northern Russia; completely off-course – migration is usually to southeast Asia; narrow pale wing-bar; prominent straight eye-stripes.

Shorelark
Eremophila alpestris
16.5cm (6½in)
Scarce winter visitor to coasts of eastern England; breeds in Scandinavian uplands; has bred occasionally in Scotland; black and yellow markings on head and breast.

Nutcracker
Nucifranga caryocatactes
31.75cm (12½in)
Rare winter vagrant, chiefly in south and east England, from southern Scandinavia and Siberia; large influx of birds in 1968 came from Siberia; dark brown, flecked with white.

Rustic bunting
Emberiza rustica 14.5cm (5³/₄in)
Rare passage migrant, chiefly in autumn; recorded mainly in northern isles of Scotland; breeds in northern Russia and winters in Asia; like reed bunting, with white underparts.

Little bunting
Emberiza pusilla 13.25cm (5¹/₄in)
Rare passage migrant, usually in autumn, mainly to Fair Isle, other Scottish islands and east coast of England; breeds in northern Russia and normally migrates southeast.

Lapland bunting
Calcarius lapponicus
15.25cm (6in)
Scarce autumn and winter visitor, mainly in northern and western islands and on southeast coast; has bred in Scotland; breeds from Arctic America to Siberia.

Arctic redpoll
Acanthis hornemanni
12.75cm (5in)
Very rare winter vagrant, mainly to Fair Isle and northeast England; breeds in northern Scandinavia and Russia; spreads south in winter; white rump and underparts.

Two-barred crossbill
Loxia leucoptera 14.5cm (5³/₄in)
Winter vagrant, mostly to east of Britain; breeds in northern Russia; winters around Baltic and in central Europe; double white wing-bars; same size as chaffinch.

Great snipe
Gallinago media 28cm (11in)
Irregular winter visitor and autumn passage migrant from Scandinavia, most often in Scotland and on south and east coasts of England; normally migrates to southern Africa; larger than snipe with much more white on sides of tail.

Wood sandpiper
Tringa glareola 20.25cm (8in)
Has bred annually in northern Scotland since 1959; occurs mainly as autumn passage migrant in southeast England; breeds in northern Europe; winters in Africa.

Broad-billed sandpiper
Limicola falcinellus 16.5cm (6½in)
Rare spring and very rare autumn migrant from Scandinavia, most sightings recorded in southeast England; usual migration to eastern Mediterranean and southern Asia; like dunlin in autumn plumage, with prominent pale eye-stripes.

Spotted redshank
Tringa erythropus 30.5cm (12in)
Regular spring and autumn passage migrant from northern Scandinavia, mainly in small numbers on coast of southeast England; winters in Africa; a few winter in Britain; longer-billed than common redshank, without wing-bars; loud 'tu-ip' call.

Visitors from southwest Europe and Africa

Fewer birds are likely to visit the British Isles from southwest Europe than from western or northern Europe, because Britain is not on the main migration routes from this region, as it is on those from north and west Europe. In winter, most of the southwest European birds travel south or southwest from their breeding areas, towards or into Africa.

Many of the southwest European birds are very infrequent and irregular visitors – wanderers that have reached Britain by overshooting their normal breeding range when returning from their winter quarters. Others are young birds, scattering in the short interval between the end of the breeding season and the beginning of the southward migration.

Most of the birds shown here, including the collared pratincole, scops owl and subalpine warbler are Mediterranean species. The Alpine accentor is, as its name suggests, a bird of the mountains. Its nearest breeding areas are the Alps and the Pyrenees. The Alpine swift breeds throughout much of southern Europe, north to Switzerland.

Until recently, of all the southwest European visitors, only the black-winged stilt and the bee-eater, which have both nested three times, had ever been known to breed within the British Isles. Now, however, following a remarkable surge in numbers in the 1990s, little egrets are widespread and breeding in substantial numbers in several southern counties.

If few birds from southwest Europe ever wander to Britain, fewer still are likely to come from Africa. Indeed, of the birds shown here, only the cream-coloured courser and ruddy shelduck may have done so. Equally, the few that have reached the British Isles may have come from southwest Asia since both species inhabit that region too.

Short-toed lark
Calandrella brachydactyla
14cm (5½in)
Vagrant, most often to Fair Isle but now annual in southern and eastern England in spring and autumn; short straight beak; underparts almost white, unstreaked.

Bee-eater
Merops apiaster 28cm (11in)
Vagrant, mainly to southeast in summer, but also recorded in spring and autumn; has occasionally nested; bred in Sussex 1955; brilliantly coloured in chestnut, yellow, blue-green and black.

Roller
Coracias garrulus 30.5cm (12in)
Declining vagrant, mainly to southern England on spring and autumn migration; used to breed as far north as southern Sweden; blue-green plumage, with chestnut back.

Subalpine warbler
Sylvia cantillans 12cm (4¾in)
Vagrant, mainly on coasts in spring and autumn; in spring has blue-grey back, pink breast and narrow white 'moustache' stripe; paler than Dartford warbler.

Alpine accentor
Prunella collaris 17.75cm (7in)
Rare vagrant, mainly to southern England in autumn; like a large, pale dunnock, with black spots on whitish chin and throat; streaked red-brown back.

Black-eared wheatear
Oenanthe hispanica
14.5cm (5¾in)
Very rare spring and autumn vagrant to widely scattered counties; largely black and white, with prominent black face-patch; sandy coloured back, with white rump.

Cream-coloured courser

Cursorius cursor 23cm (9in)
Rare vagrant from African or Asian deserts, most often to southern England in autumn; pale sandy plover-like bird with black wing-tips; runs rapidly on open ground.

Collared pratincole

Glareola pratincola 25.5cm (10in)
Vagrant, mainly to south and east England; mostly in May; long forked black tail, short bill; chin and throat light buff; back is grey-brown in spring.

Black-winged stilt

Himantopus himantopus
38cm (15in)
Rare vagrant, has bred a few times in England, very irregularly, since 1945; thin straight bill; black and white plumage, long pink legs.

Alpine swift

Apus melba 21cm (8¼in)
Vagrant, mainly to southern England in summer; large pale brown swift with white underparts except for a brown band across the breast; in flight looks like a giant white-bellied swift.

Ruddy shelduck

Tadorna ferruginea 63.5cm (25in)
Rare vagrant to many coastal counties, possibly from North Africa; birds seen singly could have escaped from waterfowl collections; goose-like, with deep buff plumage and pale head.

winter   summer

Scops owl

Otus stops 19cm (7½in)
Very rare vagrant to scattered parts of Britain, mainly during April–June; probably overshooting on spring migration; smallest owl with ear-tufts likely to be seen in Britain.

Whiskered tern

Chlidonias hybrida
24.75cm (9¾in)
Rare vagrant, mainly to southeast England on spring and autumn migration; black cap, white cheeks; resembles a dark Arctic tern; bill, legs and feet dark red.

Little egret

Egretta garzetta 56cm (22in)
Several hundred pairs now breed after remarkable increase; widespread on coasts around Britain and Ireland, still rare far inland. All-white heron, black legs and yellow feet.

Greater flamingo

Phoenicopterus ruber 127cm (50in)
Possible vagrant, autumn and winter, England; pink and white plumage, very long legs and neck; most seen in Britain are escaped Chilean flamingos, which have grey legs with pink joints.

Squacco heron

Ardeola ralloides 45.75cm (18in)
Rare vagrant, mainly to southern England in early summer; breeds in many parts of southern Europe, Asia, Africa; buff back and conspicuous white wings in flight.

Visitors from eastern Europe and Asia

Until 1832, the huge and bulky great bustard, a turkey-sized bird quite unlike any other in Europe, used to breed in Britain, but this strong and wary bird was driven out, probably by human interference. It is almost certainly lost to these islands for ever as a breeding bird, and today it occurs only as a very rare vagrant from eastern Europe, usually in winter, although attempts to reintroduce it continue in Wiltshire.

The breeding range of many of Britain's eastern European visitors has its western limit on the North Sea in Denmark or northern Germany. These include the red-necked grebe, little crake, barred warbler and red-breasted flycatcher. For others, including the black stork, great bustard, greenish warbler, red-footed falcon, scarlet rosefinch and white-winged black tern, the limit is not so far west, although both the great bustard and black stork have separate breeding populations in Spain and Portugal.

The eastern European visitors seen most frequently in the British Isles, usually on the east coast, are the red-necked grebe, a winter visitor, the barred warbler, usually an autumn passage migrant, and the Mediterranean gull. This gull is a bird of remote origin in the Black and Aegean Seas, but in recent years an increasing number remain all year and a few hundred pairs breed on the English south coast.

Every year small numbers of yellow-browed warblers and Richard's pipits make a surprising journey from beyond the Ural Mountains to the east and south coasts of Britain. Normally they migrate to their winter quarters on a course that takes them nowhere near Britain. The red-breasted goose occurs much more rarely but is liable to get caught up in migrating flocks of other geese, such as white-fronts, which carry it off its proper course. When the flock of white-fronts reaches its wintering area, the stray may attach itself to a particular pair or family. It is hard to see why other eastern birds should wander so often and so far off their regular route. Some seem to be tracing the normal line of travel but in the wrong direction, a phenomenon known as

'reverse migration'. Richard's pipits and yellow-browed warblers have both become much more regular autumn visitors in recent years.

The rose-coloured starling can also be classed as an Asian bird. Its main breeding area extends deep into Asia, and although it also breeds as far west as the plains of the Danube, it is much more likely to come to Britain from its customary locations in Asia.

Glossy ibis
Plegadis falcinellus 56cm (22in)
Vagrant, mainly in autumn and winter on coasts of southern England and Ireland; plumage has bronze gloss; very round-winged in flight; long downward curving bill.

Black stork
Ciconia nigra 96.5cm (38in)
Rare vagrant, chiefly to southern England in May–June, but many other months except winter; breeds from eastern France eastwards, also Iberia; black plumage, white breast.

Great bustard
Otis tarda 101.5cm (40in)
Exceptionally rare vagrant to widely scattered counties, mainly in winter; bred in England until 1832; wings of both sexes show black and white markings when they fly.

Scarlet rosefinch
Carpodacus erythrinus
14.5cm (5³/₄in)
Scarce autumn visitor in a variety of English counties, but most numerous in northern Scottish islands; plump, with heavy bill and distinctive sharp 'chup' call. Bred Scotland 1982 and 1990.

Rose-coloured starling
Sturnus roseus 21.5cm (8½in)
Very irregular visitor, recorded especially in northeast Scotland, eastern England, mainly in June–August, also autumn; pink with black head, wings and tail.

Red-footed falcon
Falco vespertinus 30.5cm (12in)
Irregular visitor, especially in late spring, chiefly to eastern and southern England, but has occurred elsewhere; legs and patch round each eye are bright red.

Red-breasted flycatcher
Ficedula parva 11.5cm (4½in)
Regular but scarce autumn passage migrant on east and south coasts; breeds eastward from Denmark, winters in India and Near East; white patches at the base of the tail.

Barred warbler
Sylvia nisoria 15.25cm (6in)
Fairly frequent autumn passage migrant found on the east coast of Britain; winters in North Africa and Arabia; a large warbler with grey back and long tail.

Greenish warbler
Phylloscopus trochiloides
10.75cm (4¹/₄in)
Increasing but rare autumn visitor to coastal counties; breeds on south side of Baltic; distinguished from chiffchaff by voice and single pale wing-bar.

1 Yellow-browed warbler
Phylloscopus inornatus
10.25cm (4in)
Regular but scarce autumn passage migrant, northern islands and east coast.

2 Richard's pipit
Anthus novaeseelandiae
17.75cm (7in)
Rare but regular late autumn migrant on coasts of Britain and on Fair Isle.

White's thrush
Turdus dauma 27.25cm (10³/₄in)
Exceptional vagrant, mainly in winter to southern England, but also recorded in Scotland and Ireland; breeds in Siberia; black crescents on upper parts and underparts; black and white band under wing is distinctive when it flies; similar to mistle thrush, but larger and more boldly patterned.

Red-breasted goose
Branta ruficollis 54.5cm (21½in)
Rare vagrant in winter from west Siberian tundra, usually after being caught up in flocks of other geese and carried off its proper migration route; black and white, with red-brown throat and breast; white patch between eye and delicate black bill.

Red-necked grebe
Podiceps grisegena
43cm (17in)
Scarce but regular winter visitor, to eastern counties; has bred 2–3 times; neck is darker than great crested grebe's; bill yellow at base.

White-winged black tern
Chlidonias leucopterus
23.5cm (9¹/₄in)
Rare vagrant, mainly in spring and autumn to south and east coasts; white wings in summer.

Mediterranean gull
Larus melanocephalus
38cm (15in)
Big increase on coasts from Wales south and east to northeast England; breeds on some southern estuaries; adult has all-white wing-tips.

Little crake
Porzana parva
19cm (7½in)
Rare vagrant, mostly in spring but also summer months, to many coastal counties of south and east, especially in East Anglia.

Visitors from the Arctic

Many birds take advantage of the brief Arctic summer to breed within the region stretching from Greenland through Iceland, Spitsbergen and Lapland, and across Arctic Siberia. Most are marsh and water birds. Not many strictly land birds breed in the Arctic because of the lack of food.

A few birds not only breed but also spend the winter in the far north, on the fringe of the ice-pack. The king eider and ivory gull are among these. The rest usually fly south to warmer latitudes or spend the winter at sea. The Orkneys and Shetlands are the first landfall for many of these northern birds. Even the colourful king eider drakes are recorded there quite frequently, especially in years when the Arctic winter is particularly severe and the polar ice-cap extends further south than usual.

Other visitors, such as the glaucous gull and Greenland and Iceland forms of the gyr falcon, are most likely to be seen in the northern islands, but sometimes they also penetrate further south into Scotland, England and Ireland as they move away from their breeding grounds. The weather, and the availability of food, determine when and how far into Britain these birds come.

The Arctic-breeding waders are more common, for their migrations take many of them far south of Britain, to parts of Europe and Africa. The purple sandpiper is a regular visitor to rocky shores around the entire coastline and has bred in Scotland. The little stint and curlew sandpiper can be seen in autumn, resting or feeding on the coast before continuing on their long journey to Africa, adults a month or so before the juveniles. The pomarine and long-tailed skuas, grey phalarope, Sabine's gull and little auk normally winter at sea. The little auk regularly comes south into the North Sea, and is occasionally driven ashore in numbers by storms. The others migrate to warmer waters, usually following routes that keep them over the sea, but gales may drive them to land. Some Sabine's gulls, many of which breed also in the North American Arctic, are regularly blown on to the western coasts of Britain in the autumn,

and sometimes remain all winter.

The navigational ability of birds is so remarkable that it seems unthinkable for it ever to go wrong, but this does happen from time to time. The Pechora pipit, for example, breeds in Arctic Russia and normally migrates in the autumn to southeast Asia, on a journey that takes it through China. Yet occasionally, at migration time, Pechora pipits turn up in Britain thousands of miles off course, almost always on Fair Isle.

Sabine's gull
Larus sabini 13cm (13in)
Scarce but regular visitor, mainly in autumn to Atlantic and Channel coasts; breeds Greenland, Spitsbergen, Arctic Russia; winters in South Atlantic; forked tail.

Glaucous gull
Larus hyperboreus 68.5cm (27in)
Scarce winter visitor in north and east England, but regular in Shetlands and on Scottish mainland; breeds Iceland, Arctic Russia; pale grey back and white wingtips.

Ivory gull
Pagophila eburnea
44.5cm (17½in)
Rare winter vagrant to coastal counties but chiefly in Shetlands and Orkneys, from Spitsbergen and elsewhere in Arctic; normally winters on Arctic coasts; pure white plumage.

Long-tailed skua
Stercorarius longicaudus
53.25cm (21in)
Regular, scarce autumn passage migrant from Lapland, off east coast of England; winters at sea; very long tail feathers.

Pomarine skua
Stercorarius pomarinus
51cm (20in)
Uncommon, regular passage migrant along both eastern and western coasts; breeds in Arctic Russia and Spitsbergen; winters off west coast of Africa.

King eider
Somateria spectabilis 56cm (22in)
Rare visitor from Greenland and Arctic Russia, where it breeds and winters, mainly to Scotland and the north in winter; drake has orange bill and blue-grey head.

Little stint
Calidris minuta 13.25cm (5¹/₄in)
Mainly autumn passage migrant on eastern seaboard, moving from Arctic to winter quarters in Africa; seen on return passage occasionally; whitish breast and short bill; cream streaks on back.

Temminck's stint
Calidris temminckii
13.25cm (5¹/₄in)
Scarce passage migrant from Lapland, seen in both spring and autumn, mostly in southern and eastern counties; has nested on a few occasions in northern Scotland; also Yorkshire; pale legs.

Curlew sandpiper
Calidris ferruginea 19cm (7½in)
Regular passage migrant, mainly in autumn down east coast, moving from breeding grounds in Siberia probably to Africa; also seen irregularly and in smaller numbers on return passage; like dunlin, with white rump.

Red-throated pipit
Anthus cervinus 14.5cm (5³/₄in)
Rare but regular migrant, mostly in May or autumn in Scottish islands; from Lapland or further east; winters mainly in East Africa and southern Asia.

Pechora pipit
Anthus gustavi 14.5cm (5³/₄in)
Rare vagrant from Siberia, most often seen on Fair Isle in autumn; usual autumn migration route through China to Southeast Asia; like tree pipit, with two pale streaks down back.

Purple sandpiper
Calidris maritima 21cm (8¹/₄in)
Winter and autumn visitor from Iceland and Arctic to rocky coasts, especially in north and west; has bred in Scotland; slate-grey back, yellow legs and bill.

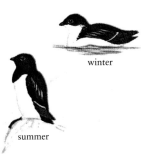

winter

summer

Little auk
Alle alle 20.25cm (8in)
Winter visitor from Spitsbergen, to North Sea coast south to Norfolk but is irregular round other coasts; outside breeding season usually remains at sea near pack-ice; very short bill.

summer

winter

Grey phalarope
Phalaropus fulicarius 20.25cm (8in)
Regular passage migrant from Iceland, in autumn and rarely in spring, on coasts of Ireland, Wales, southwest and south England; normally winters in South Atlantic.

Gyr falcon
Falco rusticolus 53.25cm (21in)
Three geographical forms occur – Iceland, Greenland and Scandinavia and Arctic Europe; white form of Greenland gyr is the most frequent visitor, but still very rare.

Visitors from North America and the oceans

Every year numbers of North American birds are carried across the Atlantic by cross-winds while they are making their autumn migration – in most cases southward down the east coast of Canada and the United States. The majority of these birds are waders, such as the long-billed dowitcher, the lesser yellowlegs, and the buff-breasted sandpiper, pectoral sandpiper and white-rumped sandpiper. These are the most numerous of the score or so of American waders that have been recorded on British shores. The next most numerous group is waterbirds, such as the American bittern, Iceland gull (which comes from Greenland, despite its name), snow goose, blue-winged teal, American wigeon and surf scoter.

Land birds also make the journey. The yellow-billed cuckoo is among those most frequently recorded, and in recent years there have been sightings of the American robin, Baltimore oriole, red-eyed vireo and white-throated sparrow. Since 1951, more than 50 species of American land birds have been recorded in Britain for the first time. It is now accepted that even small birds can fly across the Atlantic in the right conditions, aided by strong winds at high-altitude, although several species have been seen on board ships. Those that cross at least partly on board ship are usually accepted as wild birds, but birds deliberately brought to Britain are not, and their release is illegal.

The regular appearance in waters off the British Isles in late summer or autumn of small numbers of sooty and great shearwaters is one of the highlights of the year for British birdwatchers. The sooty shearwater breeds only on remote islands in the southern oceans, around New Zealand and south of

South America. Its nearest breeding places to Britain are around the Falkland Islands. The great shearwater breeds only on the Tristan da Cunha group in the South Atlantic. Both species migrate in large loops round the Atlantic each year, and the fringes of their migrations just touch the British Isles.

The appearance of Cory's shearwater is less remarkable because it breeds as near as the Berlenga Islands off the coast of Portugal, as well as in Madeira, the Canaries and the Azores. What is remarkable is that it is the least frequent visitor of the three rare shearwaters, appearing as a late summer wanderer in the Western Approaches.

Snow goose
Anser caerulescens 71cm (28in)
Winter vagrant mainly in Ireland;
breeds across Arctic America and
usually winters in western states; two
forms, one white with black wing-tips,
other dark with white head.

American bittern
Botaurus lentiginosus
76.25cm (30in)
An infrequent vagrant from North
America; occurs in Britain usually in
autumn; breeds from Arctic to
California, winters in southern states
and Central America.

Great shearwater
Puffinus gravis 45.75cm (18in)
Regular late summer and autumn visitor off Outer Hebrides, southwest Ireland and southwest England; breeds in islands of Tristan da Cunha group; dark cap and white patch on upper part of tail.

Cory's shearwater
Calonectris diomedea
45.75cm (18in)
Late summer wanderer, off southwest England on post-breeding dispersal from Madeira and other Atlantic islands; lacks great shearwater's black cap; pale bill.

Sooty shearwater
Puffinus griseus 40.5cm (16in)
Regular late summer and autumn visitor in small numbers round all coasts; breeds around New Zealand and south of South America; sooty brown plumage with paler tract under long, narrow wings.

Iceland gull
Larus glaucoides 56cm (22in)
Scarce winter visitor, mainly to northern isles; breeds in Greenland, and winters south to New York and in Iceland; smaller than glaucous gull, with more black on young bird's bill.

Lesser yellowlegs
Tringa flavipes 25.5cm (10in)
Irregular but increasing autumn vagrant, recorded in many counties; breeds widely in Canada and winters from southern USA to Argentina; bright yellow legs.

Long-billed dowitcher
Limnodromus scolopaceus
29.25cm (11½in)
Rare but annual autumn vagrant; breeds in eastern USA, winters in southern USA and northern South America; grey with white rump and lower back.

Pectoral sandpiper
Calidris melanotos 23cm (9in)
North American sandpiper most frequently reported on this side of Atlantic; mainly autumn vagrant from Canada, chiefly to eastern counties of England and Scillies; normally winters in South America.

Buff-breasted sandpiper
Tryngites subruficollis
20.25cm (8in)
Rare and declining vagrant, autumn, usually to eastern and western coastal counties; breeds in Arctic tundra, winters on South American pampas; buff plumage; usually seen on dry ground.

Yellow-billed cuckoo
Coccyzus americanus
30.5cm (12in)
Rare and declining vagrant from North America, usually to western Britain in autumn; breeds in North America, winters in South America; chestnut on wings, white marks on tail.

Surf scoter
Melanitta perspicillata
51cm (20in)
Scarce winter vagrant from northwest Canada, mainly to northern isles; usually winters on Atlantic and Pacific coasts of USA and on Great Lakes.

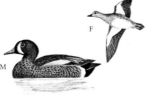

Blue-winged teal
Anas discors 39.5cm (15½in)
Over 100 winter vagrants recorded in all parts of British Isles; breeds in east and central North America; winters in Bahamas, West Indies, South America.

American wigeon
Anas americana 51cm (20in)
Rare winter vagrant, mainly in western areas; normally breeds in North America, winters in Central America; head pattern distinguishes it from European wigeon.

Birds introduced to Britain

Birds deliberately introduced to Britain are mostly gamebirds, brought here to be shot, although the little owl is a notable exception. Others are ducks and geese that have either been released or have escaped from collections and succeeded in establishing themselves. Those that are firmly established and self-supporting are given a place on the list of British birds, albeit in their own special category. These include the pheasant, golden pheasant, mandarin duck, ruddy duck, Egyptian goose and Canada goose. The capercaillie was a true native but died out and has been re-established by introductions, as has the white-tailed eagle more recently. The ring-necked parakeet, an escaped cage bird, has become firmly established in much of southeastern England and is slowly spreading. A number of introductions have, in contrast, been failures, including the bobwhite quail and Reeves's pheasant. Even budgerigars bred for several years on the Isles of Scilly, but have now disappeared.

Lady Amherst's pheasant
Chrysolophus amherstiae
58.5cm (23in)
Ornamental pheasant from East Asia, breeds in tiny numbers in Bedfordshire; dark green and white cock; hen brown, with yellow eyes and grey legs.

Reeves's pheasant
Syrmaticus reevesi 91.5cm (36in)
Ornamental pheasant from Asia; bred near Inverness during last century but died out; recently re-introduced to Scottish Highlands; largest pheasant in Britain, tail over 2m (6ft) long.

Ring-necked parakeet
Psittacula krameri 40.5cm (16in)
Since about 1970, this long-tailed, green parrot has become established in the southeast and is spreading slowly north and west.

Bobwhite quail
Colinus virginianus 24cm (9½in)
North American gamebird, released for shooting in several areas but none have become established; white markings on face; perches in trees.

Golden pheasant
Chrysolophus pictus 58.5cm (23in)
Ornamental pheasant from East Asia; small numbers, escaped or released, nest in Breckland and elsewhere; brilliant red and yellow cock; hen paler brown than hen of common pheasant.

Mandarin duck
Aix galericulata 43cm (17in)
Ornamental duck from China; breeds wild in southeast England – mainly Surrey and east Berkshire – Perth and elsewhere; drake has orange-chestnut wing-fans; duck grey-brown.

Ruddy duck
Oxyura jamaicensis
39.5cm (15½in)
North American duck, escaped from waterfowl collections; declining with recent attempts to reduce population but still nests in central and south England.

Egyptian goose
Alopochen aegyptiacus
63.5cm (25in)
Ornamental waterfowl from Africa; wild breeding populations are established in north Norfolk and elsewhere; dark brown patches on face and breast, brown ring at base of neck.

Bird Society

For birds in the wild, life is a continuous struggle for survival, and all the
ways they have developed to live together are directed to this one end.
Bird behaviour can be studied in the laboratory, and much has been learnt
in this way, but laboratory theories must be tested against observation in
the field. The emphasis in the following pages is on how birds behave in
their natural surroundings and among other birds.

Living together
The units of bird society

Some birds begin to live socially while still inside the egg. About three days before hatching, the embryo chicks of grouse, for example, begin to cheep. There is evidence that this is a form of communication from egg to egg, with the function of synchronising hatching. The birds that cheep always leave the nest within a few hours of hatching, and those that cheep the loudest tend to be those that hatch more or less together.

Cheeping can also be a form of communication between adults and chick, as in the case of the guillemot. The chick cheeps as it begins to hatch and the parent birds answer back, so that the chick learns to recognise their calls even before it has hatched, and later responds only to these.

As a general rule, birds that are born naked, blind and helpless do not cheep inside the egg, but they begin to communicate with their own species soon after hatching – as soon as they sense the presence of their parents and open their bills to beg for food.

One mate or several?

More complicated forms of social behaviour follow later – courtship, song, threat and fighting all involve association, interaction and, above all, communication with other birds. The main intercommunicating units of bird society are pairs, families, flocks and colonies, and for some species even sleeping is a social activity, with large numbers gathering in roosts.

The great majority of birds are monogamous – that is, males have one mate during the breeding season. A simple biological reason for this is that young birds usually need the full-time attention of both parents if they are to survive, but this reason does not apply in every case. Cuckoos lay their eggs in other birds' nests, and neither sex has any responsibility for rearing the young, yet cuckoos are monogamous. So, too, are ducks, although the males usually have nothing to do with raising their young. In both these cases, monogamy can be explained by complicated factors involving the timing of breeding and the availability of mates.

Other kinds of pair association are polygamy, in which one bird, usually the male, has several mates, and promiscuity, in which no pair bond is formed and the birds meet only for mating.

Forming a pair bond is broadly related to the availability of food. Taking the world's birds as a whole, the relatively few polygamous species are mainly seed-eaters, producing young at a time of year when seeds are in plentiful supply. The few that are promiscuous live mainly on plants and fruit – again the kind of food that is readily available when the young hatch. Birds that feed their young on insects are rarely anything but monogamous. Since the young are helpless for the first few days after hatching and unable to catch insects for themselves while they remain in the nest, the parents have to do it for them. However, among British birds, wrens and pied flycatchers, both mainly insect-eaters, are sometimes polygamous.

Long-lived pair bonds

Most monogamous birds (the robin may be taken as typical) pair with a different mate each new breeding season, but some long-lived birds, especially seabirds, pair for life. Studies of the kittiwake, which lives for an average of nearly 14 years, show that old-established pairs usually rear more young than

Pecking order among rooks

In small flocks of rooks, every bird has its recognised position in a social hierarchy known as a pecking order. Birds high in the order eat before those lower down. In times of food shortage, this ensures that at least the highest ranked birds survive. There may be fighting from time to time, especially when the system is being established, but in the long run bickering over food – which wastes time and energy – is reduced. Woodpigeons also have a pecking order. The system is similar to that of farmyard hens, in which the hens actually peck one another.

Piping of the oystercatchers
*The exact meaning of the piping performance
of oystercatchers is not clear, but the ceremony
takes place when the birds are excited – in
courtship or territorial encounters. Small groups
of oystercatchers, often in pairs, run up and
down with their bills pointing at the ground, at
the same time uttering far-carrying piping calls.
This behaviour seems to stimulate other birds
to start parading and calling.*

those birds that change mates in successive seasons. Gannets, which live for an average of 16 years, fulmars (14 years) and shags (nearly 16 years) benefit in much the same way by choosing the same mate for season after season. Other examples of birds that pair for life are jackdaws and greylag geese. In both species, young birds pair up in the spring following the year of hatching, and stay together for a year before they begin breeding. If a jackdaw's mate dies, the survivor will look for a new partner, but a greylag goose in the same situation will remain single for the rest of its life.

Another reason for jackdaws being thought of as unusual is that they are among the few British birds that remain paired during the winter. Even when they join up with wandering feeding flocks, paired jackdaws will keep together. Mistle thrushes, stonechats and marsh tits also form pair bonds that last through the winter. Neither of the first two species joins flocks, though, and marsh tits will do so only if a flock of tits invades their territory.

Most pair bonds are disbanded outside the breeding season. The birds that formed them either become solitary – like the kingfisher, the robin and many birds of prey – or join winter feeding flocks.

Pheasant's harem

Among the few species of British birds in which males mate with more than one female, the pheasant is an outstanding example. The cock pheasant runs a harem of up to half a dozen hens. Another example is the farmyard cockerel. In both cases, the hens disperse separately to nest after mating.

Male wrens and pied flycatchers may take one or a number of mates. Studies of the wren suggest that the reason for this variation within a single species is linked with the supply of food. Wrens tend to be polygamous in rich habitats, such as woodland, and monogamous in poorer habitats, such as moorland. Polygamy has also been reported in the case of the bittern and the corn bunting, but no cases have been found in Britain of females of any species taking more than one mate.

A minority of British birds have no sustained pair bond at all, but are promiscuous. They meet only for mating, each bird usually copulating with more than one member of the opposite sex. Among British breeding species, only the capercaillie, black grouse and ruff are known to be promiscuous. As with polygamy, promiscuity is possible only when the young can be reared by a single parent. Taking the world's birds as a whole, this situation is usually found in groups where chicks are born covered with down, and are able to run and feed themselves soon after hatching. When it occurs in species the young of which are born helpless, the food supply is abundant and reliable, consisting mainly of seeds, fruit or green plants.

Breaking away from the family

Contrary to popular belief, family life is not well developed among the majority of British birds. The family is usually a temporary unit, staying together only until the young can fend for themselves, that is for a few days or weeks after they leave the nest.

In some cases, for instance among the gannets, Manx shearwaters and swifts, there is no family life at all once the young are able to fly. Young tawny owls, on the other hand, are fully dependent on their parents for food for up to three months after fledging.

In a few other species the family stays together after the young are able to support themselves, and remains together for most or all of the time until the next breeding season. This situation is found mainly among swans and geese. Families of mute swans may be watched throughout the winter on lakes, rivers and streams in many parts of the country. Even more strikingly, Bewick's swans migrate in family groups from their breeding areas abroad and travel to the British Isles, where they stay together all through the winter.

Many British birds form integrated feeding flocks for at least part of the year, and a few, such as starlings and linnets, feed in flocks throughout the year. Winter flocks, ranging over the countryside and

Grouping of avocets
A little-understood social gathering is the 'grouping' of avocets, in which small numbers of birds, often paired, bow low, sometimes forming a circle with their long, upcurved bills facing inwards. The bowing is usually followed by fighting between the different pairs – mainly of a ritualistic nature – in which the male and female of the same pair keep close to one another.

along the coastline, include birds that have arrived from abroad as well as those that are resident in Britain all year. The flocks may be mixed or consist of a single species, as with starlings, woodpigeons and many ducks. Rooks and jackdaws often forage together, and tit flocks may contain not only tits of more than one species but also other small woodland birds, such as goldcrests and treecreepers.

Lapwings, dunlin, knot and other waders sometimes form mixed flocks when flying or roosting, but usually separate when feeding. Much the same thing happens with finches – chaffinches, linnets, goldfinches, siskins and redpolls may mingle in flight, but normally feed separately.

A flock may sometimes be composed of birds of one sex, as with tufted ducks and pochards, or of juvenile birds only, as with starlings in late summer. Other flocks contain pairs, for example jackdaws, and yet others are made up of families, and these include geese and swans.

Benefits of flocking

The reason why some birds associate in flocks instead of feeding on their own has been much disputed but three factors, often in combination, help to explain flocking in many species. The first is simply that there is safety in numbers. This is of particular benefit to birds that feed in open, exposed places, such as fields and estuaries. A predator, which would have little difficulty in taking a solitary bird, can be distracted and confused by sheer numbers when attacking a flock, and if a predator is sighted or makes an attack, one bird flying up or calling will warn the rest.

Secondly, if birds feel safer in flocks, it is highly probable that they feed more efficiently, because they can concentrate on what they are doing. The third factor is the availability of food. Some groups, such as the seed-eating finches and rooks, seek food that is abundant and easily taken in some areas, but scarce in others. Flocking concentrates them quickly in the favourable areas.

Winter feeding flocks are not simply disorganised collections of birds. They are integrated through positive social behaviour. In most flocks, cohesion is established by individuals following one another, both while feeding and when in flight. Many species have conspicuous flashes or bars, usually of white, on the wings, tail or rump, which may act as 'flock markers'. These are particularly well developed in groups that carry out complicated flight manoeuvres, such as the waders, and also in the finches. Visual markers are reinforced by special calls, especially flight calls, by which the birds keep in touch with one another.

Keeping apart in flocks

In addition, many species organise their flocks through each bird maintaining its own distance, so that it does not come into bodily contact with other members of the flock. In this way, regular spacing is preserved, and each individual has room to move, feed, look about and take wing unhindered.

Relationships between the birds in these flocks are not based on individual recognition. The flock is essentially a collection of anonymous members – unlike the small flocks of rooks or woodpigeons, in which individual recognition between birds is necessary to establish a pecking order of precedence in feeding.

Group displays

Many birds gather for group displays during courtship, but in some cases the exact meaning of the display is far from clear, because the majority of birds taking part are already paired.

Two of the oddest ceremonies involve groups of monogamous waders – oystercatchers and avocets. Oystercatchers have a piping performance in which small groups of birds, often in pairs, parade up and down uttering calls. Avocets have a grouping ceremony in which a number of birds form an inward-facing circle, bowing to one another as a preliminary to ritualistic fighting.

Screaming parties of swifts are another example of group displays involving paired birds. On fine days, a number of them swoop together in the vicinity of the nesting colony, all uttering a high-pitched squealing.

Just as mysterious are the noisy winter gatherings of magpies. Up to about 100 birds spring and dash about, flirting wings and tails to exhibit the white parts of the plumage, as well as performing slow-motion flights. Jays have somewhat similar spring gatherings, but mainly in smaller numbers of about three to 30 birds. It is widely believed that the purpose of these meetings – 'crow marriages' – is to enable unpaired birds to find mates. However, this interpretation does not account for the presence of paired birds, which are always in the great majority.

Living in colonies

About 13 per cent of the world's birds nest in colonies, but in Britain the proportion is twice as high. This is because these islands attract so many seabirds, and seabirds as a group are the most colonial of birds, often returning year after year to traditional safe sites on cliffs and rocky islands.

Broadly speaking, there are two main types of colonial species – those that form compact colonies, such as gannets, rooks and herons, and those that form loose colonies, with nests spaced further apart than the lie of the land seems to demand, such as finches, reed warblers and avocets. For hole-nesters, including jackdaws, starlings, house sparrows, tree sparrows and swifts, the closeness of the nests depends largely on the distribution of suitable cavities for them to use.

Most colonial birds defend as much territory as they need for a nesting space, but some hold much wider, well-defined areas within the colony. The Canada goose defends land on the lake island where its nest is situated and also on a stretch of mainland opposite, where the pair feed. The reed warbler defends, on average, some 250m² (300sq yd), but the pair feed largely outside this area.

Colonies of land birds are usually fairly small – fewer than a dozen pairs may make up a colony of finches, for example – but there are exceptions. A colony of rooks may include thousands of birds. The largest rookery in Britain used to be in Aberdeenshire, with up to 9,000 pairs. Grey herons nest in treetop colonies numbering from a handful to more than 100 pairs, such as in Northward Hill, Kent.

Seabirds often mass in staggering numbers. The largest colony of fulmars in the British Isles is on St Kilda in the Outer Hebrides, with a total of nearly 40,000 nests. The largest colony of gannets – up to 52,000 nests – is also on St Kilda. Skomer Island, off the Pembroke coast, has a colony of 95,000 pairs of Manx shearwaters, and colonies of guillemots thousands strong inhabit the Scottish islands. Black guillemots and shags, on the other hand, breed in relatively small colonies. As for black-headed gulls, one colony in Cumbria once held 16,000 pairs, and several kittiwake colonies used to exceed 20–30,000 pairs, but these have declined. The biggest is on the Bempton Cliffs to Flamborough Head stretch of the Yorkshire coast.

The most crowded seabird colonies are those of gannets and guillemots. Gannets leave no more than 1m (3ft) between one nest and the next. Guillemots have no true nest and crowd closer still on their cliff-ledge sites – so close that their loomeries, or bazaars, have been referred to as bird 'slums'.

Hole-nesting seabirds, such as Manx shearwaters and puffins, which can excavate their own cavities, often nest so close together that the ground is honeycombed. The smaller storm petrels and Leach's petrels use ready-made holes and have to make do with what is available, so that their colonies can be compact or loose. Colonies of skuas, and most terns and gulls, on the other hand, are deliberately loose.

Why nest so close together?

The function of colonial nesting is much disputed among ornithologists and it is impossible to give clear-cut answers to questions such as why are some

Colony under the ground
Puffins dig nesting burrows up to 3m (10ft) long, hacking at the ground with their powerful bills and scooping out earth with their large feet. They burrow even into hard, stony ground, although not so far as into cliff-top turf. A puffinry may number thousands of pairs, and the ground can become so honeycombed that it will collapse in parts of the colony. Beyond a certain point, puffin colonies begin to decrease in size, because the birds literally dig themselves out of a home.

species colonial rather than solitary nesters? Why do some species form compact colonies and others loose ones? Why do some species hold territories extending beyond the nest site itself?

However, a comparison of colonial and solitary nesting species indicates where the answers lie. Firstly, typically colonial species take food that is locally abundant but widely scattered – such as fish from shoals, fruit or seeds. They would not be successful if they established separate nests and territories, because these might not correspond with their food supply.

Secondly, the young of most colonial birds stay in the nest for some time after hatching, and living in large groups gives them some protection.

Another factor encouraging the development of colonial breeding could well be the shortage of suitable sites for nests. However, the significance of this factor has probably been exaggerated by some naturalists, especially when applied to seabirds.

The continuing existence of a colony at a traditional site indicates that the site is safe, and although nest sites may not be scarce, traditional and safe sites are by no means common. Colonies are safe places because they are often inaccessible to predators, because one alert bird can warn all the others if danger threatens and because birds will sometimes join in a communal attack on any intruders.

The synchronisation of egg-laying is important, too – it means that there are fewer losses to predators than if eggs and young were available, and vulnerable, over a longer period, as they would be if the birds laid at different times. This synchronisation is thought to arise from the close proximity of the birds – the theory being that courtship displays by a few may create a mood that runs through the entire colony.

How colonies work

A closer look at some colony-dwelling birds will show how these various factors – feeding, safety and the availability of nest sites – work out in practice. Colony-dwelling finches feed on seeds in small flocks in the breeding season and form small colonies, often not far from good supplies of their food. Another finch, the chaffinch, includes a large proportion of insects in the diet of its young, and is territorial, not colonial.

The fish-eating heron is usually a solitary feeder and seems to be colonial so that it can use safe, traditional sites – and possibly so that it can gain information about the location of food, through watching other members of the colony.

Some species vary their social patterns to fit their surroundings. On many lakes where there is a narrow band of fringing vegetation, great crested grebes are territorial birds, with their nests spaced well apart; but on lakes where cover is scarce, or where there is one particularly safe area, such as a reedbed, these birds nest in loose colonies. The sea-feeding, ground-nesting eider duck also forms colonies, mainly on islands free of ground predators. Eiders nesting on the mainland, however, do so solitarily, relying on camouflage and spacing out of the nests for protection.

It is only to be expected that birds feeding on shoals of fish will be colonial, for their food supply is abundant but scattered.

Safety is also an important factor for seabirds, and the relative security of the breeding area has an influence on the structure of the colony. Seabirds that nest in inaccessible places, such as on cliff ledges, tend to form dense colonies to make the most of the space available, for example gannets and guillemots. Those nesting in less safe places, such as marshes and sandbanks, tend to form loose colonies.

Gathering on cliffs
Kittiwakes, like many other gulls, nest on cliff ledges. They build large nests, mainly of seaweed, to take two, three and sometimes four chicks. If the ledge is too narrow, the birds still cling to the protection of the cliffs, building nests that jut out over a dizzying drop. The birds pair for life, and return year after year to the same ledge site, settling in compact colonies of several thousand pairs.

Examples are gulls and terns. While most seabirds merely defend their own particular nests, gulls and terns go further and join forces against many predators, including carrion crows, foxes and stoats. Sandwich terns have another anti-predator adaptation. They often nest within colonies of common terns or black-headed gulls, depending on the communal defence behaviour of these more aggressive species.

Where birds sleep

Choosing the right place to sleep is a life-and-death matter for birds. In their efforts to outwit predators and survive the rigours of wintry nights, some birds creep into cracks and crevices. Others fly miles across country, flocking together in hundreds of thousands, and some even cat-nap in flight. The sleeping site, whether occupied by one bird or by thousands, is called a roost. Rooks regularly travel anything from 10 to 16km (6 to 10 miles) from the roost and back again in a day. Starlings range even further into the countryside – normally between 19 and 32km (12 and 20 miles), and sometimes they will go as far as 48km (30 miles).

As long as a roost proves safe and sheltered, birds are reluctant to forsake it, and usually move away only in response to severe disturbance or to fluctuations in their food supply.

Keeping out the cold

Loss of heat at night is a major problem for all creatures. A solitary bird roosting in an exposed place on a cold night may freeze to death. Its body can lose heat to the surrounding air faster than it can be replaced, sending the bird into a coma from which it may never recover.

All birds must maintain a constant body heat to survive, although in emergencies nestling swifts can live through a temporary drop in temperature by going into a state of torpidity in which their bodily processes are slowed down. For most birds, the daytime is one long meal, broken only by such necessary actions as searching for food, preening, courtship and defending territory. When night falls they must use the heat stored up by the food taken in during the day. When they are sleeping and most likely to lose heat, birds fluff up their contour feathers to form an insulating layer of warm air. They reduce the area of their bodies exposed to the night air by hunching up (pigeons), tucking their heads behind their wings (robins) or pressing their bills into the side of the neck (grebes).

Great tits and blue tits sleep in cavities in trees or buildings, to avoid draughts and to prevent heat from escaping from their bodies. Long-tailed tits and goldcrests crowd into a small space, sometimes ten at a time, and huddle together for warmth. As many as 80 swifts have been seen clinging to the side of a house – presumably for the same reason. Quails roost together in clusters with their heads pointing outwards, ready for a quick getaway if danger threatens. In the Cairngorms in winter, the ptarmigan digs a hole in the snow in which to sleep. The warmth of this roost, like that of an igloo, depends on the fact that ice and snow are poor conductors of heat.

Birds are vulnerable to their natural enemies while they are asleep, and many species flock together for protection. Young birds and migrants that are unfamiliar with the countryside follow the lead of more experienced birds in seeking places that are relatively safe from predators. The fact that thousands of starlings or thrushes sleep in one location in the territory of a single tawny owl means that fewer individuals are likely to be taken by owls than if they were scattered, with a few pairs in the hunting grounds of individual owls.

Counting birds

In winter, flocks are at their biggest. Winter roosts of starlings, swollen by newly arrived juveniles and migrants from the Continent, commonly contain up to 500,000 birds, and one or two hold more than a million. One of the largest in Britain, at Denver, near King's Lynn in Norfolk, is thought to harbour several million birds, but even these numbers are dwarfed by comparison with the flock of bramblings that filled two small pinewoods near the town of Thun in Switzerland in the winter of 1950–1. Their numbers were calculated at more than 70 million – nearly 12 times the entire human population of the country.

Calculating the size of roosts is a specialised job, although the beginner can get some idea of the numbers in smaller flocks by finding a good vantage-point on the regular flight-lines into a roost and counting the birds as they fly in. The reliability of an estimator's figures improves with experience.

In the case of starlings, fairly accurate estimates can be made, because these birds fly into their roosts in a stream of relatively constant density – that is, a section taken from the beginning of the stream will contain roughly the same number of birds as a section of the same length towards the end. The experienced estimator may therefore photograph part of the stream to determine how many birds it contains, calculate the length of the stream and arrive at a fairly reliable figure for the total number of birds.

Starlings are the most numerous of Britain's flocking birds. Large numbers of them roost in the countryside, travelling at dusk along familiar flight-lines to roost in trees, reeds or along sea-cliffs, and returning to their feeding grounds the same way the next morning.

Roosts in towns

Starlings are equally familiar in towns. On winter evenings, the roar of traffic around London's Leicester Square used to be practically drowned by the chattering of thousands of starlings as they flew in from the country and settled on building ledges. Greater London was once the home of around 3 million starlings. Although starling numbers are now reduced, the scene is repeated in towns all over Britain, mainly in the north – in Bradford and Leeds, for example. Altogether there are some 70 urban roosting sites, on buildings, bridges and among trees in parks. Many of them are now much smaller, but the largest can still contain more than 50,000 birds.

The rook is another well-known social roosting species. In spring and summer, rooks sleep in small rookeries, but in autumn and throughout the winter, birds from a number of colonies gather together, often accompanied by jackdaws, at a single 'super roost'. In eastern England, an average rook/jackdaw roost contains about 10,000 birds.

Carrion crows and ravens may establish roosts of their own – a recent raven flock in the Hebrides was 1,200 strong – as well as sometimes sharing roosts with rooks and jackdaws.

The social roosting habits of various gulls have changed remarkably over the last few decades. The number of gulls roosting inland, mainly on lakes, reservoirs and flooded gravel-pits, has greatly increased.

Exchanging information

For most of these birds, sleeping flocks are a continuation of daytime feeding communities, but other birds that feed alone or in small groups during the daytime will sometimes flock together at night. The individual gains protection and possibly information about feeding sites – birds that return hungry may join the feeding party of more successful individuals the next day.

Pied wagtails, for example, tend to feed alone by day, although there may be other pied wagtails not too far away, but at night they roost socially throughout the year, especially in winter, mainly in reedbeds. Many roosts consist of at most a few hundred birds, but larger roosts of 1,000 or more are known, some in towns. One famous roost of wagtails, in O'Connell Street, Dublin, sometimes holds well over 3,000 birds.

Conversely, many birds sleep singly even when they feed in groups. By choosing well-concealed roosts, spaced out in countryside that they know intimately, they make themselves less conspicuous to predators. In summer, great tits sleep alone in thick foliage in the woods, although the females roost in the nest-hole while incubating and before the young grow so big that there is no space left. In winter, all great tits use holes in trees or buildings, which protect them against enemies and help to keep them warm.

Woodpeckers roost singly, in holes of their own making, throughout the year. These are often old nests, but in winter the birds sometimes excavate special roost-holes. Treecreepers used to sleep in cracks and crevices in trees and behind bark, or in shallow niches in rotting tree stumps, which they excavated with their long, curved bills. In many parts of the country, however, this species has recently taken to roosting in hollows scooped in the soft, thick, spongy bark of the giant Wellingtonia, a redwood tree introduced to Britain halfway through the 19th century.

Sleeping on the wing

Ornithologists have often watched swifts taking off at dusk after a day of activity, and flying out to sea. Although it seemed highly improbable, they found that many birds appeared to stay on the wing all night. Some remarkable detective work has been done to show that this is, in fact, what happens.

The first step was to note how many birds took off in the evening, and confirm that not all of them returned before nightfall. Observation also showed that none of the birds came back to roost during darkness. An ornithologist finally clinched the argument by flying over the sea in a light aircraft. He found dozens of the birds still airborne.

Swifts, it seems, are able to sleep – or at least to cat-nap – on the wing, probably as they glide high above the water between spells of flapping to gain height. Sooty terns must have a similar ability. These birds spend much of their life over the ocean, often miles from land, yet they can never settle on the sea because their plumage easily becomes waterlogged by salt water. They even have to snatch small fish from the surface, to avoid getting wet.

Most birds sleep during the night, when they are unable to feed, leaving the hours of daylight for foraging and nesting. The process is reversed in the case of night-hunting birds, such as owls. They need the cover of darkness to enable them to catch their prey, and therefore they sleep during the day.

Waders feed along the seashore and regulate their lives not according to the light but by the tide. Probing in mudflats with their bills, they can locate food without the aid of light. So they eat when the tide is low and sleep when it is high, irrespective of the time of day.

Why birds sing

From dawn chorus to evensong

Naturalists no longer dismiss the idea that birds may sing from sheer high spirits, but it is difficult to reconcile too sentimental an interpretation of birdsong with the utilitarianism of a bird's way of life. Singing uses time and energy that could be spent finding food and, at the same time, advertises the bird's presence to predators, but birds would have ceased singing long ago if the survival value of conspicuousness did not outweigh its dangers.

Song is just one element in the vocabulary of birds. Each bird also has a number of calls – more than a dozen different sounds for many species, each with its own meaning.

Songs and calls

It is often difficult to draw a precise line between a song and a call. Songs tend to be complex arrangements of notes, uttered rhythmically, while calls are generally short groups of up to four or five notes, and are aesthetically less pleasing, to human ears at least.

A bird can communicate many things by the sounds it makes. It can state its species, sex, individual identity, even its condition. It can trigger off sexual excitement, curiosity, alarm or fear in another bird. It can attract a mate or drive off a rival. It can pass on news – where food is to be found or where there is a possible nest site – and alert others to the presence of predators.

The purpose of the song is usually to lay claim to a territory and to attract a mate – the two instincts that shape the lives of a great number of birds at the beginning of the breeding season. Just as distinctive plumage patterns and elaborate displays minimise the likelihood of cross-breeding between different species of ducks, so distinctive songs prevent cross-breeding between similar-looking songbirds, such as the chiffchaff and willow warbler. At the same time, a bird's song is a statement of its sex – in most cases male. In only a few species, such as the robin, in which both male and female hold territories in winter, does the female sing. The song is interpreted differently according to the sex of the hearer – the same sound attracts unmated females and repels intruding males.

Territorial songs are long-range warnings from one bird to another. They must be loud and clear to be effective – certainly loud enough to be heard beyond the boundaries of the territory. A reed warbler's song can be heard about 274m (300yd) away, and its territory is usually about 250m² (300sq yd).

Driving home the message

The song needs to be persistent to make its point, so birds repeat their song-phrases hundreds of times a day. By dusk, the yellowhammer may have made its 'little-bit-of-bread-and-no-cheese' sound more than 1,000 times. The sustained warbling of a skylark, delivered as the bird climbs into the sky or sinks gently earthwards from the apex of its flight, will go on for minutes on end, for ten to twelve minutes in every hour of daylight. One bird was heard singing for 18 minutes without a pause, although three to four minutes is more usual.

Many species – the mistle thrush is one – choose commanding song-posts high in a tree, to ensure that their songs cover the widest possible area. Others add a visual effect to the advertisement by describing distinctive patterns in the sky. The whitethroat, a small warbler, performs what is almost a song-and-dance act when it accompanies its outburst of squeaky song by flying straight up from the hedge for a metre or so before dropping back again. Song-flights are particularly characteristic of ground-living birds, such as larks and pipits, which breed in open, treeless countryside.

Battle of nerves

Rival birds seldom resort to physical combat – the risk of injury is too great to make this a practical way of settling an argument. Instead, they have evolved patterns of behaviour that achieve results without exposing them to danger. Their territorial songs, like their elaborate threat displays, are battles of nerves, each bird working out the tension built up by two conflicting impulses – the impulse to fight and the impulse to flee. A bird singing in defence of its territory pays careful attention to the songs of other birds defending theirs. A robin or a wren, for instance, will pause after each phrase, allowing rivals time to get in their 'answer'. By song 'duels' with its neighbours, a bird gets to know who and where its rivals are.

There is scientific truth in the belief that a cuckoo's call announces that spring has arrived. Birdsong is inextricably associated with the season in which it is delivered, and although some birds may sing at any time of the year, they are never more vociferous than in spring, when establishing a territory. As summer approaches, and paired birds turn their attention to building nests, laying eggs, incubating and raising their young, the songs of many species become more intermittent or subdued, or even cease altogether.

Some birds, such as crossbills, may sing softly as they prospect for nest sites, and the male redstart sings as it displays before a nest-hole. Male wrens may sing snatches of song as they build nests, and other birds sing as they change places during incubation, or while they tend the young. These sounds are believed to confirm and strengthen the bond between male and female.

Spring song erupts in response to hormone-induced changes in a bird's body – particularly the increase in size of its internal reproductive organs – caused by the extra hours of daylight. In autumn, too, physiological change seems to spur some birds into song. In winter, most birds fall silent, although the robin is a notable exception. Both male and female robins defend winter territories, and sing defiantly at one another until they start forming pairs, usually sometime in December.

Dawn chorus

In the daily cycle, as in the seasonal cycle, light is the key factor affecting birdsong – night changing to day has the same song-producing effect on birds as winter changing to summer. More birds sing for the 20–40 minutes around dawn than at any other time. It is hard to find a biological reason for this, but one advantage in so many birds singing at once is that each bird can find out what is going on around it.

Birds do not generally sing as soon as they are awake. They may first stretch, like other creatures, preen their feathers and fly off to a song-perch. The blackbird is often the first to break into song, starting about 40 minutes before sunrise, closely followed by the song thrush, woodpigeon, robin, mistle thrush, turtle dove, pheasant, willow warbler and wren, usually in that order. Just as most birds sing less in the cold, dark months of the year, so the dawn chorus starts late if a heavy grey overcast dawn retards the lightening of the sky.

Night singers

Very few species sing continuously throughout the day. Most quieten down after the initial exuberance of the dawn chorus, and are subdued by about midday. A resurgence occurs in the evening, and for most species silence falls with the night, although robins sing for long periods under artificial lighting.

Birds that roost together frequently sing together before settling down for the night. Starlings flying to their roosts raise a great chorus of twittering and wheezing as they wheel through the sky. The reasons for their flight manoeuvres and choral performance are not clear to scientists, but one suggestion is that they are conferring about the local food supply. If food is due to run out, a large percentage of the starlings will move on to a place where food is more abundant.

Night birds usually sing for the same reasons as daytime species. The call of a tawny owl, for instance, is a statement of identity and a summons to its mate, but the reason why nightingales sing by night is harder to establish. Like many other small songbirds, they migrate by night, and since the males arrive from their winter quarters in April, some ten days ahead of the females, it may be that the males sing by night to compete for the females as they arrive. However, two facts do not fit in with this theory – nightingales sing by day as well as at night, and other night migrants do not sing at night.

Sounds inherited and learnt

The whitethroat inherits from its parents a complete vocabulary of call-notes and songs. No learning is necessary. If a whitethroat lived its whole life without hearing another whitethroat sing, it would still develop all its calls and songs, and each one would be perfect in pitch, volume, rhythm and quality. This has been proved by experiments in which birds were reared from birth in soundproof

Aerial theatre
In spring and summer, the sky becomes a stage on which the male tree pipit performs to attract a mate. With wings fluttering like those of a butterfly, it flies steeply up from its treetop perch and begins to sing as it reaches the top of its climb – usually about 18m (60ft). Still singing, it floats down with its wings raised and tail spread, finishing with a shrill 'seea-seea-seea' as it drops back on to the perch from which it started, or one nearby.

Drumming of the snipe
The snipe begins its territorial display by swooping down from the sky at an angle of about 45°, with its outer tail feathers – which are stiffer than the central ones – held at right angles to its line of descent. Air rushing past makes them vibrate and causes the drumming sound by which the bird draws attention to itself.

isolation. Other birds are born with the innate ability to sing songs that are characteristic of the species in all but a few details, which have to be learnt. For example, when a chaffinch first establishes a territory, its song is incomplete and it learns the flourishes by imitating other males.

Learning by imitation is the starting-point for one of the great mysteries of bird behaviour – mimicry. Many wild birds incorporate in their songs the notes of other birds and even the sounds of inanimate objects. Some 30 British birds are reputed to be mimics. The most gifted of them all is the starling, and marsh warblers, reed warblers and blackcaps can be very skilled. The starling may reproduce the sounds of such unlikely birds as tawny owls, partridges and domestic fowl, and there is a reliable account of one bird imitating the ringing of a telephone so effectively that it deceived the owner of the house on which it was perched.

Early warning system

Most birds live in constant danger of being taken by predators. It is not surprising, therefore, that their language includes a highly effective anti-predator alarm system. The first bird to spot potential danger raises an alarm that alerts all within hearing.

The danger may come from the air or the ground, and many birds have evolved calls that differentiate between the two kinds of menace. Alarms calling attention to aerial predators are usually brief, high-pitched and difficult to trace to a source. Birds hearing one of these calls scatter into cover. The alarm summons to mob a ground predator, or one spotted in a tree, contains clues to the whereabouts both of the caller and the predator.

A few birds have an even more sophisticated alarm system. Jays have several different sounds for danger, and sometimes give specific calls for specific predators. Often these resemble the cries of the predator itself. A chittering call draws attention to squirrels, a popping noise – perhaps in imitation of a gun – to humans, and a shrill 'kik-kik-kik' to kestrels.

While the song of each species must be very different, so that no confusion can arise, their alarm calls are often very similar. The first bird to spot a hawk warns all birds within hearing, not merely those of the same species as itself. Aerial predator warnings given by the reed bunting, blackbird, great tit, blue tit and chaffinch are all very similar.

How sounds are produced

Most birds make sounds by means of the syrinx, a voice organ situated near the lungs. It consists of a resonating chamber and associated membranes. Air from the lungs is driven through these membranes, which can be relaxed or tightened and moved in relation to the resonating chamber, to change the character of the sound produced. Muscles change the shape of the syrinx, and the quality of the voice alters accordingly. The entire system is different from that of mammals, which produce sound in the larynx, situated in the throat, and use their lips and tongues to give form to the sound. Versatile singers are usually those with the most intricate syrinxes, but this does not always hold true. Crows have highly developed syrinxes and are poor singers.

The smaller the bird, the higher-pitched its voice is likely to be. The firecrest, goldcrest and wren, all of them small, have some of the highest-pitched voices among British birds. The wren's voice vibrates at about 4,000 cycles per second – the equivalent of the top note on a piano – and its delivery rate is too fast for a human ear to take in every note. In 5.2 seconds, it sings 56 notes, producing a tune that becomes intelligible to human ears only if the song is slowed down on a tape recorder. At the other end of the scale, the bittern's boom is one of the lowest-pitched notes uttered by any British bird.

In addition to vocalising, some birds use instrumental techniques. The flight-music of the mute swan comes from vibrations set up by its wing-beats. The sound may help flocks to keep together, as do the vocal flight-notes of the other European swans, whooper and Bewick's.

The bleating or drumming of the snipe – the humming sound created as the bird dives through the air – is also a mechanically produced sound, but communicating mechanically has nowhere reached a higher degree of sophistication than among woodpeckers. Using the same technique as when they feed, they signal their presence and identity to one another with a sharp drumming, tapped out with an identifiable rhythm on trees.

The drive to establish territory
A system of land ownership

A blackbird attacking its own reflection in a window or a car's wing-mirror is following a behaviour pattern as deeply ingrained as the urge to mate or to find food. Its aggression is connected with the defence of territory, and this is as important for the survival of the bird and its species as are eating and breeding.

By marking out an area of land and defending it against males of its own species a bird can gain monopoly access to food, nesting material and nest sites, as well as a place where it can court its mate and rear its young unmolested by rivals. There is usually no need to defend territory against birds of a different species, because they seldom take exactly the same food and they are not rivals for mates – although they may be for nest sites.

What is a territory?

The simplest definition of the word 'territory' is 'any defended area' – a treecreeper defending its winter roosting cavity at one extreme, and a golden eagle on its home range at the other. A home range is an area the boundaries of which are not clearly defined, where birds keep apart from rivals of their own species by mutual avoidance rather than by disputes.

Size of territory	
GREAT CRESTED GREBE	Area around nest – 1ha (2½ acres); lakes
RED GROUSE	2–6ha (5–15 acres); moorland
LITTLE GREBE	0.3ha (¾ acre); ponds
PTARMIGAN	3ha (8 acres); barren high ground
LAPWING	1ha (2¼ acres) and air-space above; farmland
LITTLE RINGED PLOVER	Up to 0.4ha (1 acre) and air-space above; gravel-pits
TAWNY OWL	24–28ha (60–70 acres); broadleaved woodland
REDSTART	Just over 0.4ha (1 acre); broadleaved woodland
WHEATEAR	0.4–3ha (1-8 acres); islands
WILLOW WARBLER	0.07–0.4ha (⅙–1 acre); commons
REED WARBLER	About 250m² (300sq yd); reedbeds
MARSH TIT	0.4–6ha (1–16 acres); broadleaved woodland
YELLOWHAMMER	About 0.2ha (½ acre); hedgerows
CORN BUNTING	Just over 0.8ha (2 acres); farmland

These figures are based on studies of bird populations in restricted areas, and do not necessarily hold true for all birds throughout a species' range. The habitats in which they were studied are also given.

A pair of golden eagles may hunt over a home range of more than 72km² (28sq miles). Partridges, too, are home-range birds.

By strict definition, many colony-dwelling birds are territorial, even though they may defend just a metre or so of space at the nest site, as is the case with gannets. Black grouse can be described as territorial when they defend a patch of ground at their courtship arenas, but for the sake of convenience, the term is best confined to birds defending larger areas.

Size of territory varies considerably from species to species, and also within a species according to local conditions, such as richness of the food supply or density of cover. Great crested grebes, for example, defend anything from a few square metres around the nest to several hectares, depending on the distribution of cover.

Staking a claim

The means by which most birds advertise and enforce their territorial claims are song, special displays and, against persistent interlopers, threat or actual fighting. For a few species, including ravens and kestrels, mere physical presence is enough to stake a claim.

Most territorial species have a definite code of conduct, with the territory owner showing aggression only within its own defended area and fleeing when it is discovered trespassing in another bird's province. In an experiment to test the strength of this code, a robin was put in a cage within its own territory. It put a rival robin to flight by singing and displaying its red breast, but when the roles were reversed, and the caged robin was moved into the other bird's territory, it shrank back and would have fled if flight were possible.

A territory owner is usually secure on its own patch, although determined intruders can sometimes annex part or even all of an occupied territory by sustained hostility, especially in crowded habitats.

In many species, boundaries are sharply defined by natural features, such as trees, bushes, clearings or woodland edges. A boundary is also defined by a bird's behaviour – fear of its neighbour and its urge to attack the other bird are in balance.

Territory sizes can often be worked out by direct observation on colour-ringed or wing-tagged birds, or by counting the total of males or pairs and dividing it into the occupied area. Another method, often useful with birds holding small territories, is chasing the bird and watching how far it goes before

Six ways of sharing an area of woodland

The songs of a great variety of species ring through broadleaved woods in spring and summer. These are just some of the ways in which 2.5 hectares (6 acres) might be divided up.

CHAFFINCHES *Very common in this kind of wood, their territories include clearings and isolated trees from which they sing.*

BLACKBIRDS *The number of blackbirds and other thrushes is small because they need a better shrub layer in which to feed. Their territories extend beyond the wood.*

WREN *This is a poor wood for wrens because there is no shrub layer. The entire area might support just one bird, with a large amount of 'edge' territory.*

BLUE TITS *The lack of a shrub layer does not worry blue tits. They feed in the trees, and several pairs have territories in this wood.*

GREAT TITS *As for the wren, this wood is not particularly suited to great tits. Their territories are large because there is no good shrub layer in which to feed.*

ROBINS *There is little dead ground between the territories of the highly aggressive robins, and a few areas are in dispute between pairs.*

it encounters a neighbour or turns back. The borders of a robin's territory in a garden can be discovered by taking out a mirror and noting where the bird attacks or retreats from its own reflection.

The rule that territorial rivalry occurs only between birds of the same species has a few exceptions. In areas where ringed, little ringed and Kentish plovers breed close together, especially on the Continent, they defend territory against one another. Disputes have been recorded between reed

and sedge warblers, and garden warblers and blackcaps. However, these rival species are closely related. They take the same kind of food, and their songs are similar, and it is not unusual for them to hold overlapping territories.

Some birds that stay in Britain all year round, such as great tits, reed buntings, coots and ringed plovers, establish their territories in late winter and early spring after a winter spent as members of a flock. Other residents, such as blackbirds and wrens, which do not spend the winter in flocks but keep in touch with their territories throughout the year, start to defend them again more seriously at the same time. Summer visitors, such as yellow wagtails, whitethroats, willow warblers and wheatears, set up territory later in the spring, after journeying from winter quarters abroad.

Choosing a spot

Generally speaking, the male bird is responsible for establishing a territory and defending it. The female joins him and usually accepts the boundaries of the territory as they are, although there are odd cases of a male having to adjust the boundaries to take in the wanderings of its mate (reported of the blackbird), or because she nested outside the original territory (reported of the snow bunting). Red-necked phalaropes are exceptional because the female chooses a territory and attracts a mate. She is more brightly coloured than the male, and many of the usual roles of the sexes are reversed.

In winter-flocking species, such as buntings, the males leave the flocks first and start to set up their territories by visiting them for increasing periods over a number of weeks. Finally, the male makes the break and stays in the territory, where it is later joined by a female.

Among summer visitors, such as nightingales and warblers, the males arrive first and establish territories almost immediately. The females, following them, arrive ten days or so later. In a few species, such as the great crested grebe, the birds form pairs in open water and then seek and establish a territory together. Much the same thing happens with various ducks, such as the mallard. Certain gulls, such as the herring gull, pair in loose 'club' areas before establishing their real territory in the colony. The black-headed gull, however, has a definite 'pairing territory' where a male stays until it has a mate. The pair move to the real breeding territory later. Similar pairing territories have been recorded in the greenshank.

Moving out for food

Many songbirds live more or less entirely within the boundaries of the breeding territory throughout the breeding season and find all or most of their food there, including food for their young. Some – reed warblers, for example – move outside the territory to find food. Ducks and many waders leave the breeding territory after the young have hatched, and take them away to a more suitable feeding area.

Only a few British species defend territory in winter and, if they are residents, this is usually the same, at least in part, as the one held in summer. The best-known example of a winter territorial bird is the robin. Male and female birds hold separate plots, and both sexes sing to advertise their territories, which are only half the size, on average, of the summer ones. In effect, male and female divide the summer territory between them, although in practice former mates need not necessarily be neighbours and they do not always pair up again in a combined territory the following year.

The male wren also maintains a winter territory, retiring to part of its former breeding area from late summer onwards. Other species that hold individual territories in winter are the rock pipit, the great grey shrike (a rare winter visitor) and many birds of prey.

Very few species defend a joint winter territory. Marsh tits do so and will not tolerate neighbouring pairs, although they join passing tit flocks while these are within the territory. Well-established blackbird pairs also tend to stay together in the former breeding territory throughout the winter, although they may visit better feeding places during the day. Pairs of stonechats occupy a common territory in winter – often the former breeding area, but some pairs move right away from their summer haunts and settle in a new place.

Value of a home patch

A system of territory-holding means that birds are dispersed more widely in suitable habitats than if the population crowded in without restraint. As a result, competition for food, nest sites and safe roosting places is much reduced. Isolation from competitors is especially important for owls and many insect-eaters, which specialise in catching hidden prey by skilled hunting techniques. Such birds often need to feed their young at frequent intervals, so it is important for them to be able to find food fairly near the nest, and familiarity with a restricted area probably enables the territory owner to find food more easily than if it had to forage more widely over a greater and largely unfamiliar area.

Another advantage is that once a female has entered a territory, pair formation – and later copulation – can proceed with minimum interference from rivals. Holding a territory may also be important in maintaining the pair once it has been formed, by compelling the birds to remain together in a circumscribed area, rather than encouraging them to wander at will. In some species, joint defence of the territory together with mutual display afterwards probably helps to strengthen the pair bond.

Finally, the spacing out of nests in a territorial system makes them harder for predators to find. In fact, concealment may well be a major function of establishing a territory in many ground-nesting birds, such as plovers.

Threat and fighting

How disputes are resolved in the competitive world of birds

Competition between birds for territory, nest sites, food and mates inevitably produces hostility, but natural selection ensures that only rarely does this hostility lead to full-blooded fighting – birds with an aggressive drive that leads them to risk being killed or maimed usually do not live long enough to breed.

When conflict threatens, all animals are torn between aggression and fear. Instead of fighting, most birds show their hostility by an elaborate system of bluff and threats – intimidating calls or physical displays that stop short of violence. In many species, a single hostile encounter is sufficient to decide which bird has unquestioned priority in any future dispute.

Disputes over territory

Rivalry between birds of the same species is at its most intense and frequent during the breeding season, when the sex hormones make them more aggressive and they have to contend for territory, mates and nest sites. The establishment and defence of territory, in particular, is a major cause of threats and fighting. A bird is most aggressive near its nest, and is inclined to fight off all intruders. Further away, towards the edges of its territory, this aggression is balanced by fear of the rival from the neighbouring territory, and threat displays usually take the place of violence. A bird's urge to defend its own territory and respect that of its rival is deeply ingrained.

Conflicts can break out when food is scarce, particularly among flocking birds, such as finches, starlings, rooks and jackdaws. These disputes become serious only when the shortage is severe enough to reduce the birds' fear of one another. When a great tit finds food, it threatens other members of the flock that come too close, either by partly opening and raising its wings or by holding its head low and pointing it at the rival. One tit will rob another by flying at it and taking its place as it moves away from the food. The supplanted bird will occasionally retaliate, but usually it simply flies away and begins the search again.

Although the intensity of the struggle for food depends on how scarce it is, a time may come when there is no longer any point in fighting. A starving robin, for example, will not divert itself from the search for food by attacking another robin that encroaches on its territory in hard weather.

Warning off rivals

Apart from disputing for food and territory, birds will defend themselves if attacked by predators. They will also fight or threaten one another for a host of lesser causes, such as roosting perches, nest sites, mates and – if they are flocking or colonial birds – to maintain a set distance between themselves and their neighbours.

Birds have many ways of avoiding conflict and the need to fight – they stake their claim to a piece of territory as ostentatiously as possible, and often treat intruders to spectacular displays of force. These displays are aimed at showing that here is an aggressive bird of the same species, often of the same sex, which will attack if provoked. The effect is usually to make the intruder afraid, and encourage it to withdraw. Noisy and dazzling flying displays are used by many species to advertise their choice of territory. The male little ringed plover flies round in wide circles, arcs or figures-of-eight, crying 'cree-a, cree-a, cree-a'. If it encounters a rival doing the same thing, its cry becomes a mechanical-sounding buzz, and it flies threateningly at the other bird, stalling before it with wings quivering in a 'V' shape.

Markings that warn
When threatening, a ringed plover bends its legs and displays its dramatic black and white markings.

Threat in a colour
The yellow wagtail frightens rivals by stretching itself and showing off its brilliant yellow plumage.

Some birds do not even need to come face-to-face in order to compete for territory – robins have been observed to do it all by singing. The intruder enters alien country and sings. The occupant replies from a distance. The intruder comes deeper into the territory and sings again. At this, the occupant flies to within about 5m (5yd) of the newcomer, still hidden in the foliage, and replies more vigorously, staking its claim in forceful and direct fashion. This is often sufficient to put the intruder to flight.

Threats at close quarters

If song and flying displays fail to frighten off a rival, birds have a formidable repertoire of menaces to fall back on. At close quarters they make themselves look as big and fearsome as possible. They puff out their feathers, stiffen their crests or crown feathers, and show off any special plumage marks, colours or patterns, following up with a series of menacing movements, evolved from the first stages of jumping or flying up.

The robin stretches itself up, fluffs up the red feathers on its breast and displays them to its rival. In a similar way the great tit shows off its broad black chin, and breast-stripe bordered with yellow. The ringed plover crouches forward on bent legs, showing off its black chest-patch, ruffling its back feathers and spreading its tail to show the white outer feathers.

Many birds enhance their postures by making the best display of their markings. The most striking feature of the yellow wagtail is the brilliant yellow of the feathers on its head, breast and belly. So the bird turns full-face towards its rival and stretches, to display its plumage to the full. The jay, on the other hand, can make itself look more daunting by standing sideways and ruffling and spreading its feathers to increase its size.

The shag adds movement to its armoury of threats. It makes its crest and the feathers on its neck and head stand up, draws the head and neck slowly back, and then suddenly darts them forward at the rival, opening its bill wide and exposing its vivid yellow gape.

Frightened to death

Although this threatening behaviour seldom leads to fighting in earnest, it is extremely successful in settling disputes. Most of the time it takes the form of stylised gestures, but is none the less frightening to the birds concerned. Several cases have been reported of birds – including the blackbird – dying of ruptured hearts or blood vessels as a result of the emotional excitement of these mock battles.

Faced with an aggressor, birds are frequently uncertain what to do – whether to fight, submit or bluff it out. As the struggle between aggression and fear goes on within them, they often adopt postures curiously irrelevant to the hostile situation, many of which are drawn from other activities. Gulls will start preening themselves or feeding. Waders, such as the oystercatcher and the avocet, adopt the sleeping position, with the head turned away sideways and the bill hidden. Some birds have a special 'quandary' posture. Sandwich terns and gulls, for instance, stand with heads bowed, as if staring at their feet. This posture may be a preliminary either to submission or to an attack.

Styles of fighting

Real battles are liable to break out in extreme circumstances, however, particularly when one bird threatens another's nest during the breeding season. Then the males usually do the fighting, although their mates may occasionally join in, either tentatively trying to peck at the enemy, or attacking the enemy's mate.

In species where the sexes are difficult to tell apart, such as the great crested grebe, male may occasionally fight female, but most fights are between birds of the same sex, and only rarely do they fully engage more than two birds.

Menacing plumage
The jay turns sideways to meet an enemy, ruffling and spreading its feathers to make itself look bigger.

Taking refuge in 'sleep'
Unsure whether to fight or flee, the oystercatcher hides its bill in its plumage, as if going to sleep.

Fights are usually brief and relatively bloodless. Among the exceptions to this general rule are the spectacular battles between two mute swan cobs. In this case, the birds fight breast to breast in the water, necks intertwined, beating each other powerfully with their wings. Each one's ultimate objective is to seize the other's head and push it under the water. These battles may last until both birds are exhausted.

Less protracted fights take place between perching birds. These flutter breast to breast, grappling with their bills. Plovers fight like this, but they also use their feet. Gamebirds, such as pheasants, have spurs on the backs of their legs with which they hack at each other, using vicious downward blows. Pigeons beat each other with their wings.

Grebes grapple in the water with bills interlocked, each trying, like swans, to drown the rival by forcing its head under the water. The great crested grebe has a long, pointed bill with which it tries to spear its enemies by coming at them under water. Coots lie back on the water, supporting themselves on wings held back, and strike out with the long, sharp claws on their toes.

Herring gulls and great and lesser black-backed gulls seize each other by the bill and pull vigorously. Male gannets spreadeagle themselves, grip each other by the bill and push vigorously in the hope of toppling one another over the edge of the cliff. Where a ledge is narrow, the dispute will be quickly decided, but in flatter parts of the colony the struggle can be prolonged and damaging – one gannet in every few hundred is blind in one eye as a result.

Birds usually direct their hostility at other birds, but many will attack any animal that comes too near the nest, including human beings. Seabirds can be particularly ferocious. Skuas and some terns will fly straight at an intruder or dive at its head, striking out viciously with their feet. They have been known to draw blood from a man's head. A breeding

Some of the most dramatic battles of the bird world take place between male mute swans. When the fight is over, the losing bird submits to being pecked on the back of its head and neck.

fulmar's form of defensive attack is to shoot an oily, evil-smelling liquid from its mouth over anything that comes too near.

Submission and retreat

A game of bluff, or an actual contest, usually ends when one bird concedes defeat, most obviously by flying away. When flight is impossible – for example, when a bird is cornered – a fresh set of stylised postures and movements comes into play, frequently the opposite of those that carried the threat. The conceding bird remains motionless, head withdrawn, feathers fluffed up, and does its best to conceal the markings that at other times are used to frighten its enemies.

A submissive great tit ruffles its plumage and leans forward from the normal perching position to minimise the effect of its black frontal markings. A finch will do the same, but a mute swan that is beaten in combat lies prostrate in the water or on the bank with its neck stretched out, and submits to being pecked on the back of the head. Once the winner has established its victory in this way, however, it soon gives up the attack.

Skirmish on a ledge
Two gannets, with their bills interlocked, battle to topple one another over the edge of a cliff.

Battle in the water
Long, sharp claws are used by these fighting coots to give vicious effect to each blow of their feet.

Finding and keeping a mate
The bizarre world of bird courtship

Breeding season colours

PUFFIN

HOUSE SPARROW

Top: *A puffin in the mating season (left), and at other times. The bright colours help it to attract a mate.*
Bottom: *A male house sparrow in the breeding season (left) also shows distinctive markings.*

In the breeding season, birds inhabit a strange and colourful world of ritual and response, where song, plumage and stereotyped display help in attracting and courting a mate. Using these three elements, a bird can convey a number of messages – where it has established a territory; when it wishes to pair up; which sex and species it belongs to; where it has found a possible nest site; when it is ready to mate.

The distinctive displays of the males normally prove attractive only to females of the same species. By this means, the chances of cross-breeding are reduced, and with them the danger of producing infertile eggs or sterile hybrids.

Breeding plumage

Many birds have evolved special plumages and ornaments – crests, plumes and wattles – to emphasise their displays. The robin has its red breast, the jay its blue and black wing-patch, and the great tit a black, white and yellow head and breast. Herons have plumes, and grebes and ruffs use a variety of head ornaments in display. Even the male house sparrow, unrelievedly drab for most of the year, has distinctive head markings during the breeding season – a darker beak and bib, whiter cheeks and brighter colouring at the sides of the head.

The bill of the puffin flares into vivid reds, yellows and blues throughout the nesting season, and the plumage of many male ducks consists of an almost permanent multicoloured display. Among most of the ducks that nest or winter in Britain, there is, for much of the year, a striking difference between the plumages of males and females. The males are brightly coloured but the females are inconspicuous in drab browns and greys, more like one another than like their own mates.

The bright plumage of the male ducks lasts through the winter and into summer, until the association between paired birds ends. Then the female nests and rears the young unaided. From midsummer to early autumn, the male moults into a dull, female-like 'eclipse' plumage, which makes it less conspicuous to predators during the vulnerable period when it is unable to fly.

In many species in which male and female plumages are alike, birds are often aggressive towards one another in the preliminary stages of courtship. The male discovers the sex of the bird to which it is displaying only by the other bird's reactions to the display. If an aggressive response is maintained, it means that the other bird is also a male.

Ceremonial rituals

Courtship displays are often mutual between birds of similar plumage, particularly between large birds, such as many seabirds and freshwater birds. Often male and female play identical roles simultaneously, as in the greeting and nest-relief ceremonies of herons, when the birds meet after separation.

The so-called triumph ceremony of the Canada goose is one of the most spectacular examples of mutual display. Male and female run together and, with heads held low and necks extended, call loudly. In the head flagging ceremony of black-headed gulls, the birds threaten one another with heads low and the brown facial mask showing. Then suddenly they stretch up their necks and turn their heads, so as to present the white nape and hide the facial mask. The great crested grebe has an intricate courtship dance in which both sexes take part. Not all birds with similar plumages display together, however. In starlings, wrens and various pigeons, display is left to the male alone.

Most courtship begins in the spring, before nesting gets under way, and the male usually takes the initiative. Exceptions are the red-necked phalarope and the dotterel – both species in which the female is the larger, brighter sex, and the male has taken over the usual female duties of incubation and tending the young. There are also exceptions to the rule that birds start to pair up in the spring. A female robin will join a male during the winter, sometimes linking their territories together. Great crested grebes begin forming pairs in winter, even

Head flagging
Both male and female black-headed gulls take part in courtship displays. They start threatening one another, then suddenly turn their heads away.

Triumph ceremony
Canada geese provide an odd display during the breeding season, racing along together with necks outstretched while calling loudly.

before they have a territory. The male and female associate first in open water, and only then establish a territory.

Ducks, too, pair up in winter. Their early courtship is communal, although they are monogamous birds. Their displays are staged on water, and the chief role is played by the brightly coloured males. The display parties of some species – especially the mallard – may consist wholly or largely of males at times, but these are still part of courtship, because they are intended for the females.

Later in the season, the sexual energies of male mallards may lead them to pursue a duck with which they are not paired and attempt to mate by force. The drake flies after the duck until she has to land, then tries to copulate without going through the normal ritual. The female mallard displays a characteristic gesture of repulsion, coughing out single sharp calls, drawing back her head and ruffling her feathers.

Synchronising sexual rhythms

The reproductive cycles of birds that breed outside the tropics are set in motion by changes in the length of the day. This response to variations in the amount of daylight is known as 'photoperiodism'. Linked with alterations in the food supply, it leads to the secretion of hormones that have a profound effect on bird activity. Outside the breeding season, the internal sex organs of birds are small – a weight-saving adaptation – but at breeding time there is a remarkable increase. The testes of house sparrows and starlings enlarge by between 300 and 500 times. Those of the brambling increase at least 360 times. In female starlings, the weight of the oviduct – the egg-laying passage – increases a thousand-fold.

Change of sex

In nearly all birds, only one of the female's two ovaries – the left one – plays a part in producing the egg. The right one remains small and undeveloped. If the working ovary becomes diseased or damaged, the right one can develop – but not as an ovary. It will become a testis, a male reproductive organ. It is even possible for a hen that loses the left ovary through disease after raising chicks, to change sex and father more chicks.

A healthy female's readiness to mate, as well as being affected by length of daylight, also depends on the male. In many species, courtship is largely responsible for inducing the necessary changes in the female's body and making it ready both to ovulate and to accept the male for copulation. The amount of daylight required to trigger off the correct glandular response varies from species to species. Rooks, for instance, respond to the short days of February and March. They lay their eggs in late March and April, which means that their young

Mutual preening
Two jackdaws strengthen the link between them by preening feathers on each other's heads.

Gentle caress
A pair of woodpigeons alleviate mutual fear and aggression by caressing one another.

Gift of food
Like a parent with a nestling, a male robin brings food in its bill and passes it to the female, so helping to strengthen the bond between them.

Presenting a fish
A male kingfisher brings its mate a gift of food, presenting a fish head first so that the female can swallow it without choking. This ritual precedes copulation.

hatch in April and early May, to coincide with the peak availability of earthworms. Other species, such as summer-nesting whinchats, respond to longer periods of daylight. This is because their main food supply becomes available later in the year.

Overcoming hostility

Courtship displays also help to establish a bond between male and female once they have started to associate as a pair. They do so by breaking down the aggressiveness and fear birds feel towards others, even the opposite sex. Such feelings arise out of the need to threaten and fight rivals for territory, food and mates. A bird cannot help feeling the same way towards its mate until they know one another better.

The presence of hostility in courtship sequences is well illustrated by the male grey heron. The male's early display to a female includes postures identical to its threat behaviour towards rival males. When the female adopts the correct appeasing posture, the male's feelings of aggression subside.

In general, though, true courtship displays are basically different in form from threat displays. They also help to promote individual and species recognition. Individual recognition is especially important for colony-dwelling birds, with many birds of the same species living close together. Their courtship often begins after the male has taken up a nest site, where it is joined by the female. The male's hostility towards rival males in defence of its site makes it, at least at first, also aggressive towards any would-be mate. Later, however, the male and female often display together at the site. The displays of the grey heron, gannet and shag may be taken as typical of the courtship of the larger colony-dwelling birds.

Strengthening the bond

Once birds have paired, the bond between them – so important for most species if they are to be successful in raising young – is strengthened by special displays, such as mutual preening, courtship

feeding and showing a nest site. The bond can be further strengthened by the joint defence of territory against rival birds.

Scientists prefer the term allopreening (from the Greek word *allos*, meaning 'other') for what is usually called mutual preening, because it covers cases in which one sex preens the other, as with cormorants, as well as those in which the preening is truly mutual, as with shags and gannets.

Among native British birds, allopreening is characteristic of gannets, cormorants, shags, grey herons, water rails, moorhens, coots, kittiwakes, guillemots and razorbills; all pigeons and doves (in which it is usually called caressing); little owls (and probably other owls); swifts, house martins, bearded tits, ravens, rooks, jackdaws and choughs.

The preening is largely confined to the head and neck of the other bird. Before it starts, a special preening invitation posture may be assumed by one partner. The coot has a very well-developed invitation display, in which one of the birds ruffles out its black head feathers, arches its neck downwards and points its bill towards its feet. It freezes in this posture, and when the display is performed on river, lake or pond, the entire head of the soliciting bird may disappear underwater for a few seconds. Sometimes both birds take up the invitation posture side by side, each one waiting for the other to react.

Outlet for aggression

Since allopreening is confined largely to those areas of plumage that a bird cannot reach with its own bill, there is no reason to doubt that the behaviour is of some use in feather care. In some groups, pigeons for example, the preening bird will detach dirt and parasites from its mate's plumage and eat or discard them.

However, it seems certain that allopreening has more than this utilitarian function and is also an important form of bond-strengthening behaviour.

At times, it is an outlet for aggressive tendencies. Instead of pecking its mate, the other bird uses its bill for preening. Similarly, preening invitation displays are often submissive demonstrations of peacefulness.

Courtship feeding

This behaviour between paired birds is more widespread than allopreening. It occurs chiefly among species in which the female carries out the duties of incubation. Sometimes it is practised just during the early stages of the breeding cycle, but in most species, the male continues to bring food to the female during incubation.

The form of ritual varies greatly. In general, the female behaves like a begging chick and the male feeds it as a parent would. In fact, the habit may be of some value in preparing a bird to feed its young. The food may be passed directly from one bill to the other, as with robins, kingfishers and terns; it may be regurgitated from bill to bill, as with crows, finches and pigeons; regurgitated on to the ground first, as with gulls; or picked up and then replaced on the ground, as with red-legged partridges.

Among day-hunting birds, particularly the harriers, prey may be transferred from male to female in an impressive aerial manoeuvre. At the other extreme, no food may be passed at all in some cases, with the birds symbolically going through the motions of giving and receiving it.

When birds 'kiss'

The courtship feeding of finches is usually extremely stylised in the early stages, with male and female merely touching or scissoring bills in a kind of kiss. As the breeding cycle progresses, the feeding tends to become more complete. In the bullfinch, for example, the male has frequently reached the stage of regurgitating food into its mate's bill by the time of nest-building, and this continues throughout incubation. Chaffinches are exceptional among the finches since courtship feeding has not been observed among them.

Presenting a nest site
The male lapwing flies over its territory (left) to attract a female, and attempts to mate. Then it starts scraping out a hollow in the earth, as if showing the mate where they might build their nest.

Formal ritual
Bills meet, but no food passes. Courtship feeding between hawfinches is at times completely ritualised.

Male and female pigeons share the work of incubation – unlike finches – and their courtship feeding usually consists of formal billing. The male offers its open bill to its mate and the female inserts her own. Sometimes this is followed by feeding by regurgitation. This billing, together with ritual preening behind the wing, is part of pigeons' mating ceremony. Similarly, the male kingfisher brings a fish and gives it to the female before copulation. In many other species, such as the robin, courtship feeding is independent of mating, although it often occurs at the same stage of the breeding cycle.

Most naturalists once regarded courtship feeding as a bond-forming display. Now, however, it is recognised as having great value for some species in providing the female with extra nourishment, necessary to form eggs. This is especially important for species that nest early, when suitable food may be scarce. In the majority of courtship-feeders, the female incubates the eggs on her own, and ritual feeding by the male makes a contribution to her nourishment right up to the time when the brooding of the young is over.

Nesting invitations

In colony-dwelling birds, the male often attracts a female to its nest site. In many other species, however, the male first attracts the female to its territory and they choose a site together. Special courtship displays serve to show the mate likely nest sites. These displays are especially well developed among birds that nest on the ground or in holes in trees. In ground-nesting lapwings, for example, after mating or attempted mating – which may have been preceded by a display flight over the territory – the male runs off and starts scraping out a hollow in the earth. As it bends forwards to scratch, its tail is fanned and elevated to show off a black and white pattern, accentuated by the chestnut undertail coverts.

Little ringed plovers have a scrape ceremony in which the male shows off its conspicuously patterned tail while turning in a hollow. As the

Chase and display in wren courtship
A series of vigorous chases (top), said to start when the female entices the male, accompanies the courtship of the wren. Later, male attracts female to the nest by singing loudly, with tail and wings quivering (bottom).

female approaches, the male stands on the rim, motionless, with its tail fanned over the scrape. The female then initiates what has been called 'symbolic nest relief', slipping under the male's tail into the hollow. The male moves ceremonially away, picking up little stones and tossing them over its shoulder towards her.

Among woodland hole-nesting birds, nest-showing displays are often associated with bright and conspicuous patterns. The male redstart indicates its chosen hole by song and flight and also by displaying at the entrance. It sometimes shows off its red breast and black and white forehead or, more usually, turns round and fans out its chestnut tail.

The great tit displays its black and white head pattern and the black and yellow of its breast conspicuously against the dark entrance of the nest cavity.

Site-showing in the case of the highly camouflaged wren, on the other hand, is not linked with a bright display plumage. The male attracts a female to the domed nest it has built by a special nest-invitation display – singing loudly, with tail and wings outspread and quivering.

Mating displays

Many species have special displays to indicate their willingness to copulate, which stimulate the partner to respond. Male kingfishers and pigeons have what seems to human eyes a particularly charming habit of giving a present of food to the female.

These mating displays are not always performed just by male birds. Often, females offer soliciting displays. The female blackbird points its bill and tail up almost vertically, sleeking its feathers and running a little in front of the male, giving a soft, high-pitched call. The male, stimulated to follow, gives broken snatches of song in response, fans and trails its tail, raises the feathers of rump and crown and stretches its neck. Copulation follows if the female permits.

The male redstart has a remarkable, attention-grabbing pre-mating display, in which it squats on a branch in front of the female with head low and neck stretched out, uttering a high-pitched hissing note. Its wide-open bill reveals its eye-catching yellow gape as it fans out its tail and presses it down, opening its wings and quivering them, with their tips nearly touching above its back.

Redstarts also engage in vigorous sexual chases, flying rapidly in and out of the trees in their territory, especially after unsuccessful mating attempts. Sexual chases are characteristic of warblers, buntings, sparrows and many other songbirds. The pursuit of the female by the male is probably basically aggressive, although both sexes may well be sexually stimulated by it. The female wren is thought to entice the male to chase.

The male little ringed plover approaches the female with its body in the horizontal position, then gradually stretches up into an exaggerated upright posture with head high and chest pushed out. When close to the female, it stamps with one foot at a time, often lifting each one so high that it strikes its own breast. If the female crouches, the male mounts. After mating, the birds run swiftly away from each other, probably as fear reasserts itself, although this behaviour may also be a useful safeguard against predators.

A female shag solicits by sitting in the nest with tail cocked while bending down and moving nest material. During mating, the male grips the female's neck in its bill and shakes gently. Gannets are more vigorous, with the female meekly submitting to being bitten firmly on the back of the neck. Among herons, mating often follows the presentation of a stick by the male, which also preens its mate's head, and the two birds engage in mutual billing.

Most birds have no external reproductive organs, although in a few species, including some ducks, geese and swans, the male has a penis. In the majority of birds, the ducts leading from the testes of the male and the ovaries of the female end in their respective cloaca openings. In copulation, the male stands on the female's back, the cloacae are brought together, and sperm passes from male to female.

Courtship in action
Love-hate displays by the grey heron

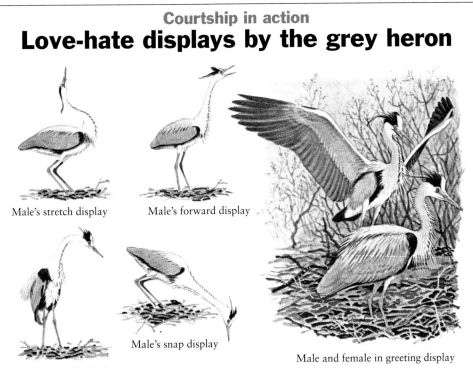

Male's stretch display

Male's forward display

Male's snap display

Male's upright display

Male and female in greeting display

Grey herons breed early in the year, and the male guards and advertises its treetop nest by repeating a loud and harsh 'fronk' and giving a stretch display – a posture that seems basically hostile, although it is for the benefit of females as well as rival males.

The male stretches its neck up, pointing the bill vertically and giving the first part of a special call, a short 'hoo'. Then it lowers itself down on the nest and curtsies by arching its head over its back, giving the second half of the call, a gurgling 'ooo'.

If a female alights near the site, the male goes into the forward display, a posture used to frighten off rivals. With head and plumes erect, it coils back its neck and then stabs its head forward towards the female, opening its bill and giving the threat call, a loud 'gooo'. It may also assume the upright display when the female is approaching, standing erect, with head and bill arched downwards, and often uttering a soft 'gog-gog-gog' call. If the female stands her ground or returns repeatedly, the male becomes less aggressive, with fewer forward displays and more and more snap displays, indicating willingness to pair up. The male stretches its neck forward with the bill pointing down, lowers its head to the level of the nest – or below – by bending its legs, then opens its bill and snaps it shut.

Once the female is accepted at the site, the male starts flying out and returning with twigs. This leads to mutual greeting displays as it alights, calling 'arre-arre-ar-ar' with neck erect and crest and plumes spread. The female repeatedly stretches up then sinks down on the nest, eventually taking the twigs and adding them to the structure.

Other greeting ceremonies, involving the raising of the wings and plumes, also occur when the birds take over from one another at the site.

Mating often occurs several times a day over a period lasting from just before egg-laying begins until the last egg is laid. Great crested grebes copulate eight, nine or ten times a day for ten to 14 days. In other species, copulation can be far less frequent. Carrion crows and magpies mate once a day, early in the morning, taking ten to 20 seconds.

Grebes, and some other birds, sometimes go through the mating ritual long before the female is ready to produce eggs, in which case the behaviour helps to maintain the pair bond. Among some other species, gannets for instance, copulation may start again at the end of the breeding season, although this time the female is not fertilised.

The only mechanism in place to prevent mating between birds from the same family is the scattering of younger birds to find territories of their own. Inbreeding is more likely to occur among colony-dwelling birds than among those that nest apart but, in any case, it carries no threat to the species. Any genetic mistakes would be quickly wiped out by natural selection.

Courtship in action
How the shag attracts a mate

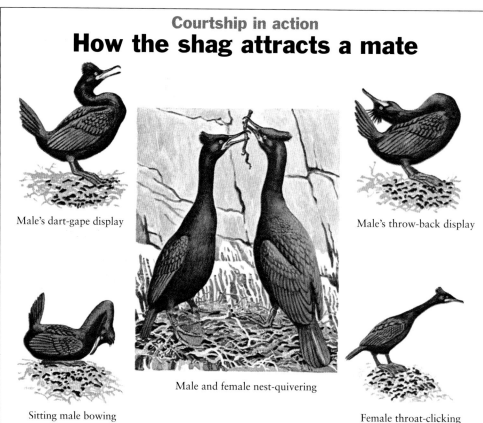

Male's dart-gape display

Male's throw-back display

Male and female nest-quivering

Sitting male bowing

Female throat-clicking

Shags are found at their nesting colonies mainly between March and August. Early in the season the male directs displays at both male and female birds but only females respond, by approaching in the correct way.

In the first display, the dart-gape, the male fans and cocks its tail, pushing out its chest. Then, with neck arched, it draws back its head and repeatedly darts it forwards and upwards, while opening its bill to show the vivid interior of its mouth.

This is followed by the throw-back display, which the male performs mainly when the other bird is looking at it, or starts to approach. Arching its neck so that the back of the head rests on its back, or is parallel to it, the male points its bill upwards or slightly backwards while vibrating its throat pouch.

When a female comes close, the male starts bowing, usually in a sitting position, pointing its bill towards its toes and cocking its tail sharply. The female usually stands behind the male and stretches its neck over the male's back, throat pouch lowered and vibrating to make a special clicking sound. Afterwards, the female preens the male on the back of its head and neck.

In the early stages of pair formation, male and female often perform a nest-quivering display, both holding the same item of nest material, first with necks stretched up and then with heads lowered to the level of the nest.

With the exception of the dart-gape and throw-back, which are exclusively male displays, all the other rituals are performed at various times by both sexes.

Competition for females

Most birds form monogamous pairs, at least for part of the breeding season, but in a few species, such as black grouse and ruff, the males take no part in any of the nesting duties, and meet the females only for mating. Among many of these promiscuous species, intense competition takes place between males for females, and this has resulted in the evolution of marked differences in size and appearance between the sexes. The males are usually larger and brighter and have evolved elaborate plumage characteristics

matching their highly ritualised displays. The females are dull in plumage, mainly because they need to be camouflaged from potential predators when nesting.

The males establish communal display grounds or arenas, usually called leks, to which the females are attracted in the early days of the breeding season. In ground-living birds, leks are situated conspicuously in the open, often on a rise or hill. The site is traditional – used for generation after generation – as long as it proves to be safe, and there may be

The noisy arena of the black grouse

Female

Blackcocks in threat display

The male black grouse, the blackcock, is strikingly different from the female, the greyhen. The blackcock has glossy black plumage, a lyre-shaped tail, white wing-bars, wrist-patches and undertail coverts, and a red wattle above each eye.

In its advertising display, the male inflates its neck and chest, erects the wattles, droops its partly open wings and fans its tail over its back so that the undertail coverts form a shield of white at the rear. Then it carries out formal encounters with its neighbours, sometimes remaining stationary and at other times making little mincing runs or jumping up and down. Blackcocks frequently call, usually either crowing, a wheezy, tearing sound, or 'rookooing', a musical, dove-like bubbling sound. Occasionally, males fight, and courts can change ownership as males on the outskirts of the lek try to force their way to the centre. The mature and more vigorous males, occupying the central positions in the lek, secure by far the most matings – as many as 80 per cent in some leks.

The greyhen moving through the lek is courted by each male in turn. The blackcock parades round, often tilting its tail and body, although it may also sink down in front of the female. Mating follows if the female crouches.

more than one lekking ground in a district. Males collect at their own lek, and there are usually plenty of them. This crowding increases the attractiveness of the lek to females, and so helps each male's chances of mating. It probably also ensures greater safety against attacks by predators. Lekking usually begins early in the day – often before dawn – and may last all morning, but at least one species, the great snipe, gathers only at night.

Within the lek each male holds a small, fixed territory, or court, in which it displays not only to females when they are present but also to other males. Highly ritualised threat displays are directed at males to emphasise the boundaries and ownership of the courts. They also serve to make the lek more conspicuous in order to attract more females.

A female entering the lek moves between the courts while all the males display, selects one and they mate. The female may go on to mate with other males. No cases have been recorded of a male rejecting the female. Females may also visit more than one lek for mating.

The territory system within the lek ensures each established male is confined more or less to its own court, and, as the displays are basically static, there is relatively little interference with mating once the female has stepped into any one court. The fighting and threat are for territory, not for females – although, of course, no lekking bird will attract a female unless it has first established a territory.

Among British breeding birds, only the black grouse and capercaillie, both gamebirds, and the ruff, a wader, mate in leks. The habit is shared by one species that used to breed in Britain, the great bustard, and two vagrant waders, the pectoral sandpiper and the great snipe.

Courtship in action
Threat and invitation by the gannet

Male advertises for
a female

Either sex may use a
pelican posture

Male and female in mutual fencing

Male bites female's
neck; female faces away

Both sexes adopt sky-
pointing posture

Some gannets are present at their nesting colonies from January to November each year, but the peak period of occupation is between March and September. Older, experienced males return to their former sites, but attempts to re-establish themselves can be challenged, and threats and fighting between males over positioning can be fierce and frequent. The male proclaims ownership of a site by a bowing display, dipping its bill from side to side, with wings held out, while giving a repeated threat call, a loud 'urrah-urrah'.

The bird's advertising display to prospecting females, which fly over repeatedly before landing, is like a low-intensity form of the bowing, consisting mainly of shaking the head from side to side, with wings closed.

When a female comes close, the male responds by neck biting, seizing her neck in its bill. Any female that is interested does not retreat or attack but behaves submissively, turning away the head and presenting the nape to the male in a facing away posture. During such an encounter, the male also assumes the pelican posture, with its bill tucked down against its breast. This seems to be a gesture of appeasement.

The male eventually surrenders the site to the female, at first repeatedly flying out and landing back beside its new-found mate, and later also bringing nest material. When they are together at the site, male and female will both assume the

pelican posture. When they move about while maintaining this posture, they raise their closed wings so the elbows are held up.

This way of holding the wings is even more characteristic of another display, sky pointing, a pose often taken up as a bird prepares to walk away from its mate or its nest. The bird stretches its neck with the bill usually pointing skywards but with the eyes focused forwards, and begins raising its feet slowly on the spot, showing the conspicuously coloured lines on the toes, before turning to fly or walk away. A special groaning call accompanies the display.

Throughout the breeding cycle, from the early stages of pair formation until after their single chick has fledged, gannets perform a special greeting ceremony whenever one of the birds joins its mate at the site. The returning bird calls as it comes back to the nest, and its mate starts to shake its head rapidly.

Whether the male is returning to the nest, or is already there, it almost invariably gives the female a neck bite and the female responds by facing away. Then they stand breast to breast and put on a display of mutual fencing, rapidly scissoring their raised bills together.

Calling goes on throughout the whole of this greeting display, and the bill actions are interspersed with downward movements of the head by both birds.

Courtship in action
Display parties of the mallard

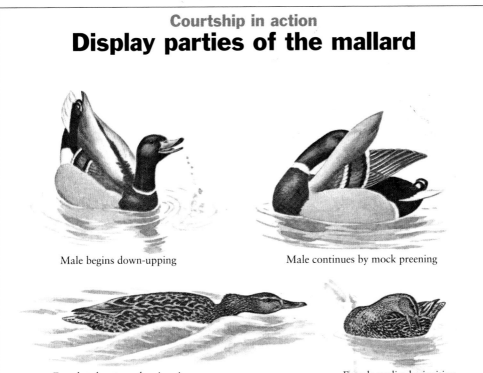

Male begins down-upping

Male continues by mock preening

Female takes to nod-swimming

Female replies by inciting

These dabbling ducks tend to congregate on rivers, lakes and ponds, and courtship displays often take place almost as a group activity. Display bouts often start with preliminary shaking, in which one male in a group draws in its head, then repeatedly rises up in the water, thrusting and shaking its head. This activity is particularly infectious. Once one bird starts, the others usually follow suit as the mood to court spreads through the group.

Shaking is commonly followed by grunt whistling, in which the bird first shakes its bill in the water, then rises up with its neck arched downwards and its bill close to the surface. In this position, the mallard draws its bill towards its breast and sends up a shower of water droplets. At the height of the movement it utters a sharp whistle followed by a grunt.

Shaking may be followed by head-up-tail-upping, in which the male whistles and raises and draws back its head, lifts folded wings over its back and cocks its tail.

Another display is down-upping, in which the male dips its bill rapidly in the water, jerks up its head, raising a little spurt of water, and then whistles and quacks.

There is also mock preening behind the wing. In this display the bird partly lifts one wing on to its back to show its bright wing-patch, turns its head behind the wing and runs its bill along the quills near the wrist joint. This produces a loud rattling noise.

When courting, the male mallard often points its head towards a particular female during grunt whistling or at the end of a head-up-tail-upping display, then starts nod-swimming round its intended mate, with head low and neck kinked. Then it raises its head again and attempts to lead the female by swimming away with head feathers compressed sideways, giving the head a high-peaked, shiny look.

The female mallard is mainly an onlooker at these courtship assemblies, but will also swim in among the males, drawing their attention by nod-swimming round as many of them as possible.

Even more commonly, the female will perform inciting movements, aimed at a particular male, while swimming after it. At the same time, the female may symbolically threaten another male, turning its head over its shoulder and uttering a special querulous call with open bill.

After a male and female have started to associate more definitely together, they will still attend winter courting parties during what is termed the engagement stage of the pairing. However, they direct their courtship rituals mainly towards each other. Later on in the cycle – at nesting time in February or March – they go off on their own to copulate.

Males of duck species related to the mallard, such as the teal and pintail, have similar displays, each with its own sequence and special features to aid species recognition.

The dance of the great crested grebe

Advertising
A single bird calls attention to itself – and to the fact that it is looking for a mate – with far-carrying croaking calls.

Discovery ceremony
One bird approaches the other in a shallow underwater ripple dive, then rises up beyond it in the ghostly penguin display. The second bird faces it in the cat display, and then they head-shake together.

Stages in the head-shaking ceremony
1. Two birds meet and approach one another with heads lowered threateningly. Then they raise their heads and spread their head ornaments while giving a ticking call and shaking their down-pointed bills from side to side.

2. They straighten up more, with tippets less fully spread, and both alternately waggle and sway their heads.

3. One or both of the birds starts habit-preening – dipping back its head to flick up one of its wing feathers.

Inland lakes and reservoirs provide the setting for the courtship of the great crested grebe. Ceremonies begin in midwinter, especially from January onwards, when the birds start forming pairs and taking up territories. They continue for weeks or even months, keeping together for the breeding season. Males and females play identical or interchangeable roles in this extravagant ritual of posture and display. Head-shaking is the most common ceremony. It may be preceded by advertising and the discovery ceremony, and followed by the penguin dance or the retreat ceremony. Other activities include fish offering and inviting.

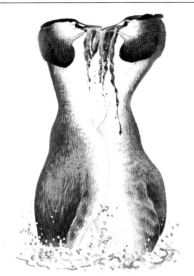

Penguin dance
After head-shaking, the birds dive to collect weed, then surface and swim towards one another. Suddenly they rise breast to breast from the water, vigorously paddling their feet and swaying their bills, still full of weed, from side to side.

Stages in the retreat ceremony
1. During the head-shaking ceremony, one of the birds suddenly dashes away, patter-flying across the water past its mate.

2. The fleeing bird subsides into the cat display, pauses, then turns to face its mate, which has also assumed a partial cat display.

Fish offering
Sometimes the male gives its mate a courtship gift of a small fish.

Inviting
This display on the water is identical to the one performed later, on the nest, by birds soliciting copulation.

Nests and their builders
From simple hollows to complicated feats of construction

Blackbird's cup nest
After establishing a foundation by lodging material in a bush, hedge or tree, the female blackbird builds a strong and secure nest of grass, roots, moss and twigs with a lining of mud and dried grass.

A nest is a shelter in the battle for survival – a cradle in which eggs and helpless nestlings can be relatively safe from their enemies – but where the instinct to build this cradle comes from is not clear. Reptiles, from which birds evolved, are not as a rule nest-builders – nor, for that matter, is the building instinct found in all birds. Cuckoos manage well enough without it, and so do a handful of other species that have their own nest sites but do no building.

A bewildering variety of places are chosen by British birds for their eggs, ranging from the nightjar's unadorned patch of clear ground to the intricate suspended nest of the goldcrest, and this variety provides a living laboratory of evolution, packed with clues that, if they do not solve the mystery of how nest-building originated, at least allow scope for intelligent guesswork.

Origin of nests
The earliest birds, following the pattern of reptiles, probably laid their eggs in holes in the ground or in trees, covering them with earth or leaves. As competition for food and territory drove their descendants into more open country, the safest place for eggs would often have been a depression or a simple scrape in the ground, and those that moved into marshland would have looked for a patch of firm ground sheltered by grass. The first cup nests may have been formed as parent birds, turning on the eggs or going through courtship rituals, moulded the surrounding vegetation into primitive, cup-like shapes.

It is quite reasonable to suppose that, as birds extended the range of their habitats, the strength of associations imprinted on their nervous systems over millions of years made them instinctively seek to recreate platforms of grass and other materials, and

so resulted in them building primitive nests. Varying degrees of intricacy in the construction of nests are related to the different demands made on each species by the need to protect its eggs and young.

Types of structure
The simplest nest of all is, in fact, not a nest at all. For instance, the tawny owl lays its eggs in a tree-hole, and the stone curlew makes use of a depression in the earth. The guillemot deposits its egg on a ledge, and the nightjar needs only a clear space on the ground. Although these were probably the earliest forms of nest, the birds themselves are not necessarily more primitive than others. The nest-building instinct can atrophy, return and wither away again as a species evolves.

Nests that call for some building fall broadly into two types – the simple nests made by nidifugous (nest-leaving) birds, and the more intricate nests of nidicolous (nest-attached) birds. Chicks of nidifugous birds are able to quit the nest and run on the day that they hatch, while nidicolous nestlings are born naked and helpless.

The nests of ducks, geese, swans, waders, gamebirds, grebes and divers – all of them nidifugous birds – are basically simple in design, and are sometimes little more than scrapes in the ground, but when they are built on water, such as those of the moorhen or coot, for all their simplicity, they may be quite substantial. Only slightly more elaborate nests are required by many seabirds, such as gulls, terns and skuas, because although their young remain there to start with, they are able to leave within a few days.

Nests reach their greatest intricacy among the passerines, or perching birds. These birds are basically woodland dwellers, and the building instinct possibly evolved at a stage when they had even more enemies among rodents and snakes than they have now. Blackbirds and song thrushes build cosy cup nests, and a few other woodlanders or former woodlanders gain added protection by building a dome over the cup. House sparrows, and very occasionally tree sparrows, do this when they nest in the open. Dippers will build a dome unless the nest cup is in a deep cavity, and magpies protect the cup with a dome of sorts by giving it a canopy of twigs. Wrens, willow warblers, wood warblers and chiffchaffs build more intricate domes, but none can compete with the long-tailed tit's beautifully made 'bottle' of lichen-covered moss, with the entrance hole placed near the top.

Simple nests on the ground and on water

Ground-nesting birds build simple nests, relying on camouflage for safety. The nightjar's nest is so simple, in fact, that it is a mere scrape in the ground. The lapwing's is only one stage more complicated – a rough lining of grass placed in a muddy hollow. Birds that nest on water may need substantial nests, but the nest construction is still basically simple – as with the great crested grebe's floating platform of water-weeds, reeds and rushes. When a grebe leaves the nest, it usually covers its eggs with weed, although there is not always time.

GREAT CRESTED GREBE

NIGHTJAR

LAPWING

Choice of location

The part played by male and female in selecting a site varies from species to species. In some 75 of the most common British breeding birds, both sexes share in site selection; in about 50 the female selects a site on her own; and in about 25 the male appears to play the leading role, although – as with the pied flycatcher, the redstart and the great tit – the female may make the final decision. The general rule is that when the plumage of the male and female differs dramatically, and when the cock bird expends a lot of energy in defending the territory by song, the female takes the major role in site selection or nest-building.

Female only selection reaches its extreme in the black grouse. The sexes meet just for mating, and the blackcock may not even know where the greyhen has made the nest. When males take the lead in selecting nest-holes, they display from their chosen site. The pied flycatcher pops its head out to show a white frontal blaze, and the redstart, facing into the hole, fans out its bright orange tail. Among waders, the male often makes several scrapes by turning its breast round on the ground, and the female chooses one. Occasionally, as with the pied wagtail, male and female may choose different sites. The female has the final say.

Each species has its preferred niche for nesting, and some have preferred heights. The sites may vary in different regions. Tree-nesting ravens are common in Wales and western England but rare in Scotland, where they nest on high moorland or cliffs. In Britain, it is rare to find small birds nesting high in trees. Just a few finches – in particular the goldfinch and, in conifers, the crossbill and the siskin – normally build their nests near the treetops. If all

the different species that might nest in a tall oak were to do so at the same time, the tree would provide a vertical panorama of bird-life. There might be a crow nesting near the top, a woodpigeon lower down, a mistle thrush in a fork or near the end of a bough, a blackbird in the shoots from the bark, a treecreeper behind loose bark, an owl, jackdaw, stock dove or woodpecker in large holes, and a tit, nuthatch or redstart in small ones.

The sites waders choose are the result of balancing the need for cover against the need for a good view from which to see predators coming. Open sites are favoured by lapwings, avocets, ringed plovers, little ringed plovers, dotterels and oystercatchers. A tuft of grass, which acts as one side of the nest, is usually preferred by curlews, whimbrels and golden plovers. The greenshank looks for a place where a stone or a dead branch will form one side of its nest, and the woodcock chooses a light cover of dead bracken. The black-tailed godwit, red-necked phalarope, redshank, common sandpiper, dunlin and snipe generally keep their nests well hidden in grass. Several of these species may well nest in the same small area. Snipe, redshanks and lapwings occupy neighbouring niches in southern England.

Rivalry for sites

To protect their helpless young, woodpeckers, hoopoes, swifts and kingfishers nest in holes. Some doves, birds of prey and seabirds nest on ledges, and some birds take over disused nests that others have built. There is often rivalry for sites among hole-nesters, and the same cavity may be used in successive years or even in the same season by different species.

Some birds build in more than one site. Male wrens may build as many as half a dozen nests. The female lays in just one but has nests in reserve should anything happen to the main one.

A ladder hung on a wall provides a series of identical sites that can confuse nest-builders. Song thrushes or blackbirds will build several nests between the rungs, sometimes not finishing any, sometimes laying in one and sometimes in two. This can also happen when two natural sites look alike. If the sequence of stimuli goes wrong, a bird may build several nests, yet not lay in any of them.

Attachment to one place

Many species show a strong preference for particular sites. A grey wagtail will return year after year to the ledge of a bridge, an oystercatcher to a scrape on a rocky headland, or an eagle to its eyrie. Long-term paired birds may ring the changes on just two or three sites over the years. If one partner dies, the other will often find a new mate and use the same sites.

Some birds persist in returning to an unsuitable site. Terns have been known to build below the spring tideline, so that their nests are washed away when the tide reaches its seasonal maximum – yet they go back for more of the same punishment.

Nests themselves are often used again, too. Blackbirds and house sparrows frequently use the same nest three times in one season, relining it each time. Herons' nests expand enormously through annual additions of material, and eagles' nests may be built up over the years.

Birds that nest in colonies – for protection and to be near their food supply – may use a site for hundreds of years. Gannets, for example, have been established on the Bass Rock, at the mouth of the Firth of Forth, at least since the 15th century. Colony-dwelling birds may move their sites according to local conditions, though. Tree-felling has driven herons and rooks from some areas, and terns are notorious for deserting their colonies.

Some birds try to find a nest site similar to the one where they were hatched. A number of wheatears, for instance, used to make for some old tins on Dungeness beach where their parents nested, and mallards for the heads of pollard willows by the Thames. However, ringing shows that young songbirds seldom return to their exact birth places.

Adaptation to man-made sites seems complete in Britain in the case of swallows, almost complete with swifts, and predominant among house martins. House sparrows, starlings and jackdaws often nest on man-made sites, and many birds will use nest-boxes. Robins, among other species, may even rear their broods in motor vehicles.

JACKDAW

WOODPIGEON

BLUE TIT

GREAT SPOTTED WOODPECKER

LITTLE OWL

Nesting season

The timing of nest-building depends on how the female responds to the stimulus of courtship. Weather is another factor – rain softens building materials and makes them easier to work into the nest. The earliest nester among British birds is the golden eagle, which starts building in the autumn before it lays. The first to lay its eggs is the crossbill, which lays in January and feeds its young on seeds. The latest to start nesting is the hobby, which usually uses another bird's old nest, and lays in June or July.

The time taken to build a nest varies. At the start of the season, building activity may stop if the weather becomes too cold, but at the height of the season a new nest may be built in a day, if the original has been destroyed. Starlings have been known to build nests in a few hours in the engine of an aircraft.

Nidifugous birds abandon their nests as soon as the chicks are dry from the eggs. Other birds stay until the young are fledged. After the nesting season,

CARRION CROW

STOCK DOVE

MISTLE THRUSH

NUTHATCH

TREECREEPER

REDSTART

BLACKBIRD

Panorama of bird-life in an old oak tree
Such a big tree might provide nest sites for a wide variety of birds, each with its preferred niche. The little owl, great spotted woodpecker, blue tit, jackdaw, stock dove, nuthatch and redstart choose cavities in the trunk and branches; the treecreeper finds a crack in the bark; the blackbird, mistle thrush and woodpigeon nest in forks at different levels; and the carrion crow builds high up, out of reach of its enemies.

old nests may be used as roosts – sleeping places – by the original builder or by another species. Roost sites, in their turn, may be chosen as nest sites.

House sparrows build special winter nests, giving rise to the belief that they use the same nest all the year round. Rooks start nest-building again in the autumn, but seldom lay eggs. In mild autumns, blackbirds and starlings may lay again. The red-legged partridge hen, uniquely among British birds, may lay two clutches a few days apart, brooding one while the male broods the second in another nest.

The materials used in nest-building are mainly gathered from surrounding vegetation – twigs, heather, seaweed, grass, straw, lichen and moss, leaves, bark fibres, flower-heads, rotten wood, and anything else available. Animal materials include wool, hair, feathers, down, cobwebs, bones, dung, droppings and, in the case of the song thrush and the swift, saliva. Some birds use mineral materials, such as mud, and, in the lining of a ringed plover's scrape, pebbles.

Collecting materials

Many birds take their nesting material from the immediate vicinity. Grebes, for instance, build their floating platforms from what they can find conveniently near, and swifts snatch dry grass stems and feathers from the air, then work these materials with their saliva into a shallow cup under the eaves. Female ducks pluck the down from their own breasts, and there are records of a turtle dove's nest consisting entirely of small pieces of wire, and a crow's nest of sheep bones.

Some birds will even reach out for materials from the nest site. At the other extreme, long-tailed tits, which may use up to 2,000 feathers for a nest lining, often go hundreds of metres in search of them. Some birds are pilferers. Tits take the lining out of crows' nests, a sparrow will pluck feathers off a pigeon, and jackdaws will even pluck wool from a sheep. Chaffinches, when they are disturbed, will dismantle their own nests and use the same materials to rebuild them elsewhere.

Construction methods

Each sex's share of the work varies as much in nest-building as it does in site selection, incubation and care of the young. The female always takes some part in the building. Even in species such as the red-necked phalarope and the dotterel, where the task of incubation is left to the male, the female still helps with the simpler construction. The male's share varies from none, as with the black grouse and most ducks, to building the main structure while the female adds the lining, as with the wren. Male finches accompany the females to the nest, but do not normally help to bring material.

The limitations of a bird's intellect are clearly revealed by the jackdaw, which drops sticks across a cavity and relies on their lodging securely in place. If the hole is too wide, the sticks simply fall through, piling up at the bottom, and the foundation is lost.

The first stage in building a complicated nest in the fork of a tree or bush depends on the material lodging securely enough to make a foundation. A blackbird, for example, will crouch on the

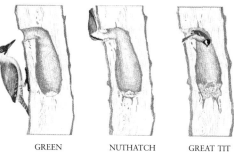

GREEN WOODPECKER   NUTHATCH   GREAT TIT

foundation and work the new material into shape by rotating round the site, pushing with its breast and beating its feet in short bursts, to press the material down. After about ten bursts, the bird will have rotated two or three times round the site. The nest cup is formed by compacting the material, not by weaving it – although the bird will use its beak to pull odd strands into the cup. A very small young bird, if held in a cupped hand, will instinctively make the same movements, proving that this way of pressing with the breast is inherited. Simple as the process may seem, it cannot be reproduced by comparatively clumsy human fingers.

Once the cup is the right height, it is lined with soft material. The song thrush is the exception among British birds, preferring a hard lining. Blackbirds and several other birds specialise in mud linings, with a finer lining of dried grass on the inside. This is why blackbirds' nests sometimes support live mosses.

Cup nests in trees and hedges are usually built under the shelter of overhanging leaves, which keep them dry. In addition, the parent birds protect their nests and eggs by brooding during rain, but storms and high winds can still wreck a nest, leaving birds to rebuild.

Among cavity nests, those made by kingfishers and sand martins are remarkable. A kingfisher will fly at a sandy bank time and again, pecking out sand until it has made a dent to which it can cling. It then excavates a tunnel about 60cm (2ft) long, rising slightly to a nest-hollow at the end. The sand martin, small-billed and weak-footed, still manages to dig a tunnel 60cm (2ft) long or more.

Shelduck, Manx shearwaters, storm petrels and puffins all excavate burrows. Most woodpeckers are superbly equipped to hack out tree-holes, but some hole-nesters, such as ducks and owls, are not and must look around for ready-made nest sites.

Generally, hole-nesters do little beyond covering the floor, once the hole is made or found. Those that build a fairly elaborate nest inside a hole, such as the blue tit, have probably taken to hole-nesting fairly recently in the history of their species.

Goldcrest's hanging nest
This smallest of Britain's breeding birds weaves an intricate nest of moss and spiders' webs, suspends it from a conifer branch and lines it with feathers. Both sexes take part in the building.

WRYNECK   STARLING   STOCK DOVE   LITTLE OWL

One home for seven birds
Many species of birds nest in tree-holes, but not all do the hard work of hacking out the holes themselves. Woodpeckers are the best equipped birds of all to do this, and after a woodpecker has made the original cavity, other birds may use it as season follows season, enlarging it or blocking up part of the entrance if necessary. Some hole-nesters do little actual building – they simply cover the floor of the cavity with nesting material.

The mud nests of swallows consist of pellets with small straws or grass stems running through them. Something as small as a bump or a single nail can provide the initial site. The cup is then built up, with a first lining of grass and a second of feathers. The house martin builds in similar fashion, but under the eaves of buildings. Its nest is also deeper and has a small hole near the top. Goldcrests construct hanging nests by weaving material round tiny twigs at the end of a conifer bough. The reed warbler weaves round reed stems.

Moorhens, grebes, coots and some ducks usually build rafts for nests, and since these float on water, they have to be fairly substantial. Moorhens and coots sometimes build in overhanging branches, extending the nest upwards if the water rises.

Some birds bring fresh greenery to the nest after the eggs are laid, and in the case of eagles and buzzards, after the young have been hatched. The reason for this is not certain – it may be either for decoration or for purposes of hygiene.

Nest size

This depends largely on the number of eggs in the clutch. A partridge needs a large nest because it can sit comfortably on up to 20 eggs, whereas the slender waders are in difficulties when their clutch exceeds their usual quota of four.

Size also depends on whether the nest is built up year by year. Golden eagles, which start adding new material in the autumn, will eventually build up a nest 2m (6ft) across and weighing more than a tonne. At the other extreme, the whitethroat's nest weighs barely 28g (1oz).

Rivalry between species breaks out over both nest sites – especially among hole-nesters – and the construction itself. A wren may try to build in a nest cup begun by swallows. Ducks of different species may try to oust one another from a site. Sometimes females of two species will lay their eggs in the same nest – blackbird and song thrush, great tit and blue tit, for instance. Usually the first-named of the pair wins in each case.

Sharing and take-overs

Jackdaws, house sparrows and tree sparrows sometimes find a ready-made nest site in rookeries or heronries. All they have to do to become lodgers in a heron's nest is to find a hole in the side, and line it for their own use.

Nest take-overs occur more frequently. Falcons and owls regularly nest in the old nests of ravens, crows or magpies. They never make a nest of their own, and occasionally they even oust less aggressive birds from a nest.

Spotted flycatchers and, less often, redstarts, use the former nests of song thrushes and blackbirds – only the lining is their own. Gulls may nest in the down of an eider duck's nest, and house sparrows may use a blackbird's nest as a base for their own. Birds' nests may even be taken over by mice and bees.

Swallow's bracket nest
A nail on a barn wall can provide all the support a swallow needs for its snug, if untidy, cup nest. Both sexes share the building work, collecting small straws and grass stems,

sometimes catching them in the air, and picking up mud to make into pellets. The nest takes shape as pellets are placed on top of one another.

Eggs: the beginning of life
A complete world inside the shell

To produce young by laying eggs has certain advantages. It means that, at the earliest stage of its development, a young bird has a sheltered environment that supplies all its needs while the mother bird remains free and unencumbered to search for food or escape from predators.

Birds share this method of reproduction with spiders, fish, frogs and most reptiles, among other creatures. In mammals, further evolution has made it usual for the embryo to develop inside its mother's body. The fact that birds, so highly evolved in many ways, have retained such a primitive way of giving birth to their young is an indication of the over-riding importance of any factor that keeps down their weight.

Food for the developing chick
At the centre of the egg is the yolk, densely packed with nutrition for the developing embryo, which begins as a germ cell on the yolk's upper surface. About half of the yolk is made up of fats and proteins, and the rest is water. The amount of yolk in the egg varies from about 20 per cent in the case of birds that hatch naked, blind and helpless, to around 35 per cent for those that hatch with a covering of down and are strong enough to run about within a few hours.

When the egg is moved, the germ cell must remain on top of the yolk if it is to develop properly. This is achieved by a kind of tough skin, the vitelline membrane, which covers the yolk and continues on either side of it in a twisted strand called the chalaza. The ends of the two chalazae are attached to the shell membranes, and with the vitelline membrane they suspend the yolk and allow it to rotate, to compensate for any movement of the egg.

Surrounding the yolk is the albumen, or white. This is liquid with a central gelatinous layer attached to the shell membranes at either end, which cushions the yolk if the egg is jarred. Albumen is 90 per cent water and has great powers of water retention – a vital necessity, since the pores on the outer shell, through which oxygen is supplied to the embryo, could easily allow water vapour to escape. Albumen also contains an additional store of protein.

Two strong membranes surround the egg contents, and on these the shell is formed. The membranes prevent many harmful bacteria from entering the egg, and the albumen can prevent the growth of any that penetrate this first line of defence. As the egg cools after being laid, it shrinks slightly and the two shell membranes pull apart at the larger end, leaving an air-space. The hatching chick breaks the inner membrane with its bill and takes its first breath of air from this space while still in the egg.

The shell consists of crystalline material, mostly calcium carbonate (lime), around a fine network of protein fibres. The calcium carbonate needed to form the shell normally comes from grit in the female's diet, but if the diet is deficient, it will be taken from the bird's own bones. If the female cannot provide enough calcium for the shells by one means or another, her eggs will not have the usual hard shells when they are laid, but will be soft-shelled and soon damaged.

Why eggs are egg-shaped
The strongest possible egg, the one with its arrangement of shell crystals offering the most resistance to pressure from outside, would be as round as a table-tennis ball, but a perfectly spherical egg would be too small for adequate development of the embryo. The diameter of an egg is limited by the diameter of the oviduct down which it must pass when it is laid. It has been suggested that the egg is spherical when it enters the oviduct but that its shape is modified as it is forced out. The pressure would be greatest at the leading end of the egg, and this would account for most eggs having one end more pointed than the other.

Some species lay eggs that are especially distinctive in shape. The eggs of waders and ledge-nesting auks are pear-shaped, for example; those of grebes, shags and divers taper towards both ends; owls and many other birds of prey lay eggs that are almost round; and the eggs of swifts and swallows are long, with blunt ends. The reasons for these differences in shape are not always known, although in some cases the variation seems to serve a purpose. The pear shape of the guillemot's egg, for example, ensures that if the egg is moved, it rotates in a small arc round its tip instead of rolling away. Since guillemots lay on cliff ledges, with no nesting material to protect their eggs, this shape has definite survival value. In other cases, the shape of the egg may be dictated by the shape of the parent bird's body. As an example, diving birds, with their long, thin bodies, lay elongated eggs.

How big?
Eggs are roughly related in size to the size of the birds that produce them. The mute swan, the largest British bird, lays the largest egg – about 11.5 × 7.5cm (4½ × 3in) – and the goldcrest, the smallest

Shapes of eggs

The tawny owl's egg comes nearest to the ideal shape for maximum strength, but most birds lay eggs that are rounded at one end and taper towards the other.

TAWNY OWL – spherical

SHOVELER
usual shape

GREAT CRESTED GREBE
long and thin

GREENSHANK – pear-shaped

British bird, produces the smallest egg – about 13 × 10mm (½ × ²/₅in). However, there are many complications within this general rule. One is that the smaller the bird, the larger the egg is in relation to it. The goldcrest's egg is a little over a seventh the total weight of the bird, and many other small songbirds lay eggs weighing a ninth as much as themselves.

At the other end of the scale, the eggs of cormorants and shags are about a twenty-fifth of the bird's weight. The reason why small birds lay disproportionately large eggs is probably that the smaller the egg, the greater is its surface area in relation to its volume, so the more heat and moisture it loses at the surface. As well as laying relatively heavy eggs, small birds also tend to lay more eggs than larger birds. The goldcrest may produce ten or more – a total of nearly one and a half times its own body weight.

Birds of similar weight may produce eggs of very different sizes. Blackbirds and snipe weigh roughly the same, and so do mistle thrushes and water rails, but the snipe and water rail lay much larger eggs than the two songbirds. This is related to the fact that their chicks are precocial – that is, they hatch covered with down and so need a greater food supply in the egg for their extra development. However, quail and many other gamebirds produce precocial chicks, but do not lay unduly large eggs.

This in turn may be because gamebirds lay large clutches and cannot provide enough material for larger eggs.

How many?

Most species produce one set of eggs – a clutch – each season, although for some, two or three are normal. Those that regularly produce more than one brood are often resident species, such as blackbirds, finches and sparrows. They have a long breeding season because they are not involved in migration. Time, weather and availability of food determine whether an extra brood is reared. In fine weather, blackbirds breed from March until late summer, and may raise three broods, each taking 14 days to incubate and about the same to fledge.

A clutch may be lost through the bird deserting it when disturbed by a predator, but the longer the bird has been sitting on the eggs, the more reluctant it is to leave them – possibly because, for many species, it would be too late to start laying again.

Various ideas of what controls the size of the clutch have been put forward, including amount of food likely to be available when the young are in the nest; the amount of food the female can obtain when she is laying; and the number of eggs the bird can comfortably sit on to incubate. It may be related to the number of young that can be raised successfully, but it does not always follow that the larger the

Partridge's clutch
How many eggs a bird can cover probably sets the limit on the size of its clutch, although the maximum number are not always produced. A partridge may lay 12 eggs, but clutches containing as many as 18 not being unusual, and in one case 23 were probably laid by one hen.

clutch, the larger the number raised. If the parents have difficulty in finding food, some of their young may starve, so that the final number raised may be less than if the clutch had been smaller to start with. This has been well demonstrated in a study of swifts carried out in Oxford. It was found that in poor summers the birds raised fewer young from broods of three than from broods of two.

Some birds will carry on laying if eggs are taken from the clutch. By continually removing eggs so that the clutch was never completed, experimenters tricked a wryneck, which normally lays eight or nine eggs, into laying 48 eggs in succession, and a house sparrow, which normally lays three to five, into laying 51. The most extreme example of such additional laying is the domestic hen – 361 eggs

have been laid in 365 days. Its ancestor, the wild jungle fowl, lays about six eggs, and left to itself, a hen will lay about a dozen eggs before incubation.

The trick does not necessarily work in reverse. Common songbirds lay their usual number even if eggs are added to the nest, but pigeons, which lay two eggs, will lay just one if an egg is put into the nest when they are about to begin laying.

The stimulus that prepares a female for laying is the presence of its mate, and most birds will not produce eggs unless they have a mate and a nest site. The domestic hen, after centuries of selective breeding, is now an exception and regularly lays infertile eggs without having a mate. Some solitary females of species kept in captivity, such as ducks, budgerigars and pigeons, have been known to lay infertile eggs, but this may be because they have come to regard their owner or keeper in the same light as they would a mate.

How eggs get their colour

The colouring and marking of birds' eggs is produced by just two basic pigments – a blue and a buff-brown. When the blue is present, it pervades the whole shell and without it the shell is white. Brownish colouring may be present on or just under the surface. On white shells this produces the yellow-buff-brown range of colours, and on blue shells it produces the green-olive range.

Markings on the shells are made by a single chemical substance, which may appear as black, brown or red-brown. Spots of this substance are

RAZORBILL

PUFFIN

CHIFFCHAFF   **GARDEN WARBLER**

Why colours change

When species that used to nest in the open take to nesting in better-concealed places, their eggs become whiter with fewer markings. This is illustrated by comparing an egg of the ledge-nesting razorbill with that of the burrow-nesting puffin, or an egg from a chiffchaff's domed nest with one from the more open cup nest of a garden warbler.

Tree pipit eggs
Differences in colour and the amount of patterning may be adaptations to suit the variety of surroundings in which the tree pipit nests.

Patterns that give protection

SHORE NESTERS *Sand and shingle beaches or freshwater margins are the likely sites for these eggs. Their pale colours and finely speckled patterns give them ideal camouflage as they lie in bare scrapes in the ground. On shingle, it is scarcely possible to spot the eggs from more than a short distance away.*

LITTLE TERN

COMMON SANDPIPER

RINGED PLOVER

MARSH, HEATH AND MOORLAND NESTERS *Dark chocolate blotches camouflage the eggs of these birds. Their nests are seldom very substantial, often little more than a scrape in the ground, possibly with a lining of local vegetation.*

LAPWING

STONE CURLEW

BLACK-HEADED GULL

NESTERS IN THE OPEN *Eggs laid in open places on the ground are usually heavily marked and dull in colour. These three birds make little or no attempt to collect nesting material, but use what is at the site. The nest may therefore be scanty and the eggs are exposed and vulnerable until incubation begins.*

RED GROUSE

GOLDEN PLOVER

MERLIN

incorporated within the shell as its thickness builds up, and may appear as pale grey, mauve or blue patches on the surface. These marks do not dry until some time after the egg has been laid, and may be smeared into streaks during the laying process.

Eggs are probably coloured and marked for reasons of camouflage, but a surprising number of birds – and not only large birds with little to fear from enemies – lay white eggs. Most hole-nesting birds – owls, swifts, woodpeckers, kingfishers and martins, for example – lay white or pale blue eggs. This may be because their eggs are too well concealed to need camouflage, but it also has the positive advantage for the bird that its eggs show up well inside the dark nest.

Other birds, including pigeons, may have no need for camouflaged eggs because they begin incubation as soon as the first egg is laid and the eggs are seldom exposed.

White eggs with red-brown spots are typical of many small birds, such as tits and treecreepers, that nest in holes or domed structures. The spots appear to have no function, and it has been suggested that they represent an intermediate stage in the evolution of a white egg from a patterned one.

Camouflaged eggs of similar colouring tend to occur in the same type of surroundings. Blue eggs are found in shaded places, such as hedgerows or holes, and buff-brown eggs on open ground. The amount of patterning depends on whether a species usually lays in an exposed place or has a well-concealed nest.

Some species produce eggs that vary considerably in colour and pattern. The tree pipit is one of these, and another is the guillemot. These birds huddle in masses on cliff-sides where there is little need for camouflage, and it is the variations that help each bird to identify its single egg among the many on the bare ledge.

Minor differences between the eggs of individual birds are normal, and in some species, crows for example, there may also be variations between eggs in one clutch. The golden eagle lays two eggs, one of which is often distinctly patterned, the other almost free of patterning. A robin's clutch of six or seven eggs often contains an odd one out, and the last egg in a common tern's clutch of three normally differs from the other two. There are no known advantages in these variations, and they may arise simply because the pigment that gives the eggs their colour runs out.

The race to maturity

How birds survive the dangerous weeks from hatching to adulthood

At hatching, many species are incapable of fending for themselves and spend their first few weeks in the warmth and shelter of the nest. These birds, which ornithologists call 'altricial', develop rapidly, however, conquering difficult habitats, building complex nests and competing against aggressive rivals for food and mates. An altricial bird is born with the one instinct necessary to ensure its growth and survival – it opens wide its mouth, stimulating the parents to provide an almost constant flow of food.

Another large group of birds, known as 'precocial', are born at a more advanced stage of development. They hatch with their eyes open, are covered with a coat of protective down and are able to run about almost at once. They leave the nest soon after the last of the brood has dried, although many may stay with the parents near the nest site for some time afterwards.

Since birds evolved from reptiles, the young of which are also precocial, it seems that this state is the original or 'primitive' one for birds, and that the altricial state is the more 'advanced' one. Although the young of many species combine features of both, these two types of development represent basically different adaptations to the problem of keeping the young alive in the dangerous period after hatching, when they are most vulnerable to predators.

In general, precocial young (chicks) have a longer incubation period, are born in more exposed nests on or near the ground, move away from the nest quickly and are less dependent (if at all) on an abundant supply of food provided by the parents. Altricial young (nestlings) often have a shorter incubation period, are born in less accessible nests in trees, remain there for some time and cannot survive without constant feeding. These two methods of surviving infancy are reflected in the different ways chicks and nestlings feed and grow.

The nestling emerges from its shell poorly developed in almost every respect except one – its digestive system. It is an eating machine. The robin grows from 2g ($^1/_{14}$oz) to 20g ($^7/_{10}$oz) in less than 12 days, and the cuckoo from 2g ($^1/_{14}$oz) to 50 times that weight in three weeks. From a starting weight of about 70g (2½oz), the gannet reaches more than 4kg (9½lb) in ten weeks.

Frequency of feeding

To make this growth possible, one or both of the parents must work hard at finding food and bringing it back to the nest. Frequent small feeds prove the most efficient for increasing the size of nestlings. The great tit has been known to bring insects to the nest 900 times a day, or 60 times an hour – a high rate like this is possible only if the food supply is abundant and near to the nest. Birds of prey tend to bring fewer, but larger, feeds.

Birds that have to travel far from the nest in search of food cannot make frequent feeding trips. Instead, they often bring back large feeds stored in throat pouches or in a sac in the throat, called the crop, and regurgitated for the young. Parent gannets average three feeding sessions a day between them for their single nestling, which puts its head inside the parent's mouth as the food is regurgitated. Swifts are fed by regurgitation every two hours on average, although they are capable of living for a day or longer without food in a state of torpor – almost suspended animation – when bad weather drives away the insects that their parents normally catch for them.

Many parent birds show a remarkable ability to vary the amount of food they collect according to the needs of their brood. They will frequently increase the amount of food brought back to the nest as their offspring get bigger and hungrier. The female pied flycatcher will even react to the death

THREE-DAY OLD LAPWING CHICK

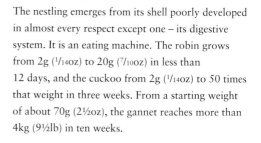

THREE-DAY OLD BLACKBIRD NESTLING

Young – alert or helpless
Alert and covered with down, the lapwing chick runs and feeds itself three days after hatching, but the blackbird nestling is blind, naked and dependent on its parents for food.

of the male by collecting as much food herself as both did before. The larger the brood, the more frequently the parents bring food, but individual nestlings in a large brood seldom get as much food as those in a smaller one, and are often smaller and presumably weaker as a result when they leave the nest.

Enriching the diet

To achieve maximum growth, nestlings often need richer food than an adult's diet would provide. The house sparrow's mainly seed diet, for example, lacks the protein needed for rapid development, so the parent bird catches insects to feed its young. A study has shown that animal matter makes up less than 5 per cent of the diet of an adult bird, but nearly 70 per cent of the diet of its young.

Pigeons have become better adapted to a seed diet. They are unique in producing a milk, similar in composition to the sort that mammals produce. This milk, which appears as a cheesy mass in the crop, is rich in protein and is given to the young about twice a day, and the nestlings themselves store it in their own crops.

Among the great majority of British birds, both parents feed the nestlings. In species such as the blackbird, in which only the female broods, the male often takes on the larger part in feeding at first. However, among those songbirds that are sometimes polygamous – the wren and pied flycatcher for example – the female often has to rear the brood alone. In some of the day-flying birds of prey, such as the sparrowhawk, and in many of the crow family, the female and young are entirely dependent on the male for food for much of the time that the young are in the nest.

Different feeding techniques

The method of feeding the young varies between different groups of birds. Most songbirds, and many other species, simply bring items, such as insects, in the bill and push them more or less intact into the wide-open gapes of the nestlings. Hawks, owls and other birds of prey tear up the food when the young are small and feed them on tiny morsels. Shrikes dismember prey for their nestlings in the same way. The male kestrel catches the prey and brings it to the female to tear up in small pieces and feed to the young. If the female dies, the male goes on providing prey for the young, but often does not take over the task of tearing it into small pieces. So if the young are too small to do it themselves, they may starve in the nest, surrounded by food. The young of petrels, shearwaters, gannets, cormorants, shags, pigeons, swifts, some woodpeckers and some songbirds are fed by regurgitation.

Crying out for sustenance
Nestlings, such as these blackcaps, prompt their parents to feed them by opening wide their bills. The bright pink interior – the gape – stimulates the parents to feed them.

The feeding of precocial young is far less complicated. They come from eggs containing a higher proportion of yolk (up to 35 per cent) and any remaining from the growth of the embryo is taken into the stomach and rapidly absorbed before hatching. The fat from the yolk is stored, partly in the liver and partly under the skin, and provides a reserve, enabling the bird to survive without food for several days after hatching if necessary.

Early days

Chicks, being better developed than nestlings when they are born, develop less quickly, and so need less food. Many of them play a part in foraging for their own food, and some are led to it by the parents. Those that nest on or near the ground, or near water, feed on small creatures, such as insects and spiders, or on vegetable matter that can easily be picked up. Young gamebirds will instinctively peck at green objects, and this helps them to find their first food items, such as aphids, without any previous experience.

Not all chicks can feed themselves from birth, however. Sometimes it takes considerable skill to catch the kind of food they need. The precocial young of grebes, terns and auks, for instance, eat fish, and those of nightjars eat insects taken in flight. The chicks of all these species need to be fed by the parent birds at first. A pair of great crested grebes with four chicks will bring on average about 20 small fish an hour throughout the day for the whole of the twelve-week rearing period, reaching a peak of some 40 feeds an hour on some days and in all providing well over 20,000 fish.

Some chicks – those of skuas and gulls, for example – leave the nest but cannot find food nearby, so they too have to be fed by their parents. They stay near the nest while the parents travel considerable distances in search of food.

Birds that feed their young seem to do so partly because they are stimulated by their offspring's begging and partly in response to an instinct that asserts itself in the breeding season. On rare occasions, that instinct can produce odd results –

Delivering rations
The hungry young herring gull begs for food by pecking at the red spot on its parent's bill. This prompts the parent to regurgitate the food it has collected on to the ground, and pick out pieces to feed to the young. When it gets older, the chick takes food for itself from the parent's bill.

adult starlings, for instance, have been known to bring food to the nest and deposit it there as much as a week before the eggs hatch – and it may subside in swallows and martins at the end of the season, to the point where they desert the young and begin migrating.

In any case, the feeding instinct is powerfully supplemented by the begging of the young. Mouths wide open, they call and may move in the nest. At first, nestlings will gape blindly upwards whenever the nest is jarred as if the parent has just landed, but not when it is shaken by the wind. They have sensitive yellow flanges at the sides of the bill, and will beg for food when these are touched by the parent. Later, when they can see, nestlings gape and call whenever the parent is in sight.

Begging for food

Gaping is made more effective by markings on the inside of many birds' mouths. These markings attract the parents' attention and provide a target at which they can aim the food they have brought. Crows have bright pink interiors to their mouths; woodlarks and skylarks have three black spots; and bearded tits have rows of white, peg-like projections that stand out against the black background and red surround of the mouth.

Most nestlings give calls to encourage the parents to feed them. Young pigeons are known as 'squeakers' from the high-pitched hunger-call they give. The young gannet pesters the parent by pointing its bill upwards, swaying its head and making lunges at the adult's bill. When older, it also utters a 'yipping' begging call.

Among chicks that are fed by their parents, young great crested grebes swim towards whichever one has a fish, 'peeping' vociferously and splashing up the water behind them with their feet. This begging

behaviour of older chicks also serves to prevent the adults from attacking them, by showing that the chicks are submissive.

Parents make no attempt to share out food, but feed the nearest or highest begging head, which is usually that of the strongest hungry youngster. When a nestling has received enough food, it tends to subside, and another takes the best position. If any nestling gapes unnecessarily and receives food it does not need, the adult will sometimes withdraw any the young bird has not promptly swallowed. As long as the parents can maintain a sufficiently rapid rate of feeding, all the young will get a more or less equal share of food, but as soon as there is a food shortage, the shares become unequal. Among chicks that hatch at different times, the first-hatched and the biggest and strongest will usually get the giant share of available food, while the others will often starve. When all the young hatch out at the same time, the whole brood is likely to weaken and die. A cuckoo that has not pushed the host bird's eggs or nestlings out of the nest is usually strong enough to win any battle for food. Among predatory species, the weakest nestling will sometimes be eaten by its parent or another nestling when food is short.

How young are reared

Unable to control their own temperature for some time after hatching, young birds are dependent on their parents for heat. The degree of brooding (warming) needed differs between chicks and nestlings. At first, nestlings take on the temperature of their surroundings, and until they can maintain a constant temperature – at between one and three weeks – they need the almost constant warmth of their parents. A drastic drop in the temperature of the surrounding air will kill them. Chicks are less liable than nestlings to lose warmth, because their temperature control starts while they are still in the egg, but the insulation of the adult state is acquired more slowly – often at between two and three weeks – and chicks need to be brooded, at least intermittently.

Most species brood their young by crouching over them, which is particularly effective in cup-shaped nests, but other methods have evolved where conditions require them. Parent cormorants brood their young with their feet, in the same way as they incubate eggs. Grebes shelter their chicks among the feathers of the back, because of the wetness of the nest. Most chicks, however, are brooded on the ground. Brooding and sheltering are especially important at extremes of temperature and on wet days, to prevent either chilling or overheating. Species such as hawks, herons and many songbirds with open nests often shield their young from the hot sun by spreading their wings over them.

The parents of nidifugous chicks lead them away from the nest site after hatching. In some species, such as lapwings, the family remains in the parents' breeding territory, but in others, such as oystercatchers and many ducks, the chicks are led right away from the nesting area to a more suitable feeding ground. This may mean a long and dangerous overland journey, during which the chick's yolk supply will tide it over until food is available. In large towns, mallard broods sometimes attract attention when they cross roads and hold up the traffic while on their way to water.

Adult waders sometimes pick up their young and carry them across obstacles, such as walls, ditches and fences. The parent woodcock or redshank flies with one chick at a time, holding it tightly between its legs and, in the case of the woodcock, keeping it in position with the bill. Adult great crested grebes carry their chicks on their backs for up to three weeks after hatching, their bodies providing a sort of floating nest, dry and safe from predators. In an emergency, they will even submerge with the young still aboard, deliberately imprisoning them under the wings to stop them rising to the surface. The mute swan also carries its young on its back at times during the first weeks after hatching.

Keeping the nest clean

The accumulated droppings of a brood reared in the nest for two or three weeks would be a serious hazard to health if left there, and any close to the nest can give away its position to predators. Droppings from the young of many songbirds, particularly those in less well-hidden nests, are enclosed in gelatinous capsules. When the nestlings are young these are eaten by the parents, and later they are taken and deposited some way from the site. The parents will also clear the nest of uneaten food and even dead nestlings. Species less vulnerable to predators are not so careful. The young of hawks and kingfishers defecate over the side of the nest, or in the entrance tunnel. Many seabirds make no attempt to clear the nest at all.

Young birds grow to adult size remarkably quickly compared with reptiles or mammals – in as little as two weeks in the case of some of the smaller, open-nesting songbirds, such as whitethroats – but it is difficult to say when they are fully grown, because there is seldom any clear indication. Even when a bird has reached adult weight, it is often not fully developed in other ways – it cannot fly, perhaps, or has not yet got its body feathers.

In addition, the young of some birds that gather food far away from the nest go on gaining weight even after they reach the adult norm – the gannet becomes 50 per cent heavier, for example. This

Bigger than the parent
Some young increase their body weight so much that they become heavier than the parent bird. At seven weeks old, this Leach's petrel weighs 70g (2½oz), its parents 43g (1½oz). The extra weight may be needed when the fledgling begins to fend for itself and may go without food for days.

excess weight consists of stored fat, which tides the fledgling over when it leaves for the sea, until it can feed itself.

The problem is further complicated by the fact that birds' features do not develop symmetrically. If one is especially important to a species, that one will grow at a faster rate than others. Cover-haunting birds, such as moorhens, have only rudimentary wings for many weeks, although the body and legs grow quickly. Grouse chicks, which need to flutter or fly at an early stage to avoid capture by predators, have wings that are capable of some flight before the rest of the feathering is complete.

How much of this development goes on in the nest depends mainly on how safe the nest is. Precocial young may leave in a matter of hours, but altricial nestlings stay for anything from 13 or 14 days in the case of the blackbird to as long as eight weeks in the case of the swift, which is reared in a much safer nest in a hole or crevice. Seabirds tend to have longer nesting periods, with gannets staying in the nest for up to 14 weeks.

When families break up

Altricial birds are still dependent on their parents after they leave the nest, and the fledglings are fed and protected until they complete feather-growth and can forage for themselves. How long this takes depends on the availability of food. Blackbirds can find the insects and worms they need after about 20 days as fledglings. Tawny owls, on the other hand, have to be fed by their parents for up to three months after leaving the nest before they can catch prey.

It is even harder to determine the total length of time that chicks spend with their parents, although some, such as swans and geese, are known to stay together as a family unit throughout the whole of the winter after they are born. In the majority of species, however, the chicks probably become independent shortly after they are able to fly.

The struggle for food
Feeding techniques of specialists and all-rounders

Birds live at what, for humans, would be fever heat – at a normal temperature when awake of about 41°C (106°F), rising as high as 43.5°C (110°F) during exercise. To maintain this temperature, and to provide energy, which it burns at a furious rate, a small bird may take about one-third of its body weight in food every day. A larger bird needs about one-seventh, because it loses heat less quickly – heat is lost through the surface, and large creatures have less surface area in relation to their volume than small ones. Doubling the size of a bird halves the rate at which it loses heat.

Food taken by an insect-eating or flesh-eating bird is broken down by acid secretions and crushed by the muscular walls of the gizzard. In some species, further digestion takes place in one or two long, thin sacs, which open low down in the gut. Birds that live mainly on vegetable food have a more elaborate digestive tract. The elastic walls of the lower gullet expand into a crop where food can be stored for later digestion. The crop of the woodpigeon in winter may hold 85–114g (3–4oz) of grain or clover leaves. The gizzard of a seed-eater or a leaf-eater is very muscular. In the folds of its rough, horny lining it grinds food against grit, which must be regularly swallowed to provide additional crushing machinery. Vegetarian birds have two large intestinal sacs, and these are essential for adequate nutrition – if a red grouse's sacs are obstructed by disease or parasites, it will starve to death in the midst of plenty.

Feeding skills

Most birds can use their bills to pick a minute gall-wasp from a leaf, dig a 5cm (2in) hole to reach a beetle pupa, tug an earthworm from the ground, swing a snail-shell against a stone or pick up a ripe cherry. Surprisingly little use is made of the feet in feeding. Only hawks and owls actually seize their prey with their feet, but tits, shrikes, ravens, crows, jays, magpies and crossbills hold morsels with their feet when breaking them up. Gamebirds regularly dig with their feet in litter and soft earth, and thrushes do so occasionally.

Nuthatches and great spotted woodpeckers wedge nuts in cracks of trees before splitting open the shells. Herring gulls have developed an even more sophisticated method of getting at food – they pick up mussels then drop them from the air to shatter the shells on the shore.

Grey herons stalk through the shadows seeking prey, which they stab with their long bills. Kingfishers catch their prey with a shallow dive from a perch. Ospreys and gannets hurtle down from the sky. Grebes and divers propel themselves underwater with their feet, searching for food, and auks – razorbills, guillemots and puffins – 'fly' underwater, using their wings for propulsion.

Killing prey

Owls and falcons use sheer speed to fly down their quarry. Peregrines, which strike with the claws, in full flight, will kill birds heavier than themselves, but most species that kill on the ground take relatively small prey – in a rough-and-tumble with large prey, their feathers might get broken. The quarry is despatched with a bite at the base of the skull.

Kingfishers batter the heads of the fish they catch on the perch. This not only kills the fish but probably makes it easier to swallow.

Song thrushes are well known for their habit of carrying snails to favourite anvil stones to be broken open. Apparently, they can tell whether shells are empty or full, not by their weight but by the sound made when they hit the anvil. Dry and empty shells are often found unbroken beside the stones.

Feeding times vary with size and season. In winter, a small bird has to feed right through the day to secure enough fuel to maintain warmth during the night, while many larger birds take a midday break, sometimes accompanied by a nap. Some birds of prey can secure a day's food in one or two kills, and will hunt at the same time, along the same tracks, day after day.

Day and night control the feeding routines of most birds, but surface-feeding ducks and many waders follow the ebb and flow of the tide. Woodcock, snipe and dabbling ducks living inland may feed at any time of the day, but prefer the night time. Among owls, the short-eared owl is unusual in being largely a daylight hunter. Blackbirds in autumn and starlings in spring take earthworms in the early morning hours, and other kinds of food later in the day.

Song thrushes have two periods of snail-eating – midwinter and high summer – but this reflects not so much the availability of snails as the lack of other, preferred foods. Summer drought locks worms and insect larvae below the baked surface of the soil, and hard frost causes a dearth of anything else to eat. In a mild winter, thrushes will not eat snails, and in a rainy summer they will eat very few.

During the first day after a snowfall, ground-feeding birds are often scarce. This is possibly because more heat is lost while seeking food than while at rest, and it is not worth losing the extra heat on the offchance of finding food. Only when their reserves of fat have been used up are birds driven to seek food, or perish.

The urge to forage

Birds have an innate drive to hunt for food, which is stimulated by appetite. At times, hunger is completely satisfied before the urge to forage is exhausted, and then the bird will abandon the prey it secures. A song thrush will leave a large earthworm to burrow back into the soil, a peregrine will knock down a moorhen and fly on with never a backward glance. When jays and tits store nuts and acorns, they may be discharging an unsatisfied foraging drive, but for the nutcracker the storage of food is essential for survival through the winter. Tits have been known to fly into houses and tear paper, and this may also be attributed to an unsatisfied urge to hunt in a particular manner – presumably for prey that shelters under thin bark.

Working together

Cooperation in hunting by birds of a single species is rare, but one example is the cormorant. At times, a score or more will fish strung out in a line, diving more or less simultaneously, and presumably each bird turns some fish towards its neighbours.

Mixed flocks of tits, warblers and treecreepers roam through the woods in late summer. One suggestion for why this should be so is that each bird unconsciously acts as a 'beater' for the others, but it may be that the main advantage of this social feeding is the warning of attack provided by so many pairs of eyes. In hard weather, little grebes accompany mute swans and coots, presumably

gleaning small organisms driven from the weeds that the bigger birds root up. Blackbirds and robins follow the track of a mole.

Some birds take advantage of the feeding habits of others without offering anything in return. Chaffinches will pick the pips from the cores of crab-apples hacked open by fieldfares, and greenfinches will nibble the actual fruit. A few species are piratical, living at the expense of other birds. Great skuas steal fish from other seabirds. When a fish-carrying gannet is sighted, one or two skuas close in to hustle and mob it until it regurgitates its load of fish. In recent years, the black-headed gull has also become parasitic, stealing earthworms from lapwings. Blackbirds sometimes snatch earthworms from song thrushes. In one spring, it was calculated that the song thrushes lost nearly one-tenth of their catch to blackbirds.

Birds that hunt for themselves from a young age begin by pecking at any small object that contrasts with its background, and so learn to distinguish the edible from the inedible. Some birds that are fed by their parents may learn to recognise food by the appearance of what is brought to the nest, but a swift, which is fed in the dark with regurgitated insects, must either learn by experience when it takes to the wing or have an inborn tendency to pursue flying insects.

Avoiding competition

When food is short, birds may face competition not only from members of their own species, but also from birds of other species. One method of avoiding harmful competition is for each species to have its own special habitat. Shags, for example, tend to work rocky and open shores, while the closely allied

Differences in diet between two related birds

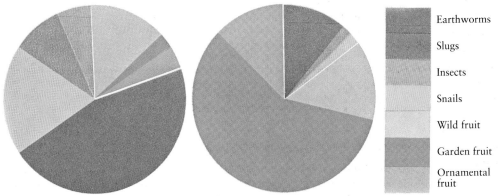

SONG THRUSH – mainly a flesh-eater   BLACKBIRD – mainly vegetarian

Earthworms
Slugs
Insects
Snails
Wild fruit
Garden fruit
Ornamental fruit

The diets of song thrushes and blackbirds, which are both members of the thrush family, include similar items, but in strikingly different proportions. In the above diagram, white lines divide animal foods (in various shades of brown) from fruit (in different shades of green). From this, it's easy to see at a glance that animal foods make up more than three-quarters of the song thrush's diet, but less than a quarter of the blackbird's.

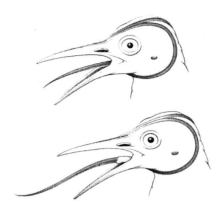

The woodpecker's tongue

Thanks to an ability to extend its tongue four times the length of its upper beak, the green woodpecker can winkle out an insect from about 13cm (5in) behind the bark of a tree. After the bird has chiselled through the bark, its tongue flicks into holes made by wood-borers and hooks the insects out on backward-pointing barbs. The tongue itself is the end portion of a flexible system of bones and tissue – known as the hyoid – that wraps up and around the woodpecker's head and is anchored near its right nostril.

cormorants fish in estuaries and along sandy beaches. Even when the two species do meet, they show different dietary preferences. Shags usually pursue the smaller species of fish while the slightly bigger cormorants go after the larger ones.

In English woodland, five species of tits may share one habitat, often working in mixed flocks. In a winter feeding party, there are often different levels for food-gathering. Great tits hunt largely on the ground; marsh tits in the shrub layer up to about 6m (20ft); blue tits and coal tits at all heights from just above the ground to the treetops; and long-tailed tits at higher levels than the marsh tits.

When great tits do leave the ground, they prefer to hunt in sycamores. Blue tits spend a lot of time foraging in oaks, coal tits in conifers and marsh tits in hazels and elders. Even on the same tree, different species have their feeding niches – blue tits, for example, probe among buds and along slender twigs, while marsh tits feed more on larger limbs and branches.

All distinctions of feeding habits between different tits break down when there is a temporary superabundance of food. For instance, when a woodland area suffers a plague of the defoliating caterpillars of the winter moth, an 18m (60ft) oak may harbour 200,000–400,000 caterpillars, and all kinds of species make the most of this time of plenty, deserting their usual niches.

Even when two closely allied birds take the same foods, their diets may be very different. For example, worms, slugs, insects and fruit appear in the diets of two members of the thrush family – the song thrush and the blackbird. Yet animal foods occur nearly five times more frequently in the song thrush's diet than in the blackbird's. Snails figure prominently in the diet of the song thrush, but blackbirds cannot crack the shells of large snails, although this could never be guessed from an anatomical comparison of the two birds. Other differences in their diets are equally strange. Song thrushes eat great numbers of yew berries, while blackbirds eat very few; song thrushes prefer large beetles, such as cockchafers, while blackbirds prefer ants.

Most birds drink when they have the opportunity, but some survive on 'metabolic' water – water released in the digestion of food. Seabirds can, and do, drink seawater and get rid of superfluous salt by secretion of highly concentrated brine from glands situated at the base of the beak. Crows and sand-grouse bring water to their young by transporting it in the throat or soaking their breast plumage.

All birds conserve water by producing very highly concentrated urine, almost a paste of uric acid crystals, and in very dry weather by reducing song and, with it, evaporation of moisture from the lungs.

All-purpose and specialist bills

Gulls and crows, nature's scavengers, take a relatively wide range of both animal and vegetable foods with their all-purpose bills, but other birds, seeking to avoid competition within their preferred habitat, have become increasingly specialised feeders and depend on a fairly narrow selection of foods.

If their methods of feeding differ, species that are otherwise alike in size and general structure may show striking differences in the design of their bills. Conversely, species that are not alike in other ways may have similar bills if they share roughly the same feeding habits. This is because of the process known as convergent evolution, which produces similarities of design between unrelated species if they face similar challenges. The kingfisher and the heron, for example, feed by spearing fish, and both have evolved dagger-shaped bills.

The rook, a specialised feeder on insects and earthworms, has a longer bill than that of its nearest relative, the carrion crow, which takes worms much less often. Other soil feeders have taken this development even further – the snipe, woodcock, curlew, black-tailed godwit and dunlin, which probe for food in soft mud, have extremely long bills, and each species avoids competition with the others by probing at a different depth.

All the finches have the hard, conical bills typical of seed-eaters, but the bill of each species is slightly different from the rest. The most powerful, that of the hawfinch, can crack a cherry stone. At the other extreme, the thinner-billed goldfinch extracts the seeds of teasels by boring for them.

The many shapes of bills

SHEARING
Wigeon uses short, wide bill to crop grass and plants.

PRISING
Oystercatcher strikes into shell of prey and levers it open.

FILTERING
Avocet skims insects from the surface of mud or shallow water.

TEARING
Golden eagle's strong, hooked bill is designed to tear flesh apart.

PROBING
Woodcock uses long, thin bill to probe for worms in soft earth.

HAMMERING
Green woodpecker chisels into bark for hidden insects.

GRASPING
Red-breasted merganser grips slippery fish in serrated bill.

SPEARING
Grey heron's long, dagger-like bill is well suited to spearing fish.

SIFTING
Spoonbill sifts animal organisms from shallows with spatulate bill.

INSECT-EATERS

Whitethroat has forceps-like bill.

Treecreeper probes tree bark.

Swift gapes to catch insects.

SEED-EATERS

Hawfinch cracks cherry stones.

Redpoll eats small birch seeds.

Crossbill picks seeds from cones.

Care of the plumage

How birds keep their feathers in peak condition

Feathers are not everlasting or indestructible, and although they are replaced periodically in moulting, an efficient all-the-year-round system of feather maintenance is vital to a bird's well-being and survival. Two groups of feathers need special attention – the flight feathers of the wings and the 'steering' feathers of the tail. If the primaries and secondaries of the wing become damaged or excessively worn, their aerodynamic efficiency is diminished. This, in turn, imposes strain on the bird's energy and resources, reducing its general ability to cope with the challenges of life. It becomes less efficient in feeding and also in escaping from predators.

Preening

Birds have an elaborate system of feather care, and spend as much time as possible on it each day – not only in special sessions, but at any odd moment they have to spare from other activities. The most important form of feather care is preening, a habit shared by all birds, whereby the bill is used in two main ways. With the body feathers fluffed up, a bird 'nibbles' individual feathers between the tips of its bill, working from the base of the quill outwards in a series of tiny and precise pecking movements. The bird also draws feathers one at a time through its bill, with a single, quick pull of the head – particularly the wing and tail feathers, which are awkward to reach and require special attention.

By such preening movements, the bird removes foreign matter from plumage and skin, works in fresh oil from the preen gland just above the tail, puts any disarranged feathers back in place and repairs feather vanes and webs by 'zipping up' any barbs and barbules that have come apart.

Preening also removes parasites, especially feather lice and mites. Birds that are ill or have malformed or damaged bills, preventing adequate preening,

often carry an abnormally large number of parasites, which eat away the feathers and affect general health. Birds are liable to attract several groups of parasites – blood-sucking flies and louse flies, feather-eating feather lice, and ticks and feather mites, which live on either feathers or blood. None of these parasites, as far as is known, is harmful to humans handling the birds, and some birds are at times free at least from feather lice. One study of 249 chaffinches showed that 51 per cent carried no feather lice; other figures were 51 per cent for robins (172 examined), 59 per cent for blackbirds (out of 54), 55 per cent for great tits (out of 172) and as many as 90 per cent for blue tits (out of 704). Infestation by parasites varies according to the time of year, and is at its height just before the breeding season.

Scratching

A bird cannot, of course, preen its own head. Instead, it must scratch with one foot while it balances on the other. This rather crude method seems to serve most species in keeping the head feathers in good order. Birds have two different ways of head-scratching – direct and indirect. In direct scratching, the foot is simply lifted up to the head, along the outside of the body. In indirect scratching, a wing is drooped and the foot on the same side is brought up over the shoulder to the head. As a general rule, the method of head-scratching is characteristic of each species and family of birds. The majority of British songbirds and related groups, such as swifts, nightjars and kingfishers (but not woodpeckers), scratch indirectly. Most others do so directly, except for the plovers (but not turnstones), oystercatchers, stilts and avocets.

A few birds, such as the cormorant, gannet and heron, are equipped with a pectinated claw – this takes the form of a special comb on the inside edge

Preening
A male blackbird (left) 'zips up' its wing feather barbs while its mate nibbles feathers under its tail.

Direct scratching
With wings closed, a lesser black-backed gull reaches a leg forward to scratch its head feathers.

of the third toe. The birds use this claw to scratch the back of their head and neck.

In a few groups, including some crows, bearded tits, martins and pigeons, paired birds preen one another's heads. This behaviour, which is termed allopreening, is often an important part of courtship, but in some species at least, it is also extremely useful in helping to keep the head plumage in good order.

Bathing

A bird may preen some of its feathers at any time of day, often because of some temporary irritation, but birds preen more completely as part of an elaborate toilet sequence, which begins with bathing. As well as cleansing, the main object of bathing for many birds seems to be to dampen the plumage so that preen oil may spread more effectively.

Land birds bathe in shallow water, including puddles and the edges of streams or ponds, where they can stand safely. A bird-bath will attract songbirds, such as blackbirds or song thrushes. The bird sits with its body feathers fluffed up and first dips forward with head, breast and wing joints in the water, at the same time shaking its bill violently from side to side and flicking its wings forward. Then it squats back, with tail and belly in the water, and flicks its wings upwards to send the water splashing and showering.

A bathing bird alternates between these two sets of movements several times – but does not spend very long over the dip because of the risk from predators. At the end, it shakes its feathers vigorously, to throw off the water, then moves away quickly.

Waterbirds, such as ducks, grebes and various seabirds, spend more time over bathing because they are usually safe on open water and can dive to escape from predators if necessary. Ordinary surface bathing in these species consists of repeated head-ducking, scooping water up on to the back, then rubbing the head against the flanks. They also beat their wings vigorously in the water, raising sheets of spray. More elaborately still, ducks, swans and geese will roll over, somersault and dive while bathing. Grebes kick vigorously under the surface, and gannets roll over sideways with one wing lifted.

After bathing, waterbirds start to dry themselves by shaking their feathers, in the same way as land birds, and also flapping their wings. Cormorants and, to a lesser extent, shags perch on rocks and stretch out their wings to dry after bathing.

Swallows, swifts, various terns and other birds that are most in their element when flying, bathe from the air by repeatedly plopping to the surface for a brief moment, without actually alighting. Kingfishers launch from a perch over the water, dip momentarily under the surface and fly up again.

As well as bathing in standing water – in which they often wallow, unlike other land birds – pigeons bathe in the rain, lying with one wing lifted. Many songbirds, such as tits, bathe clumsily against dew or rain-soaked vegetation. Skylarks never bathe in standing water, but lie down in the rain with both wings extended.

Oiling

After its bath, the bird oils its plumage, applying a feather dressing in the form of a secretion from its preen gland. Oiling waterproofs the plumage and maintains its heat-insulting properties, and so is particularly important to waterbirds and very small land birds.

The preen gland is situated just above the tail. Nipple-like in shape, with the opening facing upwards, it is surrounded in some species by a ring of special feathers, which act as a wick in dispensing the oil. Blackbirds, song thrushes and almost all other songbirds oil their feathers in the same way. The bird twists its tail sideways, reaches back and nibbles at its preen gland, stimulating the flow of oil. Usually it oils its head first. It does this by scratching its oil-covered bill with its foot and then, quickly and carefully, using its foot to spread the oil over the feathers on its head. Then it quivers its oily bill, and to a lesser extent its oily head, under the wings,

Indirect scratching
A chaffinch scratches its head by drooping a wing, then bringing its foot up over its shoulder.

Bathing
Fluffing up its body feathers, a song thrush bathes by splashing in shallow water.

A great crested grebe rubs its head on its preen gland, stimulating the gland to produce oil.

Sunning
A blackbird spreads its wings and tail in the sunshine – possibly to keep down the number of feather parasites.

paying particular attention to the primary flight feathers. Oil is spread over the rest of the plumage during the thorough preening that follows.

Many long-necked waterbirds, such as grebes and geese, use their heads as an oily 'mop'. They first rub their heads on the preen gland to collect the oil, and then over flanks and back, gradually spreading oil over the rest of the plumage.

Powdering

There are exceptions to the usual sequence of bathing, preening and oiling. Gamebirds, for example, never voluntarily bathe in water, and others, including some pigeons, do not oil themselves. Pigeons powder themselves instead, using their powder down. This consists of specially modified body feathers that grow continuously and disintegrate into a fine powder of minute dust particles that permeate the plumage, especially when the birds preen. Many other species probably possess a little powder down.

Birds of the heron family have the down distributed in well-defined patches on the body. The heron has a set of three such 'powder puffs', and the bittern has two. These birds powder themselves carefully after their heads and necks become soiled by fish and eels. Bitterns are especially fond of eels, which wriggle and lash when caught, spreading their slime on the bird. The bittern first rubs its head on

the powder puffs, then dusts its befouled feathers with the particles of down, after which it combs itself, scratching off the powder and slime with its pectinated claw. Oiling and preening follow, and perhaps a repeat of the whole process.

Sunning

Most species sun themselves, lying with tail and one or both wings spread. Blackbirds, song thrushes, robins, starlings and other garden birds all indulge in this behaviour. Sunning could be regarded simply as a cooling device, helping the bird to lose heat through exposing sparsely feathered areas to the air and breeze. Certainly, sunning may have this function in, for example, incubating birds unavoidably caught in strong sunlight. Reed warblers have been reported to behave in this way.

However, the majority of birds that sun themselves are deliberately seeking the sun. It has been argued that they derive great pleasure from sunning, but even if this is true, it cannot be the behaviour's biological purpose. Birds' instincts have developed for survival value, and birds stretching in the sun are vulnerable to predators.

Sunning is associated with preening and scratching, which suggests two possible functions. It may help to de-louse the bird by making its feather parasites move about the plumage so that they are more accessible when the bird preens; and

Powdering
A bittern rubs its head into its breast, gathering powder down to clear fish slime off its feathers.

Dusting
House sparrows make scrapes in the ground, then work dust into their feathers.

ultra-violet light from the sun may affect the properties of the preen oil on the bird's feathers in some beneficial way.

Dusting

A minority of bird groups, notably gamebirds, such as pheasants and grouse, dust themselves in dry, fine earth, grit or sand. They scrape hollows in the ground and work the dust up among the feathers, shaking it all out before preening.

Dusting has also been reported among owls, hoopoes, certain hawks and nightjars and among a few songbirds, including wrens, skylarks and – as every gardener with a seedbed or newly sown lawn knows – house sparrows. Several sparrows at a time may pit the earth with their dusting scrapes.

The value of dusting as a part of feather care is not fully understood. Certainly, it does not seem to serve the same main purpose as bathing in water – that is, to facilitate oiling. As with sunning, together with the associated preening and scratching, it probably helps to combat parasites.

Anting

The most bizarre feather-care habit of all is anting. This seems to be confined to songbirds and has been reported in at least 22 British native species and well over 200 species in all.

A great deal has been written at secondhand about anting but much of this information is unreliable. First-hand observation has shown that when birds behave in this way, they always use worker ants of formic-acid producing species. In Britain, this is mainly the common garden ant (*Lasius niger*), the yellow hill ant (*Lasius flavus*) and, probably, the wood ant (*Formica rufa*).

The ants are used in two main ways. In the first, the active or direct method, the bird picks up one or more ants in its bill, lifts one wing, presses its tail sideways to steady the wing and rapidly applies ants to the underside of its primary feathers, near their tips. It rubs them on its feathers, spreading formic acid and any other body fluids of the ants, together with its own saliva. Chaffinches and meadow pipits use a single ant at a time, but starlings and magpies collect a billful before starting. Magpies appear to be the only direct anters among British birds that apply ants to the tail as well as to the primary feathers.

In the second form of anting, the passive or indirect method, the bird allows live ants to run over its plumage, deliberately arousing them so that they aggressively squirt out their formic acid. The jay leans back on its tail, with its wings spread out in front of it. The blackbird, song thrush and mistle thrush half squat among the ants with wings outspread, and the carrion crow and rook lie down, spreadeagled, and wallow among the ants.

Among garden birds, especially starlings and blackbirds, anting may best be seen in late summer, when ants are swarming for their mating flights.

The purpose of anting is by no means clear. Some ornithologists believe that birds do it purely for the sensuous pleasure of having their skins stimulated by formic acid, but there is no doubt that formic acid is an insecticide. This was proved when a Russian scientist counted the feather mites on four meadow pipits that had been anting with wood ants and, for control purposes, on four others that had not. He found dead mites only on the birds that had been anting. The surviving mites on the anting birds were crawling at random on the birds' plumage, whereas those on the birds that had not been anting remained undisturbed among the barbs of the feathers. Out of 642 live mites taken from the anting birds, 163 died within twelve hours, but of 758 taken from the other birds, only five died within the same time.

So it seems that anting may kill some of the bird's feather mites sooner or later, and make the survivors more accessible for preening. It may also have other beneficial effects that are not yet fully understood, especially in connection with the all-important primary feathers, which are the main targets for anting.

Direct anting
The starling's technique is to gather a billful of ants and rub them on its flight feathers.

Indirect anting
A jay allows worker ants to run over its plumage, vigorously squirting out formic acid.

Index

Figures in **bold** type refer to full-page illustrated entries, giving profiles of the birds and distribution maps.

The Book of British Birds

Project Editors Marion Paull, Caroline Boucher

Art Editor Simon Webb

Designer Keith Miller

Assistant Editor Rachel Weaver

Consultant Robert Hume

Maps Jenny Dooge

Proofreader Ron Pankhurst

Indexer Hilary Bird

READER'S DIGEST GENERAL BOOKS

Editorial Director Julian Browne

Art Director Anne-Marie Bulat

Managing Editor Nina Hathway

Head of Book Development Sarah Bloxham

Picture Resource Manager Christine Hinze

Pre-press Account Manager Dean Russell

Product Production Manager
Claudette Bramble

Production Controller Katherine Tibbals

Origination by Colour Systems Limited, London
Printed in China

AUTHORS

Phyllis Barclay-Smith, CBE

Jeffrey Boswall

Dr Philip J K Burton

Dr Bruce Campbell, OBE

Dr John Carthy

Dr C J F Coombs

Dr Peter M Driver

John Gooders

Dr C J O Harrison

The Rev P H T Hartley, MA, BSC

David Holyoak

Dr R K Murton

Dr Ian Newton, FRS

Richard Perry, BA

K E L Simmons, BA

Robert Spencer, BA

Kenneth Williamson, FRSE

ARTISTS

Norman G Barber

Raymond Harris Ching

Kathleen Flack

Eric Fraser

Robert Gillmor

Hermann Heinzel

Rosemary Parslow

Philip North Taylor

Sydney Woods

The Book of British Birds is published by The Reader's Digest Association Limited, 11 Westferry Circus, Canary Wharf, London E14 4HE

Copyright © 2009 The Reader's Digest Association Limited

Copyright © 2009 Reader's Digest Association Far East Limited

Philippines Copyright © 2009 Reader's Digest Association Far East Limited

Copyright © 2009 Reader's Digest (Australia) Pty Limited

Copyright © 2009 Reader's Digest India Pvt Limited

Copyright © 2009 Reader's Digest Asia Pvt Limited

The Book of British Birds was first published in 1969. This edition has been fully revised and updated.

We are committed both to the quality of our products and the service we provide to our customers. We value your comments, so please do contact us on **08705 113366** or via our website at **www.readersdigest.co.uk**

If you have any comments or suggestions about the content of our books, email us at **gbeditorial@readersdigest.co.uk**

ACKNOWLEDGMENTS

front cover naturepl.com/Charlie Hamilton James

back cover rspb-images.com/Ernie Janes

1 naturepl.com/T J Rich

2-3 naturepl.com/Pete Cairns

4-5 naturepl.com/Bernard Castelein

7 naturepl.com/Ross Hoddinott

30 ShutterStock, Inc/David Peta

39 ShutterStock, Inc/Rex Rover

57 iStockphoto.com/saints 4757

81 ShutterStock, Inc/Kevin Eaves

97 ShutterStock, Inc/Gail Johnson

113 ShutterStock, Inc/Richard Bowden

137 iStockphoto.com/AVTG

147 ShutterStock, Inc/Peter Blottman

173 naturepl.com/Ross Hoddinott

199 ShutterStock, Inc/Terence Mendoza

213 iStockphoto.com/swilmor

231 ShutterStock, Inc/Libor Piska

251 Frank Lane Picture Agency/Markus Varesvuo/
      Minden Pictures

265 Photoshot/Mike Lane/NHPA

ISBN 978 0 276 44549 1
Book Code 400-441 UP0000-1
Oracle Code 250013806S.00.24